MASTER SHIPBUILDERS
OF NEWFOUNDLAND AND LABRADOR

VOLUME TWO:
NOTRE DAME BAY TO PETTY HARBOUR

CALVIN D. EVANS

WITH

PHILIP EVANS

P.O. Box 2188, St. John's, NL, Canada, A1C 6E6
WWW.BREAKWATERBOOKS.COM

LIBRARY AND ARCHIVES CANADA CATALOGUING IN PUBLICATION
Evans, Calvin D.
Master shipbuilders of Newfoundland and Labrador / Calvin Evans ; with Philip Evans.
Includes bibliographical references and index.
Contents: v. 2. Notre Dame Bay to Petty Harbour
ISBN 978-1-55081-569-6 (v. 2)
1. Shipbuilding--Newfoundland and Labrador--History. 2. Ships--Newfoundland and Labrador--History. I. Evans, Philip, 1977-, author II. Title.
VM27.N45E83 2013 623.82'0309718 C2013-901008-4

Canada Council for the Arts Conseil des Arts du Canada Canada Newfoundland Labrador

We acknowledge the support of the Canada Council for the Arts, which last year invested $157 million to bring the arts to Canadians throughout the country. We acknowledge the financial support of the Government of Canada through the Canada Book Fund (CBF) and the Government of Newfoundland and Labrador through the Department of Tourism, Culture and Recreation for our publishing activities.

PRINTED AND BOUND IN CANADA.

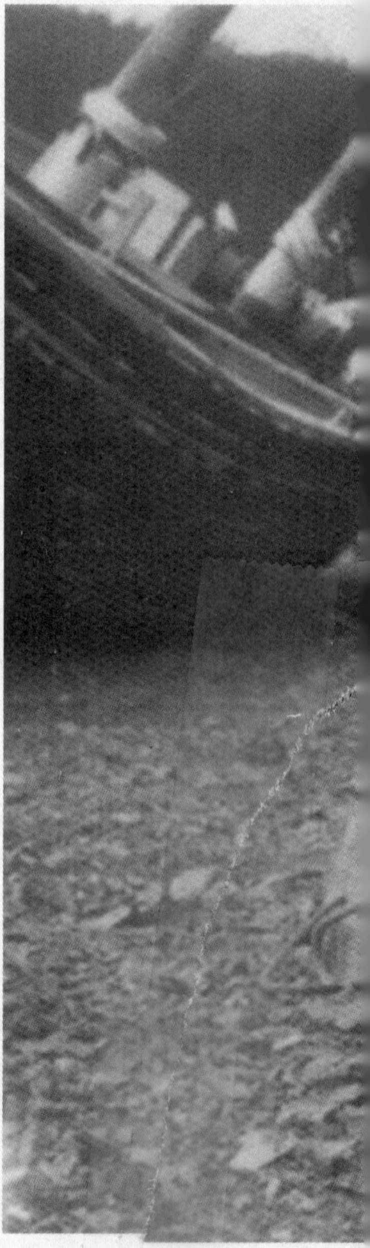

FRONT COVER: John H. Forsey's 228-ton *Jean & Mary* constructed and awaiting launch at Marystown in 1919. (Courtesy of The Marystown Heritage Museum)

BACK COVER: Capt. John Hann Blackmore (sitting on a log) in his shipyard at Port Union. (Courtesy of Don Blackmore)

ECHOES OF THE PAST: JOHNNY MARSHALL AND DON TULK CAULKING A BOAT AT HARBOUR BUFFET. NOTE THE CAULKING MALLETS AND THE LONG STRAND OF OAKUM WOUND AROUND THE CAULKER'S LEFT ARM.

(Photo used by permission of the Maritime History Archive, Memorial University of Newfoundland.)

CONTENTS

CONTENTS

THE 55-TON SCHOONER *GLADYS C.* BEING CONSTRUCTED AT EVANS' POINT, NORTHERN ARM, IN 1906. NOTE THAT EACH MEMBER OF THE BUILDING CREW IS HOLDING A TOOL.
L TO R: ROBERT HUMPHRIES, EDWARD EVANS JR., JABEZ EVANS, MATTHEW COOK, FRED EVANS, ROBERT EVANS (THE MASTER BUILDER), SAMUEL EVANS, AND BENSON EVANS. THE VESSEL WAS LOST SOMEWHERE IN TRINITY BAY IN 1930.
(Photo Courtesy of Angus Evans.)

PREFACE

SOME OF MY FONDEST childhood memories have to do with being surrounded by the shipbuilding tools and artifacts of the Evans family. My grandfather Samuel was a shipwright, and his and my great-grandfather William's tools were housed in the family workshop. There were huge bins full of trunnels, ship's knees, blocks and tackle; walls covered with a variety of saws, axes, augers, planes, and C-clamps; and a sealing gun hung securely on a long wall. Underneath Jacob Evans's house next door were neat coils of bank line and a variety of half models for ships the Evans family had built. Next door, on the other side, was Robert Evans's workshop. Since Robert was still an active builder, his workshop was considered by small boys as an inner sanctum, and we dared not enter, but our hungry eyes surveyed the vast array of gleaming, polished tools. Farther along the road in the opposite direction and at the water's edge was Luke Manuel's shipbuilding site and his two-storey workshop. Luke was long gone and the workshop was securely locked, but cracks in the weathered building allowed us to catch glimpses of what must have been a marvellous collection. Many of the Evans tools and artifacts are now exhibited in the Botwood Heritage Centre, and only two artifacts remain in possession of the family, both used during their fishing on the Labrador: the large box-compass with its sliding wood cover and the leather-bound, retractable "spy-glass" which extends to about forty inches.

Regrettably, not a single tool or artifact of the Manuel family of the Bay of Exploits, possibly the most prolific family of shipbuilders in the history of Newfoundland, is displayed publicly. Many of their trade tools were taken to the mainland by visiting relatives as heirlooms of a quickly disappearing family tradition and heritage. Many other valuable artifacts went to private collections.

As a boy growing up in Northern Arm in the Bay of Exploits, I spent much time in the house and stores of my great-uncle Job Manuel, my grandmother's brother, but he never once spoke about his shipbuilding exploits. Neither did Robert Evans, our next door neighbour. If it had not been for my questioning Robert in 1955 (he was then eighty-plus years old) and taking detailed notes, he probably would never have shared this information. Were these men excessively modest, or did they regard shipbuilding as simply something they were taught to do, a trade born of necessity, nothing particularly special? It must surely have been the latter. Many other men around Newfoundland were doing the same thing. The same kind of thinking was evident in our several conversations with Henry Vokey of Trinity. There is a special kind of satisfaction in working with the natural product, in Henry's words, "Nothing but wood." Henry's hard, gnarled hands speak eloquently of that love and satisfaction.

The lost tools and artifacts of the Cox family of New Bay serve as a kind of modern-day parable of what has happened with much of the traditional material culture of Newfoundland. The Cox family workshop was built at the edge of the sea among their stores, wharf, and other fishing structures. As family members aged and died off, the ocean and weather took their toll until the premises gradually collapsed and fell into the sea. Metal tools sank to the bottom where they rusted away. Wooden tools and artifacts drifted out to sea where they became derelicts on some distant shore. Thus has much of our tangible and visible cultural history been lost forever.

The tools and artifacts that remain form the only tangible evidence of the master shipbuilders' accomplishments. Many of these were fashioned in the family carpenter shop or the blacksmith shop, and here the builder displayed his innovative skills in crafting truly distinctive artifacts. Each tool bore a distinctive mark of ownership, often the initials laboriously carved in a wooden handle or filed in the metal, so these could not be claimed by other workers but could be returned to the right tool box at the end of the work day. Fortunately many of these artifacts have been preserved by thoughtful families, and some of them are now mounted in professionally-designed exhibits such as in the Grand Bank Fishermen's Museum, the Winterton Boat Building Museum, and the Botwood Heritage Centre. The exhibition of tools in the Trinity Museum is disappointing because it lacks the organizational touch of the professional curator, yet Trinity was perhaps the prime shipbuilding site in all of Newfoundland. Carbonear fortunately has the one remaining Rorke Store with an amazing pictorial display of the early fishery and shipbuilding as well as the dramatic ship's knees which support the ancient building. The Harbour Grace Museum displays only a few significant pictures depicting its historic role as a major shipbuilding site. We look in vain for similar exhibits in Monroe, Heart's Content, New Perlican, Hant's Harbour, Rocky Harbour, and Bay D'Espoir.

Only a few remnants of ancient shipbuilding sites remain, such as at Monroe, Trinity Bay, but these are fading fast. Still visible there in 2010 were several deep hollows in the bank where the Stone family's ships were laid in the stocks. One of our hopeful expectations from this project is that local heritage groups will be motivated to identify specific shipbuilding sites in their communities, erect appropriate signage, and incorporate these sites into their walking trails as a way of remembering and honoring those who were skilled founders of communities and early employers. There are still many Newfoundland communities once much involved in shipbuilding without a heritage centre or museum to exhibit the tools and artifacts associated with the trade. One significant example is New Harbour where the Newhook family of shipbuilders featured prominently in local economic history for several generations.

Were shipbuilders actually founders of communities? While they were not the primary founders, they still played a significant role in settlement formation, along with merchants and ordinary fishermen-planters. This was particularly linked to the practice of winterhousing as families moved from outer coastal settlements to the heads of bays from October to May each year, primarily to build ships and boats for pursuit of the fishery. Rev. Joseph Parkins's account of a month-long journey from Exploits Islands to the upper Bay of Exploits area, as described in detail in the *Twillingate Sun* of April 13, 1883, furnishes a fine account of this practice with an emphasis on shipbuilding in various locations. The Evans family had been using this area for shipbuilding at least thirty years before Parkins's visit, first living in winter tilts and then permanently settling at Evans's Point by 1876, thus becoming the founders and first settlers at Northern Arm. They had brought with them several other families who worked with them as ship's carpenters and Labrador fishermen. The Manuel family had used Ship Cove, in Botwood, for many years as a shipbuilding site but soon settled with the Evanses at Northern Arm. Not only were these two families the founders of Northern Arm, but they were also the economic engine that provided labour and sustenance for many others. The upper storey (third floor) of the Evans residence housed the men who came from surrounding communities to assist them in the harvesting of timber and then helped with the construction of their vessels, who returned in June to accompany them to the Labrador for the summer fishery and again in the fall to assist with the curing of the catch. The Evanses had three shipbuilding sites in Northern Arm; the Manuels had two sites and a sawmill and eventually established a local merchant firm. Additionally, the Manuels provided a house which served as a school during weekdays, a chapel on Sundays, and a social and community centre on occasion.

Likewise at Moreton's Harbour, the Horwood family of Carbonear set up a shipyard in the late eighteenth century and constructed vessels for the cod fishery and the seal hunt. Then came the Knight family of St. John's and the Small and Osmond families, all of them fishermen-shipbuilders and founders of this community. The story is repeated again and again throughout Newfoundland.

The distinction between fisherman, planter, and shipbuilder is almost impossible to make. And the *McAlpine* and *Lovell Directories* from 1871 to 1897 are so subjective and inconsistent in categorizing occupations that they are of little help. While most of the Newhooks of Trinity Bay are classified as fishermen in the *McAlpine Directory* of 1870-71, the reader should note in the Appendix to Chapter Four, Volume One, that most men in Bonavista Bay during this period—particularly in Gooseberry Islands, Flat Islands, Flower's Island, Bennett Island, Indian Arm, and Bloody Bay—are classified as shipbuilders. Perhaps the compiler visited these places during the shipbuilding season and saw all these men at work in the docks. The ship registers are the only reliable source for occupational classification, and many men whose occupation was given as fisherman, planter, trader/dealer, etc.

were also the builders of these particular vessels. The building of a ship was simply a means of getting to where the fish were and therefore incidental to whether the man was designated as fisherman, planter, or trader/dealer. Shipbuilding occurred in so many coves and harbours it is impossible to name all of them, thus the common use of general designators such as Trinity Bay, Bonavista Bay, Notre Dame Bay without any possibility of determining where the actual construction took place. The ship registers generally make a clear distinction between the person who owns the ship and the person who built the ship. These are often the same, but he may, for example, have been one of five brothers or the owner/builder. The infamous 1854-77 gap in the records, when shipbuilders' names are not recorded, deprives us of important information during what some describe as the golden age of shipbuilding in Newfoundland.

A definitive history of early shipbuilding in Newfoundland (1500-1800) has not yet been written, and that was not my intention. My focus has been primarily the approximate period 1800-2000, the period covered by the ship registers available to me. Any references to early shipbuilding in the published literature have been incorporated into the opening sections of each chapter, but this must surely be only a smattering of ship construction that occurred during that 300 year period. My primary interest has been the shipbuilders themselves rather than the types of ships they built, though I have supplied that information where it has been available.

This two-volume set, *Master Shipbuilders of Newfoundland and Labrador*, was designed as a tribute to the men who developed or were gifted with such considerable skills with wood that they fashioned truly excellent wooden ships for the Labrador and Grand Banks fisheries and for transporting the finished products to European and South American countries from at least the 1600s to the 1940s, as well as to skilled boatbuilders who constructed smaller vessels for the pursuit of the inshore and near-shore fisheries of Newfoundland and Labrador. The first volume of this set, published in 2013, is subtitled *Cape Spear to Boyd's Cove*. The present volume completes the remainder of Newfoundland and includes Labrador.

Apart from a very few of the better known and well-publicized of these shipbuilders, the names of the vast majority have long been forgotten or were never known to a broad public audience. All of them deserve a significant place in our history, for they played a role during the early years of our colony and province in helping to form some of the hundreds of coastal communities and a way of life still remembered in broad outline, but deserving of an even better reconstruction. We can recapture some of that way of life through the eyes of shipbuilders and other artisan classes which have now almost entirely disappeared.

I committed a great deal of forethought as to how I would present this material to the reader and considered that any approach would be fraught with difficulties. Nevertheless, I decided on the regional approach, "one bay at a time," with a view to highlighting the most prominent of these shipbuilders and shipbuilding families chronologically within these regions. Because there are so many shipbuilders and so much information about them, both volumes are necessarily heavy, fact-filled presentations. These are reference works written in narrative form and therefore do not comprise a unified narrative of the shipbuilding industry. I would recommend that these volumes be used as a reference source, taking small portions at a time, rather than reading them sequentially, and using the Index as a starting point for individual shipbuilders or families. My role, as I see it in these volumes, is to make available primary data of use to other writers; I am thus a compiler as much as, or more than, a writer. I would be delighted if others would use these offerings as a starting point for their own historical or imaginative writings.

These two volumes contain many details about individual shipbuilders and shipbuilding families and the communities where these builders lived and worked. The primary sources for these data are the ship registers deposited at the Maritime History Archives at Memorial University, the Registry of Shipping in St. John's, the National Archives in Ottawa, newspapers published in St. John's, Harbour Grace, and Twillingate, and the published literature. As discovered since the publication of Volume One, in briefly reviewing the early fishery and early settlement, I did not adequately consider the more recent scholarship on these topics.

Little new information on early shipbuilding has come to light since the publication of Volume One; one remarkable exception was of the construction of the entire superstructure on the 180-ton Spanish galleon *Trinidad* which was built in Spain in 1574 and sent to Labrador for the crafting of the "bridge deck and its upper part" (Barkham 81-82). More data on this is found in Chapter Three on Labrador.

Lloyd's Registers for the eighteenth century note several ships built in Newfoundland but with no information about builders or place of construction. These ships are all designated "Plantation-built" and noted to have been constructed in Newfoundland. The records for the 1750s and 1760s were checked carefully and spot checks were made following this period. The 130-ton *Aurora* was constructed in 1752; the 50-ton *Ann* in 1753 for Joliff; the 80-ton *Dispatch* in 1754 for Joseph White; the 100-ton *Beckford* in 1755 for Pitts; the 150-ton *Alex & John* in 1757 for Crosbie; the 70-ton *Betty* in 1760; the 30-ton *Billy* in 1762 for William Spurrier; the 250-ton *Escape* in 1763 for Pike & Green; the 90-ton *Bee* in 1763 for Bayley & Co.; the 70-ton *Betsey* in 1765 for Anthony Mery; the 120-ton brig *Neptune* in 1768 and the 50-ton *Penguin* in 1769. Some of the owner names are familiar from Volume One. For example, the *Dispatch* would probably have been constructed at Trinity for Joseph White, and the *Billy* and the *Ann* would probably have been built at Oderin or Burin for William Spurrier and Peter Joliffe. Some of these men may have been agents for British merchants or the merchants themselves. Some spot checking of the Lloyd's Registers was done following this period, but no substantive information was found except the names of a few ships: the *John* in 1753, the *Industry* in 1773, the *John* in 1782, the *James* in 1783, and the *Jane* with no date. These ships were registered in British ports.

Helpful comments from several interested readers have furnished additional information to what was presented in Volume One.

In Volume One, I mentioned Murley Berkshire of Random Island as one of the "finished carpenters" on the renowned Splinter Fleet at Clarenville in the 1940s. Since then I have corresponded with Murley, who is now ninety-three years of age. The names of only four of the master builders and two of the finished carpenters were identified in Volume One. Murley has now furnished additional details. The superintendent of construction was a Mr. Hayes, likely from Nova Scotia, since we know that William J. Roue (the designer of the famous *Bluenose*) was also the designer of these ten remarkable ships. After a short period, probably after the second ship was launched, Mr. Hayes was succeeded by a Mr. Pentz from Nova Scotia. Murley began work after the first ship, *Clarenville*, was launched in the spring of 1944 and was laid off in August 1946. He did not work in the dock. About 150 men were involved in the building operation. After the ships were launched, they were taken to the railway wharf, and Murley was one of the "finished carpenters" who built the superstructure on each vessel, consisting of the cabins, bridge, and forecastle (crew's quarters)—i.e., everything above decks. The men worked during the entire period under the superintendence of Max Sinclair from Gin Cove. Bramwell Smith from Hodge's Cove was Murley's foreman. Two other foremen were Alonzo Frampton of Gin Cove and Colin Baker of Snook's Harbour. Five of the finished carpenters were Eleazer (Lees) Hiscock, Ezekiel Cooper from Clarenville, Ernest and Gordon Wiseman from Shoal Harbour, and Watson Bowering from Apsey Brook. Other carpenters were Ross Laite from Petley, Hayward and Lindo Smith from Apsey Brook, and George Wiseman and Norman Blunden from Shoal Harbour. Boyce Smith of Elliott's Cove was one of the engineers installing the engines. The rigging of the vessels was also done under the superintendence of Max Sinclair. The riggers were Charles Laite of Petley, Jake Morgan of Seal Cove, and William Burt of Elliott's Cove. The government's intention was that these vessels would be built with Newfoundland materials; much of the birch and spruce was harvested near Glenwood and sawn at the mill in the dockyard.

New information has also come to light on the famous shipbuilder Michael Kearney through my correspondence with one of his descendants, Anna Kearney Guigne, a Folklorist and Adjunct Professor of Music at Memorial University. The shipbuilder extraordinaire Michael Kearney was actually Michael Kearney Junior. His father, Michael Kearney Sr., was employed by Holdsworth & Co. in the early years, operated a salmonry at Biscay Bay in Trepassey Bay about 1804, and moved to St. John's sometime after Michael Jr's birth in 1811. Holdsworth & Co. was an important merchant firm of Dartmouth, Devon, with its Newfoundland headquarters at Ferryland and pursuing an extensive trade along the Southern Shore. The John Kearney who crafted the 84-ton *Messenger* at Bay Bulls in 1820 must certainly have been Michael's uncle, his father's brother, so we will designate him as John Kearney I. Daniel Condon of St. John's married Michael's daughter, Margaret, and at age twenty-three he became an apprentice of Michael Kearney and learned the trade of shipbuilding from his father-in-law. Condon became a significant shipbuilder and shipowner in St. John's, constructing the first steamer in Newfoundland.

Michael Kearney and John Lambert, another prominent St. John's shipbuilder, purchased waterfront property on the south side of the harbour, probably in 1845, and the *Public Ledger* of January 7, 1845, mentions both an upper and lower shipyard. During 1845, three other vessels were under construction in the "lower shipyard." By 1850, however, Kearney was declared insolvent, and from that point he appears to have used the Mudge's dockyard or the merchant's property for whom he was building.

At the launch of his 180-ton brig *Thomas Ridley* at Carbonear in 1852, Michael Kearney gave a public address which was commented on in the *Harbour Grace Weekly* and repeated in the *Royal Gazette* of February 5, 1852:

> Kearney...compared the fishermen of Newfoundland to the miners of California, enabled as they had been to preserve the country from irretrievable ruin, notwithstanding the thousands of pounds that were absurdly sent away year after year to other colonies for vessels far inferior to those that could be built in this Island. He appealed to the hardy sealers of the Bay whether in a tempestuous night and amid rolling icebergs, they wouldn't feel as comfortable on a Newfoundland built vessel as they would on board vessels from neighbouring provinces, although the price of the latter might be a few chalks lower.

Kearney's comments are particularly relevant to the arguments made in Chapter Nine of this volume. For additional information on the Kearneys, see Chapter Eight of this volume.

Gilda Parsons, a retired teacher and a descendant of the Humby family of Summerville, has provided corrective information about her ancestors. Her paternal grandfather was Edward Humby II who constructed the 98-ton *Golden Stream* in 1935 and several other ships. He was the son of Eli Humby, not of Henry William Humby, as I had suggested in Volume One. Eli and Henry William were brothers, sons of Edward Humby I who built thirteen ships and rebuilt two others between 1876 and 1903. Edward I died in 1912. Edward Humby II was interviewed by historian and model shipbuilder Robert Halliday several times before Edward died in 1995; the interviews were taped for CBC.

In Volume One I leaned too heavily on D. W. Prowse as a source in establishing an historical context and did not sufficiently take into account the more recent scholarly writings on the early fishery and early settlement in Newfoundland. I have now read *Newfoundland in the Nineteenth and*

Twentieth Centuries as well as *Early European Settlement and Exploitation in Atlantic Canada* and checked other available sources.

Ships were being registered in St. John's as early as 1804, but these references were found only when the ship was re-registered at a later date. It appears that attempts were being made for ship registration as early as 1786, but it is not until 1813 and 1817 that we begin to see a few fulsome records. By 1818, the records become detailed and regular. In the twenty-sixth year of King George III (1786), an "Act for the further Increase and Encouragement of Shipping and Navigation" was passed by the English Parliament, and this was very probably what occasioned the first registration of ships in Newfoundland. This was also called the Merchant Shipping Act and required that any ship with a deck and of more than fifteen tons burthen be registered with the Customs Office at its home port. This was undoubtedly the Act that Capt. David Buchan was following in 1819 or 1823 when he supervised the registration of Margaret and John McCarthy's ship *George* at Harbour Grace. There was an Act passed in the fourth year of the reign of King George IV (1824) entitled "An Act for the Registering of Vessels," and this caused a spate of re-registrations in 1825 from which we derive a great deal of detailed information on prior shipbuilding in the colony. The year 1825 also almost exactly coincided with the collapse of the English migratory fishery, and the work of exporting codfish was then being taken over by the St. John's merchants and merchants of the south coast. What is known about shipbuilding in Newfoundland before 1813 is sparse indeed and is confined to occasional references in re-registration of ships and in the published literature such as D. W. Prowse (165, 378, 402, and 711) or Lloyd's Registers for the 1700s. Of particular importance is Prowse's statement that the 1718 Parliamentary Report indicates that "nearly all the Poole vessels engaged in the Newfoundland trade were built in the Colony. Spurriers built barques, brigs, and ships at Oderin, Burin, and St. Lawrence" (165). Some scholars question Prowse's statement about 1718 and suggest it could possibly have applied to 1817 or 1818, but in the ship registers during this latter period, only two ships were found to have been built for British merchants and these were crafted at Harbour Breton and Trinity. Prowse's two sentences in a footnote (165) are not time-connected in my judgment; the way they are written appears to imply that William Spurrier Sr. was the builder of some of these ships, yet Spurrier very probably did not come to Newfoundland until the 1750s. Prowse also lists thirty ships constructed in Newfoundland in 1804, a variety of schooners, sloops, luggers, brigs, and "ships," ranging in size from 31 tons to 232 tons (711). He unfortunately missed six additional vessels built during 1804 in Conception Bay (*Volume One* 58). All ships constructed during the early period were registered in British ports.

It has been pointed out that Nimshi Crewe's assertion that Charles Newhook I "was brought out from Europe to Newfoundland about 1777 by the mercantile firm of Benjamin Lester, to be its master shipbuilder at Trinity" needs to be questioned. There appears to be no corroborative evidence to maintain that claim. Crewe also asserted that Rev. George Lester-Garland had stated that Charles I was mentioned in Lester's letter books, but no specific letter was cited. Indeed, according to Gordon Handcock, there are no extant letter books in the Lester papers for 1777. Some of my conclusions about shipbuilding at Trinity in the very early period are rather conjectural, but the question still remains: If the amazing Newhook shipbuilders were not trained by Charles I, by whom were they trained? They must have learned the trade from Lester's other master builders. Thomas Stone, Lester's agent and formerly his chief clerk, supervised shipbuilding at Trinity from 1776 until the 1790s, and Lester's diaries contain many references, some not always favorable on this topic, but no entries mention Charles Newhook I. Lester frequently complained that ships built by Stone and sent to Poole had faults. In particular, some were not properly caulked or fitted. The second generation of Newhook shipbuilders certainly outperformed their teachers.

Indicative of the kind of error that can easily be made in research of this kind is the case of James Burden of Salvage (*Volume One* 160). He was presented as one man but they were actually father and son, the father building ships from at least 1867 to 1881. James Burden I was listed as a planter in 1867, a merchant in 1878, and a trader/dealer in 1881. He may well have constructed other ships during the period when shipbuilders' names were omitted from the registers, 1854-77. He died in 1894. The son James Burden II of Salvage was noted in the *Free Press* of February 1908 as "building a new schooner for the fishery. He is the only one building here."

My hope is that new information will become available as a result of the publication of these two volumes, information that will either support what I have written or correct and even refute some of the claims I have made. This has been an enormous undertaking and keeping all the factual information under control and consistent has been a challenge. I simply want to pay tribute to these amazing men who contributed so much to the establishing of early communities and to a burgeoning shipbuilding industry in our colony and province.

There are thirteen distinct areas of Newfoundland and Labrador covered in these two volumes. I have followed the divisions used by the Atlantic Canada Shipping Project at Memorial University in the 1950s and 1960s. These generally correspond with the large bays, but there are several long coastal stretches such as the south and southwest coast. The south and southeast Avalon Peninsula are combined into one district. The St. John's merchant firms discovered the mighty timber stands of Notre Dame Bay, Green Bay, and White Bay in the early period and sent professional shipbuilders there for a winter to construct large vessels for transport of their products. As timber stands became depleted in Conception Bay, builders moved along the coast to Trinity Bay and Bonavista Bay. The timber resources of Bay D'Espoir were also discovered in the early period, as were the regions at the head of Fortune Bay and Placentia Bay. Certain regions of the west coast yielded timber for the crafting of many ships, some of considerable size.

The tonnage of vessels is consistently given throughout the narrative, but this should be supplemented with information about the dimensions of the vessel. Research shows there is no specific formula for calculating the size because there are several variables depending on the kind of ship in question, but at least there are reasonably accurate comparisons. A 15-ton ship was found to measure 40 feet long, 14 feet wide, and 6 feet deep. The dimensions for a 22-ton ship were 42 x 15 x 6, for a 50-ton ship 63 x 19 x 8, a 77-ton ship 72 x 22 x 8, and a 100-ton ship 78 x 24 x 9. The 125-ton brig *Scotch Lass*, constructed by Michael Kearney at Ferryland in 1838, was 73 feet long, 19 feet wide, and 13 feet deep. The 190-ton brig *Gratia*, constructed by Garrett Curtis at Renews in 1838, was 86 feet long, 19 feet wide and 14 feet "deep of hold." Some of the dimensions of the three-masted schooners were as follows: the 372-ton *Attainment* of 1917 was 137 feet long, 32 feet wide, and 11 feet deep; the 428-ton *Marie Louise H.* of 1919 was 140 feet long, 32 feet wide, and had a depth of 14 feet; the 149-ton *Nancy Lee* of 1920 measured 116 x 29 x 11.

The average life of a wooden ship has been calculated to be about nine years. When the vessel is well-maintained and regularly refurbished, the average life rises to about fifteen years. There were many exceptions to this rule-ofthumb, however. Robert Evans's 39-ton *Defender* lasted for thirty-eight years (1901-39), and his 48-ton *Reliance* served from 1903 to 1936. Thomas Palfrey's tern schooner *Mollie Fearn* had a long life of thirty years. Michael Kearney's 180-ton brig *Thomas Ridley* spent thirty-three years in the trading business. Matthew Hudson's 32-ton *Three Sisters* lasted for thirty-six years. Joseph Matterface of Boat Harbour built the 19-ton *Joseph M.*, which served for thirty-seven years. John Dunphy's 27-ton *Mary Nagle*, built in 1895, lasted for forty-two years, and Benjamin Foote of Placentia Bay constructed vessels which lasted for forty-four and sixty-seven years. It is not at all exceptional to find in the registers many vessels which served for more than thirty years.

I would say that ninety per cent of the vessels constructed in Newfoundland were carvel-built and the seams caulked with oakum, the builders using the moulded and rounded model, the layered model, or the three-stick method so enthusiastically presented by Jerome Canning during his workshops at the Winterton Boat Building Museum. There were exceptions, of course, as illustrated especially in various newspapers of the day. For example, in 1907 the 63-ton ketch-rigged schooner *Cecil Belle* which had been started at Gambo by W. R. Strong and finished by Thomas French and Amos Piercey was noted by the *Free Press* to be

> "of peculiar build and rises very high aft…due to the rake of the stern timbers being in a continuous line with and forming a part of the upward curve made by the planking under the vessel's quarter. The object of this no doubt is to reduce to a minimum the retarding effect of the 'dead water' when sailing."

In that same year, 1907, Thomas A. Winsor of Exploits Islands built the first "knockabout" schooner in Newfoundland, using American plans. The schooner was about 50 tons, had no bowsprit or jibboom, and regularly reached the great sailing speed of 15 knots. Likewise, the south-coast builders were greatly influenced by American schooners for their sailing qualities and used American plans in designing their ships. William Wakely of Haystack had designed and crafted several small schooners in the 40-ton range in the early 1900s on which the *Free Press* of 1907 commented when the *Pandora* arrived in St. John's:

> "Mr. Wakely's own design…is a departure from the old model. One prominent feature is the shape of the hull aft. She is hollowed

> on each side so as not to cause so much suction from 'dead water' as the ordinary craft, a fact which adds considerably to her sailing powers."

There are many other instances in the literature which demonstrate the shipbuilder's innovative skills and willingness to adapt the model to the needs of changing times.

Throughout both volumes of this set, occasional reference is made to the kinds of woods used in the construction of ships. No such references occur in the Newfoundland ship registers, which seems strange indeed. About Lloyd's Registers it is asserted that when no reference is made to the kind of wood used it is to be assumed that the wood is oak. Most references to the woods used in the construction of Newfoundland ships were found in newspapers, in the literature pertaining to the trade, through family recollections, from merchant account books, or even eyewitness accounts. A Newfoundland forestry book published in 1974 states that there are only two existing Newfoundland hardwoods: white birch and trembling aspen. Dr. Wilfred Grenfell's romantic and exaggerated references to Newfoundland schooners being crafted out of the softwoods fir and spruce should be discounted as inaccurate. It is doubtful fir was ever used except possibly for the crafting of cabins. Spruce was used in a judicious manner, usually alternating with juniper and birch in the framing timbers of the vessel, and sometimes as masts because of their tall, straight, knot-free nature. For example, William Carberry's 45-ton schooner *Lady Braham* at Burgoyne's Cove in 1907 had masts of local spruce, the mainmast being 56 feet high and the foremast 54 feet high. In that same year, it was stated that Alfred Vey's 40-ton *British Empire*, built in Random Sound, Trinity Bay, had masts of pitch pine and American spruce.

The Newfoundland forests were well-stocked with juniper, birch, pine, and black spruce and up until at least the 1920s with an abundance of witchhazel (yellow birch, *Betula lutea*) which oozed an oil-like substance that made it ideal for underwater planking. For example, the *Free Press* reported in 1918 that Adam Chalk's 504-ton *Bella Scott* at Botwood had "bottom planking 3 and ½ in. witch-hazel—which is considered the finest timber our country produces." Yellow birch still exists in Newfoundland but only in rich, moist areas and in exceedingly small stands in the Bay D'Espoir area, western Newfoundland south of Deer Lake, and a few regions on the Avalon

Peninsula, but it is seldom if ever used today. Many large staunch and sturdy vessels were crafted with Newfoundland woods, particularly in the early years. For large vessels built in the later years, local woods were usually supplemented by imported oak, particularly Baltimore white oak, English elm, BC fir, California fir, pitch pine, American spruce, American beech, and Demerara greenheart. Shipwrecks on the coast sometimes furnished oak and other hardwoods which were reclaimed for the construction of new ships or the rebuilding of damaged vessels. Nothing was wasted.

Newspapers of the day make frequent references to newly built ships being brought to St. John's for registration and noting some special characteristics. For example, the 26-ton *Speedwell* constructed at Lance Cove, Trinity Bay, in 1907 by William Taverner was "full-timbered with juniper, spruce and birch, planked with hardwood." At Norman's Cove that same year, John Piercey's 40-ton *Alice C.* was "strongly-built, planked with hardwood," and Patrick Seward's 27-ton *Native Lass* at Heart's Ease had "hardwood plank with spruce decking." The 62-ton *Ronald Barry* constructed in 1918 at Green's Harbour by James Green had "a hard pine deck, plank and ceiling and was built for the bounty." Many other ships were noted to have hardwood planking and to be "full-timbered" with birch and juniper and sometimes with alternating spruce. "Full-timbered" means the timbers were placed especially close together for sturdy construction. For example, Robert Evans's 372-ton three-masted schooner *Attainment* at Thwart Island in 1917 had timbers that were only five inches apart.

From an earlier period, Garrett Curtis's 190-ton brig *Gratia* at Renews in 1838 was "built of juniper and witchazel." Michael Kearney's 130-ton brig *Mary Hounsell* of 1842 was noted to have been built of "White-hazel and Juniper" and the "Stem and Stern-post each in one length, all the growth of this island." Jonas Newell Newhook's 248-ton *Fleet Wing* of 1857 was framed entirely with local juniper but its "topsides, rails and covering boards of Baltimore white oak, keelson of white oak and Demerara greenheart with greenheart treenails." And Henry Vokey's schooner *J. & B.* in 1970 had a juniper hull with decks and masts of BC fir, cabins of solid mahogany, and deck railings of oak.

These few references give a flavour of the selection of woods from a surrounding productive forest, and in some instances supplemented by imported timber, all available for purchase from St. John's merchant firms.

Many other references to the woods used will be found throughout this two-volume set.

Chapter Nine of this volume offers a corrective to the assertions of John P. Parker about the Newfoundland tern (three-masted) schooners of the early twentieth century. Parker was a respected writer, ship master, and superintendent of harbour pilots in Nova Scotia who, in his influential 1960 book *Sails of the Maritimes*, asserted that these Newfoundland schooners were "not a success," that "the wood was not of good quality" and of "unseasoned timber of poor grade," that they were "built hurriedly" and "without great capital investment," that "they were too light in design and were insecurely fastened," that "the pumping was primitive," and that they were "constructed by men who were expert only at building smaller craft." I attempt in that chapter to counter Parker's conclusions.

In spite of my almost thirty-year effort in collecting and organizing material on Newfoundland shipbuilders, I believe there is much material that has not yet come to light. Perhaps the publication of these two volumes will encourage local historians, family researchers, and other interested readers to delve into and reveal other sources to complement what I have done. That would make all my efforts worthwhile.

CHAPTER ONE

NOTRE DAME BAY
INCLUDING BAY OF EXPLOITS, HALL'S BAY AND GREEN BAY

A SMALL PART OF Notre Dame Bay—from Crow Head, Twillingate, to Boyd's Cove—was covered in Volume One. It is difficult to determine a satisfactory dividing point in the western section of the Straight Shore, so an arbitrary decision was made to include Fogo Island and New World Island as well as Chapel Island and Dunnage Island and the Dildo Run in the former area.

It is challenging to make a clear distinction between the two areas for a number of reasons. Many of the shipbuilders who lived in the former area did most or all of their shipbuilding in Notre Dame Bay, Bay of Exploits, Hall's Bay, and Green Bay, and several of them eventually settled in this area. It is therefore complicated at times to pinpoint clearly the builder's place of residence because he may have lived in Twillingate, for example, but winterhoused (living in tilts) in Notre Dame Bay for several consecutive years. In an e-mail of January 11, 2014, Gordon Handcock writes, "The migration links between the fishing areas and the timbered areas were an important factor in the settlement of the latter.... In time many of the former ship-building and wintering sites became principal settlements." Also in the early years, the terms Notre Dame Bay and Green Bay were often used interchangeably, creating some confusion for readers.

This is a huge area and in the early years was exceedingly well-timbered down to the water's edge. J. B. Jukes, the visiting geological surveyor, described the area in his 1840 book *Excursions in and about Newfoundland*:

> The trees…grow so closely together, that their twigs and branches interlace from top to bottom, and lying indiscriminately among them, there are innumerable old and rotten stumps and branches, or newly fallen trees, which, with the young shoots and brushwood, form a tangled and often impenetrable thicket… Every step through these woods is a matter of toil and anxiety, requiring constant vigilance to avoid falling, and constant labour to procure standing room…. In the heat of summer, while the woods are so thick as to shut out every breath of air they are at the same time too low and too thinly leaved at top to exclude the burning rays of the sun, the atmosphere being rendered close and stifling by the smell of the turpentine which exudes from every pore of the trees. (20-21)

It was to such a pristine area that the early entrepreneurs and shipbuilders came. Men such as John Slade, Thomas Colbourne I and John Colbourne of Poole, George Skeffington of Bonavista, the firm of Richard and Netlam Tory and William Pittman ventured into this vast area and beyond in the early years despite the threat of harassment from the French who had been ceded fishing rights along the French Shore from Cape Bonavista northward and the native occupiers of much of this area, the Beothuk. The temptation of wood for shipbuilding, as well as furs and salmon fishing of the great rivers, was too much to resist. And along with the pursuit came conflict, particularly with the Beothuk who succumbed eventually to the aggressive tactics of Europeans and Newfoundlanders and were cut off from their coastal food supplies.

One of the additional difficulties in dealing with this area is the very common use of broad terms to describe both where the shipbuilder lived and where he built his ships. The ship registers are replete with general terms such as Notre Dame Bay, Green Bay, Bay of Exploits, and all too often with nothing more explicit than that, so it is impossible in these cases to determine which particular part of this extensive area the builder reported to the registrar. This is a particular problem in dealing with this region and is not quite as difficult in any of the other areas.

The mighty timber stands of the Notre Dame Bay/Bay of Exploits/Green Bay area must have been familiar to the St. John's merchants from an early period. Merchants were, in fact, sponsors of shipbuilding from the very beginning and often sponsors of early settlement. Humphrey Cole, a St. John's merchant, had ships built there in 1822 and 1825. Thomas Knight I of St. John's built a ship in Green Bay in 1831, James Woods and John Ackrell in 1833, James MacKay in 1836, Henry Knight in 1838, and Thomas Ashman in 1839. These were mostly large ships, taking advantage of the available massive timber stands.

Resident builders were constructing ships there even before that. The builder of the 116-ton brig *Invulnerable*, built at Burnt Bay in 1816, is unknown, but the vessel's owner was from St. John's. William Skinner was the builder of the 49-ton *Amity* constructed at New Bay in 1819. This vessel was registered in Poole and was owned by Thomas Every of Fogo, the local agent for John and Thomas Slade of Poole. Skinner resided at Fogo and in 1841 built the 28-ton *Experiment* in Green Bay.

John Peyton Jr. had two shipbuilding sites in the Bay of Exploits, one at Indian Point opposite the mouth of the Exploits River and one at Exploits Islands. He brought two shipbuilders from Christchurch, England, at the beginning: Robert Crabtree and James Bemister. It is not known how long they stayed. In 1819, Peyton engaged Garrett Curtis of Salmonier, St. Mary's Bay, to supervise operations at both his shipyards. A local man, John Fudge, built the 37-ton *Liberty* for Peyton in the Bay of Exploits in 1820. Curtis remained with Peyton for eleven years and during this time built seven ships for him: the 75-ton *Ann*; the sister ships the 118-ton brig *Worcester*, which was sold to St. John's merchants Thomas H. Brooking and Richard Robinson, and the 150-ton brig *Amprilite*; the 34-ton *Joseph* built for Brigus merchant Charles Cozens; the 71-ton *Elizabeth*, which was sold to James Stewart, merchant of Greenock, Scotland; the 56-ton *Hope* for merchants John Brine and Nathaniel Smith of St. John's and Greenspond; and the 61-ton *Kate*, which was built for J. J. Grieve, merchant at St. John's. Four of these ships were built in the Bay of Exploits; the *Elizabeth* was built at Twillingate and the *Hope* was built at Greenspond. Shipbuilding must have been a profitable business for John Peyton.

Curtis left John Peyton's employ sometime after 1833 and moved first to Renews, where he built several large ships, and then he returned to Salmonier, where he continued building until at least 1852. He built at least sixteen ships during a thirty-two year period and may have continued building during the period when shipbuilders' names were omitted from the records, 1854 to 1877.

William Snow I built the 42-ton *Snow Drop* in the Bay of Exploits in 1823 for David, Robert, and James Slade, merchants at Fogo. This is the only time Snow's name appears in the records. It is the same with John Reans whose name appears only once when, in 1833, he built the 109-ton brig *Mary Jane* in the Bay of Exploits for J. J. Grieve, a St. John's merchant. Reans was very probably an English shipbuilder rather than a local man.

James Sevier of Exploits Islands built three ships in the Bay of Exploits between 1827 and 1835: the 28-ton *Nightingale*, the 69-ton *Actor* in 1830, and the 139-ton brig *Adelaide*. The last two ships were built for St. John's merchants and the last one for Charles and Thomas Bennett, and Humphrey Cole was the master. Cole was a shipbuilder himself, and one wonders if James Sevier was a professional builder brought from England. Joseph Seeviour (note the variant spelling of the name) may have been a brother of James; he built the 49-ton *Active* in the Bay of Exploits in 1847. Both men were designated as planters.

John Foote and William Menchenton were early residents of Exploits Islands and had their shipyard on the island, where all their ships were built. They were co-builders of the 55-ton appropriately named *John and William* in 1826. Both men were planters. John was the master builder of the 86-ton *Sisters* in 1829, and William was still his partner. In 1838, William built the 59-ton *Mary Jane*. The John Menchenton, who built the 82-ton *Mary Jane* in 1849 in Green Bay for William Menchenton, and the William Foote, who built the 76-ton *Euchidas* in Green Bay in 1849 for John Foote and the 43-ton *Beaver* in 1859 for himself, were undoubtedly sons of the older men.

John Cook of Fortune Harbour built the 53-ton *Dove* in 1828 and sold it the same year to J. B. Bland, St. John's merchant. In 1834, he and George and James Cook, probably his sons and all of them planters, co-built the 100-ton *Industrious* at Fortune Harbour. John Cook's name also appears in the record with the designator "Sr."

From this point onwards, we will deal in this narrative section only with the most prominent builders; occasional builders are found in the Appendix to Chapter One. Shipbuilders are presented in family groups only if there were three or more significant builders and more than one generation.

THE ROWSELL FAMILY

Early members of the Rowsell family in Notre Dame Bay achieved both fame and infamy in connection with the Beothuk; one brother, George, was favoured by the natives, and the other, Thomas I, was regarded as their enemy and eventually killed by them in 1789. Local sources say the first Rowsell to settle in Hall's Bay, William Rowsell I, was a shipbuilder from England.

In 1831 at Hall's Bay, John Rowsell Jr. built the 33-ton *Brothers* for his own use. His partner was his father, John Rowsell Senior. In 1844 Joseph Rowsell constructed the 21-ton *Sally Ann* in Green Bay. George Rowsell, a farmer/planter at Twillingate, built the 21-ton *Father and Sons* in Green Bay in 1846, and Thomas Rowsell Sr. and Jr. were his partners in this venture. In 1849 John Jr. constructed the 41-ton *James* for a St. John's merchant. Also in Green Bay, in 1856, William Rowsell II fashioned the 49-ton *Six Brothers* and his partners were Esau and Mark Rowsell, the latter being appointed master of the vessel. Twenty-three years later in Seal Bay, William Rowsell constructed the 37-ton *Emma*. We do not know how many ships William built during the period when builders' names were omitted from the records.

The same thing applies to Thomas Rowsell. In 1858 he built the 46-ton *Five Brothers* in Green Bay, and in 1876 he built the 19-ton *Elizabeth Jane* for which he collected the government bounty of $57. He probably constructed several ships between these dates, but the ship registers are silent from 1854 to 1877. In 1884 Thomas constructed the 18-ton *Arina* somewhere in Notre Dame Bay, and when he sold it in 1889 the record notes that he was a resident of Ward's Harbour. This was probably Thomas Jr., referred to above. Levi Rowsell of Ward's Harbour, and possibly one of Thomas's four brothers, built the 28-ton *Niagara* in Hall's Bay in 1877. In that same year, John Rowsell II of Burnt Islands crafted the schooner *Gladiator* somewhere in Exploits Bay, and Edward Rowsell was appointed master. The vessel was built for Exploits merchant, Josiah Manuel, and Manuel was paid the bounty of $99. And finally, in 1884, Henry Rowsell of Leading Tickles built the 35-ton *Isabel* for a local trader/dealer.

THE MANUEL FAMILY

The Manuel family was by far the most prolific family of shipbuilders in the Notre Dame Bay area and along the northeast coast. In fact, they were the most prolific family of shipbuilders in the whole of Newfoundland and Labrador. Most of their vessels were of small to medium size, and it was not until the early 1900s that one member of the family master-built a few of the large three-masted vessels.

Joseph Manuel II was the progenitor of the Newfoundland clan that remained on the island and is reputed to have come to Newfoundland in 1785 with brothers Samuel I and William and their father Joseph I. John Manuel I is reputed to have owned a fleet of fishing vessels which had been coming to Newfoundland for many years before this. However, it was not until 1833 that the Manuels began their illustrious shipbuilding ventures. The three brothers, Thomas I, James II, and Luke I, co-built the 28-ton *Plover* at Twillingate that year; James I was the fourth partner. And in 1844 Thomas built the 56-ton *Triumph* for a St. John's merchant. Thomas was master of this vessel as he was of the 102-ton brigantine *Charles*, which had been built in the Bradore Lakes in Nova Scotia and which he purchased in 1850. When Thomas crafted the 62-ton brigantine *Challenge* in 1852 for St. John's merchant Thomas Row (Roe), he also became master of that vessel. Then comes the gap in the records, and we know nothing more of his building record, but we know that he continued as a ship's captain for several years.

Samuel Manuel II and John Manuel II of Burnt Island, Green Bay (presumably Exploits Islands), co-built the 50-ton *Ann and Elizabeth* somewhere in Green Bay in 1840, and in 1846 John Manuel of Exploits constructed the 39-ton *Elizabeth* in Green Bay, and Samuel was his partner. In 1852 John built the 39-ton *Jane* for Edward Downton, an Exploits planter.

In 1853 Simon Manuel of Exploits began his illustrious building career which lasted for thirty-six years, and in that time he produced nineteen ships. His first ship was the 59-ton *Dante* built in Green Bay in 1853, and his partners were his brother Josiah and his father Joseph II. He constructed many of the well-known Manuel ships such as the 47-ton *Olive Branch*, the 57-ton *Dauntless*, the 50-ton *Royal Arch*, the 56-ton *Pert*, the 60-ton *Lizzie*, and the 33-ton *Niobe*. The Customs' Returns for 1875 and 1876 note that Simon collected the government bounties of $120 for the *Lizzie* and $150 for the *Royal Arch*. He must have operated somewhat independently within the Manuel family since he is noted also as having collected the bounty on three other ships: the 65-ton *Billow* of 1877 ($195), the 40-ton *Jessie* of 1883 ($120), and the 40-ton *Family Trial* of 1886 ($120). Simon's largest ship was the 70-ton *Reynard* built in 1888, and his smallest ship was the 25-ton *Little Willie* crafted for merchant Edwin J. Duder in 1884. All his ships were built in the Bay of Exploits or Green Bay, and in the early years, those two terms were often used synonymously. Two ships were noted as having been built at the Exploits River, and it is quite possible that most of Simon's ships were built in what is known today as Botwood harbour. Simon's last ship was built at Burnt Bay in 1889, the 55-ton *Nora Creina*, and constructed for Edwin J. Duder. Simon was then sixty years old. Throughout his career he was listed as a planter and served as master of most of the ships he built. In the latter years, he was living in St. John's and returning to the Bay of Exploits to construct his ships.

James Manuel II of Exploits built two ships in Green Bay: the 86-ton brigantine *Veloz* in 1858 and the 50-ton *Northern Light* in 1864. Since the notorious gap occurs during this period, nothing further can be determined about his building career. It is known that in 1848 he was master of the 49-ton *Rover*, which had been built in Nova Scotia by Thomas Miller Sr. of Placentia.

Josiah Manuel became the most famous of the seven Manuel brothers, sons of Joseph II and Elizabeth (Milley) Manuel of Exploits. Josiah was a planter during the first seven years of his building career and during this period built three ships: the 30-ton *Ruby* in 1868, the 41-ton *Archibald* in 1871, and the 39-ton *Road Ash* in 1874. By 1875 Josiah had become a trader/dealer, and that year he constructed the 22-ton *Maria* at Exploits Islands. The Customs' Returns for 1876 indicate that Josiah built the 38-ton *Maud* that year and was paid a government bounty of $114 for the ship. This small vessel lasted for a remarkable twenty-seven years and was broken up at Random Island in 1903. In 1877 Josiah crafted two ships in the Bay of Exploits: the 38-ton *Rose* and the 48-ton *Edith Jane*. Even after he had become a merchant in 1880, he continued to supervise the construction of ships on Exploits Islands and produced the 33-ton *Pert* in 1880, the 49-ton *Jabez* in 1881, and the 54-ton *C.A.M.* in 1882 for which he was paid a bounty of $162. The *Twillingate Sun* of January 20, 1881, describes Josiah as a boatbuilder, but he was much more than that. From 1893 to 1905, the year before his death, Josiah maintained an intense building activity with the 58-ton *Hearty* and the 20-ton *Swan* in 1893, the 35-ton *Skip Jack* in 1894, the 26-ton *Brisk* in 1897, the 34-ton *Our Bobs* and the *Baden Powell* in 1900, the 66-ton *Duchess* in 1901, the 68-ton *Reciprocity* in 1903, the 85-ton *E. P. Morris* in 1904, and the 82-ton *M. P. Cashin* and the 44-ton *Dyama* in 1905. Over a period of thirty-eight years, Josiah built twenty ships and carried on a busy trading and supply business along the northeast coast. He was the prime example of a merchant shipbuilder and in the latter years closely supervised the construction of ships in close proximity to his extensive business properties on Exploits Islands. Between 1876 and 1904 he collected bounties of more than $6,295 for ships constructed by and for him.

Josiah employed at least twelve shipbuilders in the Bay of Exploits area between 1877 and 1906 to construct ships for him. These were John Rowsell, James Lyver, Francis Luff, George Luff, Francis Wells, James Wells, Lionel Hynes, James Snow, Henry Warford, Samuel Rose, Absalom Chalk, and Josiah Purchase. Several of the Manuel brothers and cousins were also building ships for Josiah's extensive fishery and supply business throughout these busy years.

The *Daily News* of February 15, 1896, commented:

> If every settlement in Terra Nova boasted such men as Josiah Manuel and Thomas Winsor of Exploits, poverty would be at a discount. Mr. Manuel is building 2 schooners and repairing a third. Mr. Winsor is also building one. This gives employment to a large number throughout the winter and will enable them to go to the fisheries free of debt. Instead of drawing supplies on their summer account they are earning them. Exploits is a snug little place, her sons and daughters are most hospitable, and withal industrious. The people deserve to succeed and will do so. No settlement knows better how to build schooners and no schooners are better built than the Exploits ones.

Josiah died in St. John's in January 1907 at the residence of his son-in-law John C. Crosbie. The newspapers of the day paid high tribute to the "Merchant Ship builder." A special train from Lewisporte brought "Mrs. Josiah Manuel, Miss Janet Manuel, Mr. Chesley Manuel, Messrs. G. W. Gushue, J. Penney, A. Yates, B. W. Morris and several others to attend the funeral obsequies of the late Josiah Manuel." The *Free Press* continued:

> Josiah Manuel conducted business in Green Bay for 40 years, on the French Shore, in the Straits, with Exploits the place where he was born as his headquarters. As a shipbuilder he ranks with the foremost...for the number of schooners built and the beauty of their lines and their durability and seaworthiness. At least 100 schooners have come from his docks and there are 7 on the stocks at present. A life-long Conservative...[he developed] pneumonia and congestion of the lungs while on a visit to the city...This is the passing of no ordinary man...much of the prosperity of northern Newfoundland is due to him.

Mrs. Josiah Manuel died in August 1916 at age 81.

Josiah's brother Luke (Luke Manuel II) moved to Northern Arm in the 1870s and built ten ships over a period of thirteen years, between 1876 and 1888. His first ship was the 40-ton *Osprey*, and for it he was paid a government bounty of $120. Luke was my grandmother's father. His ships were between 40 and 84 tons. Being a devout Methodist lay reader and Sunday school superintendent, Luke named several of his ships after people "who built up Christianity in the western world," in the words of Robert Evans. Luke crafted the 61-ton *Gideon Ousley* in 1877, the 56-ton *Wilberforce* in 1879, the 46-ton *Sammy Hick* in 1884, and the 54-ton *Barbara Heck* in 1886. The *Sammy Hick* lasted for a remarkable forty-eight years and was lost at sea in 1932. The Customs' Returns between 1877 and 1886 indicate that Luke collected a bounty of $510 on three of his ships.

John Manuel III began his shipbuilding career in 1876 with the 44-ton *Princess* for which Josiah was paid a government bounty of $88. John's second ship was the 52-ton *Medeanne*, also constructed for Josiah. John continued building until 1902. He built fifteen ships over a period of twenty-six years. All his ships were constructed in the Bay of Exploits, specifically one at Kite Cove, two at Thwart Island, and three at Fortune Harbour; other specific locations are lacking. His largest ship was the 91-ton *Jenette*, and his smallest was the 25-ton *Janet*. Nine of his fifteen ships were fashioned for Josiah Manuel: the *Princess*, the *Jenette*, the *Janet*, the 50-ton *Artist*, the 43-ton *Olivette*, the 55-ton *Hecla*, the 76-ton *Royal Huntress*, the 55-ton *Shamrock*, and the 55-ton *Wigwammer*. The 25-ton *Notre Dame* was built in 1892 for Mary Ann Quirk of Fortune Harbour. And one ship built in 1889 bore the playful name *Can't Help It*. The *Twillingate Sun* of May 4, 1883, noted that John Manuel was a boatbuilder.

Jonathan Manuel of Exploits built nine ships over a period of twenty years, between 1878 and 1897. All nine of his ships were constructed for Josiah Manuel, including his largest ships: the 68-ton *Flying Mist*, the 63-ton *Meteor*, the 61-ton *Enchantress*, and the 56-ton *Larkspur*. His ships were built in the Bay of Exploits and specifically one at Exploits River and one at Burnt Bay. The general designator "EXP" in the ship registers covers a very large area, and it is always more interesting when one can locate the specific building site.

George Manuel was one of the seven famous Manuel brothers. He was master of Bowring Bros.' 473-ton steam-sail vessel *Curlew* twice from 1877 onwards. He was thirty-two years old in 1877. In 1888 he was vice-master of

THE SEVEN MANUEL BROTHERS OF THE BAY OF EXPLOITS, ALL MASTER SHIPBUILDERS. SEATED L TO R: LUKE, JOSIAH, AND SIMON. STANDING L TO R: PERCIVAL, GEORGE, THOMAS, AND JONATHAN. THE MOST PROLIFIC FAMILY OF SHIPBUILDERS IN NEWFOUNDLAND, THE MANUELS PRODUCED AT LEAST THIRTY-THREE BUILDERS AND MORE THAN 200 SHIPS. (Photo Courtesy of Winston Manuel.)

the 293-ton *Plover*. His shipbuilding career began in 1879 with the construction of the 52-ton *Mayflower*. The next year he built the 56-ton brigantine-rigged *Henrietta*. By 1883 he had relocated from Exploits Islands to Kite Cove (later renamed Laurenceton), and the *Twillingate Sun* of May 4, 1883, calls him a boatbuilder. In the thirty years between 1879 and 1908 he crafted fourteen ships, including the 65-ton *St. Clair*, the 50-ton *Tulip*, the 47-ton *Zada Belle*, and the 36-ton *Medallion* in 1908, his last ship. He built only two ships for his brother, Josiah Manuel: the 26-ton *Ajax* in 1895 and the 35-ton *Rapid* in 1896.

Solomon Manuel constructed six ships over a period of thirty-one years. His first ship, the 19-ton *Lavinia*, was built at Exploits Islands in 1878, and shortly after that he settled at Kite Cove where in 1881 he built the 33-ton *Harmony* for Josiah Manuel. By 1907 Kite Cove was being called Laurenceton, and here he fashioned the 28-ton *Alexandra E.* that same year. His largest ship was his last, the 50-ton *Oakland*, which he built in 1909. This ship was rebuilt by James T. Feltham at Bragg's Island in 1929 and had an engine installed in 1944, thus lasting more than thirty-five years.

Jacob Manuel, a descendant of the Twillingate branch of the Manuel family, had located in New Bay, specifically at what later was called Cottrell's Cove, by at least 1882. His first ship was the 46-ton *Sisters* crafted in 1876 for Edward Moore of New Bay who collected the bounty of $138. In 1882 Jacob built the 59-ton *Amelia* for local merchant Edmund Moore. His other two ships were constructed in 1884 and 1894 for local planters.

Samuel Manuel III had located in Kite Cove by 1882 and built there the 16-ton *Gipsy* in 1882 and the 15-ton *Patience* in 1883, both for St. John's merchants John Duder and Edwin J. Duder. His place of residence is given as Burnt Arm in 1900 when he constructed the 33-ton *Ladysmith* at Exploits Islands. This was corrected to Kite Cove the next year where he built the 55-ton *Ettie Elliott*. Kite Cove and Burnt Arm are virtually the same community.

Andrew Manuel I had the incredible record of building at least sixteen ships in twenty-one years, from 1875 to 1896. He started with the 64-ton *Lady Hill* in 1875 and then crafted the 100-ton *Mary Jane* in 1876. J. & J. Clark collected the government bounty of $128 for the first vessel; Bowring Bros. collected $300 for the second. After twenty years in the trade, the *Lady Hill* was transferred to Pictou, Nova Scotia, in 1900. The record for Andrew falls silent until 1881 when he builds the 72-ton *Flamingo*; he concluded his career in 1896 with the 25-ton *Rattler*. His largest vessels were the 100-ton *Mary Jane* of 1876 and the famous 84-ton *Mandamus*, which he built in 1895. This vessel and eight others were fashioned for Josiah Manuel. About the *Mandamus* the July 10, 1895, edition of the Daily News raved: "The *Mandamus*...can be enumerated in the category of the best modelled, best finished, and most substantial class of vessels now built in this colony...such a splendid craft...can compare favourably with any vessel of similar tonnage in Canada or the United States." The *Evening Telegram* of January 14, 1922, remembered the *Mandamus* as "the largest banker of the Newfoundland fleet" when it was constructed twenty-seven years earlier. The naming of the 69-ton *Anti-Confederate*, in 1888, undoubtedly reflected Josiah's political views. The 61-ton *Mitchie*, built in 1887, was named after Josiah's daughter who married John C. Crosbie and subsequently became Lady Crosbie. All of

Andrew's vessels were built in the Bay of Exploits, and several of them lasted for more than thirty years, which is truly remarkable.

Azariah Manuel's building career began in 1882 with the 16-ton *Condor*, which he constructed at Scissors Cove, and ended in 1913 with the 19-ton *Brandt* built at Salt Pond. During this thirty-two year period he crafted eleven ships, all of them for merchants: Edwin J. Duder, Mark Osmond, Josiah Manuel, Frederick Moore, Thomas A. Winsor, and William H. Winsor. By 1906 he had settled at Salt Pond, but he built ships also at Burnt Bay, Exploits River, Thwart Island, and Lewisporte (a later name for Burnt Bay). Two of his most noteworthy ships were constructed for Josiah Manuel: the 45-ton *Mischief* crafted in 1902 and the 39-ton *Mikado* in 1904. His largest ships were the 57-ton *Nerett* built in 1908 and the 55-ton *Robin* in 1907.

Eight additional Manuel men constructed at least one ship each during the period 1884 to 1906. Thomas Manuel II built the 38-ton *Jim Jr.* in 1884 for Josiah Manuel; Percival Manuel, Josiah's youngest brother, built the 33-ton *Fraulin* in 1884, and his partner was the master mariner George Manuel, another brother. Percival later moved to New Brunswick and then to the United States and worked in shipyards in both places; Titus Manuel, in 1876, built the 48-ton *Brothers* (for which Josiah collected a bounty of $144) and in 1889 fashioned the 31-ton *Pansy*, both for Josiah Manuel (a grandson once told me that a merchant had given Titus a certain amount of money to build a ship, and when it was completed the following spring, Titus had made not one cent of profit!); Eleazer Manuel built the 58-ton *Carmena* in 1893; Peter Manuel, in 1896, crafted the 16-ton *Brothers* for Josiah Manuel; Philip Manuel (another of my grandmother's brothers) built the 56-ton *Energy* at Northern Arm for Josiah Manuel; John Manuel IV of Jackson's Cove, Green Bay, constructed the *Ripple* in 1902; and Ambrose Manuel built the 41-ton *Mapleleaf* in 1906 for Josiah Manuel. All these vessels were crafted in the Bay of Exploits, except John Manuel's *Ripple*.

Richard Manuel built his first ship, the 31-ton *May*, at Exploits Islands in 1896 and his second, the 34-ton *Swallow*, at Marshallville in the Bay of Exploits in 1901. Over a period of twelve years he constructed a total of six ships. His first four ships were built for the Exploits merchant Thomas Avery Winsor, and his last ship, the 55-ton *N. Duncan*, was constructed in 1907 for Chesley and Jabez Manuel, sons of Josiah Manuel who took over the business after their father's death in 1906. The *N. Duncan* was named after the Canadian writer Norman Duncan who stayed with the Manuels at Exploits several times and who was the author of *Dr. Luke of the Labrador* and many other books.

Chesley and Jabez Manuel also became merchant shipbuilders but never rivalled their father, Josiah. Jabez constructed three ships for the family firm: the 17-ton *Fitz* in 1904, the 52-ton *Emily* in 1905, and the 65-ton *George Wheatley* in 1906, all built before his father's death. Chesley Manuel built the noteworthy 76-ton *Fog Free Zone* in 1907. From then onward both men devoted their full time to the business. Two of the additional shipbuilders they employed were Elijah Burt of Peter's Arm, who in 1907 built the 49-ton *Express*, and Jonas White of New Bay, who built the 24-ton *C.C.C.* in 1908.

Caleb Manuel was a descendant of the Twillingate branch of the Manuel family and had settled at Lewisporte by 1900. Here he crafted the 54-ton *Bonanza* in 1900, the 63-ton *Lewisport* in 1901, and the 74-ton *Encore* in 1902. He completed his building career with the 86-ton *Louisa A. W.* in 1906. This vessel was re-registered at least four more times, was rebuilt by James Feltham of Deer Island at Trinity in 1934, and was re-registered in 1939, probably with an engine installed. The ship thus lasted thirty-three-plus years.

Job Manuel was my grandmother's brother, and I knew him well when I was a young boy growing up in Northern Arm. He was a kind, soft-spoken man, always busy. Job was the son of Luke II and began his remarkable shipbuilding career by constructing two ships in his first year: the 41-ton *Klondyke* and the 64-ton *Challenger*. He followed this up with the 102-ton *Dictator* in 1900 and the 63-ton *Duke* in 1901. Then came the 83-ton *Drummer's Tax* in 1902. All these vessels were built for Josiah Manuel, Job's uncle. There followed a pause of five years as Job was setting up a business in Northern Arm, Bay of Exploits. In that year, 1907, he constructed the three-masted 120-ton schooner *Nina L.* at Northern Arm. The vessel was built for Chesley and Jabez Manuel who sold it later to John C. Crosbie. Assisting Job in this venture were a number of local builders: his brothers Philip and William, Robert Evans, my grandfather Samuel Evans, and very probably Alfred Manuel and Jacob Evans. Capt. Charlie Moore was sent to Northern Arm to inspect the vessel for Crosbie and to supervise its rigging. Andrew Horwood commented, "The vessel was a beautiful little thing but was plagued from the very beginning." After several unfortunate incidents—having a man die after falling from the mast during the rigging, being caught in a storm and thrown over on her side so the cargo had to be jettisoned, being caught off the Newfoundland coast during a raging forest fire when the crew were almost overcome with smoke, being trapped in the Mediterranean just beyond the Straits of Gibraltar for fifty days by an unyielding westerly wind—the *Nina L.* was abandoned during a severe Atlantic storm on December 12, 1911.

SHIPBUILDING CREW OF 1907 AT NORTHERN ARM, BAY OF EXPLOITS, GATHERED FOR THE CONSTRUCTION OF THE 120-TON THREE-MASTED SCHOONER *NINA L.* THE MASTER BUILDER JOB MANUEL IS SEATED IN THE CENTER OF THE FRONT ROW. SEATED SECOND FROM THE LEFT IS ROBERT EVANS, ANOTHER MASTER BUILDER. (Author's Collection)

Job Manuel's next three vessels were also built for Chesley and Jabez Manuel: the 58-ton *Scotch Cure* in 1907, the 69-ton *Diver Jack* in 1908, and the 38-ton *Eye Opener* in 1912. Newspapers of the day stated that the *Scotch Cure* was constructed by "Job Manuel & Brothers." This would have included Philip and Alfred Manuel.

There followed another period of inactivity for Job Manuel as a shipbuilder, and then in 1917 he began a period of intense activity at Norris Arm where he crafted four three-masted schooners for Michael E. Martin of St. John's and the Norris Arm Shipbuilding Co., a subsidiary of the Newfoundland Shipbuilding Co. bankrolled by a group of Norwegian financiers from New York with headquarters at Harbour Grace, in 1917, while developing a pulpwood operation at Glovertown. Job Manuel built the 339-ton *Pauline*

Martin in 1917. She was abandoned in the North Atlantic on December 9, 1918; no other details could be found. The 491-ton *Kathleen* was crafted in 1918 and carried an initial mortgage of $70,000. Job Manuel was ably assisted in the final stage of constructing the *Kathleen* by a group of shipwrights sent out from St. John's. This probably had to do with the caulking of the vessel as happened in 1917 at Thwart Island with Robert Evans's tern schooner *Attainment*. At the time of construction, the *Kathleen* was accepted for classification by the Bureau Veritas of Paris, France (the equivalent of the British Lloyd's). The 151-ton *Neerod* was built in 1919 and was tragically lost at Carbonear Island just three months after being registered on December 11, 1919. The 169-ton *Rose M.* was also constructed in 1919 and had a short, unfortunate life. While she was returning to the Bay of Exploits after her registration in St. John's she was badly damaged in December 1919 at Thwart Island but was repaired and then laid up for most of the following two years because of "trade conditions." In August 1921 she took a load of herring from Twillingate to Halifax, and on her return she loaded codfish at Fogo for Portugal and was wrecked and totally lost at Horta in the Azores on January 14, 1922. An Inquiry was held into the loss of the *Rose M.*, and the captain was judged to be negligent; in fact it was discovered that he held no certificate of competency or service, and though the mate was an experienced seaman, he too was judged to be negligent.

There were a few Manuel shipbuilders in the later years, and they deserve an honourable mention. Andrew Manuel II of Lewisporte built three vessels on the west coast. In 1929 it was the 520-ton wood-lumber barge built at Humbermouth. It had one mast, two bulkheads, and was motor-powered. In 1934 Andrew built the 62-ton *New Commission* at Piccadilly, and in 1937 he crafted the 133-ton *Sylvia Hansen* at Humbermouth. This latter vessel had two masts and had an engine installed in 1944. In 1940, back in Lewisporte, Andrew built the 15-ton *Runnymede* for Marmaduke Manuel, mariner. In 1950 at Lewisporte, Marmaduke Manuel fashioned the 12-ton passenger boat *Miss Bridgeport*. Harold Manuel of Cottrell's Cove and Northern Arm, a long-time harbour pilot at Botwood and grandson of Jacob Manuel, built the 15-ton *Phoebe M.* at Triton in 1987 and fibreglassed it in 1990, and this vessel was still in use in 2013. Harold also built the *Betina* at Northern Arm and several boats as well.

So there is the record of the Manuel family of shipbuilders. There were at least thirty-three shipbuilders in this amazing family and a total of 178 ships built over a period of about 150 years. Considering the notorious gap in builder information in the ship registers from 1854 to 1877, a time of intense shipbuilding in Newfoundland, we may safely add another thirty to fifty ships to this list. A remarkable feat indeed.

THE EVANS FAMILY

The Evans family of Exploits Islands, Northern Arm, and Harry's Harbour are the second most prominent family of shipbuilders in Notre Dame Bay, though they did not come close to the Manuel family in terms of production. The Evans and Manuel families were intertwined through marriage, church activity, and work projects. Edward Evans Sr. is believed to have been a deserter from a British man-of-war ship performing fishery protection service around the island of Newfoundland and along the coast of Labrador in the late 1830s or by 1840.

Because Edward Sr. was a deserter, he made a concerted effort to stay out of the limelight, and the records on his shipbuilding before the 1870s is very sketchy. Only when his sons were old enough to be listed as partners in a shipbuilding venture did Edward allow his name to appear on the registration form. Edward had been a warrant officer on the British ship and is believed to have been the head of the carpentry division. He therefore brought these skills with him to his new country when he fell in love with a young Newfoundland woman, Caroline Ball, and deserted his ship the following year. He had settled at Exploits Islands by about 1840.

With the fear of being caught as a deserter, Edward probably worked for other master shipbuilders in the early years or persuaded the men for whom he built ships not to identify him as the builder. The gap in builder information from 1854 to 1877 certainly suited his situation, whether he was aware of it or not. Finding a place off the beaten track, he may well have worked with the Foote family who had a sawmill at Peter's Brook in the Bay of Exploits and who built ships at that location. Seeking further seclusion in the mid-1850s he took his young family to Green Bay, and a son born there was baptized by an itinerant Church of England minister in 1857.

According to family testimony, Edward built the *Sarah Jane* about 1870 for Jimmy King of Western Bay. It is known that Edward had connections to the Evans family of Western Bay, and he probably spent the first year after his desertion with them. He later built a small boat which had been painted black and named *Jim Crow*; he would use this boat to escape into the nearby woods of Northern Arm whenever an official-looking ship was seen to be entering

Botwood harbour. Edward built the 56-ton *Morning Star* in 1873, and his four sons were listed as partners: William, Edward Jr., Solomon, and Henry. This ship was lost on the Labrador in 1902, thus lasting for twenty-nine years. In 1876 Edward Sr. built the 77-ton *Search* and again his four sons were listed as partners. These are the only known vessels to have been constructed by Edward Sr., though the ship registers credit William Evans as being the master builder of the *Search*, probably because he registered the vessel at St. John's. Robert Evans, in 1955, affirmed unequivocally that Edward Sr. was the builder. Edward had constructed his ships first in the Rattling Brook area of Norris Arm and then on what later came to be called Evans' Point at Northern Arm, and the family moved from Exploits Islands to Northern Arm about 1876, so the vessel named *Search* was very probably connected with the search for a new home.

In 1881 when Edward's grandson Robert became seriously ill, Edward and Robert's mother, Hannah, took him aboard the *H.M.S. Druid* to see the ship's doctor when the ship was anchored in Botwood harbour while Capt. William Robert Kennedy and several of his officers were away exploring the upper reaches of the Exploits River. We can only imagine with what trepidation Edward went aboard this ship which was engaged in the same business as the ship from which he had deserted about forty years earlier. Edward died the next year, in 1882.

Though William was the eldest son, it was the second son, John, who built the first vessel in the second generation. He had moved, with members of the Dorey family into which he had married, from Black Island to Harry's Harbour, Green Bay, about 1874, two years before all other members of the family moved to Evans' Point, Northern Arm. John was twenty-nine years old when he built the 32-ton *Mary Jane* somewhere in Notre Dame Bay, very probably in the Western Arm of Green Bay. When he constructed the 15-ton *Harp*, in 1877, he was settled at Harry's Harbour. There followed at least six other ships in the next twenty-three years, including the 67-ton *Delta* in 1889 and the 80-ton *Sarah Jane* in 1885. With this last vessel, John had built larger than his father. In 1906 John crafted the 31-ton *Lotus* for St. John's merchant Augustus F. Goodridge. The ship register gives the following specifications about the vessel: "One deck. Square stern. Billet head. Carvel build. 2 bulk-heads. Trunk. Raised deck." This was probably characteristic of all the Evans vessels and was undoubtedly traceable to Edward Sr., his father. John's descendants claim that he built other vessels, but these could not be found in the ships registers: the *Daisy*, the *Randolf C.*, the *Mary*, and the *Lucifer*. This last vessel must have been either a very contrary vessel or, more probably, was named after John's young sister, Luciana, and the family recollection is mistaken.

William, the eldest son, became the family's master builder at Northern Arm, constructing only one ship before his father died; however, the Customs' Returns of 1876 differ from the ship registers and give William credit for being the master builder of the 77-ton *Search*. The ship registers are very probably correct. The merchant Edwin Duder collected the bounty of $231 for this vessel. William's first vessel was the 65-ton *Telephone* built in 1881. His father and two brothers were his partners. This vessel was sold to merchant Augustus F. Goodridge in 1903 and then in 1904 to Robert Ehlers of Bristol, England, and was lost in 1906, thus lasting for twenty-five years. William crafted seven more ships between 1884 and 1899: the 51-ton *Zingra* in 1884, the 57-ton *Galatea* in 1886, the 79-ton *Genesta* in 1888, the 70-ton *Glad Tidings* and the 63-ton *Geranium* in 1889, the 54-ton *Marguerite* in 1892, and the 49-ton *Percy L. D. Knee* in 1894, built for Capt. Job Knee, master of the coastal boat *Clyde*, and named after his son. William's last vessel was named *V. M. B. S.* and bore the initials of his four daughters. When Rev. Joseph Parkins of Exploits Islands visited the Evans family at Northern Arm in the winter of 1883, he commented on one of their "experiences of muscular energy" which consisted of harvesting a spruce tree:

> The cutting down of which 3 of them had been employed for 5 hours and a half. Its trunk, as they said, was the largest they had ever seen in the country, which, when cut up, would be very useful as timbers in the body frame of a new schooner.

These timbers were very probably used the next year in the construction of the 51-ton *Zingra*. Parkins's comment is a confirmation of what J. B. Jukes had observed in his 1840 visit to this region.

Solomon Evans built only one ship, the 32-ton *Viola* in 1892. Almost immediately after completing the ship, he became ill and died, and his brother Edward Jr. registered the ship at St. John's. The family recollection is that Solomon sprained himself badly during the construction of his ship.

Henry Evans built eight or nine ships between 1897 and 1908. He was forty years old before he built his first ship, the 38-ton *Cabot*, and he returned to the place of his birth to do this—North West Arm, Green Bay (now Burlington). The Evanses had a connection with the Mills family of North

West Arm when Julia Jane Mills came to Northern Arm as an eighteen-year-old teacher in 1889, and died there in the spring of 1890. She was the sister of Eleazer Kenneth Mills, who in 1929 built the *Bessie Marie*, the last three-masted vessel constructed in Newfoundland. Henry Evans's largest vessel was the 75-ton *Ethel E.*, built in 1905 at Northern Arm. His last vessel was the 51-ton *Boethuk S.*, built in 1908. This vessel changed hands four times, and her final owner was Edward Humby of Summerville, Bonavista Bay. She was broken up in the mid-1940s, and I saw her old "bones" in Summerville harbour in 1955. She had been in use for well over thirty years. Henry was the only member of the Evans family to collect a bounty on his ship, the *Cabot*, and for this he collected $152, that is, $4 per ton; the bounty on all their other ships was collected by the merchants for whom they built: Edwin J. Duder and George J. Carter. Henry's ship *Alan Carter*, built for merchant George J. Carter and named after Carter's son, was lost in the great storm of July 28, 1908, between Indian Harbour and King's Bay on the Labrador coast. Henry did not even have time to register the vessel before leaving for the Labrador. Dr. Wilfred Grenfell arrived immediately after the storm and salved the American-built *Pendragon*, buying it from an agent on the beach and selling it to "my good friend" Henry Evans for $80. Six years later, in 1914, Henry was lost with this ship and all his crew while on the way to the Labrador. The northern coasts and Labrador were packed with ice throughout spring and early summer, and Henry, sailing at night, must have run into the ice off the Brehat shoals where wreckage from the ship was picked up at a later date. Henry was acknowledged to be the greatest ship's captain in the family, and perhaps he dared too much on that last voyage. He also had a true singing voice and raised all the hymns in the church at Northern Arm in the days before organs became popular.

Edward Evans Jr. was a shipwright for many years, but he is only given credit for master-building two ships: the *Daffodil* in 1898 and the *Strathcona* in 1907. He named this latter ship after Dr. Grenfell's vessel because the good doctor had arrived on the scene when Edward was in great pain from blood poisoning in his hand. When Dr. Grenfell later saw the new ship, he gave Edward a flag for the vessel; the pennant was so long that it dragged in the water when the vessel was at rest. Edward was generally satisfied to assist his son Robert in Robert's distinguished career as a shipbuilder.

In 1935, when he was fifty-three years old, Roland Evans of Harry's Harbour, son of John, built the 38-ton *Miss Green Bay*. Roland was a merchant at that time; he is reputed to have built a second ship, though the ship registers do not confirm that. Roland's brother Elisha also built a ship, according to his son Jack, but this could not be confirmed from the ship registers.

And so we come to the third generation of Evans shipbuilders.

Robert Evans of Northern Arm, son of Edward Jr. and grandson of Edward Sr., had a distinguished career as a shipbuilder. He told me in 1955 that when his uncle William finished his own building career with the construction of the *V.M.B.S.* in 1899, he undertook the task of training Robert as a master shipbuilder. William and Robert were both small men and perhaps that affinity was the deciding factor. Robert's father, Edward, was by contrast a very tall man, like his father, Edward Senior.

HENRY EVANS (1897) AND ROBERT EVANS (1901), MASTER SHIPBUILDERS. THE EVANS MEN HAD THEIR PHOTOGRAPHS TAKEN BY THE CELEBRATED ST. JOHN'S PHOTOGRAPHER SIMEON H. PARSONS ON THE OCCASION OF BUILDING THEIR FIRST VESSEL. (Author's Collection)

Robert's first ship was the 39-ton *Defender* fashioned in 1901 at Northern Arm. Over a period of forty-one years, this vessel changed hands seven times; was rebuilt and enlarged in 1926 at Fair Islands, Bonavista Bay, by Malcolm Rogers; had an internal combustion engine installed in 1939; and was sold in 1942 to Samuel Roberts, merchant at Triton. The ship lasted for forty-one-plus years. Perhaps with memories of the famous Jonas Newell Newhook, Robert named his second vessel *Fleetwing*, though she was only 26 tons. After building three more ships at Northern Arm—the 48-ton *Reliance*, the 36-ton *Gertie B.*, and the 55-ton *Gladys C.*—Robert moved to Moore's Cove, New Bay, for the winter of 1907-08 and built the 67-ton *Gertie Moors* for the merchant William Moore.

Robert was also one of the shipwrights assisting Job Manuel when he constructed the three-masted vessel *Nina L.* at Northern Arm in 1906-07, as a family picture showing the construction crew attests.

According to *Free Press* reports and the Diary of the Rev. Robert Samuel Smith of New Bay, Robert and his wife lived in Moore's Cove during the entire period of building the *Gertie Moors*. The local correspondent to the *Free Press* noted in his regular columns the progress on this vessel, indicating that Robert had started construction by November 1907 and near the end of January 1908 "Mr. Evans is making quite a show already in William Moore's dock." The vessel was launched in August, and the correspondent wrote, "She is a splendid looking boat and well-built, and neither her owner nor builder need to be ashamed of her." Back in Northern Arm in 1909, Robert built the 55-ton *Change*, named because of the change of government that year. There is a picture of the beautiful white-winged *Change* in John T. Rowland's book *North to Adventure*, but there it is incorrectly identified as the *Pendragon*. Rowland was working for the summer with Dr. Grenfell at St. Anthony and along the Labrador coast. The *Change* was the first of the Evans vessels built with mill-sawn lumber from Ritchie & Baird's sawmill that had been established at Evans' Point the previous year.

It was seven years before Robert Evans resumed shipbuilding. The tragedy in 1914 of losing Henry Evans and his entire crew in the *Pendragon* sobered the Evans family and turned their attention away from the sea. In 1916 William Horwood, of the Horwood Lumber Co., invited Robert to come to St. John's to look over some three-masted vessels in the harbour and persuaded Robert to begin construction of a ship on Thwart Island in the Bay of Exploits. A large group of men were gathered on the island in the fall of 1916 to begin the construction of the 372-ton three-masted vessel *Attainment*. Much of the wood had already been cut on the island, including birch, juniper, soft pine, and spruce, but a large amount of imported wood was brought to the site, in particular oak, pitch pine, and hard pine. Local witchhazel was supplied in abundance, and the "deadwood" had been cut on the island. "Deadwood" consisted of large blocks of hard timber which are laid upon the keel of a ship especially at the stern. My father-in-law, Gordon Locke of Tizzard's

Harbour, was a fifteen-year-old boy at the time and had come to the site with his father, Alexander Locke, a master carpenter, and Gordon was my source of information about the building. Following are the recollections of a teenager when Gordon was eighty-eight years old. The keel was made of oak, and the sections were forelocked and bolted together (scarfed). The stem and prow were made of local birch. Some of the trunnels were three and four feet long; they were squared at the top, and young Gordon observed that, unless the men hit them dead centre with their malls, they tended to split and had to be discarded. He persuaded Robert Evans to allow him to trim the squared top to prevent spoilage. The stern post and prow sections cut from "deadwood" were so heavy that a pair of horses was required to pull them to the job site. These were then bolted and forelocked into place at the stem and the stern and the planking was later attached to these. Juniper and hard spruce were used for the body frame, and the timbers were only five inches apart. Birch was used for planking the bottom part of the vessel, and pitch pine and hard pine were used as the men progressed upward. The vessel was planked inside as well as outside. The vessel was so high, scaffolds had to be constructed inside in order to complete the planking. Soft pine was used to construct the rice decks and the poop decks. Iron knees were used to connect the top beams to the sides of the vessel. The rudder trunk was ploughed and keyed so it would not leak.

Gordon's recollections about the steam box are important because he was taught by Robert Evans how to use it and was later put in charge of it under Dickie Chalk's general supervision. The steam boiler stood eight to nine feet high. An injector pushed the water upward from its source in a nearby brook into digesters which were kept covered with netting to keep stones and leaves out. The steam box stood four to five feet high and was about twenty feet long. Planks were pushed into the steam box on rollers, three and four planks at one time, and remained there for twenty-five to thirty minutes. The steam box was sealed at one end, and a door at the working end was sealed during the steaming process. The resin from the pitch pine would run out on the ground. Planks were about three inches thick and eight to nine inches wide. The last thing Gordon did at night was to shut down the boiler and assure that it was full of water by siphoning it up from the brook. The tubes in the boiler were kept clean with a sponge and wire brush, and the exact amount of pressure maintained at all times. Young Gordon must have learned the trade well since three years later he was placed in charge of a sawmill owned by the French family at Birchy Bay.

A large covered platform was built at the site with a drafting board made of match lumber. This is where Robert laid out his blueprints and did his calculations with divider and rule to construct a pattern by scale for each section of the vessel as the work progressed. About 150 to 160 men worked on the site in various capacities, sawing and shaping timbers, building structures for the men and the horses, working in the dock, handling supplies delivered to the site from Campbellton, St. John's, Harbour Grace, and elsewhere. Apart from a short break for Christmas, the men worked on site from October to the following September. When the *Attainment* was launched in September 1917, she "ran a mile up the bay" and when taken in tow by the coastal boat *Clyde*, men on board the *Attainment* could look down on the deck of the other vessel. The skids had been greased the previous day, but certain dignitaries had not arrived, so the launch was postponed, and the skids were greased a second time. So when the launch took place, "there were two streaks of flame down along the skids." It is reported that upwards of 500 people attended the launch, coming in motorboats from Campbellton, Lewisporte, Botwood, Laurenceton, Exploits, Moreton's Harbour, Horwood, and Springdale. Mrs. William Horwood christened the *Attainment* as the vessel slid from the stocks. The vessel was towed to Campbellton to have the three spars stepped-in and to be rigged. A correspondent at Campbellton wrote, "She is a splendid vessel of about 300 tons and has a birch bottom with hard pine topsides, and a remarkably strong deck of 4 by 4 inch hard pine. All the fastenings are of galvanized iron and she is in every respect a credit to the builder."

On November 24, 1917, the *Attainment* was taken to St. John's by Capt. Andrew Roberts, carrying a cargo of almost half a million feet of lumber. When she arrived at St. John's a reporter wrote:

> The *Attainment* is a splendidly built schooner, nothing but the best material being used in construction, while the work was done by the most skilled shipwrights, a staff from the city doing the caulking. She is built along very fine lines and should be a fast sailer.

In January 1918 she left St. John's to take a load of fish "across the pond" and returned with a load of salt. By September 1918 she was sold to Campbell & McKay, a new fish-carrier company in St. John's, and in October left with a load of salted dried codfish for Pernambuco. This was the beginning of a most spectacular triangular voyage from St. John's as far south as Bahia and

Santos, where she loaded coffee for Le Havre, France, then to a British port to load coal for Cadiz, and then brought a load of salt back to St. John's. This extended journey lasted for about sixteen months. On her return she went on dock in St. John's for repairs and maintenance and then headed for Parrsboro, Nova Scotia, to load deals (pine or fir lumber); she was in ballast, but perhaps not sufficiently. She was wrecked in a severe storm on Long Island in the Bay of Fundy on April 25, 1920, when a northeast gale with snow and "a terrible sea" drove her ashore. All the crew members, including the captain's wife, were saved by a breeches buoy rigged with help from the shore. What role, I wonder, did those two large loads of "the demon salt" play in the *Attainment*'s early demise?

In the fall of 1919 Robert Evans began the construction of another three-masted vessel for the Horwood Lumber Co. at Campbellton. This was the 149-ton *Nancy Lee*, launched in the summer of 1920. She was for a time transporting lumber from Horwood's sawmills in Notre Dame Bay to St. John's, then made several trips south to Pernambuco, Maceio, and Barbados and several trips "across the pond," and once took a cargo of dried codfish all the way through the Mediterranean to Turkey; newspapers reported that it was the farthest east that a Newfoundland schooner had travelled up to that time. On October 1, 1925, she left Horse Harbour, Labrador, with 5515 quintals of codfish in bulk for Seville, Spain. Her carrying capacity was just over 2500 quintals of fish, and she was loaded with more than twice that amount; it was at least the third occasion when she was seriously overloaded. For twenty-five days in mid-Atlantic, the ship was battered by a severe storm which became "a torment of fury." Her rails, bulwarks, and stanchions were carried away in the storm, and the pumps were fixed when the men became totally exhausted from the strain. The Scottish liner *Benvorlich* came to the rescue on October 25, but it was a hazardous job rescuing the men in a roiling sea. The schooner was set on fire before the crew left. The *Nancy Lee* must have been a sturdily built vessel to have survived previous cases of overloading.

Robert Evans was at one point offered the job of head shipwright at the St. John's Dry Dock, but his wife vetoed the move, and he remained at home in Northern Arm for the remainder of his life. Apart from building several boats, Robert's last vessel was the *Oscar*, a large barge or scow built for the Shell Oil Co. at Botwood in 1937 for use at the airbase in servicing planes for B.O.A.C, Pan-American Airlines, and American Export Airlines. E. J. Gulbrandsen of St. John's had been brought to the site to install the oil tanks in the refuelling scow. Robert also built the B.O.A.C. building on the airbase in Botwood where the town's museum is located today. He built wharves for the military at both Botwood and Wiseman's Cove, and also constructed a house for his brother, Jabez, at Northern Arm, using remnants from Major Sidney Cotton's hangars at Botwood dating from the early 1920s. When he built his last boat at Northern Arm about 1940, my brothers and I spent many hours silently observing his every move, and we were there for the launch over a steep bank with the use of several blocks and tackle secured to large trees. Then in the 1950s, Robert turned his hand to constructing several motorized model schooners and derived much pleasure from sailing them in the bay.

Jacob Evans, Robert's cousin, was the last of the Evans shipbuilders. He would have been trained as a shipbuilder by his father, William Evans, as was Robert. While Jacob is given credit in the ship registers for master-building only one ship at Northern Arm, the 49-ton *Beulah* in 1907, he would have been a master carpenter on ten or eleven other ships which the Evanses built at Northern Arm. In 1941 the *Beulah* was sold to the Ministry of National Defense, and the register on her closed in 1944, so she was active for thirty-seven years. Jacob also very probably assisted Job Manuel in the construction of the three-masted schooner *Nina L.* at Northern Arm in 1906-07.

Jacob would almost certainly have been working with Robert Evans on the 372-ton *Attainment* at Thwart Island until mid-1917 when he moved to Harbour Grace with the new Newfoundland Shipbuilding Co., which was being financed by Norwegian millionaire Christopher Hannevig out of New York. The Company bought the property at Ship Head where the old whale factory had been located and moved into Harbour Grace with a large professional staff and orders for thirteen ships by October 1917. In the first two years they built the 430-ton, three-masted *Armorel*, the 498-ton, three-masted *J.O.*, the 613-ton two-masted *Dellecnac*, and the 226-ton, one-masted *Harbour Grace*. Then came a series of events which signalled the beginning of the end for the company: the government's attempt to withdraw the bounty on ships over 120 tons, a major fire on the shipbuilding site which destroyed much of the premises and several of the seven berths where ships were under construction, the devaluation of the Norwegian kroner, and the loss of the *Dellecnac* in a transatlantic voyage during her first year. In the court inquiry on the *Dellecnac* that followed, Jacob Evans is described in the newspaper accounts as "Shipbuilder Evans," indicating the trusted position which he held in the company. Whether he can be accorded the title of master builder of the four large vessels cannot be determined. There are no other shipbuilders listed in the array of experts: an on-site managing director, two assistant managers, a superintendent, a mineralogist, a civil engineer, a fishing expert, a forest candidate, and a lumber expert.

Three other vessels were constructed by the Newfoundland Shipbuilding Company in the first two years: the 12-ton *Grace Aneta* which was still being used as late as 1937, a vessel called *No. 2 Transport* whose size is not known, and a 250-ton, flat-bottomed wrecking steamer.

Two of the partially-completed ships which were saved in the Harbour Grace fire were the 127-ton, three-masted *Monchy* and the 99-ton, two-masted schooner *Vickers-Vimy*. The *Monchy* was launched in 1919 and sold to Cyril W. Tessier, a St. John's merchant, and the *Vickers-Vimy* was launched in 1920 and was owned by Kenneth LeDrew of Cupids when she was lost at sea near Greenspond in 1937. Jacob Evans is clearly listed as the master builder of these two ships.

When Jacob left Harbour Grace, probably in 1921, he moved with his family first to Halifax where he worked in the shipyard for a few years. He then moved on to Boston where he was employed for several years in the Charlestown Shipyard. During World War II, after he had retired, Jacob's skills were still in demand, and he was called back to work for a time in the same shipyard.

By way of summary, the Evans family consisted of ten master shipbuilders through three generations, and they produced at least sixty-two ships. Allowing for the thirty-year period 1840 to 1870 when Edward Evans Sr. would have been an active shipbuilder, and considering the fact that names of shipbuilders were not required to be recorded during much of this period, we may add ten or twelve ships to this enviable record.

THE MILLS FAMILY

The Mills family of North West Arm, Green Bay (now Burlington), were another prominent family of shipbuilders in Notre Dame Bay. The family of five brothers—Abraham I, George, Ambrose, Joseph, and Nathaniel—had moved from Moreton's Harbour to the Green Bay area, probably in the early 1850s. According to the testimony of James Squires in 2011, Abraham first settled at "Schooner's Cove north of King's Cove and across from Barrens Point." This would be north of what today is known as Harry's Harbour.

Abraham established a fishing room there and pursued the Labrador fishery. Shortly thereafter, the family moved into North West Arm and settled in what came to be known as Mills' Cove, the only place in the Arm with water sufficiently deep to launch large vessels. Abraham launched two vessels from there: the 56-ton *Rabbi* in 1862 and the 56-ton *Proprietor* in 1881. The Customs' Returns for 1876 indicate that Abraham built the 31-ton *Albert* that year, so there were almost certainly other vessels for which there is no record. Not all ships in the early years were taken to St. John's for registration. Some were lost before they could be registered, some were registered in the person's name for whom they were built, and during much of this period, builders' names were not required to be added to the form at the time of registration.

At North West Arm in 1877, Joseph Mills built the 38-ton *Lilly Jane*, his only known vessel. In 1885 Ambrose Mills launched his 38-ton schooner *Contest*, and in the same year, a third brother, George Mills, crafted the 28-ton *Warwick William*. In 1884 Elijah Mills built the 19-ton *Village Belle* and sixteen years later went across to Jackson's Cove and fashioned the 50-ton *Kathleen* for John W. Knight, a trader/dealer.

Eleazer Kenneth Mills, son of Abraham, has at least fourteen vessels to his credit in the ship registers between 1899 and 1930. Eleazer is best known as the builder of the last three-masted vessel constructed in Newfoundland, the 152-ton *Bessie Marie* of 1929. She was built for Ashbourne's Ltd. of Twillingate and was used first as a fishing schooner, then as a freighter transporting cargo around the coast, and went annually to the seal hunt. In her later years, she was converted to a two-masted vessel. Alterations were made to the *Bessie Marie* in 1940, 1952, and 1956 at the Grenfell Dock at St. Anthony, as documented in Francis Patey's book *The Grenfell Dock*. At one point her tonnage was given as 201. She was still in service in 1959, and the registry did not close on her until 1977 when she was judged to be "no longer seaworthy." She had given at least thirty years of service, possibly as many as forty-eight.

There was a connection between the Mills family of North West Arm and the Evans family of Northern Arm. Eleazer's sister, Julia Jane Mills, had come to Northern Arm as a teacher in 1889 and died the following spring and was buried in the cemetery on Evans' Point. My great-grandfather, William Evans, a lay reader, would have assisted Luke Manuel at the funeral. In 1897 Henry Evans went to North West Arm and built the 38-ton *Cabot*, his first vessel, undoubtedly with the assistance of the Mills shipbuilders. He was then returning to the place where he had been born forty years earlier; Edward

Evans Sr. had taken his young family to Green Bay sometime between 1853 and 1858. By 1897 Henry's older brother, John Evans, had already built eight vessels in Harry's Harbour, just across Green Bay.

Eleazer Mills' first vessel was the 34-ton *Clara* built in 1899. In the next seven years, he constructed four more ships between 15 and 35 tons each. Then he crafted three ships for the Knight family of Moreton's Harbour, thus re-establishing contacts with the old family community. In 1915 Eleazer built the 26-ton *Mildred G. Knight* for William A. Knight, planter; and in 1917 and 1923 he built the 23-ton *Chanceport* and the 27-ton *J. S. Knight* for Joseph Knight, trader/dealer. In 1926 he launched the 85-ton *Edna Louise* for Ashbourne's Ltd., and in 1926 and 1927 constructed two more schooners for Ashbourne's Ltd., plus the *Bessie Marie* in 1929. In 1928 he built the 16-ton *Lady Bartlett* for his own use; this vessel was almost surely named after his wife, Jane Bartlett. His last vessel was constructed in 1930, the 37-ton *Speed Queen*. Eleazer was then sixty-seven years old, and he passed his tools over to his son Abraham II.

Abraham II, or Abram as he is often called in the ship registers, had actually begun his shipbuilding with the 26-ton *Daisy G.S.* in 1922. In 1925 Abraham fashioned two ships for Frederick N. Osmond, a Moreton's Harbour merchant. According to the ship registers, Abraham did not construct another ship until 1941; that was the 64-ton *Bette Myrna*, and it was followed in 1948 by the 66-ton *Earl Keith*. Local elders also give Abraham credit for building another vessel named the *Keith & Kevin*, but did not supply a date.

From other documented sources we discovered that nine other ships were built in North West Arm (Burlington), and their names were: *Louise*, *Ida M.*, *Jim B.*, *Hettie Belle*, *Emma Jane*, *Rio Grande*, *Autobiography*, *Geneva Roberts*, and *Kate*. These could not be found in the ship registers. If these local records are accurate, most of them would have been built by the Mills family or in the Mills' dock. There was only one deep water area suitable for launching in Burlington and that was in Mills' Cove. Only one other large vessel was said to have been launched in the town and that was in a site quite close to Mills' Cove. Several small boats were built and launched in Winterhouse Cove (now called Perry's Cove) on the south side of the Arm.

Keeping the Moreton's Harbour connection, it should be noted from Jill Marshall's genealogical research that William Mills, who was born in Moreton's Harbour in 1828, was a shipbuilder, and Archibald Mills, who was born at Moreton's Harbour in 1860 and died in 1944, also was a shipbuilder. William

John Mills was the brother of Abraham I and must have remained behind in Moreton's Harbour when his four brothers moved to North West Arm.

THE SCEVIOUR FAMILY

The Sceviour family (also spelled Sevier, Seeviour, Seviour, Sevior) produced eight master shipbuilders and built at least thirty-eight ships between 1827 and 1915. There were probably three generations of shipbuilders.

James Sevier of Exploits Islands (whom we met earlier in this chapter) was the progenitor of this family. He constructed the 28-ton *Nightingale* somewhere in the Bay of Exploits in 1827. His vessels became progressively larger, for in 1831 he crafted the 69-ton *Actor* for William Johnston, merchant of St. John's, and in 1835 he constructed the 139-ton brig *Adelaide* for Charles and Thomas Bennett, well-known St. John's merchants. Humphrey Cole was appointed master of this large vessel.

Joseph Seeviour built his one and only ship in 1847, the 49-ton *Active*. He was probably the brother or possibly the son of James Sevier.

James W. Seviour was the builder of the 47-ton *Busy* in 1871 somewhere in Green Bay. His partners were John and George Seviour. The *Twillingate Sun* of January 20, 1881, lists James Seviour of Exploits as a boatbuilder. In 1888 he was noted to be master of the schooner *Flamingo*.

William Sceviour of Exploits was the builder of seven ships between 1876 and 1893. His first ship was the 59-ton *William*; his second, in 1877, was the 45-ton *Star*; and his third, in 1878, was the 59-ton *Mary*. In 1880 he built the 50-ton *Sweet William* at the Exploits River, probably in what today is Botwood harbour. In 1883 he constructed the 44-ton *Goodwill*, well known in the Labrador fishery. All seven ships were built for merchants, four for the Bowrings of St. John's, one for James Ryan of Bonavista, and two for Thomas A. Winsor of Exploits Islands. The bounty was collected by the merchants. Most of William's ships lasted for twenty-plus years.

George H. Sceviour was the most productive builder of the family. He built sixteen ships and rebuilt one in the twenty-four years between 1879 and 1902, a remarkable record. His first ship was the 63-ton *Annie* in 1879 built for Charles Bowring. All his ships were of at least medium size, but by 1887 he had increased the size considerably. The *Jubilee* of 1887 was 73 tons, the *Thomas* of 1888 was 74 tons, the *Mermaid* of 1889 was 78 tons, and the *Modus Vivindi* of 1891 was 83 tons, his largest ship. The 39-ton ship *Radical* was already forty-four years old when he rebuilt it in 1894, and it was not broken up until 1925, thus lasting a remarkable seventy-five years. This ship had been built in 1850, and had probably been built by his father or uncle. George's last ship was the 33-ton *Carrie S.* built in 1902. All of his ships were crafted for merchants: five for the Bowring firm of St. John's, six for the Goodridges of St. John's, four for local merchant Thomas A. Winsor, one for Thomas R. Smith of St. John's, and for the last vessel his partners were James W., Arthur L., and Augustus R. Sceviour, probably a brother and two sons.

Abraham Sceviour built two ships only: the 62-ton *Jacinth* in 1904 and the 18-ton *Pearl* in 1905. The first ship was built at Pilley's Island and the second at Hall's Bay. Both ships were constructed for St. John's merchant James Baird. Abraham was almost certainly a part of the Exploits clan.

Robert A. Sceviour built seven ships between 1906 and 1913. All were built for Exploits merchants except the 45-ton *A. F. Goodridge*, which was built for the Goodridge firm of St. John's in 1912. This ship was rebuilt in 1930 by John Decker of Joe Batt's Arm and was renamed the *Fogota*. Robert's largest ships were his first three: the 64-ton *Pratincole*, the 65-ton *Humming Bird*, and the 69-ton *Ger-Falcon*. At the launch of the *Humming Bird* in June 1907, the local correspondent to the *Free Press* wrote, "Timbers all juniper and spruce, planked with birch and juniper, pitch-pine spars, new sails and rigging." The 33-ton *Shag* built in 1913 was rebuilt at Dunville, Placentia Bay, by Patrick Michael Tobin, thus lasting twenty-two-plus years.

Eliphaz Sceviour built only one ship, the 22-ton *Iwyll* in 1915. The record lists him as a fisherman, as were his partners Simon and Cyril Sceviour.

THE DALTON FAMILY

There were only five shipbuilders in the Dalton family of Exploits Islands, but they constructed thirty-two ships from 1840 to 1893. There may, in fact, have been only two generations of builders but they "built large." They were all planters, and for one of their ships their partners were Abraham and Robert Sevier.

Matthew Dalton Sr. built his first ship in 1840 somewhere in Green Bay, the 36-ton *United Brothers*. George Dalton was his partner and undoubtedly his brother. According to the ship registers, Matthew did not build another until 1865, the 58-ton *Sea Slipper*, well known in the Labrador fishery, but the gap in the records must be considered. John Dalton, very probably his son, was his partner in this venture, as he was in the 53-ton *Attila* in 1867. When Matthew built the 53-ton *Prime* in 1874, his partner was his other son, Matthew Dalton Junior.

George Dalton built the 53-ton *Native Lass* in 1848, and his brother Matthew was a partner as were Abraham and Robert Sevier.

John Dalton became the dominant shipbuilder in the Dalton family, and in the twenty-eight years between 1869 and 1897, he built twenty ships, another remarkable record. His first vessel was the 56-ton *Osprey*, built for his own use as a planter. In 1871 he crafted the 68-ton *Kate*, and his merchant partners were C. R. Ayre and A. Marshall of St. John's. By this time, in the ship registers, John's status is given as shipbuilder, and that status is repeated in subsequent records. In 1875 he fashioned the 69-ton *Ocean Queen* somewhere in Green Bay and Ayre & Marshall collected the bounty of $138. In 1877 John built the 46-ton *Lady Glover* for James C. Rogerson, St. John's merchant, and then became the master of this vessel for a time. This vessel was rebuilt and enlarged in 1899 by Josiah Frampton at Gin Cove, Trinity Bay. From 1877 onwards, most of John's vessels were built at the Exploits River. It is known that the Dalton's main shipbuilding site was opposite Killick Island in what is now the town of Botwood, and this may be what Exploits River means in the records. Here he built the 36-ton curiously-named *X 10 U 8* in 1877; the 52-ton *Ripple* and the 50-ton *Scilla* in 1878; the 54-ton *William Patterson* and the 85-ton *Isabella* in 1879; the 61-ton *Clara Jane*, the 51-ton *J. L. Brown*, and the 71-ton *Jessie* in 1880; and the 97-ton *Amelia Emma* in 1881. John went to Kite Cove (Laurenceton) in 1882 to build the 35-ton *Annie D.* for Moses Monroe, merchant at St. John's, and the 52-ton *Green Leaf* for Thomas and John Barbour, planters at Pinchard's Island. In 1883 John was back at the Exploits River where he built the 33-ton *Lily*, the 50-ton *Valeria*, and the 44-ton *Royal Arch*; this last vessel became very well-known around Notre Dame Bay and in the Labrador fishery. When Rev. Joseph Parkins from Exploits Islands visited his flock near the mouth of the Exploits River in the winter of 1883, he made note of the Dalton ships in the dock at Killick Island as well as other ships being constructed in the region.

John Dalton went to Fortune Harbour in 1889 to build the 92-ton *Portland* for local merchant Richard Quirk. This vessel was later sold to Waterman & Co. of Twillingate and was transferred to the Prince Edward Island registry in 1896. The *Portland* was not John's largest vessel. He built the 100-ton *Phyllis* in 1892 at Gander Bay. John closed out his shipbuilding career at Fogo in 1893 with the construction of the 84-ton brigantine *Laddie* for Robert Scott, local merchant. John's fame as a builder must have been known as far away as St. John's because the *Times & General Commercial Gazette* of March 29, 1893, wrote:

> A ship is being built at Fogo by John Dalton of Exploits Bay. She will be a first class schooner. Will be fastened with the best brand of galvanized iron…to be so expertly built that she will get a 13-year class and no doubt will be fully entitled to the $6.00 per ton which is offered for such superiorly built vessels. It is difficult to find a more competent and experienced ship-builder in this colony.

The *Laddie* was wrecked off Ferryland in 1899 but was rebuilt, restored to the registry under the ownership of Charles Dawe of Bay Roberts, and broken up in Hudson's Bay in 1916.

John's brother, Matthew Dalton Jr., built his first ship in 1875, the 42-ton *Young Bride*. The government bounty of $82 was paid directly to Matthew. This vessel was broken up at Herring Neck in 1916 after forty-one years of use. He built two ships for John Steer, St. John's merchant: the 51-ton *Snow Drop* in 1878 and the 55-ton *Lily* in 1879. In 1880 he crafted the 52-ton *Excel* for four planters at Bay Roberts. When he built the 42-ton *Hephzibah* in 1884, his partner was his father, Matthew Sr., and for this, Matthew Jr. collected a bounty of $123. His last ship was fashioned in 1892, the 52-ton *Vaudeville*, for George and Eliphaz Sceviour who were by now trader/dealers at Exploits Islands. In 1906-07 Matthew Jr. went to Cottrell's Cove, New Bay, at the request of the Rev. Robert Samuel Smith and his congregation and built the Methodist Church which still stands in 2014 in excellent condition with its open varnished ceiling and cross beams and ships knees that give one the impression of looking into the hold of a ship. Trunnels (tree-nails) were also used in the construction of the foundation, and the large timbers were scarfed (as in a ship), and are visible today both in and underneath the building. It is of interest that just down the road in Fortune Harbour, Matthew's Methodist compatriot, Jonas John Newhook (son of the famous shipbuilder Jonas Newell Newhook), had been engaged to build the Roman Catholic Church in that town in 1907. Jonas remained a Methodist (though some report he converted to Catholicism just before his death), but his wife and children were all Roman Catholic. Both church buildings are noteworthy candidates for preservation.

John A. Dalton of Kite Cove (Laurenceton) was undoubtedly a member of this family. In 1897, at Exploits Islands, he built his only ship, the 60-ton *Zephyr*. It must have been constructed for his own use as a planter.

THE PADDOCK FAMILY

The Paddock (Paddick, Paddic) family produced nine shipbuilders and twenty-seven ships in the period between 1875 and 1953. It is unclear whether these are all from the same family group and how many generations are involved, but their contribution to the shipbuilding industry is noteworthy.

George Paddick of Ward's Harbour built his first ship in Hall's Bay in 1875, the 28-ton *Ocean Traveller* for which he collected the government bounty of $56. He was an itinerant shipbuilder as his second ship and his largest was constructed in Sunday Cove Tickle, the 45-ton *Brilliant Star*. Then he was back in Hall's Bay in 1879 to build the 37-ton *Union*, in Little Bay Islands in 1880 to construct the 36-ton *Wild Rover* for merchant James Strong, and in Pilley's Island in 1892 to build his last ship, the 35-ton *Minnehaha*.

Eli Paddock (also called Elias in some records) crafted ten ships between 1875 and 1887. Four of his ships were built at Robert's Arm, five at Hall's Bay, and one at Lushes Bight. Eli eventually settled at Robert's Arm. His first two ships were found in the Customs' Returns, not in the ship registers: the 119-ton *Constance* of 1875 and the 80-ton *Frances Helen*, both built at Hall's Bay. The government bounties of $238 and $240 were collected by R. D. Hodge and T. D. Hodge, merchants of Twillingate. The large size of these two ships leads one to conclude that Eli had probably been building for several years before this, but the ship registers are silent from 1854 to 1877. Eli constructed two more ships in 1878: the 31-ton *Hilda* and the 52-ton *Rise & Go*. He built the 67-ton *Helena* for James Strong in 1887, and his largest ship was the 72-ton *Adventure* built at Robert's Arm in 1881.

John Thomas Paddic crafted his first ship, the 50-ton *Juliet*, in Hall's Bay in 1882. His second ship was built at Sunday Cove Island and his third ship, the 57-ton *Saffron*, was constructed in 1903 somewhere in Notre Dame Bay for James Strong. Strong must have had great faith in the Paddock builders.

Joseph Paddick I built two ships only, both of them in 1882, both at Little Bay Islands, both at 37 tons each, and both for James Strong. The first was the *Blood Hound*, and the second was the *Lilly of the Sea*.

Solomon Paddick constructed four ships between 1899 and 1907. His first ship was his largest, the *Fashoda*, at 85 tons, which is most unusual for a beginning builder. He probably had much prior experience in a shipyard. His second ship, the 34-ton *Cordelia Strong*, was built at Lushes Bight in 1902 for James Strong. The two others ships were crafted at Sunday Cove Island and at Ward's Harbour.

Oliver Paddick built only one ship, the 28-ton *Diadem* of 1905. This vessel was rebuilt and enlarged twenty-two years later by George Hunt at Fair Islands, Bonavista Bay, so it must have enjoyed a relatively active life.

James Paddick crafted the 28-ton *Emerald* in 1905 at Robert's Arm for James Baird, St. John's merchant. It was broken up at Twillingate in 1925.

Samuel Paddick of Ward's Harbour constructed the 26-ton *Constant* at Robert's Arm in 1906 though it was not registered until 1908. His partner was Thomas Paddick, very probably his brother. In 1926 Samuel Paddock (note the spelling) constructed the 27-ton *S. and T. Paddock* at Beaumont, and Thomas Paddock was his partner. In 1936 Samuel Paddick built the 78-ton *Betty & Molly* at Port Anson, and Thomas Paddick was once again his partner. In spite of the discrepancy in spelling, these must certainly be the same two men.

Joseph Paddock II built the 26-ton fishing vessel *Miss Beaumont* at Port Anson in 1953.

THE WISEMAN FAMILY

The Wiseman family of Little Bay Islands produced six shipbuilders and nineteen ships between 1872 and 1937; one ship was especially noteworthy, the three-masted vessel *Norma B. Strong*.

Philip Wiseman was the first shipbuilder in the family. He constructed the 17-ton *May Flower* in 1872 for his own use in the fishery. He was a planter.

In the twenty-four years between 1882 and 1905, George Wiseman crafted five ships. His first was the 33-ton *Antelope*. In 1897 he built the 23-ton *Katie May* for planter John Wiseman, and in 1902 he built the 29-ton *Ethel S.* for Walter Wiseman, also a planter, and the 27-ton *May Flower* for Joshua Parsons of Lushes Bight; the two Wiseman men for whom he built were probably his brothers.

Job Wiseman of Little Bay Islands crafted eight ships between 1899 and 1918, all of them except the first at Little Bay Islands. His first ship was the 29-ton *Minnie B.*, and it was built at Woodford's Arm. His next six ships were of modest size, ranging from 43 to 63 tons. The *Bessie S.* of 1902 was 51 tons, and the *Ettie Bess* of 1904 was 43 tons. Both the *Meta Bell* and the *Mabel* were 54 tons each, both of them constructed the same year, 1907, and the *Lotus* of 1904 was 63 tons. The *Lotus* and the 45-ton *Dunner*, built in 1913, were constructed for James Strong. In fact, it is probable that Job Wiseman was James Strong's shipbuilder and that all the ships were built for Strong and sold to various owners; the female names probably reflect names of the Strong family. That might explain why Job's next schooner, and last, the 197-ton, three-masted vessel was called *Norma B. Strong*, which was crafted at Little Bay Islands in 1918 and sold to W. S. Monroe, St. John's merchant. This vessel was very probably built for James W. Strong Ltd. for sale to Monroe. Andrew Horwood states incorrectly that the builder of the *Norma B. Strong* was W. Wiseman; it is possible that Walter Wiseman, referred to above, assisted with the construction. Horwood writes further about this vessel that she "was as good as any imported schooner. All of her life she was commanded by Captain Stephen Penney of Carbonear and was only lost for want of canvas when a succession of storms stripped her of her sails." Three times she had approached to within thirty miles of Cape Race with her load of "demon salt" and been blown off by northwest gales, successively stripped of her canvas and blown back across the ocean "battered and bruised," finally ending up in the Portuguese Azores where the crew abandoned ship and made it to shore in the lifeboat. It was February 8, 1922.

Frederick Wiseman constructed two ships at Little Bay Islands, the 35-ton *Fantome* in 1904 and the 53-ton *Lilla L. W.* in 1910. This last vessel was rebuilt at Badger's Quay in 1941 by Jesse Hunt and enlarged to 83 tons, thus lasting thirty-one-plus years.

John Wiseman of Little Bay Islands built two ships, one in 1905 and the other in 1906. The first, the 35-ton *Emerald*, was built in Hall's Bay, and the second, the 37-ton *Annette*, was constructed at Little Bay Islands.

Frederick Newton Wiseman of Little Bay Islands built the 13-ton passenger boat *Susan Joan* in 1937 though it was not registered until fourteen years later, in 1951. He was a master mariner and may have used it for other purposes prior to 1951, registering it at that time as a passenger boat.

I give these details about the Wiseman shipbuilders to support the fact that it was quite natural for such a family to construct a large three-masted vessel such as the *Norma B. Strong*. More than one member of that family were likely involved in the construction of that large vessel.

THE STRONG FAMILY

There were only three shipbuilders in the Strong family and these were probably two brothers and a son. From 1873 J. & J. Strong were supplying merchants for the inshore and French Shore fishery, and after 1894 the company became known as Mursell & Strong and expanded their operation to include the Labrador fishery.

Joseph Strong built the 22-ton *Ira H. Sankey* in 1876 at Little Bay Islands. His next two vessels were built at Pilley's Island where he was a trader/dealer: the 36-ton *Cupid* of 1891 and the 85-ton *Atalanta* of 1895.

James Strong was a trader/dealer when he built his first ship, the 42-ton *Enterprise*, in 1877 at Hall's Bay. His next two ships were constructed in 1900 at Little Bay Islands: the 39-ton *Dianthus* and the 52-ton *Pretoria*. He still held the status of trader/dealer when he built the 34-ton *Ivy* and the 47-ton *Myrtle* in 1901. This is curious because other records give James Strong the status of merchant from 1880 to 1887. Other shipbuilders were constructing ships for Strong between 1880 and 1920; these were Henry Oxford, William Shea, Samuel Short, Jacob Morrey, and Edward Boone. When Job Wiseman built the 197-ton tern schooner *Norma B. Strong* in 1918, it was very probably built for the James Strong firm in order to be sold immediately to W. S. Monroe of St. John's. Then in 1919 the 121-ton *Norman W. Strong* is built at Little Bay Islands, and the builders' names are given as "Mursel and Strong." Mursel was Richard Mursell who built the 27-ton *Experiment* in 1880, the 32-ton *Antelope* in 1882, and the 42-ton *Portland* in 1899, all three at Little Bay Islands, and who had become Strong's partner in 1894. The fact that James Strong is named as the builder may mean only that he supervised the construction being done by other master builders; perhaps Job Wiseman was one of these. In 1925 James Strong Ltd. is noted as the builder of the 140-ton *James Strong* at Little Bay Islands. By 1934, when the *James Strong* was re-registered, James Strong was living in St. John's. He was at that time serving in the government of Richard A. Squires.

William A. Strong built only one ship, the 84-ton *W. S. Monroe* in 1906 at Little Bay Islands. He was yet another merchant shipbuilder. This vessel arrived in St. John's in January 1907 to be surveyed, and according to the *Free Press* "was found fully up to the requirements called for under the bounty act. She is 83 tons and one of the best schooners built here for some time."

THE NORRIS FAMILY

The Norris family is being included here not because they were a family of significant shipbuilders, but because they are so similar to the Strong family as a significant merchant firm and produced at least one significant shipbuilder in the person of John J. Norris.

Three long arms protrude out into western Notre Dame Bay: Western Arm (present day Harry's Harbour), Middle Arm, and Southern Arm. By 1838 a fishing community had been established on Three Arms Island located in Middle Arm. Following the move of a few settlers from Twillingate, James Norris Sr. came from St. John's to Three Arms in the 1840s. James Norris Jr. was just a child at that time. By 1871, at age 20, James Norris Jr. had set up a small trading business in the area and built at least two schooners; only one was found in the ship registers—the 24-ton *Little Mary* built in 1880 at Southern Arm. David Norris, who built the 19-ton *Young Agnes* at Southern Arm the same year, was very probably James Jr.'s brother or possibly uncle. These may be the two ships that James Jr. used in the early years of his trading business. In the years between 1885 and 1909 James also had others build ships for him: William Perry of North West Arm constructed the 45-ton *Nelly May* in 1885; Charles King of Harry's Harbour the *Mary R.* in 1906; George Rice of Pilley's Island the 32-ton *Roseland* in 1906; Robert White of Harry's Harbour the 30-ton *Annie Maud* in 1906; George Wellman of Harry's Harbour the 63-ton *Loyalty* in 1907; James Jones of Little Bay Islands the 43-ton *A. Conqueror* in 1908; and Abraham Rideout of North West Arm the 25-ton *Handsome Queen* in 1909. With these vessels, Norris supplied crews for the French Shore and Labrador fisheries. His branch businesses at Conche and Coachman's Cove were operated by his sons John and Bernard. James Norris also operated a sawmill in the area.

John J. Norris, son of James Norris Jr., went to Englee in the fall of 1918 and began construction of the 242-ton, three-masted schooner *Armistice* for the A. E. Hickman Co. of St. John's. The *Evening Telegram* announced her arrival in St. John's on October 4, 1919: "The new schooner *Armistice*, built at Canada Bay by Norris...arrived this morning in tow of the tug *Ingraham*. She is said to be a splendid vessel." She would have been towed to St. John's to be rigged. It is the only vessel attributed to John J. Norris in the ship registers. It seems like a monumental task for a novice shipbuilder, but he would undoubtedly have taken several of the local shipbuilders with him, including Abraham B. Rideout, who had already built a ship for the Norris family and later built the 272-ton *Lady Baie Verte* in 1944, and possibly Robert White, who had also built a ship for Norris as well as the 222-ton, three-masted schooner *Mabel Davis* in 1918.

James Norris Sr.'s son, Stephen, was killed in France during World War I, and this deeply affected the Norris family. After the death of James Norris Jr. in 1924, the business was terminated and the family left Three Arms.

THE CHALK FAMILY

The Chalk family of the Bay of Exploits (with early connections to Moreton's Harbour and Bridgeport, NDB) produced four master shipbuilders, one of whom became quite well known as the builder of large vessels for the Anglo-Newfoundland Development Co. of Grand Falls at the port of Botwood.

Absalom Chalk crafted six vessels between 1880 and 1904. His first vessel, built in 1880, was the 32-ton *Brothers Hope*. This vessel and his next two were constructed for Mark Osmond, merchant at Moreton's Harbour. By 1893 Absalom had settled at Scissors Cove where he built the 16-ton *Otter* for R. D. Hodge, merchant at Twillingate. The 30-ton *Ortolan* was built at Lewisporte, and his last vessel, the 58-ton *Cold Storage*, was constructed at Exploits River for Josiah Manuel. All six of his ships were built for merchants.

Abraham Chalk (sometimes called Abram in the records) built four of his five ships at Scissors Cove between 1898 and 1908. His first vessel, the 15-ton *Phoebe Jane*, was registered in the name of Emma Jane Chalk of Scissors Cove. Her relation to Abraham is unknown, and this was probably the family's fishing vessel. Two of Abraham's vessels were built for planters, one for a local trader/dealer and one for a St. John's merchant. His largest vessels were the 42-ton *Gannet* and the 56-ton *Dorothy B.*

Stephen Chalk constructed the 30-ton *Laura C.* at Western Arm in 1902, and in 1910 he built the 23-ton *Meta C.* for J. W. Hodge, merchant at Fogo. It is probable that Stephen had settled at Carmanville by 1910. It cannot be determined what connection he had with the other Chalk builders.

The most noteworthy of the Chalk shipbuilders was Adam Chalk. He started small but "built large." His first ship was the 19-ton *Foam* built in 1897 at

Luke's Arm. In 1900 he fashioned the 21-ton *J.P.L.* at Farmer's Island; in 1901 the 29-ton *Ida Belle* at Loon Bay; and in 1902, also at Loon Bay, the 95-ton *Premier* for George J. Carter, supplying merchant at St. John's and Herring Neck. At Farmer's Arm he crafted the 66-ton *Energy* for Reuben Small and brothers. This vessel was built of juniper and designed for the coasting and trading business. She was surveyed by Lloyd's surveyor Mr. Wheatley in July 1907. At Chapel Island in 1907 Adam built the 40-ton *Mayflower*.

One year later, Adam Chalk was hired by the A.N.D. Co. to build a steamer at Millertown for use on Red Indian Lake. He may have built several vessels at Millertown for the company, but if so most were never registered. In March 1917 he was working on a 300-ton steamer at Millertown for use on Red Indian Lake to bring supplies to the lumbermen at their camps, to haul rafts, to transport hay and bags of oats for the horses, etc. He had already constructed the *Lady Mary*, but because she was never registered we do not know her tonnage. At that point, a local writer noted that Adam Chalk "has many fine vessels to his credit." By August 1917 he had made a start on his first large vessel at Botwood but took a few days off from the construction to visit Thwart Island in September to watch the launch of Robert Evans' 372-ton *Attainment*. Chalk hired, on the spot, many of the master carpenters who had worked on the *Attainment*, including Alexander Locke of Tizzard's Harbour as his new foreman.

In October 1918 Adam Chalk launched the 504-ton, three-masted *Bella Scott*; it had required almost a full year to complete the construction. A local correspondent to the *Free Press* reported in August 1917 that "A boiler is being installed at the dock, and plank will be sawn there, while pneumatic drilling machines will also be used to bore holes for bolts and trennails, and pneumatic hammers may be used for driving bolts, etc. in order to hasten the work." My grandfather, Samuel Evans, made hundreds of these juniper trennails, and he and my father, as a young teenager, delivered them regularly to the building site. Each trennail was tapered at both ends so that they could be cut in the middle to make two trennails. The *Bella Scott* was equipped with auxiliary engines. When Adam Chalk visited St. John's in November 1917, he was accompanied by Mr. Black, a Lloyd's surveyor, who had just completed his survey of the *Attainment* which was being sparred and rigged at Campbellton. That same local correspondent elaborated further in February 1918 on the building of the two large ships at Botwood:

> They are built of the country's best timber. The keels are 13 ½ by 13 ½ inches hard pine, with 4 inch oak shoe. Stern and stem posts are also hard pine. Keelsons are six feet wide hard pine. The timbers consist of the very best and largest birch that can be secured in the country; the clamps are of good California fir, 6 ½ inches thick; ceiling from 5 to 6 inches thick; outside planking, ten streaks of 5 inch California fir, and bottom planking 3 ½ inch witch-hazel – which is considered the finest timber our country produces. They will be fastened to stand the test of the Western Ocean. The iron used is from ¾ up to 1 ¼ galvanized. The beams are 12 by 12 and 14 by 12 inch hard pine. They are braced with iron knees on every second beam, the knees weighing about 650 pounds each. They have also poop decks and a double deck under the poop. They will be three-masted ships and will be equipped with 150 horse power auxiliary engines. Such ships as these are never built in this country before, and we feel proud of the splendid vessels that have been launched during the past season.

According to the A.N.D. Co. diaries, the *Bella Scott* loaded and unloaded cargoes at Botwood harbour for several months before her long fateful trip to South America. Loaded with codfish at St. John's in April 1919, the *Bella Scott* headed for Brazil but ran into heavy ice off Cape Race and had to return to port for repair to her head gear. While she was returning from Brazil, she caught fire near Kingston, Jamaica, and was totally destroyed on August 30, 1919.

In October 1919 Adam Chalk launched a sister ship, the three-masted, 582-ton *Sordello*. In the rhetoric of the newspapers of the day, she was said to be "a magnificent ship," "a masterpiece of marine architecture," and "the best ever turned out in Newfoundland." This ship was used for several years by the A.N.D. Co. for transporting pulp and pressed sulphite to England and bringing back china clay, sulphur, and other products. By 1928 the company's steamships had largely replaced her, and on January 3 of that year she was sold to Ashbourne's Ltd. of Twillingate; in 1934 she was converted to a hulk in Twillingate harbour for storage of supplies.

With materials left over from building these two massive ships at Botwood, Adam Chalk set to work building the 59-ton *Exploits II*, to be used as a tugboat for the Company in and around Botwood Harbour. In later years, she was renamed the *J. M. Olds*, a tribute to the much-loved doctor at Twillingate

Hospital. Adam very probably built the two large motorboats *Jupiter* and *Uranus* for the Park & Storm Co. which did waterfront work for the A.N.D. Co.

Then Adam was off to Red Indian Lake once again to build another large steamer for the Company, the 250-ton *Fleetway* which was constructed in 1921.

SIGNIFICANT INDIVIDUAL SHIPBUILDERS AND SHIPBUILDING COMPANIES

In this section we will deal in chronological order with individual shipbuilders whose production was really significant or who are worthy of honourable mention for other reasons, as well as with emerging shipbuilding companies in the later period.

Edward Downton of Exploits Islands is given credit in the ship registers with having built only one ship: the 59-ton, brigantine-rigged *Globe* in 1853 for J. J. Grieve, merchant of St. John's. Charles Downton was appointed master of this ship. The gap when builder' names were omitted from the registers covers the period 1854 to 1877, so Edward's full production cannot be determined. Edward had come to Exploits from Southhampton, England, as a shipwright, according to Dr. E. R. Seary. He was buried next to John Peyton in the cemetery at Exploits.

There were four shipbuilders in the Gillespie family of Fortune Harbour. Samuel was the first, building the 51-ton *Mary Jane* somewhere in Green Bay in 1864. The next year, Alexander Gillespie got his start by co-building with Richard Hamilton the 48-ton *Robert Grieve* for a merchant of the same name in St. John's. Alexander and Richard were both planters. Then they parted ways, and Alexander constructed five ships on his own: the 53-ton *Success* in 1875, for which Smith McKay was paid the bounty of $106; the 38-ton *Spring Bird* in 1878, at Fortune Harbour, of which he became master for Mark Osmond, merchant at Moreton's Harbour; the 27-ton *Village Bride* in 1884 at New Bay for planters Edward and William Gillespie of Fortune Harbour who collected the bounty of $78; the 41-ton *K.T.A.* in 1890; and the 24-ton *Reunion* in 1896. These last two vessels were built at Fortune Harbour for merchants. Edward Gillespie built the 15-ton *William* at Fortune Harbour in 1872; she was lost at Black Bear Island on the Labrador coast in 1890. And finally, William Gillespie constructed the 32-ton *Village Bride* in 1904 at Fortune Harbour, perhaps in tribute to Alexander's vessel of the same name. This vessel must have been sturdily built since she was rebuilt at Kingwell,

Placentia Bay, in 1926, had an engine installed in 1937, and was registered de novo in 1939, thus lasting thirty-five-plus years.

Richard Hamilton, who was the co-builder of the 48-ton *Robert Grieve* with Alexander Gillespie in 1865, struck out on his own and at Fortune Harbour in 1873 built the 30-ton *Minnie Hamilton*; Richard was then classified as a trader/dealer as he was in 1877 when he built the 32-ton *Phantom* at Fortune Harbour. His partner and fellow trader/dealer was James Byrne of Fortune Harbour. In 1887 Hamilton built his last ship—the 51-ton *Electric Light*.

William Snow II of Black Island and William John Snow are almost certainly the same person. Assuming this, Snow built nine ships between 1875 and 1900 and rebuilt one in 1911. His first ship was the 48-ton *Lily Dale* which was constructed somewhere in the Bay of Exploits, and the Customs' Returns indicate that the government bounty was collected by Martin & Brothers. This was followed the next year by the 55-ton *Welcome Home* constructed at Burnt Bay, NDB, and the bounty of $165 was paid to Charles Brett & Brothers. The 34-ton *Rosetta* was built in 1878 and the 19-ton *Arthur* in 1882. Then came the 19-ton *Isabella Jane*. Twice in the records, his name appears as William John Snow who in 1897 is the builder of the 32-ton *Matthew* at Burnt Bay for Thomas A. Winsor, merchant of Exploits Islands, and in 1900 with the 22-ton *May Flower* built at Indian Arm. In 1911 he rebuilt the 23-ton *General Booth* at Little Burnt Bay.

Thomas Avery Winsor, merchant and postmaster at Exploits Islands, crafted the 60-ton *William* in 1876. He is also credited with having built the first "knockabout" (American plans) schooner in Newfoundland in 1907. This schooner was about 50 tons, had no bowsprit or jibboom, but carried a large spread of canvas. It was noted that a schooner of the same type had been seen on the Rose Blanche grounds in the previous year and that this class of vessel had proven to have excellent sea-going powers, reaching a fifteen knot record. In 1905 at Exploits, Winsor rebuilt the 103-ton schooner *Olive*, which had been built at Summerside, PEI, in 1883. Winsor died in June 1909.

John C. Collins of Indian Islands crafted his first two ships there: the 18-ton *Napier* in 1876 and the 34-ton *Orange* in 1879. Both ships were constructed for merchant Edwin J. Duder. Collins built two more ships there and then built three ships at Noggin Cove, NDB: the 19-ton *No Surrender* in 1887, the 26-ton *Flora* in 1904, and the 27-ton *Nora C.* in 1908. He had built seven ships over a thirty-two year period.

George W. Clarke is generally associated with Springdale, but he was originally from Twillingate, and his first two schooners were built at Robert's Arm: the 45-ton *Emeline* in 1877 and the 38-ton *Rose of Sharon* in 1882. In 1896 and 1900 at Hall's Bay, he built the *Blanche* and the *Shamrock*, each of them at 18 tons. In 1902 he constructed his first large ship, the 89-ton Ettie Bess, and the place of building is given as Springdale which is undoubtedly where all his ships were built from 1896 onwards. Clarke developed an extensive business at Springdale, including a large sawmill. *Springdale* was the name given to his 91-ton vessel of 1903. In 1906 he built the 85-ton *Ethel B. Clarke*. Azariah Small of Tizzard's Harbour was one of Clarke's ship designers and master builders through the early 1900s. Small counselled Clarke that his vessels were too flat in the bottom and then built a model eight feet long out of pine plank persuading Clarke to modify his plans and build ships in the future according to these modifications. In 1913 Clarke rebuilt the 106-ton *Banbury*, which had originally been constructed at Lunenberg by John Smith in 1893. All of this was good preparation for building the 417-ton three-masted schooner *Ruth Hickman* in 1917. She was constructed for the A. E. Hickman Co. of St. John's. The *Ruth Hickman* was torpedoed in the North Atlantic, twenty days out from Spain, on May 30, 1918. The crew landed safely at Angra in the Azores. The ship registers give Clarke credit for building twelve ships and rebuilding one, but another source credits him with building sixteen schooners.

It was very probably in the Springdale area that the famous Jonas Newell Newhook performed his greatest shipbuilding feats between 1852 and 1876 in the large shipyard provided by Thomas Knight II. In the early records, the building site is simply called Hall's Bay. An anonymous correspondent during this early period mentioned that fifty-one vessels had been constructed there but gave the names of only four. He did mention "the renowned sealing vessel *Jasper*" crafted by Newhook, and though this vessel does not appear in the ship registers, it was found in the writings of Rev. Naboth Winsor. It was 60 tons and was owned in 1851 by Capt. James Burton of Bonavista North. Now we know that Newhook was building in Hall's Bay one year earlier than previously thought.

George Warr built his first ship in 1877: the 52-ton *Rise and Go*; he did not build another until 1887—the 22-ton *General Booth* which lasted for thirty-one years. George was from Little Harbour, Twillingate, but eight of his nine ships were built in the Hall's Bay-Badger Bay area. Only the 60-ton *Resolute* of 1892 was built at Twillingate. He probably settled at Pilley's Island after 1897. His largest vessels were the 59-ton *Nellie W.*, built at Sop's Arm in 1906, and the 85-ton *Swallow*, built at Pilley's Island in 1907.

Francis Warr built twenty-three ships in Notre Dame Bay between 1878 and 1904, another remarkable building record. In the later records, his name appears as Frank. He began his building career at Robert's Arm in 1878 with the 46-ton *Betsey Purchase*. In 1883 Francis constructed the 36-ton *Merley* for which he was paid a bounty of $108; this vessel was rebuilt and enlarged to 40 tons by Jonas Rice at Point Leamington in 1912 and lasted until 1926 when it was lost at sea somewhere on the Newfoundland coast: a long life of forty-eight years. All of Frank's ships except one were built at Robert's Arm, which is where he must have settled after leaving Twillingate. The one exception was the 32-ton *Tugela* crafted at Dog Island in 1900. He built several large ships such as the 73-ton *Dolly McC.* in 1901, the 75-ton *Studland* in 1888, the 93-ton *Terra Nova* in 1891, and the 98-ton *Canford* in 1890. But his pride and joy must have been the 143-ton schooner *Bobs* which he crafted in 1903 for James M. Jackman, merchant at Tilt Cove. The *Free Press* of September 22, 1903, carried this note:

> The new schooner *Bobs* arrived in port from Snook's Arm with a load of whale bone. [She is here] for registration. She is a splendid craft of 144 tons, is on her maiden voyage to Windsor, Nova Scotia and will mostly be used in connection with the Tilt Cove Stores trade. Capt. Saunders is in command.

While Francis Warr built ships mostly for merchants, he also constructed about ten of his ships for planters.

John Downton of Exploits constructed four ships between 1877 and 1884, though he was very probably building well before 1877 during the period when shipbuilders' names did not appear in the registers. He began with the 50-ton *Jane* in 1877 for which he collected the bounty of $147 and then sold the vessel to Charles Bowring, merchant of St. John's. His next three vessels were also sold to or built for Bowring: the 59-ton *Louisa* in 1880, the 46-ton *John Wickford* in 1882, and the 41-ton *Forest Belle* in 1884. John's address is given as Green Bay and Exploits Bay, but he was a resident of Exploits Burnt Islands.

James Wells of Swan Island (Swan Harbour?) constructed seven ships in total, with four of these in the Bay of Exploits and specifically two at Indian Arm and one at Campbellton, between 1879 and 1902. His first ship was the

50-ton *Ocean Traveller*. Two of his ships were built for Josiah Manuel: the 50-ton *Albatross* in 1884 and the 38-ton *Cornwall* in 1901. Five of his ships were built for merchants and two for planters.

James Snow was probably a brother of William Snow mentioned earlier. His first ship was the 35-ton *Wild Wave* of 1875, and his second, the 49-ton *Brothers*, was built at Burnt Bay in 1879 for William and Henry Dorey, planters at Black Island. James was probably settled at Burnt Bay because, nine years later, he built the 19-ton *River Stream* there. His next three ships were built at Indian Arm in 1891, at Little Burnt Bay in 1907, and at Kite Cove in 1913. In a period of thirty-seven years, he had built six ships, again an indication of the priority of the fishery over shipbuilding.

John Head crafted ten ships between 1879 and 1911. His first ship was the 27-ton *Thomas D.*, built at Burnt Bay. Then in 1880 he constructed his largest ship, the 63-ton *Prince Imperial*. Both these ships were built for St. John's merchant, Philip Hutchins. In 1894 John built the 16-ton *Jane* for Dawe P. Osmond, a trader/dealer at Moreton's Harbour. It was named for Osmond's wife. When Dawe Osmond died in 1920, Jane became a shipowner in her own right, participating in the sale of one ship and buying shares in another which she sold in 1924. John Head constructed another ship for Dawe Osmond, the 18-ton *Gypsy* in 1901 at Comfort Cove. Eight of John's ten ships were built at Comfort Cove, so it is highly likely that he had settled there. His last two ships were the 22-ton *Sir Ralph Williams* built in 1909 and the 25-ton *Lady Williams* fashioned in 1911.

George Hawkins Jr. of Triton Island builds five ships in five years and then disappears from the records, which seems very unusual. In his first year, 1880, he constructs two ships: the 22-ton *Fortunate* and the 22-ton *Young Builder*. The latter vessel was probably named in recognition of his youthful status; it was built for his father George Hawkins Senior. His five ships were constructed in five different locations: Robert's Arm, Triton Island, Little Bay Islands, Sunday Cove Tickle, and Long Tickle. His largest ship was the 43-ton *Water Lilly* built in 1882. Such a promising career coming to such an abrupt end seems to spell disaster of some kind. His first ship was lost at sea in 1886.

John J. Ridout crafted his first of seven ships at Little Bay Islands in 1880: the 58-ton *Minnie E. Strong* for James Strong, merchant of the same place. It must have been built well because it lasted for thirty years and was lost at sea in 1910. He then constructed his largest ship, the 75-ton *Lily of the North* at

Hall's Bay for a local planter. Three of his ships were built at Cutwell Arm—the 47-ton *Silver Cloud* in 1897, the 33-ton *Madonna* in 1901, and the 29-ton *Phyllis J. F.* in 1908—and one was built at Ward's Harbour. Five of the seven ships were built for merchants. His period of building was from 1880 to 1908. It is possible that the John Rideout who builds four small ships at Three Arms, Green Bay, between 1940 and 1951 is a son or grandson of John J. Ridout.

Frederick Jure settled in Kite Cove (Laurenceton) sometime before 1881 because in that year he fashioned his first ship, the 54-ton *Bismark* there. Eleven of his thirteen ships were built for the merchant Edwin J. Duder of Herring Neck and St. John's. He must have set some kind of a record for building because in 1883 he constructed three ships: the 21-ton *Hound*, the 41-ton *Iolanthe*, and the *Olivette*; in 1884 he built four ships: the 44-ton *Romeo*, the 28-ton *Juliet*, the 21-ton *Ellen*, and the 20-ton *Belle*; and in 1885 he crafted three ships, but this time at Burnt Arm (the other side of Kite Cove): the 25-ton *Alpha*, the 23-ton *Glide*, and the 25-ton *Jessie*. All this building was done in a five-year period, which is truly remarkable. Frederick must have exhausted himself because he did not build another ship until 1889, the 46-ton *Milda*. This was his last ship. It was sold to the Adventurers of England Co. headquartered in London, England. The *Twillingate Sun* of March 4, 1883, noted that Frederick Jure of Burnt Arm was a boatbuilder. And that he was!

John Hull of Little Bay Islands had a distinguished career as a shipbuilder extending over forty-five years, from 1882 to 1926, and resulting in sixteen vessels built and three rebuilt. Nine of his ships were built and three others rebuilt for James Strong of Little Bay Islands, so he was probably Strong's chief builder during this period or shared that responsibility with Job Wiseman. His first vessel was the 44-ton *Mary Rose*. He also constructed large vessels, such as the 65-ton *Magnolia* in 1887, the 87-ton *Ellen D.* in 1888, and the 80-ton *St. Elmo* in 1898. It is of interest that Martha Benson, a married woman at Little Bay Islands, held sixteen shares in this ship from 1898 to 1914. John Hull went to Hall's Bay in 1905 to construct the 35-ton *Emerald*; this vessel was broken up in 1932. He crafted the 37-ton *Dorothy Strong* and the 10-ton *William Strong*, both in 1920. The latter vessel was very probably a pleasure boat for the Strong family. The *Evening Telegram* of October 30, 1922, commented on the arrival of Hull's 36-ton *Violet Jones* in the city to be registered: "The schooner *Violet J.* is on her maiden voyage to this port. She was built last summer at Little Bay Islands by Mr. J. Hull and five helpers. The work started on May 10th. She has 700 quintals of dry fish on board. The workmanship is highly commented on by people who viewed her at Job's wharf." In 1925 and 1926, to cap off his building career, John Hull rebuilt for James Strong Ltd. the 29-ton *Daisy*, the 34-ton *Cordelia Strong*, and the 20-ton *Clover Leaf*.

It is fitting at this point to consider William Hull because he was probably a brother of John Hull though William started a bit later. Between 1892 and 1908 he constructed six ships, beginning with the 45-ton *Cecilia* and concluding with the 34-ton *Lucy S.* The *Coronet* of 1905 was his largest ship at 62 tons. Four of his ships were built for St. John's merchants, none for James Strong.

James Bowers built all of his seven ships at Nipper's Harbour between 1883 and 1920. He started his building career with the 20-ton *Alert*. By the time he built his fourth ship in 1900, the 27-ton *Cronge*, his status is given as merchant; this may account for the fact that all his vessels were built at Nipper's Harbour. His largest vessel was the 62-ton *Maryllia* built in 1906.

Thomas Colbourne II of Wild Bight and Little Bay is worth an honourable mention, though he is known to have built only one ship, the 18-ton *Annie Laura* in 1884. Thomas was born in Twillingate in 1840 and died on April 4, 1923. Fortunately his obituary, written by a friend, Thomas E. Wells, appeared in the *Evening Telegram* of April 7, 1923. Wells had known Thomas Colbourne since 1883. Part of the obituary reads as follows:

> Thomas Colbourne…removed with his family to Wild Bight in the early 70s and set to work to clear up a home in the Virgin forest among the early settlers…he followed the codfishery, as master and owner of a fishing schooner, and was a successful fisherman farmer. When the mine started at Little Bay in the 70s his uncle being Robert Colbourne the original discoverer of the Little Bay mines…Thomas gave up the uncertain codfishery and became a carpenter in the mine and worked his land, vegetables being in demand at the mine. Later he became a prospector for the Little Bay Mining Co., and he with Mr. Wilson from Nova Scotia discovered the 'Lady Pond' mine…. Thomas also built his own schooner and sailed her.

This vignette gives some insight into how early settlers of this region used their skills and initiative to survive and prosper.

Solomon Brown of Kite Cove (Laurenceton) fashioned seven ships between 1885 and 1907. All his vessels were built at Kite Cove, though by 1900 the name Laurenceton is used consistently. The 17-ton *Fiona* was built in 1885 and was rebuilt in 1910 by Peter Anstey at Twillingate, thus lasting twenty-five-plus years. Six of Solomon's ships were small, his largest being his last, the 50-ton *Nora B.*, built for George J. Carter, merchant at Herring Neck and St. John's. The others averaged 22 tons each.

Charles Tucker's period of shipbuilding lasted from 1891 to 1908, and in that eighteen-year period he built thirteen ships, an impressive record indeed. Eleven of his thirteen ships were constructed at his home in Pilley's Island; the other two were crafted at Three Arms and Southwest Arm. He first built the 33-ton *Madora* at Three Arms, and then in 1893 the 43-ton *Rival Queen*. In 1897 he built what would seem to have been sister ships: the 26-ton *Little Dora* and the 22-ton *Little Dot*, both for W. B. Grieve, St. John's merchant. By 1901 Charles had become a trader/dealer, but he continued to build ships. Five of his vessels were constructed for W.C. Job, and all but two for St. John's merchants.. His largest ships were the *Rival Queen* and the 36-ton *Lady Effie*.

James Lannon was a resident of Fortune Harbour, and all but one of his seven ships were constructed there between 1891 and 1901. That other ship was built at New Bay—the 30-ton *Bruce* in 1899. He first built the 44-ton *New Era*, and the next year he built the 55-ton *Mystery*. The aptly-named 34-ton *Fortune* was crafted in 1893. Five of his ships were constructed for St. John's merchants.

John Thomas Morey was probably a resident of Pilley's Island, but he built four of his five ships at Sunday Cove Island between 1896 and 1903. He crafted two ships in 1896: the 22-ton *Donald* and the 28-ton *Ivy Bess*. His largest ship was the 34-ton *Esther* constructed in 1897. The 26-ton *Daisy* was built for James Strong, and rebuilt for Strong in 1925 by John Hull of Little Bay Islands.

Thomas Tulk may have been from Herring Neck but built his first three of four ships at Western Arm, NDB: the 25-ton *Eva Booth* in 1901 for George Barbour, master mariner of Newtown; the 28-ton *Little Beulah* in 1904; and the 36-ton *Ethel G.* in 1905. The 15-ton *Little Maple Leaf* of 1908 was constructed at Rocky Bay; it was his last ship.

George Wellman was somewhat of an itinerant shipbuilder, constructing his first three ships at Sunday Cove Island from 1902 to 1906. His first ship was the 37-ton *Delsie Bell* built for William Ashbourne, merchant at Twillingate. In 1906 he crafted the 29-ton *E. R. Annadale*, which was lost at sea in 1934 having lasted for thirty-six years. In 1907 George constructed the 63-ton *Loyalty* at Harry's Harbour for James Norris, merchant at Three Arms. His last ship was his largest—the 77-ton *Lady Squires* built at Springdale in 1930.

The next builder is included more as a curiosity than anything else. John C. West of Simcoe, Ontario, built the 13-ton *Annie* at Red Indian Lake in 1900 for Lewis Miller, who had come to Newfoundland from Scotland in 1900 and established a very large sawmill at Millertown and another at Glenwood and a major shipping port for his lumber at Lewisporte (both towns being named for Miller). The *Annie* was a steamship with paddles, had no masts, and was equipped with an eight-horsepower engine. It was not registered until 1902. In the record, Miller is described as the Managing Director of the Lewis Millertown Co. Ltd. Perhaps John C. West had been brought in because of his expertise with steamships on Lake Simcoe. Concluding that timber in the area was over mature for sawn lumber and more suitable for pulp, Miller left Newfoundland in 1903.

All of George Luff's six ships were constructed for the Manuel family of Exploits Islands. George built over a short period, between 1902 and 1909. His first two ships were constructed for Josiah Manuel: the 40-ton *Alexandra* and the 45-ton *Harold T.*, both in 1902. Josiah died in 1907, and George Luff resumed building in 1907 for Chesley and Jabez Manuel, Josiah's sons. In three years he built the 39-ton *C.L.B.*, the 36-ton *Lom*, the 27-ton *O.K.M.*, and the 63-ton *Merry Widow*. The local correspondent to the *Free Press* waxed eloquent when the *C.L.B.* was launched on May 10, 1907:

> Are you going to the launch? This was last week's salutation and also the event of the year. On Thursday 6th Mr. Manuel's dock was the central point of attraction and the greater portion of the harbour wended their way thither. At 6:20 p.m. the trip was loosed and a fine schooner of about 60 tons slided to her Paradise. Hundreds of eyes were fixed on the spot where she took her first dip, while a large number rallied along the deck from side to side. Mr. George Luff, the ship-builder deserves a word of praise for his ability and success along these lines. The dock-yards of England could not turn out better models than those sent out from the dock-yards of Exploits. Well done, Newfoundlanders. They not only build them but rig and sail them. We hope that

> whatever party is returned to power that there will be more encouragement given to such industries and we shall soon see Newfoundland take an important place in the industrial world.

Mr. Luff must have been much encouraged, but such a promising builder disappears from the scene after a brief eight years.

James Jones of Little Bay Islands crafted only four ships, all at Little Bay Islands, but he is worthy of our attention here because he is the James Jones who became the master builder and superintendent of construction for Sir William Coaker's Port Union Shipbuilding Company. Jones began his shipbuilding career in 1903 with the 42-ton *Annie H.J.*, and his partner was fellow planter Richard Jones. In 1905 he fashioned the 91-ton *Renown* for planter John Jones. John Jones had already constructed at least one ship previously—the 75-ton *Lily of the North* in 1881 for which he had collected a bounty of $225. Three years later, in 1908, the 43-ton *A. Conqueror* was constructed by James Jones for James Norris, merchant at Three Arms. In 1910 Jones built the 63-ton *Ruby V. Jones* for George Jones, a fisherman at Little Bay Islands. This vessel was lost at sea in White Bay in 1938, thus lasting twenty-eight years. By the time he moved to Port Union in 1915 to become superintendent of the Port Union Shipbuilding Co., James Jones was classed as a master mariner with thirty-seven years at sea.

Abraham B. Rideout is worthy of an honourable mention because, in addition to constructing smaller ships, he built a particularly large ship. But he began his shipbuilding career by constructing the 25-ton *Handsome Queen* at North West Arm (Burlington) in 1909 for James Norris, merchant at Three Arms. It was sixteen years before he built the 16-ton *Piano* at Three Arms, and four years later it was the 81-ton *Grace Lorraine* at Burlington. In 1944 Abraham constructed the 272-ton, one-masted wood barge *Lady Baie Verte* at Baie Verte for Bowaters Ltd. of Corner Brook. Another builder who constructed a large ship in this area was Luke Thomas, who at nearby Middle Arm in 1948 built the 111-ton *Carol Strong* for James Strong Ltd. of St. John's.

We have already considered the Norris Arm Shipbuilding Co. as a subsidiary of the Newfoundland Shipbuilding Co. at Harbour Grace, with Job Manuel as their master shipbuilder. The Company, under the direction of Michael E. Martin, built four large ships before the parent Company went bankrupt. These ships were: the 298-ton *Pauline Martin* in 1917, the 356-ton *Kathleen* in 1918, and the 148-ton *Rose M.* and 129-ton *Neerod* in 1919.

Theophilus Wells was the master builder of the 146-ton, three-masted schooner *Percie Wells* for the Horwood Lumber Co. in 1919. The place of construction is given in the records simply as Hare Bay. There are at least four Hare Bays in Newfoundland: one on the southwest coast (Hare Bay fjord), one in Bonavista Bay, one on Fogo Island, and one in White Bay on the Northern Peninsula. Complicating matters further is the fact that this is the only vessel for which Theophilus Wells is given credit in the ship registers. The fact that the vessel was built for the Horwood Lumber Co. should narrow the site to the northeast coast, and my guess would be that Theophilus was from Notre Dame Bay and crafted the ship at Hare Bay on the Northern Peninsula. There were at least six shipbuilders in Notre Dame Bay with the name of Wells between 1897 and 1912. One of these was Zephaniah Wells who built ships at Swan Harbour and Samson's Island in 1897 and 1912. It would be just like a man named Zephaniah to name his son Theophilus. In 1921 the *Percie Wells* had brought a load of molasses from Barbados to Campbellton, and then took a load of lumber from there to New York, and was on the way back to St. John's with a load of hard coal when she went missing sometime in October 1921 and was never heard from again. She carried a crew of six.

The Anglo-Newfoundland Development Co. of Grand Falls and Botwood became a major player first in the construction of large steamers at Red Indian Lake and then in the construction of large wooden transport vessels at Botwood Harbour. We have already considered several of these under Adam Chalk, the Company's master builder for many or all of these vessels. Chalk began working for the Company at Red Indian Lake sometime after 1910 and in March 1917 was building an unnamed 300-ton steamer as a companion ship for the similar-sized *Lady Mary* which he had constructed previously and was then lying up for the winter. At Botwood, the Company launched the 504-ton *Bella Scott* in 1918, the 582-ton *Sordello* in 1919, and the 59-ton *Exploits II* in 1919. In 1921 Adam Chalk built the 250-ton steamship *Fleetway* at Red Indian Lake. The Company did not build any more ships until 1945, and then they launched the 19-ton tugboat *Sir Vincent J.* and the 19-ton tugboat *Henry S.C.* at Twin Lakes, Badger. In 1947 the Company built the 17-ton workboat *Francis H. II* at Glenwood.

Samuel Simmons of Lewisporte got his start in shipbuilding by assisting Robert Evans in the construction of the 372-ton *Attainment* at Thwart Island in 1917 and again with the 149-ton *Nancy Lee* at Campbellton in 1920. In 1916 at Campbellton he constructed the 27-ton *David Beatty* for the

Horwood Lumber Co. In 1929 at Howley he constructed two small ships, both of them 24 tons: the *Joan Tipping* and the *Nellie Roberts.* In 1930 he built the 29-ton *Jessie Hansen*, also at Howley. His last vessel was built at Piccadilly on the west coast in 1939: the 21-ton *Westbow*.

William Francis Bartlett ("Frank") was a great promoter of shipbuilding in Green Bay in the 1930s and 1940s, though he appears not to have been a shipbuilder himself. The interesting thing about Frank Bartlett is that four of his ships were registered in the name of his wife Jane at the time of building. She was thus a shipowner over a period of eleven years. It is now known, however, that three of Jane's four ships were built by George Pynn of Rattling Brook, so Pynn was one of Frank's master builders as was Philip Card of Rattling Brook. Philip Card built the 56-ton *Radio City* in 1935; as far as we can tell, it was the only ship built by him.

However, George Pynn built ten ships between 1931 and 1946 and at least three of them for Frank Bartlett: the *Arizona* in 1931, the 73-ton *Audrey Bartlett* in 1936, and the 68-ton *Tempest* in 1940. Pynn gave city names to three others of his ships: the 76-ton *Denver City* in 1933, the 84-ton *Dawson City* in 1934, and the 43-ton *Dayton City* in 1935. By 1946 when George Pynn built his last ship, the 75-ton *Louisa & George*, he was a resident of Middle Arm, Green Bay.

In the 1950s and 1960s we see the emergence of shipbuilding companies in various parts of Newfoundland. There was a concentration of these in various parts of Notre Dame Bay. It is impossible to determine who the individual master shipbuilders were in most instances.

The Weirs of Little Bay Islands had a connection with Lewisporte, at least through Reginald Victor Weir. James Weir built the 21-ton fishing vessel *Joyce & Ivan* at Little Bay Islands in 1949, and in 1956 constructed the 29-ton *Peggy Williams* as a passenger boat. From 1953 to 1966 Reginald Victor Weir constructed six ships at Little Bay Islands, and at least three of these were substantial-sized vessels: the 41-ton passenger/cargo vessel *Miss Vera* in 1953, the 42-ton *Reliable One* in 1966, and the 273-ton *Sybil Eloise*, a cargo vessel constructed for Buffett Fisheries Ltd. of Grand Bank in 1964. The other three were small fishing vessels averaging about 23 tons each. From 1967 to 1972 Reginald Victor Weir was described as a shipbuilder from Lewisporte, but four of his fifteen vessels were built at Little Bay Islands, and he is sometimes described as a shipbuilder from Little Bay Islands building ships at Lewisporte. His first vessel built at Lewisporte was the 23-ton

Western Tickle in 1967. The fifteen ships built during these later years were all fishing vessels and averaged about 25 tons each. They were built in six years, five of them in 1972. They bore such fascinating names as: *La Scie Belle*, *Conche Cruiser*, *Condor no. 1*, *Miss Mt. Carmel*, and *Endeavour II*. Twenty-one ships built in twenty years was an enviable record indeed; all of these were described in the ship registers as wooden fishing vessels. They were regarded as the preferred product for fishermen of that period.

Weir's Fibreglass Products of Little Bay Islands was probably operated by one of Reginald's sons or certainly by members of the same family. By this time, fibreglass vessels had become the preferred vessels for local fishermen. Weir's Fibreglass Products built four small vessels between 1989 and 1992, all of them described as "GRP-Fishing" and "moulded." They averaged less than 10 tons each. Their names were *Trina & Sons*, *Nicole Eugene*, *Miss Bridgeport*, and *Island Harvester*. And then came the 1992 Moratorium and the end of Weir's Fibreglass Products.

It was probably the family or certainly relatives of James Jones, of Port Union and Sir William Coaker fame, who constructed a shipyard at Little Bay Islands in the 1960s and established S. T. Jones & Sons Ltd. as shipbuilders. The family group constructed ten ships in the seven-year period from 1967 to 1973. Their largest ship was the 64-ton, two-masted *Ashuanipi* constructed in 1967. Other substantial ships were the 48-ton, one-masted *Newfie Maid* of 1971 and the 47-ton, two-masted *Judy Deanna* of 1971. All other ships were in the 19 to 27 ton range, and all were wooden fishing vessels including the *Cape St. Anthony* of 1967, the *Miss Beachside* of 1968, and the *Newfie Girl* of 1973.

Carl Raymond Wright of Nipper's Harbour crafted nine wooden fishing ships in the period from 1968 to 1975. Most were in the 25 to 27 ton range, and two of these were substantial-sized vessels: the 49-ton *Melinda Joyce* of 1974 and the 50-ton *Rodger Dennis* of 1973. All but two of these were one-masted; the other two were two-masted. Four of the vessels carried such exotic names as *Green Bay Rover*, *Cape Chidley*, *Rocky Bay*, and *Eventide IV*.

Carl Wright was very likely the person who founded Wright's Boatyard Ltd. at King's Point in 1980 and continued it until 1982. The telephone directory for 2009 listed the name of Carl Wright at King's Point. During this three-year period, the Boatyard constructed eight wooden fishing ships ranging in size from 10 to 28 tons each. Three ships were constructed in 1980, including the 27-ton *Miss L'Anse au Loup*; one ship was built in 1981; and four ships were built in 1982, including the 27-ton *Arctic Drift*, the 27-ton *Northern Tip*, and the 26-ton *Marine Fisher*.

Pelley Enterprises Ltd. was established as a shipbuilding company at Springdale in 1969. In a fifteen year period, from 1969 to 1983, they constructed fourteen vessels. Eleven of them were wooden fishing vessels and three were of steel construction. Their first ship was the 126-ton, two-masted *Sister Alex* of 1969 and was constructed for Cyril Clyde Pelley, contractor; he may, in fact, have been the owner of the enterprise. They did not build another until 1979 and then they crafted thirteen ships in a five-year period. Their wooden fishing vessels varied in size from 4 tons to 52 tons. The 52-ton *Arctic Venture* and the 40-ton *Polar Venture* were built in 1979, and the 24-ton *Arctic Clipper* was constructed in 1980. Pelley's three steel ships were the 11-ton *Iron Cow* built in 1980, the 20-ton *Miss Lumsden* of 1982, and the 24-ton *Steel Dolphin* of 1983. The *Steel Dolphin* was built at Goodyear's Cove, their only ship not built at Springdale. It is of interest that when the name *Iron Cow* was changed to *J. C. & Paul* in 1990, the ship carried a mortgage of $75,000. By comparison, the 4-ton wood-fishing vessel *Cathy Priscilla* in 1981 carried a mortgage of $61,180. Ships were beginning to cost substantial amounts of money.

It cannot be determined whether Melvin Howard Pelley, who built the 8-ton *White Shark* at Beachside in 1991, was involved with Pelley Enterprises Ltd. of Springdale. The vessel was described as GRP-Fishing, moulded, and motor-screw.

T.W.N. Limited of Nipper's Harbour operated from 1979 to 1984, and during that period they constructed twelve ships in the town, and after a lapse of five years they built one ship at Argentia. It is possible that this company was owned by the Noble family or the Wright family of Nipper's Harbour. All twelve ships crafted at Nipper's Harbour were wooden fishing vessels and varied in tonnage from 4 to 48 tons. Their largest ship, the 48-ton *Carl Venture*, was built in 1982. Their smallest ship, the 4-ton *Ocean Gambler II*, was built in 1984. Most of their ships were in the 25 ton range. Some of the most memorable names were *Sunset Bay*, *La Scie Liner*, *La Scie Star*, *Penny's Dream*, and *North Cruiser*. The 70-ton GRP-Fishing vessel *Golden Princess* was built at Argentia in 1989 but was not registered until 1991. What effect the 1992 Moratorium had on this company cannot be determined.

Lewisporte Marine Ltd. had a short life in 1979. They built three vessels that year and then ceased operations as a shipbuilding company. Their first two vessels, each about 23 tons, were wooden fishing ships and the third, the 13-ton *Jeffery Tyson*, was a GRP-Fishing vessel.

Green Bay Enterprises Ltd. of King's Point existed for only two years as a shipbuilding company and during this time built five vessels, all wooden fishing ships. They started in 1979 with the colourfully-named 12-ton *Muddy Shag*, built one more ship that year and three more in 1980. Their largest vessel was the 32-ton *Gary Michael* constructed in 1980.

Atkinson & Yates Boatbuilders Ltd. of Springdale existed as a shipbuilding company from 1987 to 1991 and during this five-year period constructed fifteen ships; twelve of them were GRP-Fishing ships, one was described as a pleasure boat, one as a yacht, and one as a passenger boat. The ships ranged in size from 4 tons to 13 tons and were motor-screw. The 5-ton passenger boat was appropriately named *Bontours*, the pleasure boat was the 5-ton *S.S. Matthew*, and the 4-ton yacht was named *Nixie*. Some of the other interesting names were *Beachside Cruiser*, *Drifter's Dream*, and *Trinity Challenger*. It is of interest that the 8-ton *Tammy & Cynthia* built in 1987 carried Mortgage A of $57,498 and Mortgage B of $52,270.91. Their last ship, the 11-ton *Newfie Nova*, built in 1991, was registered in 1992, the year when the Cod Moratorium was announced.

Yates Shipbuilding of Springdale is probably a survivor of Atkinson & Yates Boatbuilders Ltd., and their small boats are still in evidence around our coasts in 2013.

CHAPTER TWO

WHITE BAY AND THE NORTHERN PENINSULA

THE SEVERAL REGIONS included in the area from Cape St. John up around the Northern Peninsula and down along the west coast and along the south coast as far as Harbour Breton were practically invisible to the St. John's newspapers; it seems the only news consisted of reports of shipwrecks, severe storms, and the progress of icebergs down along what today we call Iceberg Alley, down through the Strait of Belle Isle, and along the west coast. It was also an area almost totally neglected by the St. John's merchants. Only in the area of the west coast-southern section were a few ships built for these merchants in the late eighteenth and early nineteenth centuries. When the English and the Jersey merchants vacated the area they were mostly succeeded by local merchants and particularly the Moulton firm of Burgeo and the Penny firm of Ramea.

As we leave the previous areas with their clearly defined bays, we enter a region where the divisions are much more arbitrary, but as a guide, we are following the divisions established by the Maritime Shipping Project at Memorial University in the 1950s.

This chapter deals with the area west from La Scie into White Bay and around the Northern Peninsula and south to Cow Head. The name White Bay had been in common use since the 1600s, the area from Cape St. John to Cape Bauld being known later as Greater White Bay. Aboriginal groups from the Labrador, particularly the Montagnais, came across the Strait of Belle Isle to trap for furs in White Bay, and an early map describes their route across the Northern Peninsula as "Path of the Savages." In the early days, this region was part of the French Shore, and the Petit Nord was the area most heavily fished by the French, even from the 1500s, with their primary efforts focussed at Cape Rouge, Conche, St. Anthony, Fleur de Lys, Fishot Islands, and La Scie. Fishot Islands appeared on a French map as "Ille de Ficho" as early as 1547 and was dubbed "Fishroad Islands" three hundred years later by English naval captains. As late as 1857 the French held eight fishing stations on Fishot Islands and had 430 men fishing there in sixty batteaux. There was a mixed French and English population throughout this period, and Martin Bromley was a *gardien* for the French and was the chief fisherman in the area in 1872. Fleur de Lys seems to have been the easternmost point of the Petit Nord, and after the Treaty of Utrecht (1713) the French carried home their fishing boats and sent back a crew two months early to prepare for the new fishing season. When they lost both Ile Royale in Cape Breton and Quebec after the Treaty of Paris (1763), they actually increased their fishing activity in the Petit Nord and northwards. The French seem not to have been interested in White Bay itself. D. W. Prowse affirms that Bonavista planters were fishing as far north as Quirpon as early as 1698. During the Seven Year's War (1756-1763), the English moved into this area in significant numbers. Poole merchants George Milner and Matthew Glover had developed a fishing station at St. Julien's by 1761. And when the war ended in 1763, there were almost 800 men and 100 fishing boats active along the coast from Fleur de Lys to Griquet, though this number seems to have declined dramatically following this. In the 1760s the English appear to have been fishing in tandem with the French at Englee, Canada (Canaries) Harbour, and Wild Cove. The French generally pursued a ship fishery, carrying their fish home green and heavily salted.

Only the bravest and most intrepid explorers ventured into this area to develop significant land-based fisheries. One of the first was John Slade of Poole in the 1760s. Slade had made his first trip to Newfoundland in 1748, and by the late 1750s he was headquartered at Twillingate and significantly involved in the Poole-Newfoundland trade with a broad focus on salt cod, seals, salmon, and furs. By 1763 Slade had a fishery operation established at Sop's Island in White Bay. Richard and Netlam Tory of Poole took over this operation from Slade within a very short time, and by 1786, after more than twenty years of operation, they were forced out by the French, assisted curiously by the British navy forces. The Torys had operated a cod fishing business at Sop's Island, a salmon fishery on Main River, and in the winters pursued a seal fishery and trapped furs. Slade had moved his operation north to Conche and Battle Harbour, Labrador; the Torys also moved to Labrador after their eviction. By 1777 Slade was managing his extensive business from Poole, leaving his nephews in charge of his burgeoning business in Newfoundland. The William Pittman who was an employee of the Torys during this period was very probably the father of "Old Billy" Pittman (1791-1864) who is regarded as the first permanent settler in the area. That distinction may in fact have belonged to the father. One of them, probably the father, was granted by the French the right to fish for salmon on Main River in the early 1800s and very probably acted as a caretaker of French Shore properties during their absence. John Gill (or Gale) was operating a cod and salmon fishery by 1820 at Granby (Big) Island and Chouse Brook. Very little specific data exists concerning these ventures, but it is known that Sop's Island was the oldest English settlement north of Cape St. John.

Information on shipbuilding in this area in the early years is sketchy at best, and there was not a lot of it. Most shipbuilders listed in the ships registers have only one or two ships to their credit, and I expect that the builders were so far away from the port of registration at St. John's that many of their ships were never registered. The nondescript "White Bay" is generally used as the building location for many of these ships. The area was also so remote from St. John's, particularly in the early years, that there is scarcely a mention of activities in the newspapers of the day or in contemporary literature.

Samuel Parsons of Hawke's Bay was the first shipbuilder found in this region. In 1821 he constructed the 53-ton *Mary* for William Genge of Forteau, Labrador, and Joseph Bird Jr., merchant of Dorset, England. Two years later Parsons "raised on" and decked the 46-ton *Jane* for merchant Joseph Bird. This vessel had been built as an open boat in the Bay of Islands in 1815. The Birds may have been father and son and one of their local planters, Genge, was fishing for them on the Labrador.

William ("Old Billy") Pittman appears in the Slade ledgers as early as 1810. By 1821 he was the skipper of a 48-ton fishing schooner, and over the following two decades he is said to have built several more schooners, but these could not be found in the ship registers. In 1820 Henry Knight of Moreton's Harbour built the 48-ton *Margaret* for Pittman who, at that time, was listed as a planter in White Bay, undoubtedly at Sop's Island. This was probably the vessel of which he was skipper in 1821. It is known that in 1826 Pittman built the 47-ton *Amity* for a St. John's trader/dealer.

Five years later, in 1831, John Gover (Gower, Govey?) was sent into White Bay to build the 117-ton brigantine *Clydesdale* for St. John's merchant J. J. Grieve. Gover was very likely an English shipbuilder brought in for that express purpose or one operating out of St. John's or Conception Bay. The enormous timber stands of White Bay were by now well known to the St. John's merchants.

William Facey of White Bay built the 27-ton *Nancy* in 1834, and when it was registered in 1836 the owner was William McCarthy, planter of St. John's. And still in the 1830s, Charles Dawe and William Hutchings of Cow Head built the 23-ton *Ant* in 1837, and when it was registered for the first time in 1846 it was owned by William Henry Ellis, merchant at Bonne Bay. Though the French occupied this entire area until 1904, Newfoundland fishermen had moved into the area in increasing numbers and by 1838 were pursuing a migratory fishery along the French Shore, most of them coming from the greater Notre Dame Bay area, particularly Twillingate, Change Islands, Moreton's Harbour, and Herring Neck. At the government enumeration in 1857, only 231 permanent residents were listed.

Only one ship was built in this region in the 1840s. That was the 23-ton *Saint Patrick* built by Patrick Duggan in 1840. The owner was Daniel Duggan, planter of Green Bay, and Patrick was master of this vessel, so he may have gone to White Bay for the sole purpose of building the ship with the Duggans' home being in Green Bay.

Only three ships were built in the 1850s, and for two of these we have specific building locations. John Johnston of White Bay constructed the 23-ton *Mary Ann Jane* in 1851 at Hare Bay, but the vessel was not registered until 1858. Though Hare Bay furnished great timber stands, it is curious that John and Michael Crowley of Hare Bay went to Green Bay in 1858 to construct their 43-ton *Brothers*. And in the same year, Henry Gillard of White Bay built the 28-ton *Frolic*, which was lost at sea in 1872, thus lasting for fourteen years.

When the White Bay area was enumerated in 1857, Basil Osmond with his eleven children was located at Gold Cove near Hampden, and his brother Joseph Osmond was living at Seal Cove. These may well have been the sons of Bazariel Osmond who was a boatbuilder for John Slade in Twillingate in the 1780s and 1790s.

James and Anthony Gardner of White Bay, like the Crowley brothers, went to Green Bay in 1864 to build the 25-ton *Greyhound*. The ship registers give John Pyne of White Bay credit for building two ships in specific locations: the 18-ton *Industry* at Canada Bay in 1869 and the 40-ton *Mary Joseph* in 1879 at Conche. This last vessel was sold to P. & L. Tessier, merchants of St. John's, and was lost on the Labrador coast in 1885. We should also consider the notorious gap in the records when shipbuilders' names were not given from 1854 to 1877, so John Pyne very probably built several other ships.

THE HOPKINS FAMILY

While at least twenty-five families in this region produced at least two or three shipbuilders, only the Hopkins family of Englee can truly be called a shipbuilding family with builders in at least three successive generations. Charles Hopkins built the 23-ton *Morning Star* at Englee in 1880 and collected a bounty of $66; she lasted until 1903 when she was lost at York Point, Labrador. Robert Hopkins built the 15-ton *Florence* in 1891 for the Alcock family of Griquet, trader/dealers. William Hopkins of Englee was probably the son of Charles or Robert and is well known as Sir Wilfred Grenfell's friend. Dr. Grenfell writes about him in his autobiography *A Labrador Doctor*:

> Will Hopkins can take an axe and a few tools into the green woods in the fall, and sail down the bay in a new schooner in the spring when the ice goes. To see him steaming the planking in the open in his own improvised boxes on the top of six feet of snow made me stand and take my hat off to him.

Dr. Grenfell confirms that William "built a vessel at our mill" in 1908.

William began his shipbuilding career by constructing the 54-ton *Kingfish* at Canada Bay in 1901 for W. C. Job, merchant at St. John's, and continued with the twin ships 42-ton *Mary M.* and the 42-ton *Maggie M.* at Englee in 1902 for Samuel and John Moulton, merchants at Bonne Bay. Then came the 41-ton Roddickton in 1903, the 69-ton *Emma E. White* in 1908, and the 39-ton *Daryl*, also in 1908, all three ships for W. H. Peters, merchant at

St. John's. The *Free Press* of December 3, 1907, reports that "Dr. Grenfell is having a new schooner built at Englee by Mr. Hopkins and a number of workmen are under his superintendence, for his cooperative stores." The *Maggie M.* was rebuilt at Catalina in 1930, thus lasting twenty-eight-plus years, and the *Roddickton* was rebuilt at Little Heart's Ease in 1926, lasting for twenty-three-plus years, testimony to the skills of the original builder.

The ship registers are silent on William Hopkins's production for eighteen years, and then in 1926 at Boyd's Arm, Canada Bay, he builds the 123-ton schooner *Nellie Reeves* for John Reeves, merchant at Englee. This vessel was lost at sea near Change Islands in 1932. Hopkins probably built several vessels during this period, but they could have been registered in the name of the new owner with no credit being given to the builder.

Willis R. Hopkins began his building career at Englee in 1938 when he constructed the 59-ton *Island Coaster*. He is very probably the son of William. We do not hear of Willis again until we see him at Wesleyville in 1961 constructing the 360-ton *Prince Andrew*. From 1962 to 1975 he was building much smaller ships at Carbonear and Harbour Grace.

John Hopkins, who may have been William's brother, built the 64-ton *Advance* at Canada Bay in 1902. Two builders, probably of the third generation, built ships at Englee in 1968; Leonard W. Hopkins built the 24-ton *Englee Twin Stem*, and Randolph Grenfell Hopkins built the 24-ton *Debbie Anne*. These were likely William's grandsons, and we should note the Grenfell name attributed to Randolph.

About twenty-five families in this region produced at least two or three shipbuilders, the Elliott family producing four builders between 1873 and 1968 at Ha Ha Bay, Raleigh, and Lock's Cove and the Randell family nine builders between 1967 and 1982 at Williamsport, Hooping Harbour, Bide Arm, Englee, and Great Harbour Deep. The Elliott family of Cook's Harbour were prolific boatbuilders before the 1980s.

John J. Norris of Three Arms, Green Bay, arrived at Englee in the fall of 1918 to begin construction of the 242-ton, three-masted schooner *Armistice* for the A. E. Hickman Co. of St. John's. Since Norris seems to have had no prior experience at shipbuilding, he was very probably the construction foreman of the project and probably brought with him shipbuilders from Green Bay who had previously built vessels for the Norris firm at Three Arms. These might have been Abraham Rideout of North West Arm and Robert White, who the previous year had supervised construction of the 222-ton, three-masted schooner *Mabel Davis*. The *Armistice* was launched in the late summer of 1919 and was towed to St. John's to be rigged. On the way to Spain with a load of fish, the *Armistice* developed a leak which the pumps could not control, and she foundered in mid-Atlantic in late December 1922. She was close to the Spanish coast, so the crew made it safely to land. The *Mabel Davis* also fell victim to the North Atlantic when she was totally lost on May 10, 1919, in Latitude 43.3 N, Longitude 40 W.

In this area, shipbuilding following the earliest period was sporadic indeed. Either their ships were not registered at St. John's or fishermen pursued an inshore or near-shore fishery primarily in small boats or trapskiffs up to the 1950s. An illustration of the excellent fishing in this area is given in the St. John's newspaper *Free Press* of November 25, 1913:

> Patrick Tobin of Gray Islands holds the record as an individual fisherman in Newfoundland for having made the biggest bill in the shortest season. A mercantile firm paid him $1,050 for his season's work—July 7 to September 15—he landed 160 quintals of cod, fishing 'cross-handed.' The fish was split and cured by Tobin's wife and self, who also made the oil ready for market. This is the largest individual bill to be made by any fisherman in Newfoundland.

While this incident indicates a prosperous fishery, it also demonstrates the necessity of cooperative efforts between husband and wife in the pursuit of the fishery.

During the 1960s there was a resurgence of shipbuilding, and about forty ships were constructed during this decade. About half that number was produced in the 1970s and half again in the 1980s.The resurgence of the 1960s and 1970s was particularly evident in the work of the International Grenfell Association at St. Anthony. Between 1968 and 1975 they constructed fifteen small one-masted wooden fishing ships between 18 and 29 tons. The managing owner of their first ship, the 24-ton *Connie James*, was

Matthew Francis Rose of St. Carols, White Bay; he was classified as a fisherman. It is not known if he was the master builder of the remaining ships. Their smallest ship, built in 1973, was the 18-ton *Fisher-m'Jig*, and their largest ship was the 29-ton *New Moon* crafted in 1974. Nothing is known of the *S.S. Wilfred Grenfell* which was built at St. Anthony in 1943; it could not be found in the ship registers, but it is possible that it was also constructed by the International Grenfell Association.

Christopher R. Decker of Roddickton constructed at least four ships in 1972 and 1973. These were also one-masted wooden fishing ships between 27 and 29 tons. They were named *Salmon Point*, *Cape Harrison II*, *Northern Peninsula*, and *Cape Fare*. It is possible that Christopher Decker was the master builder of the one-masted, 29-ton *Mae Heather*, which was constructed by Roddickton Industries in 1975 at Roddickton; this vessel was equipped with a diesel engine.

Port au Choix Shipbuilding & Supply Ltd. constructed nine of the same type of ship from 1973 to 1976. Most of these at the beginning were in the 22 to 25 ton range, but their last three vessels were the 50-ton *Rich Point*, the 32-ton *Julie La Blanche*, and the 32-ton *Skagway*. Lambert Kennedy of Port au Choix fashioned three ships at Port au Choix from 1979 to 1982. It is possible that Kennedy was the master builder for Port au Choix Shipbuilding & Supply Ltd., which had produced the nine ships in the early 1970s. Kennedy's later ships were the 14-ton *Bella Star*, the 46-ton *L. J. Kennedy*, and the 49-ton *T. J. Gould*.

Reid Products Ltd. of Bide Arm constructed three ships in 1972, all in the 27-ton range, but these were two-masted wooden fishing ships. They were named *Donald Bennett*, *Twila Jane*, and *Rhonda M. Gaye*. The Fisheries Loan Board of Newfoundland was financing this operation. It is not known if there was a connection between this operation and Sea Forest Products Ltd. of Bide Arm which produced five small wooden fishing ships in 1980 and 1981. Their first ship, the 11-ton *Donna Kay*, carried a Mortgage A for $107,700. Their next three ships were in the 10 to 12 ton range, but their last ship, the *Clarence & Noble* of 1981, was less than 7 tons.

A correspondent for Transcontinental Media, writing in the *Official 2009 Tourist Guide of the Viking Trail & Labrador Coastal Drive*, describes the boat styles and building methods for this region:

> Consequently, the steam-timbered speedboats of Port au Choix are built with raking stems while those of the Straits aren't—better for hauling cod traps. Further north, the boats were built with grown timbers for added strength. Boat styles weren't standardized, but remained as varied as the accents of the people who built them.

The correspondent then comments on Wes Pilgrim of Main Brook, a builder of trapskiffs:

> These hulking open boats were built with a transom beam stern—which allowed room underneath the boat for the propeller of an inboard engine. Trapskiffs were also made with moored timbers—Mr. Pilgrim spent many hours digging up roots to cut trees down—getting the angle of the root meeting the tree for his timbers.

Both of Wes's sons, Reuben and Bob of Main Brook, are boatbuilders in the tradition of their father. Undoubtedly, these are the descendants of Herman Pilgrim of Main Brook who, in 1981, built the 32-ton wooden fishing vessel *The Struggle.*

Though the production of ships in this area was small in comparison with other regions of Newfoundland, it was not inconsequential. Greater White Bay and the Northern Peninsula was an area that seems to have received very little publicity in newspapers of the day or in contemporary literature. It was, therefore, a largely unknown area during the period under study here. In the early twentieth century, the northern section of the west coast was dubbed Newfoundland's "Forgotten Coast" by Rev. Canon J. T. Richards, the Anglican priest at Flower's Cove, in an attempt to highlight the needs of people through a newspaper campaign. Residents of the area still complain as late as 2012 about being neglected by the provincial government.

I have heard it said by businessmen who travelled through this area in the 1970s and 1980s that the fishery was especially prosperous and that it was not uncommon for two- or three-storey houses to be graced with an elevator. The Cod Moratorium of 1992 constituted a severe blow to the fishermen of the area and to the economy in general.

The great timber stands of the region, particularly around Canada Bay, attracted the attention of St. John's merchant J. J. Grieve as early as 1831 when he sent his shipbuilder John Gover to the region to construct the 117-ton brigantine *Clydesdale*. Though the designator given in the record is White Bay, it probably conformed to what was known as Greater White Bay, and the ship may well have been built in Canada Bay. The area must have proved to be somewhat remote for the St. John's merchants, or it is possible that vessels were built that are not traceable during this early period. It was not until the early 1900s that other large vessels were found to have been crafted in the region. If a history of sawmills in Newfoundland is ever written, this region will figure prominently, particularly after 1914 when Capt. William Snow transported the Harry Crowe mill from Point Leamington to Canada Bay, taking over from Dr. Wilfred Grenfell's sawmill, and again in 1936 when the large Saunders & Howell sawmill was moved from Norris Arm to Roddickton. Many other sawmills operated in this area until quite recent years, and the Bowater Company of Corner Brook took large supplies of timber from these mills. Dr. Grenfell records that in 1908 William Hopkins constructed a ship "at our mill," indicating that the vessel was crafted with mill-sawn lumber. This information provides another piece of the puzzle as to when shipbuilders ceased using pit-sawn lumber and started using the mill-sawn product.

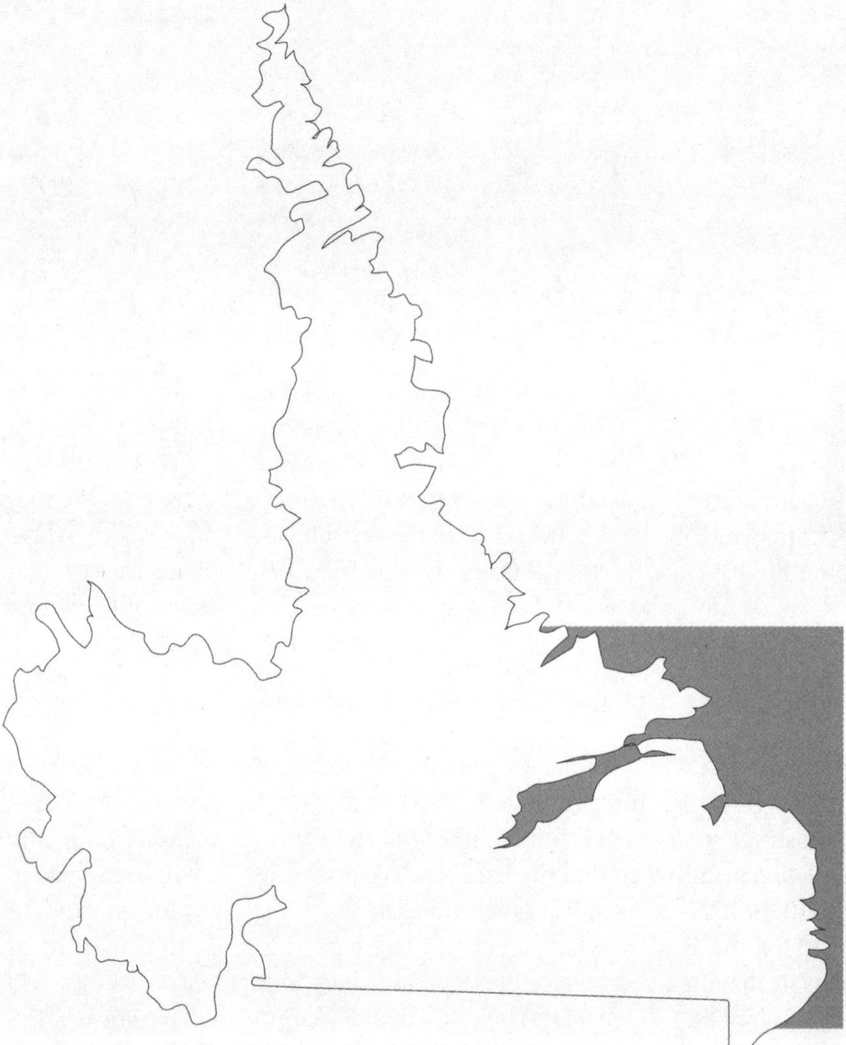

CHAPTER THREE

LABRADOR

IN THE PORTUGUESE language, Labrador (*lavrador*) means landowner, and it is believed this name was applied to the Labrador coast during the early exploration voyages. A report on the voyages of John and Sebastian Cabot written in 1516 uses the term. A Weimar map of 1530 applies the name to the area and asserts it was "discovered by the English…of Bristol…And as the one who first gave notice of it was a Labrador of the Azores, they gave it the name" (*Dictionary of Canadian Biography I*). The title of *lavrador* may well have been applied to Joao Fernandez, who is believed to have charted the Labrador and Newfoundland coasts with John Cabot in 1498.

Sebastian Cabot explored the northern sections of Newfoundland in 1508 for England, and this would likely have included Labrador. William G. Gosling, in his 1911 book *Labrador: Its Discovery, Exploration and Development*, affirmed that the Labrador coast was well known to fishermen by 1510. In 1527-28 John Rut sailed along the Labrador coast for England. In the 1540s the Basque whalers arrived to begin the trade in the Strait of Belle Isle, having already developed a cod fishery along the south coast and in the Gulf of St. Lawrence. It is believed that as many as 2500 Basque whalers came annually to the region during this period. The sixteenth century *chalupa* (boat), which was found submerged in the harbour at Red Bay and is now on display in the local museum, may well have been built there. In 1534-36 Jacques Cartier explored the Labrador and Newfoundland coasts for France, and in 1543 Jean Alfonses explored the Labrador coast for France. Capt. George Weymouth is believed to have explored what later came to be known as Hamilton Inlet as early as 1602, and John Knight apparently did the same in 1606.

Aboriginal peoples lived in the Hamilton Inlet area in the sixteenth century, and it has been affirmed the Inuit first settled near Rigolet on Eskimo Island about 1600. They would have been building boats of various kinds and sizes for many years before Europeans arrived.

The first actual reference to shipbuilding in Labrador could be referred to as "ship finishing," and this applies to the Spanish Basques in 1574. The 180-ton galleon *Trinidad* was constructed in Spain that year by master carpenter Cristobal de Artadi and was taken to Labrador for the whale fishery "specifying that the upper deck is to be finished in Terra Nova." Other details specify "that the said captain, with the artificers of the said galleon shall have the bridge deck of the said ship and its upper part satisfactorily built in Tierranova and the said Bartolome (de Garre) is to give him the nails and oakum that are needed." (Barkham 81-82). Carpenters and caulkers were members of the forty-four man crew. Labrador place names mentioned in these early documents are Buytres (Butes, Buitres), Grand Bay, Port Breton, and Port of the Vanguard. The mention of a second master carpenter, in the person of Domingo de Uriarte, may signify that another ship had been constructed or finished in Labrador, testifying to the builders' confidence in the satisfactory quality of local woods (Barkham 77, 87).

We are indebted to Capt. George Cartwright for some of the earliest references to boatbuilding and shipbuilding in Labrador. In his *Journal* of 1770 he refers to sawyers and the use of the pit saw and refers to building methods, but these are unfortunately to the building of houses, stores, and stages rather than boats and ships; however, in 1771 he refers to having "the skiff caulked and payed" (i.e., covered with pitch) and the fact that they "picked oakum"; he refers to the shallop leaving for Fogo as soon as his correspondence is completed. He writes of finding birch and larch and black spruce trees, and white spruce trees which were tall, clear, and straight, "from six, to nine feet in circumference" and refers to his schooner *Enterprise.* In 1772 he mentions the "flat" which they used for fishing the rivers (undoubtedly built in the country). Then in 1775 he makes reference to his boatbuilder and cooper (without mentioning their names), whom he was taking to Sandwich Bay, and to his sealing-skiff (which undoubtedly was built in Labrador) and refers to his old ship the *Countess of Effingham* which had been captured by an American privateer but re-taken on her way to Boston and returned to North Harbour. Later he reports that the *Countess* was unfortunately "dashed to pieces in Trinity Bay, in the spring of 1781"; that same year he had a new schooner built at Paradise, Labrador, which was badly damaged on the way to Dartmouth and was later captured by the enemy. And while in a despondent mood about his growing debts in 1783, he wrote a poem worth quoting in part because of its reference to local woods and shipbuilding:

> We'll shift the Scene, and to the Woods repair,
> And see what various Works are doing there.
> In yonder Birchen grove, there lives a Crew,
> Employ'd in mending Casks, and making new.
> This wood of Spruce, which rises to the sky,
> The fish'ry's future Shipping will supply.
> Some fell the Trees, and some saw out the Stock,
> Whilst others form the Vessel in the Dock.
> In these Employments, Winter's passed away;
> No change is found, till near the approach of May.

References to shipbuilding in Labrador after Cartwright are non-existent until the early 1800s. The first of these references is to 1806 when the 30-ton *Curlew* was built "at the Labrador." The ship registers describe it in 1818 as "square, no figure head." It was "raised on" and enlarged to 32 tons at St. John's in 1818. It was a two-masted vessel, but the name of the builder is not given. The name William Morley of Carbonear has been suggested, but this cannot be confirmed. It is known that Morley built the 87-ton *George* at St. Lewis, Labrador, in 1826. This vessel was constructed for Carbonear merchants Elson, Harrison, Slade Jr., Seager & Major.

In 1809 at Henley "on the Coast of Labrador" the 112-ton, square-sterned brigantine *Indiana* was constructed. It bore a woman's figurehead. One of Garland's shipbuilders at Trinity could have been the builder; another name suggested is Clement Noel of Harbour Grace, but these suggestions cannot be confirmed. Noel built two ships: the 76-ton *Regulator* in 1813 at Crocker's Cove, Conception Bay, and the 75-ton *Glengarry* at Harbour Grace in 1841. He served as master of both ships, so he may well have spent time at the

Labrador. The builder would have had to be a person of considerable experience to construct such a large, full-rigged ship.

The *Esquimaux* was built as an open boat at Esquimaux Bay in 1811 and decked and enlarged to 38 tons at St. John's in 1819. The owner was Robert Alsop, local merchant, but the name of the rebuilder is unknown.

John Slade of Poole and Twillingate may have had his fishing business established at Battle Harbour, Labrador, as early as the 1770s. When Richard and Netlam Tory were forced out of White Bay by the French in 1786, curiously assisted by the Royal Navy, they also moved their firm to Labrador. Samuel Prowse & Co. established a fishing business at Antle's Cove, Cape Charles, about 1812 along with his two sons (some say it was as early as 1794). It is not known how long this firm lasted, but some writers suggest it was absorbed by John Slade or possibly by the Torys. Perhaps some of the vessels named above were constructed by these firms.

The 135-ton brig *Hope* was built at the Labrador sometime before 1838, but the precise date cannot be determined. It was advertised for sale in the *Public Ledger* of December 25, 1838. It was "built of Juniper and other choice materials...[and was] sheathed with English Elm." Mr. White of Waterford, Ireland, was the builder. The vessel had a stowing capacity of 3400 quintals of fish. Robert Brine & Co. was the seller.

There is then a silence for almost forty years with no news of shipbuilding in Labrador. In 1877 William Goudie builds the 17-ton *Charlotte* at Grosswater Bay, but the ship is not registered until 1880. The owner is James Strong, trader/dealer at Little Bay Islands, and Goudie is the ship's master. Goudie was probably in the employ of Strong while living or over-wintering at the Labrador. A similar pattern continues with Joseph Harris who crafts the 17-ton *Verbena* at Goose Bay in 1883, and the owner was John McDougall, merchant of St. John's. Azariah Boone of Port de Grave overwintered at Labrador for at least one year and constructed the 21-ton nostalgically-named *I Am Away* in 1882 though it was not registered until 1884. It was unfortunately lost at Black Island, Labrador, in 1885.

Samuel Elson of Sandy Hill Bay, Labrador, must have been a resident of Labrador since he constructed three ships there between 1886 and 1890. His first ship, the 20-ton *Fanny*, was built for John Winsor, merchant of Carbonear. And the other two ships: the 15-ton *Silvanus* and the 31-ton *Ira D. Sankey* were built for James Winsor, planter of Carbonear. The first ship was registered seven years after it was built, the second eight years after, and the third six years after. Elson may have gone to the Labrador both as a shipbuilder and to supervise the Winsor operation on the Labrador coast.

To complete our look at shipbuilding at Labrador during the closing years of the nineteenth century, we note that William and James Learning were there building a ship each in 1889 and 1890 for Robert S. Munn, merchant at Harbour Grace. James constructed the 23-ton *Anna* in 1889 at Grady Harbour, and William built the 33-ton *Caber Faigh* in 1890 at Sandwich Bay. Each vessel was registered within one year of being constructed. William and James may have been local men since the Learning name has been associated with Cartwright, Labrador, since about 1852.

There are two names worthy of mention in the early 1900s. Robert White, probably from Seal Cove, Bonavista Bay, was at Mary's Harbour, Labrador, in 1902 to build the 38-ton *Minnie* for James Norris Jr., merchant at Three Arms. The best way to explain this is that Norris must have been expanding his business to include Labrador and convinced White to spend the winter there. It is curious to conjecture otherwise since Green Bay had such great timber resources readily available. White continued as a shipbuilder for Norris and in 1918 constructed the 222-ton, three-masted *Mabel Davis* at Bide Arm, Canada Bay.

The other man is Edwin C. Grant who was from Trinity but built the 28-ton *Sophie Grant* at Blanc–Sablon, Labrador, in 1911. Even more confounding is that he was a merchant builder. Was he, like James Norris, trying to set up a business in Labrador? And why did he choose Quebec Labrador rather than Newfoundland Labrador? The ship was not registered until 1914, but the ship registers tell us nothing of its fate. Perhaps Grant returned to Trinity to carry on his business. According to the *McAlpine Directory* for 1894-97, both Robert Grant and D. Grant were carpenters at Trinity. Edwin would have been a member of this family but cannot be traced further.

From 1914 to 1959 only one ship appears to have been constructed in Labrador, and that was the 17-ton *Miss Gray*. The builder was Egbert Dawson Sweetapple of St. John's, and the one-masted, sloop-rigged vessel was launched at Port Hope Simpson. Sweetapple was listed as the owner/carpenter. Residents must have been pursuing an inshore fishery in small boats which did not require to be registered. Ships built between the 1960s and the 1980s appear in the Appendix to this chapter. Most of these were small wooden fishing ships between 8 and 20 tons. The only ships of substantial size were Paul Kippenhuck's 45-ton *Blanche Marie* constructed at Square Islands in 1967 and Benjamin James Rowe's 55-ton *Bella Rosetta* crafted at Port Hope Simpson in 1970.

Reuben Carpenter of Port Union (and before that a master carpenter with the Clarenville Splinter Fleet) went to Postville, Labrador, and crafted four ships in 1976 and 1977 in a program sponsored by the Minister of Rural Development. Reuben's sons Joe and Bruce each spent a year with their father at the shipyard. The *Jenna Marie II* and the *Viola Dee* were built in 1976, and both were about 18 tons. The company in the first year was called Postville Shipyards 1976. In 1977 the name was slightly changed to Postville Boatyard 1977 (which sounds like a government initiative), and it produced two more ships: the 18-ton *Miss Postville* and the 12-ton *Miss Makkovik*. Both these vessels belonged to Her Majesty the Queen and in 1978 were sold to "the Postville Shipyard a body corporate having its principal place of business at Postville, Labrador." All the ships were eventually sold to local fishermen. To demonstrate the politics involved in this project, two of these ships had been launched and hauled out on the ice to wait for the ice to melt, but a surprise visit from a politician required that the ships be hauled back to the stocks for a photo-op and a re-launch.

Mention is made in the Appendix to Eldred Poole who built the 13-ton *St. Lewis Sound* in 1980. He is undoubtedly related to Paul Poole of St. Lewis who had a distinguished career as a boatbuilder. Paul built his first boat when he was thirteen years old in 1940. The boat was thirteen feet long. During his building career, he constructed fifty-five boats and five model boats. The largest boat was twenty-nine feet long. These were mostly motor boats, and he generally charged $200 to build a boat. It required about one month to complete the building, and these were always constructed in May or June of each year. His last boat was built in 2008 when he was eighty-one years old. The Winterton Boatbuilding Museum has listed more than 400 of such men throughout the Province.

For more than 200 years the fishery along the Labrador coast was crucial to the economy of the colony and province, and to the livelihood of hundreds of fishing families. Most of the fishing ships and collector ships were built in island coastal communities, but the great timber stands of parts of the Labrador attracted shipbuilders from the island, and merchant firms sometime sent shipbuilders there for a winter project. Additionally, many of Newfoundland's most famous ships and most celebrated captains sailed these beautiful but often treacherous coasts, and many were the shipwrecks in storms breaking upon them without warning. Most of the vessels constructed by residents of Labrador appear to have been fishing boats. Only distance from the suppliers of necessary complementary timber and the inconvenience involved prevented the Labrador from being the scene of more construction of large ships.

CHAPTER FOUR

WEST COAST
SOUTHERN SECTION

IN THIS CHAPTER WE will look at the area from Bonne Bay to Codroy and Searston, the southern section of Newfoundland's west coast. This region includes Bonne Bay, the Bay of Islands and Humber Arm, the Port au Port Peninsula with Port au Port Bay and St. George's Bay and the Grand Codroy area.

The Basques were probably the first to begin a migratory fishery in this area. They had commenced cod fishing along the south coast and southwest coast by the 1520s and whaling in the Strait of Belle Isle by the 1540s, fishing at least in the beginning for Spain. Jacques Cartier is believed to have visited this area in 1534, but the French appear not to have begun a large-scale seasonal fishery until the late 1700s. By the Treaty of Versailles (1783), the French fishing rights were extended beyond Point Riche as far south as Cape Ray, and the area from Cape Bonavista to Cape St. John reverted to the English.

Archaeological digs have confirmed the presence of prehistoric groups on the Port au Port Peninsula, particularly the Dorset Palaeo Eskimos and probably also the ancestors of the Beothuk. Aboriginal groups from Nova Scotia, the Mi'kmaq, arrived in the St. George's Bay area by 1538 according to J. D. Rogers, though R. T. Pastore dates this migration about the mid-1700s. Yet another group of Mi'kmaq came to the area about 1815. By the late 1800s their descendants had moved onto the Port au Port Peninsula.

Bonne Bay appears on French maps in 1698 and 1741, but if the French came to the area that early they would have been using it simply as a base for fishing in the waters of the Gulf. There is no record of English settlement until six families arrived in Bonne Bay from southwest England in 1807. By the enumeration of 1857 there were only ninety people living in Bonne Bay.

The French may have been fishing in the Bay of Islands area in the early part of the 1700s, and the English fishers appear to have arrived in the area by the 1760s. Settlement in the Humber Arm dates from the 1780s when several residents from England and the south coast of Newfoundland arrived. In the enumeration of 1857, only 143 residents were counted. But a large and prosperous herring fishery began in the 1850s with high demand for the product emanating from Nova Scotia and the United States. By the 1860s about ten schooners and more than 200 small boats were engaged in this fishery. And by the mid-1860s, lumbering had become a major concern, bringing interested parties from Nova Scotia and New Brunswick to settle in the region.

By the late 1700s the French were safely ensconced on the Port au Port Peninsula and were using it as a base from which to fish the rich grounds of the Gulf of St. Lawrence. The major stations for the French fishery were Isle Rouge (Red Island) and Long Point. By the late eighteenth century, several deserters from French ships had settled on the Peninsula, and these were joined by a number of Acadian families from Nova Scotia during the period 1825 to 1845. By the 1870s many others arrived from Nova Scotia to settle in the area. As early as 1842, J. B. Jukes, the geological surveyor, had characterized Flat Bay, St. George's, as "by far the most inviting part of Newfoundland," and in 1951, W. C. Wonders called it "the only natural harbour on the southwest coast of Newfoundland."

This became a unique region of Newfoundland because of its proximity to the British maritime colonies and because of burgeoning markets in the United States. Ships built in the area were often transferred to Halifax or Charlottetown, PEI, and ships which had previously been registered in Halifax were sometimes transferred to Newfoundland. The area also attracted shipbuilders from Nova Scotia who came over for periods of time to construct ships here.

The first reference to a ship built in this region occurs in D. W. Prowse's *History of Newfoundland*. Prowse lists thirty ships built in 1804, and one of these was constructed somewhere in the Bay of Islands: the 196-ton, fully-rigged ship *Marianne*. We know neither the specific location nor the name of the master builder.

When Clement Pennell registered his 38-ton *Success* in 1822, it was noted that the vessel had previously been registered at St. John's in 1811; it had been built originally in St. George's Bay, and Pennell appears to have been the rebuilder in 1822. Joseph Pennell, probably a brother of Clement, built the 47-ton *Royal Sovereign* in 1824, also at St. George's Bay.

John Henlen crafted the 35-ton *Betsey* in 1814, the 37-ton *Lucy Ann* in 1825, and the 18-ton *Snowbird* in 1844; all three vessels were constructed in St. George's Bay. Moses Henlen constructed the 20-ton *Sisters* in 1840; Edward Henlen built the 26-ton *Providence* in 1841, and John was the owner of forty-eight of the sixty-four shares. Philip Henlen built the 21-ton *Jane* in 1846 for a planter at St. George's Bay. William Henlen was the builder of the 20-ton *Mary Jane* in 1851, and his partner in the venture was James Henlen. All the Henlens were planters in St. George's Bay, and they were very likely father and five sons.

The builder of the 56-ton *Hagdown* is unknown, but it is known that the vessel was fashioned at "Cod Roy River" in 1815, and she was registered at St. John's that same year. James Hore built the 32-ton *Speedy* in 1817 at St. George's Bay but did not register it until 1822. Ralph Brake constructed the 43-ton *Hope* somewhere in the Bay of Islands in 1818, but the vessel was not registered until 1822.

The Messervys of St. George's Bay were also planters and shipbuilders. Philip Messervy built the 55-ton *Rose* in 1823 and the 24-ton *Ceres* in 1834. When the second vessel was registered in 1838, it was owned by John Benjamin Cox, a trader/dealer at Burgeo. This reveals yet another trend for this area; many vessels were built for merchants along the southwest coast, testimony to the fact that the area produced fine timber for ship construction. John Messervy, probably a brother of Philip, constructed the 29-ton *Ranger* in 1824 for Philip and in 1839 built the 32-ton *Sarah Ann* for his own use as a planter.

Francois Benoit Jr. was the builder of the 26-ton *Jane* in 1824 at St. George's Bay; the vessel was constructed for his father, Francois Benoit Sr., planter. And Charles A. Bennoit (different spelling) of Port au Port built the 32-ton *Albert F.* in 1889 at Stephenville. Were they descendants of the deserters from French ships in the late eighteenth century? The persistence of French names in the area may be testimony to this fact (e.g., Victoire Marsh who crafted the 45-ton *Royal William* in 1835 in St. George's Bay and Magloire Blanchard, one of the owners of the 27-ton *Elizabeth* at Codroy in 1874).

William Weller built the 37-ton *Nancy* somewhere in the Bay of Islands in 1824. Samuel Swyer Sr. constructed the 41-ton *Charlotte* in St. George's Bay in 1825. And William Gale built two ships: the 38-ton *Three Brothers* in 1829 at Codroy and the 20-ton *Maria* in 1838 at Codroy River. In 1833 he sold the first vessel to John Parsons, a planter at St. George's Bay. John must have had good success with the vessel since in 1844 he built a 57-ton ship with the same name. His brother and partner, James Parsons, constructed the 38-ton *Victory* in 1841 at St. George's Bay.

James Hulan constructed the 35-ton *Magdalene* in 1832 somewhere in St. George's Bay, and the vessel was registered the next year by the planter/owner Philip Hulan, undoubtedly a brother of James. These were very probably the grandsons of the famous Mrs. Anne Hulan who appears to have lived from about 1740 to 1840 and remembered Capt. James Cook who had done survey work for England around the coast of Newfoundland from 1763 to 1767; according to William Epps Cormack's report in 1822, Mrs. Hulan had a magnificent farm at the second Barachois River and had lived in the St. George's Bay area for upwards of sixty years. In 1835 Mrs. Hulan had a second distinguished visitor in the person of Archdeacon Edward Wix, a Church of England missionary from Great Britain who recorded the story of her capture in 1814 by an American privateer who confiscated her ship with a load of cured salmon and brought the ship to New York. Only through the generosity of new-found friends was Mrs. Hulan able to provision her ship for the return to Newfoundland where she concluded her business at St. John's and returned home.

John Renouf was the builder of the 38-ton *Venus* in 1835 at St. George's Bay. John Morris, also of St. George's Bay, built the 13-ton *Rambler* in 1836 for a planter at Port aux Basques, and Benjamin Kippen constructed the 16-ton *Elizabeth* at St. George's Bay in 1837 for his own use as a planter.

William Carter of Codroy River built the 12-ton *Hebe* in 1838 for Samuel Swyer, a planter at St. George's Bay, who was himself a shipbuilder in 1825. Carter also constructed the 17-ton *Snowbird* in 1841 at Codroy River for his own use as a planter. John Hall, also of Codroy River, built the 27-ton *Nancy* in 1839 and his partner was another planter.

Only three vessels were built in this area in the 1840s. Philip Dennis of St. George's Bay constructed the 41-ton *Caroline* in 1841. Henry and Edward Nicholle jointly constructed the 20-ton *John* in 1847 at St. George's Bay for their work as planters; the vessel was lost at sea in 1850. And Jonathan Davy of Codroy River crafted the 27-ton *Britannia* in 1848 for a planter in the same place.

Only two vessels were built in the area during the 1850s, and both of these were constructed by the same builder. William Curtis built the 23-ton *Morning Star* in 1853 at Codroy River, and it was sold the same year to Robert Pack, merchant at Carbonear. Curtis had probably taken his new vessel to St. John's for registration and received such a good offer from Pack or his agent that he sold it immediately; many stories are told about such opportune moments in the life of a shipbuilder. Curtis returned home and the very next year at Little Codroy River built the 24-ton *Ringdove*, which he used in his own work as a planter.

From this point onwards, we will focus on significant and prominent shipbuilders only. All others are included in the Appendix to Chapter Three.

From 1873 to 1886 Joseph J. Curling lived in the Bay of Islands area, having sailed his yacht *Skylark* from England to Newfoundland as a gift to Bishop Edward Feild after the ship *Lark*, owned by the church, had been lost. Curling at that time held a commission with the Royal Engineers after graduation from the Royal Military College. He was so moved by his Newfoundland visit he offered himself as a candidate for the priesthood and was appointed to the Bay of Islands, ordained in 1874, and later appointed as Rural Dean for the Strait of Belle Isle. Because of his engineering training, he was able to design and build many churches and schools along the west coast, but he also designed and built several ships. Though he left Newfoundland in 1886, he returned for two visits in 1887 and 1889. In the latter year, he sailed the 33-ton *Sapper* back to England, and it was transferred to the London registry that same year. The credit for building this vessel in 1885 is given to Thomas Dohman in the ship registers, but it was obviously designed by and co-built with Curling. Another vessel which he had owned while in Newfoundland was the 6-ton *Dove* constructed in 1881, and the ship registers say that George Pynn was the builder. This vessel also would have been designed by Curling. There undoubtedly were several other vessels designed if not built by Curling, but they cannot be found; some of these could have been crafted during the period when shipbuilders' names were omitted from the ship registers.

Albert Ball was a significant shipbuilder in the period 1880 to 1891. During this period he constructed four ships ranging in size from 23 to 58 tons. His partner and fellow planter in the 35-ton *Waterlily* in 1880 was William Ball. Their home was Birchy Head, Bonne Bay, where their first ship was built. The 58-ton *Caroline* was built at Norris Point in 1889 for a fisherman at that place. The 35-ton *Florence B.* and the 23-ton *Olive* were built for two merchants at Rose Blanche. Undoubtedly, Albert Ball had constructed several other vessels, most of them registered in the names of their owners without attribution to the builder or not registered at all.

James Murphy of Codroy was a contemporary of Albert Ball and constructed four ships between 1881 and 1893. Actually his first ship was a rebuilt. In 1881 he rebuilt and enlarged at Codroy River the 67-ton *Ellen* which had originally been constructed at Salisbury, Massachusetts, in 1850. This was followed in 1884 by the 34-ton *Willie R.* at Codroy River, in 1888 by the 17-ton *Unique* at Grand River, and in 1893 by the 16-ton *Dauntless* also at Grand River. The first vessel was rebuilt for a St. John's trader/dealer and the other three were built for merchants at Rose Blanche and elsewhere.

Though John Wight is given credit for building only four ships, two of these were of sufficient size to deserve an honorable mention. The *Lizzie* of 1881 was 82 tons, and the *Rosemary* of 1885 was 94 tons. In 1883 he had constructed the 23-ton *Jeremina* for which he collected a bounty of $69. Also in 1885 Wight crafted the 40-ton *Sweet Briar*. The *Rosemary* and the *Sweet Briar* were constructed at Birchy Head, Bonne Bay, for St. John's merchant John Steer. Wight was a planter in Bonne Bay and used the *Lizzie* himself, probably fishing on the Labrador.

John McLeod lived in Humber Sound and constructed four vessels and rebuilt one of these between 1882 and 1887. In 1882 he was classified as a mariner when he constructed the 47-ton *James Davis* for the Davis family of Humber Sound. This vessel was transferred to the Halifax registry in 1887. In 1882 he also built the 102-ton *Grace Carter* for Thomas Carter, merchant in the Bay of Islands. This ship was wrecked and then rebuilt and refurbished by McLeod and restored to the ship registry in 1887. She was lost somewhere in the North Atlantic in 1898. In 1883 McLeod constructed the 73-ton *Annie Allen* for the Allen family of fishermen at Bay of Islands. This vessel was lost at Low Point, Nova Scotia, in 1903, having lasted for twenty years. McLeod was sole owner of the 115-ton schooner *Narcissus*, which he built in 1884; this ship foundered at sea in the North Atlantic just two years later.

George B. Moffatt of Bonne Bay is given credit for building only one ship, but it was the 113-ton schooner *Annie G. Moore*, and the Customs' Returns state he was paid a bounty of $339; the ship was constructed somewhere in Bonne Bay in 1883. The vessel was built for two merchants and a mariner at Cape Breton Island. It burned up in Alaska in 1898. Curiously, the *Twillingate Sun* of November 2, 1883, lists Moffatt as a boat builder; was it the size of the vessel that caught the newspaper's attention? Boatbuilder and shipbuilder are virtually synonymous terms in newspapers of the day.

Thomas Dean of Norris Point, Bonne Bay, built six small to medium-sized ships in the period 1884 to 1910. His first two ships, the 24-ton *Jeremina* and the 20-ton *Lizzie*, were built for merchants in Bonne Bay. His third ship, built in 1893, was the 12-ton *Mary Ellen* and was owned by Ellen Dean, probably Thomas's wife, and the vessel was lost in 1896 "north-west of Fish Island Straits at Bellisle," yet another tragic story of danger on the Labrador coast. Thomas's last three vessels were built for fishermen in Bonne Bay; the 40-ton *May Flower* in 1903, the 21-ton *Nellie* in 1906 and the 36-ton *Hayward S.* in 1910.

Winslow C. McKay was attracted away from Nova Scotia in 1884 by Thomas Carter of Humber Sound in order to begin construction of the 92-ton *Maud Carter* which was launched in 1885. Carter was a merchant in the Bay of Islands. This vessel was transferred to the Halifax registry in 1887, so Carter was probably expanding his own base of operation. Carter probably kept McKay around to construct the 178-ton brigantine *Ellie Carter* in 1886, which was sold the next year to James Furlong, merchant at St. John's, and transferred to the Halifax registry in 1888. McKay then built the 62-ton *Mary Ita* in 1887, which was almost immediately sold to Furlong and in 1897 sold to foreigners. McKay then moved on to Gambo in Bonavista Bay and worked for John J. Murphy, building at least two vessels for Murphy: the 81-ton *St. Bernard* and the 82-ton *St. Francis*, both in 1888. The first vessel was lost off Cape Bonavista in 1919, having lasted for thirty-one years and the second vessel was lost in 1902 somewhere on the Newfoundland coast, having lasted for fourteen years. Murphy had advertised these ships as "well-built, being copper-fastened and full-timbered." By 1890 Winslow McKay had an established shipyard operating in Shelburne, NS, and built several more large schooners, especially for merchant firms on Newfoundland's south coast. His shipyard was operating until at least 1918.

Herbert John D. Carter of Humber Sound was listed as a shipbuilder when he registered the 36-ton *Miskoud* in 1890; his partner in the venture was Fred T. Carter, a fisherman. But Herbert was not the builder of this vessel; Thomas Carter is given the credit for being the master builder. Undoubtedly Herbert and Fred were his fellow shipwrights on the project. It seems likely that Thomas Carter had been inspired by the building prowess of his friend Winslow McKay. But Herbert Carter in 1905, somewhere in the Bay of Islands, built the 33-ton *Erita & Ena*, and in 1911 he rebuilt the 111-ton *Henry M. Stanley*, which had originally been built at Essex, Massachusetts, in 1890. It is of interest that both these ships were owned by women. Carrie Carter, widow of Summerside, owned the *Erita & Ena* when it was registered on July 12, 1907, but no further transactions on this vessel could be found. Grace Petipas of Summerside bought the *Henry M. Stanley* in 1911. It was a Labrador-going ship, and she sold it on July 4, 1913, to merchants at Halifax.

It cannot be determined if Patrick and John Condon of Humber Sound were related to Daniel Condon of St. John's who was the son-in-law of the famous shipbuilder Michael Kearney. Daniel Condon was a prominent shipbuilder in St. John's from at least 1862 to 1878 and a prominent businessman and shipowner following that later date. Patrick Condon of Humber Sound built the 53-ton *Daisy Maud* in 1887, and his partners John and William Condon are both classified in the record as shipbuilders. In 1888 Patrick constructed the 69-ton *Beacon Light* for Moses Monroe, merchant at St. John's. This vessel was registered de novo in 1905 when it was sold to Edward Bishop, merchant at Wesleyville. The vessel was lost at sea on the Labrador coast in 1911, thus lasting for twenty-three years. In 1890 John Condon built the 36-ton *Crustacean* at Port au Port for James Baird, merchant at St. John's. When John built the 33-ton *Alice Condon* in Humber Sound in 1895 his partners were James and William Condon. In 1903, somewhere in the Bay of Islands, John constructed the 12-ton *Ubique* for a merchant in the bay. John P. Parker, in his book *Cape Breton Ships and Men*, states that John Condon of Newfoundland was engaged to be the master shipwright of the 245-ton, three-masted schooner *County of Richmond* at Johnstown Cape Breton. Parker comments, "She was a very full vessel with an elliptical stern and fitted with a scroll at the head." This vessel was bought by W. H. Moulton of St. John's but turned out to be, in Parker's words, "an indifferent sailer." The date of construction was 1919.

The Barters of Codroy are worthy of mention though it is difficult to determine how many there were due to the similarity of first names. John Barter of Codroy crafted the 20-ton *Beatrice* in 1895, and his partner was Frank Barter, mariner. Edmund Barter of Codroy was a planter when in 1899 he constructed the 13-ton *Braganza* for a fellow planter at Grand River. When in 1908 Edmund built the 41-ton *M. Francis* at Codroy, his partners were fellow mariners John, Frank, and Eugene Barter. Edmund does not appear in the records again until 1935 when he builds the 33-ton *Margaret Flynn* and the 27-ton *Leila Gillis* at Grand River, so it remains possible that this is Edmund Barter Jr. Meanwhile, in 1911 Edward Barter of Codroy built the 11-ton *Carrie Hanham* for a fisherman at Rose Blanche. And in 1919 Edwin Barter of Codroy built the 120-ton schooner *Eliza Podway* for Edwin J. Gillis, merchant at Codroy; this vessel was involved in a collision at sea and sank in 1929. This was very probably the E. Barter of Codroy who rebuilt the 26-ton *Dorothy Mac*, which had been fashioned in 1914 by Elijah Boyde at Farmer's Arm, Notre Dame Bay. Since the handwriting in the ship registers is sometimes difficult to decipher, it is possible that Edmund, Edward, and Edwin are the same person.

William S. Wheller of Bonne Bay constructed five ships between 1901 and 1910. He began his shipbuilding career in a very ambitious manner by building two substantial-sized ships the same year, 1901: the 63-ton *Eudora Belle* for a merchant and the 78-ton *Ella Frances* for a mariner. In 1903 he also built two ships—the 37-ton *Conqueror* and the 25-ton *Assyria*, both for fishermen in Bonne Bay. He completed his building career when he constructed the 33-ton *Eva Muriel* for four fishermen brothers in Bonne Bay.

David F. Barry of the Bay of Islands built the 22-ton *Manilla* at Summerside in 1903; at that time he was classified as a fisherman. It was thirteen years before he built his second ship—the 41-ton *Outlaw* in 1916 for the Bay of Islands Fishing Company. In 1922 he crafted the 58-ton *Philomena*, and the owner was Anne A. Barry of Curling. The ship was classified as a steamer and was launched on June 12, 1922, and had a compound condensing engine installed with a Scotch boiler made by the Portland Engine Co. Limited. The *Evening Telegram* carried a column from a local correspondent who noted the new ship was "the mental product of our genial friend and fellow townsman David F. Barry, and her workmanship is also his." All the timbers used were locally harvested, and the ship's carpenters and caulkers were all from the Bay of Islands. The vessel had been constructed for Capt. James Barry of Curling, so perhaps Anne A. Barry was his wife. The ship's name was at some point changed to *Carmela Barry*. It was totally lost at Caribou Brook, Cape St. George, on August 26, 1927.

The 510-ton, three-masted vessel *Arnish* was built at Summerside, Bay of Islands, in 1917. Arnold Cluett of Belleoram was brought in to be the master builder. The master caulker was William Ruth of Summerside, "whose caulking is famed on this coast." One record says incorrectly that the large ship was built at St. George's by Joseph Flett, merchant at St. George's; another says the builders were "Flett and Tulk"; yet another record states it was Tulk, Flett & Co.; possibly Tulk was Frank, Charles, or Wilfred Tulk of Harbour Buffett, all of whom were master mariners. Merchants often partnered with master mariners as a way of guaranteeing the success of their sea ventures. Yet another record says incorrectly that the vessel was built for J. Herbert Carter of Humber Sound; presumably this is Herbert John D. Carter to whom reference was made earlier. It is just possible that Herbert Carter was the supervisor of construction on contract for Flett and Tulk and that Arnold Cluett was the master builder under his general supervision. Great difficulty was experienced in the launching of the vessel, and it was not accomplished until at least the third try. The *Evening Telegram* of June 20, 1919, notes that the vessel "had stuck last fall on her launching [and] 'Herb' [J. H.] Carter got her off." Carter was assisted in this arduous task by James Davis of Summerside and Mr. Pilley of St. George's who jointly "finished off the vessel." This was most probably the only role that Carter played with the large vessel. To Carter's credit had been the salving of the U.S. tug *Potomac*, abandoned, adrift and ice-bound in the Gulf of St. Lawrence several years previous to this launch. The *Telegram* rhapsodized about the *Arnish*'s "beauty of lines, excellency of material and workmanship. She is considered by those well able to judge the very best in the country." The vessel was not registered at St. John's until September 11, 1919, and was tragically lost at sea 120 miles east by north from Fogo less than two months later, on November 2, 1919.

George Edward Parsons of Bonne Bay built three ships between 1936 and 1945. He began his building career with the 30-ton *Dorothy M. Parsons*, and he was at that time classified as a fisherman. The next year at Trout River he built the 17-ton *Myra G. Butt*. In 1945 he completed his building career with the construction of the 16-ton *Elizabeth A. Parsons*. He was then living at Woody Point, and that is where he built his last ship; his partners were all fishermen, presumably his brothers: Samuel F., Alfred Ormsley, Andrew Nelson, and James Herbert Parsons.

THE SHEARS FAMILY

The Shears family did most of their impressive shipbuilding at Rocky Harbour, but they may have had their origins in St. George's Bay. Stephen Shears, planter of St. George's Bay, crafted the 20-ton *Rose* in 1847, and Moses Shears, also of St. George's Bay, built the 25-ton *Providence* there in 1849. Not until 1934 do we find a reference to another Shears. This was John Shears, planter at Rocky Harbour, who that year constructed the 27-ton *Ethel Pearl Shears*. John may have been the father or older brother of Gordon Shears and Clyde Shears of Rocky Harbour who compiled an impressive record of shipbuilding between 1942 and 1981. During this period they constructed at least fifty vessels, mostly one- and two-masted wooden fishing ships. Included also were a passenger boat, two tugs, two yachts, and a pilot boat.

Gordon Shears' name sometimes appears in the records as George Gordon Shears and once or twice as George Shears. The building project appears to have gone through a number of name changes, and sometimes one builder gets the credit for a ship and sometimes the other. Often they are listed as joint builders. By 1969 their company was called Gordon and Clyde Shears Ltd. In 1981 they fashioned their last ship. Their enormous record of production may account for the fact that there were so few other builders in the region during this period; the Shears brothers were supplying most of the fishermens' needs.

Gordon Shears may have started his building career alone when, in 1942, he built the 18-ton *V. D. Gimblews* at Rocky Harbour. He owned this and his next vessel built in 1948, the 13-ton *Linda Shears*, jointly with Harold Clyde Shears, and they were referred to as lumber dealers and lumber manufacturers. Gordon alone is given credit for the next seven vessels built between 1950 and 1966. These ranged in size from the 15-ton pilot boat *Humber Pilot* (which was later converted to a yacht and re-named *Rophil*) to the 33-ton tug *Birch Lake* built for Bowaters NF. Pulp & Paper Mills Ltd. in 1952. In 1958 Clyde and George Shears constructed the 17-ton *Henry & Brian*; presumably George is George Gordon Shears. In late 1966 Clyde Shears returns to the project, and his name now appears consistently without his first name Harold.

Most of their vessels during the 1960s and 1970s were in the range of 14 to 26 tons, but by the mid-1970s we begin to see a trend towards even smaller fishing vessels. Several were as small as 7, 8, and 9 tons. The builders were following the trend established elsewhere in Newfoundland, and several of these were very probably fitted with outboard motors.

Several of the Shears' vessels carried female names, a few male names, and several had very picturesque names such as the 30-ton *Pine Lake* in 1951; the 18-ton *Belle Isle* in 1966; the 23-ton, two-masted *Cape Shallop* in 1967; the 24-ton *Anchor Point North* in 1969; the 25-ton *Cape Verde II* in 1971; the 17-ton, two-masted *Miss Charlottetown II* in 1973; the 10-ton *Shallow Bay* in 1977; the 9-ton *Wolf Rock* in 1979; the 7-ton *Flowers Cove South* in 1980, which carried a Fisheries Loan Board Mortgage A for $43, 380; the 11-ton *Big Rock* in 1980; and their last ship, the 8-ton *Oggaksuk*, in 1981.

GORDON PITTMAN

Gordon Pittman of Rocky Harbour compiled an amazing record of building of at least forty-two ships between 1967 and 1990. He began with the 14-ton *Sandra & Wanda* and the same year built the 24-ton *Latona*. All his ships up until 1974 were noted to be one-masted vessels, but that same year he constructed the 40-ton, two-masted yacht *Sea Dream II*. Following that date, the ship register does not record the number of masts, so presumably they are one-masted or had no masts.

Pittman's building record was astonishing when one notes that in 1971 he built six ships, all about 25 tons; from then onwards he averaged about three ships per year; and in 1979 he produced seven ships ranging in size from 17 to 21 tons. In 1980 he took a break—in addition to producing three ships at home, he travelled to Newstead, Notre Dame Bay, and co-built with Frank Greenham the 12-ton fishing vessel *Frank & Sons*. Perhaps one should interpret this as a favor for a friend.

Pittman, along with Gordon and Clyde Shears, supplied the needs of fishermen and merchants along the west coast for new fishing ships in the period from the 1950s to the early 1990s. This is the major reason why there were so few other shipbuilders in this region during this period.

The names of some of Pittman's ships are noteworthy: the 18-ton *Corbet Island* and the 25-ton *Morning Glow* of 1968; the 19-ton *Northern Seagull* of 1970; the 25-ton *Cooper's Island*, the 26-ton *Port Verde III*, the 25-ton *Sea Fare* of 1971; the 27-ton *White Foam II* of 1972; the 9-ton *Labrador Spray*, the 15-ton *Admiral Point*, and the 16-ton *Labrador View* of 1978; the 16-ton *Gulf Foam* of 1979; the 11-ton *Ferret island* of 1980; the 7-ton *Ocean Fancy* of 1982; and the 5-ton *Rocky Point* of 1983.

Decks Awash, in August 1977, published the results of an interview with Gordon Pittman and noted that his 45-foot longliners had a beam of 15 feet (increased from 12 feet for greater stability) and that Pittman asserted his boats were better than the Nova Scotia Cape Islander type. Pittman said, "The Newfoundland boat has inflexible sawn timber, while the Nova Scotia boats use steamed timber. If you get out on the sea with steamed timbers your boat will go and come like a dog's stomach. Our boats are heavier planked too." Employing up to eight or ten men at his busiest times, Pittman's operation was pumping up to $5,000 per month into the local economy through wages, benefits, and supplies.

In 1985 Pittman took another break from Rocky Harbour and went north to Port Saunders where he rebuilt the 23-ton *Atlantic Mist* which had been built in 1978 by Bay D'Espoir Enterprises. In 1990 he crafted his last vessel, the 22-ton *B. S. Venture*, at Rocky Harbour, thus bringing his outstanding building career to completion.

Several vessels were built in this region by construction companies beginning in 1979 and ending with the institution of the Cod Moratorium in 1992, and it is impossible to determine who the individual shipbuilders were.

In 1979 Frelco Ltd. of Stephenville built the 4-ton aluminum fishing vessel with the unromantic name *Frelco no. 1*. There were no others. Wells and Park Construction Co. Ltd. of Cox's Cove constructed the 7-ton wooden fishing vessel *Corinna Cavelle* in 1979 but did not register it until 1981. Guildford's Ltd. of Stephenville was a Dartmouth, Nova Scotia-based company, and they built three GRP (Glass Reinforced Plastic) fishing ships in 1981: the 10-ton *Lillian Catherine*, the 10-ton *Virginia G.*, and the 18-ton *Atlantic Reaper*. LeGay Fiberglass Ltd. of Stephenville was a Waverly, Nova Scotia-based company and crafted the 4-ton GRP fishing vessel *Trinity Belle* in 1981. Humber Arm Shipbuilding Co. Ltd. of Benoit's Cove in 1989 constructed the 81-ton steel-fishing ship *Gallant Lady*. Only two other Newfoundland companies at the time were building steel ships: Glovertown Shipyards and the Marystown Shipyard. And finally, Kustom Fiberglass (Nfld.) Ltd. constructed three ships between 1990 and 1992, all of them GRP fishing vessels: the 27-ton *Atlantic Conquest*, the 33-ton *Island Voyager*, and the 37-ton *Roberts Sisters I*.

Just a few curiosities to mention before we leave this area: Moses Shepherd's 29-ton *Livonia* built in 1894 at Lark Harbour was lost at sea near Liverpool, England. Why was such a small schooner involved in transatlantic crossings? James Evans' 18-ton *Donalda* built at Codroy in 1905 was lost at sea in 1952, having lasted for a remarkable forty-seven years. Orestes Howell built the 18-ton, curiously-named schooner *I. G. W. T.* in 1906, and it was lost at sea in 1928 after twenty-two years of service. And finally, Andrew Arthur Hull built only one ship, the large, 149-ton *Doris V. Douglas* in 1935 at Humbermouth.

The area along the west coast-southern section related more to the British maritime colonies than it did to St. John's and the rest of Newfoundland. Trade with the maritime colonies and the United States was being carried on from very early periods. Local builders bought mainland ships and sold their locally-built ships to mainland merchants and mariners, as well as to fishermen and merchants along the south and southwest coast. Mainland shipbuilders were also attracted to this area to construct ships for local planters and merchants. We also see the emergence of builders of French extraction. In the early period, settlers came to the area from the maritime colonies as well as directly from England. It was an area with quite distinct characteristics, not the least of which was the purchase of fishing ships in the later period by local fishermen from the more prominent area builders such as Gordon and Clyde Shears and Gordon Pittman.

CHAPTER FIVE

SOUTHWEST COAST AND SOUTH COAST

IN THIS CHAPTER WE examine the southwest and south coast of Newfoundland from Cape Ray to Harbour Breton. The area from Cape Ray to Harbour Le Cou has such an affinity with the west coast-southern section they appear to belong together. Shipbuilders along the west coast, and particularly in the Codroy region, were regularly supplying newly built ships to fishermen and merchants along the southwest coast. And residents of the southwest coast, along with their neighbours, were depending on fresh vegetables and other products from the nearby British maritime colonies from earliest days. The uniting factor appears to have been Port aux Basques, which was a centre of commerce for the region due to its advantageous position near the mouth of the Gulf of St. Lawrence.

Port aux Basques itself appears to have been used from the early 1500s by the Spanish and French Basque whalers who stopped there for wood and fresh water as they entered the Gulf of St. Lawrence to begin the hunt on their way to Red Bay Labrador. They called the Strait of Belle Isle by the name Granbaya, and English maps named it Grand Bay. Maps of 1612 were calling the Port aux Basques area "bay eclaire," and maps of 1687 called it "B. S. Clara," which undoubtedly meant Bay St. Clara. The influence of the Basques may have been more far-reaching, since M. F. Howley asserted that Isle aux Morts had been named by them. It is also asserted that the Ramea Islands were known to the Portuguese and possibly other Europeans by the 1500s.

The second group of visitors to this area were the Mi'kmaq from Cape Breton, who may have arrived on the west and southwest coasts by the early 1600s (one writer has suggested 1538) and were firmly established in the Bay D'Espoir area by the early 1700s.

When Capt. William Taverner surveyed the area between 1714 and 1718 for Great Britain, he described the third group of arrivals as a "little Commonwealth" of disreputable French deserters, from Isle Royale (Nova Scotia), who were being supplied by French ships and who were curiously trading their fish products with the settlement they had abandoned.

Though fishermen from France had been forced to withdraw from Cape Breton, Hudson's Bay, and Placentia by the Treaty of Utrecht in 1713, it was probably a few years before the French had become established in the Port aux Basques area in order to take advantage of the rich fishing groups of the Gulf, so they should be considered as the fourth group of visitors. It appears to have been considered by the English as a remote area at this time. Since the French were well established at St. Pierre et Miquelon, they were exploring much of the south coast, including the Ramea Islands, the McCallum area, the Rose Blanche Bank, and La Poile; the latter area being patrolled by French soldiers well into the 1800s in order to discourage settlement by the English. The French, the Spanish, the Portuguese, and the English appear to have been exploiting the south coast and southeast coast fisheries from the early 1500s. From Placentia, the French had been fishing the area of Connaigre in tandem with the English from the 1600s, and Cape Negre was included in the French census of 1686 and had a population of seventy-two, including three families and many fishing servants. Working from Placentia, the French also fished in Hermitage Cove in the late 1600s and the early 1700s; it was one of their eight fishing stations in Hermitage Bay, Placentia Bay, and Fortune Bay. From earliest times, the French, again in tandem with the English, used the great timber resources of Bay D'Espoir to repair and possibly build ships. Harbour Breton was very probably originally named Havre Bertrand by the French fishing out of Placentia and was included in their census of 1687 but had no resident families.

The English came to this area later than the French, and their first intrepid explorers appear to have been English merchant firms and the merchant/traders of the Jersey Islands. The English should therefore be considered as the fifth group of visitors. These English and Jersey firms set up fishing stations all the way from the Burin Peninsula to the Burgeo-La Poile area sometime in the 1700s. There may have been a few individual efforts before 1763, but even in that year there were fewer than forty boats engaged in the fishery from Hermitage Bay to Cape Ray with a winter population of about 100 and a summer population of about 200. This list is by no means complete, but it should be noted that when Capt. James Cook surveyed this part of the coast, probably in 1766, he saw only five fishing stages at Port aux Basques and one fishing stage at Harbour Le Cou.

Newman & Co. of Totnes, Devon, and later Dartmouth, under Richard Newman, appears to have been an exception to the rule of a later English arrival. Richard apparently had been granted fishing rights on the south coast as early as 1601. By 1672 Newman had established a fishing station at Pushthrough, and by 1679 the company had permanent settlers living on plantations at Harbour Breton, Gaultois, and Hermitage. The Philip Nicolle Co. of the Jersey Islands would probably have been the second merchant firm to establish fishing and trading stations along the south coast, though an accurate date is impossible to specify. They were probably established there about 1789. In 1803 they brought at least forty fishing servants to the area, and by the 1830s they were encouraging settlement along the south coast and particularly in the La Poile and Burgeo area, though Burgeo had seen its first settlers in the late 1700s. The Robert Newman Co., successor to Richard's company, had developed fishing stations at St. Lawrence by 1784, at Burin and Little Bay by 1793, and by 1800 had nine fishing stations between Burin and Hermitage Bay. Newman & Co. appears to have reached as far as Burgeo by the 1840s. By the early 1850s they had built four large stores, a shop, an office, and two cookrooms at Burgeo and were employing at least forty-four people by the end of that decade. Bishop Feild described Newman's premises at Harbour Breton as "complete and comfortable, and consequential as wealth can make it." Newman & Co. expanded and entered into various partnerships through the years with fishery operations centered on the south coast, in St. John's, and in Conception Bay. After more than 300 years of operation, they closed out their last branch at Harbour Breton in 1907.

The rich timber resources of Bay D' Espoir were being exploited by both the English and the French from earliest times for the repair of ships, but not until 1804 do we find references to shipbuilding in the region. It is hard to imagine that no serious shipbuilding occurred there for the previous 100 years; any ships built there would have been registered in European ports, so there is no way to be certain. Since the English regained control of the south coast in 1713, they must surely have been building ships in the 100 years between that date and the first specific references in the ship registers to shipbuilding on the south coast (1804, 1813, and 1818). Of the thirty ships built in Newfoundland in 1804, according to D. W. Prowse, one each were reported for Bay D'Espoir, Oderin, Trepassey, Capelin Bay (southeast coast of the Avalon), and Great Placentia, and one for the Bay of Islands. Actually, Prowse's list is incomplete; he curiously missed seven ships which were constructed in Conception Bay that year. In 1804 at "Bay Despair," the 94-ton schooner *Fanny* had been constructed, but neither the name of the firm nor that of the master builder is known. This vessel would have been registered in England. Registration of ships at St. John's was not regularized until the early 1800s, and it is not until 1818 that we have specific and fulsome information on Newfoundland-built ships. According to Archdeacon Wix's report in 1835, Nicolle & Co. had stationed a winter crew at Swanger's Cove, harvesting timber for shipbuilding at Jersey Harbour. At the same time, Newman & Co.'s winter crew was stationed at Southeast Arm doing the same. But both firms were building ships in Bay D'Espoir well before that date.

There was also a sixth group of visitors to Newfoundland's south and southwest coasts—the Americans. It was not until the 1783 Treaty of Versailles that the fishing rights of the Americans were clarified, but they had been fishing these coasts many years before that. They were now permitted to fish on the Grand Banks and other Banks and in the Gulf of St. Lawrence. There were many recorded incidents of American interference with both English and French fishers, including destruction of their fishing equipment. The American Treaty Shore, as defined in 1818, included the area from the Ramea Islands westward to Cape Ray and from there north to Quirpon Island, from Mont Joli northward on the Labrador coast, and an area around the Magdalen Islands. Their fishing was restricted to three miles offshore, and they were allowed to enter unoccupied harbours only for water, wood, shelter, and ship repair. It proved to be a troublesome agreement, and American privateers operated in the region at will as we have already seen with their capture of Mrs. Anne Hulan's ship and cargo in 1814.

Of the six groups of visitors who came to this coast, only the Mi'kmaq and the English remained to become permanent residents. The English were a mixture of "youngsters" sent out to occupy fishing stations along the coast, merchants' servants, hardy planters, and rugged entrepreneurs, and perhaps a few deserters. It must have been a daunting prospect for many of these people, but they persisted in their endeavours.

The first detailed record found about shipbuilding in this region was the 47-ton *Sisters* built at "Harbour Britain" in 1813 by Thomas DeCaen. The record notes the vessel was "British Plantation Built," square-sterned, and had no gallery and no head. It was registered in Poole, and the registering officer was George Richard Robinson while the master was Charles Patten. The owners were Samuel and John Clark of Poole, merchants. When this vessel was registered de novo in 1824, she belonged to William Vallance and Richard Hunt, merchants of St. John's.

Prowse affirms in his *History of Newfoundland* that, from 1815 to 1817, Newman & Co. "built several fine vessels at Great Jervois, which were highly commended by Trinity House for their excellent models and staunch construction, all constructed out of timber obtained in Bay Despair." Great Jervais (also called Jervois, Jervis, and Jarvis) was located at the Head of Bay D'Espoir and was probably originally named Grand Jervais by the French. The names of the vessels referred to by Prowse cannot be determined. It is known, however, that John Oxford built three ships there in 1818 and 1819: the 122-ton brig *Hawk* in 1818, the 128-ton sloop-of-war *Kite*, and the 68-ton *Stag* in 1819. The *Hawk* was owned by Henry Hanson of St. John's, an agent and ship's husband for four merchants whose names are unknown. The *Kite* and the *Stag* were noted to be "of London," so they may have been owned by Newman & Co., and the *Kite* was built to mount between ten and thirty-two guns.

The third prominent master builder was Thomas Silk, who operated in Jersey Harbour, about three kilometers northeast of Harbour Breton. In 1818 Silk built the 48-ton *Fishhook*, and the record states it was "square with a Billet head." He constructed the 38-ton, one-masted smack *Nautilus* "of Fortune Bay" in 1819. And in 1822 Silk built the 124-ton brigantine *Juno* for Philip Nicolle Jr., merchant of the Jersey Islands. Undoubtedly the first two were also built for Nicolle & Co.

The fourth prominent builder was Thomas Power, who constructed two ships at Bay D'Espoir (probably at Great Jervais): the 48-ton *Chance* in 1820 and the 96-ton brigantine *Saint Patrick* in 1831. In this latter venture, Power was assisted by John Hurdle. The owners of the first vessel were Christopher Spurrier, his nephew William Jubber Spurrier, and his uncle Peter Joliffe, merchants of Poole. The Spurriers, father and son both named William, had been operating out of Burin at least from the 1790s; the son died in 1800, the father in 1809, and then Christopher took over the family business. While the Spurriers built ships at Burin and Oderin, they also used the Bay D'Espoir area as a significant shipbuilding site, and Power appears to have been their master builder. The *Saint Patrick* was co-owned by Joseph Ryan, merchant of St. John's, and Catherine Morris of Burin, widow of Geoffrey Morris, merchant of Poole and Liverpool. Catherine also co-owned two other vessels. Back at Burin in 1838 Thomas Power built the 27-ton *Speculation* for Patrick Morris, merchant of Burin.

In addition to assisting Thomas Power with the construction of the 96-ton brigantine *Saint Patrick* in 1831, John Hurdle branched out on his own and built the 118-ton brig *Calypso* at Burin in 1833 for Joseph Ryan and Catherine Morris of Burin, and Hurdle then travelled to Carbonear, Conception Bay, to build the 23-ton *Native Lass* for James Doyle, mariner. Hurdle was an itinerant builder, yet another indication that he was a professional builder brought in from England or Ireland.

William Conch built two ships at Harbour Breton in the 1830s: a 75-ton brig in 1831 and the 96-ton schooner *Snipe* in 1839. The record notes that the first ship was "To process to Portugal and from there to this Port," (i.e., St. John's). Both these ships must have been registered in England.

These six master builders were very probably brought in from England or Ireland for the specific purpose of constructing ships. After short periods of time, they disappear from the records.

An open boat which was built in Bay D'Espoir in 1820 was decked and rebuilt as a 50-ton vessel called *Billow* at Mortier Harbour, Placentia Bay, in 1825. The 18-ton *Dart*, which had been crafted as an open boat at Hermitage Bay in 1823, was in 1827 decked at Little River by William Hooper of Lamaline; he must have been overwintering there.

From the 1830s to the 1850s, there were several master builders who each constructed only one ship according to the ship registers. Because it is such an early period, they are noted here with only the basic information. In the 1830s there were five such builders. Three of these were building in Hermitage Bay: Nicholas Harrison, a trader/dealer, in 1836 built the 51-ton *Hope*; in the same year, planter John Pittman constructed the 17-ton *Mary Ann*, and his partner was fellow planter William Pittman; and in 1838 planter Matthew Crotty of St. Lawrence built the 21-ton *Mary Ann*. Henry Whiffen constructed the 52-ton *John & Phyllis* in 1838 for Chambers & Butler, merchants at Placentia, and William Anderson of La Poile built the 17-ton *Two Sisters*.

Seven ships were built in this region in the 1840s. William Bragg of Grand Bay constructed the 13-ton *Favourite* in 1840. Also that same year in Hermitage Bay, John Buffett built the 19-ton *John and William*, but the ship was not registered until 1844. Eighteen years later, Buffett, who was now settled at Jersey Harbour, fashioned the 21-ton *Julius Caesar* at Bay D'Espoir. This builder was moving around and may have been an employee of one of the merchant firms; it is hard to imagine that he constructed no ships in the intervening seventeen-year period. John Butt, planter of Port aux Basques, built the 18-ton *Britannia* in 1840, and it was broken up thirty-two years later. Thomas Jeynes of the Ramea Islands constructed the 19-ton *Mary* in 1843 at White Bear Bay. Benjamin Buffett, planter at Hermitage Bay, constructed the 23-ton *William and Harriet* in 1845, and this vessel was lost at sea on the west coast in 1869 after twenty-four years of use. John Evans, planter of Cape Ray, rebuilt the 23-ton *Freedom* in 1849; this vessel had been built in Prince Edward Island in 1844. And finally for the 1840s, the 58-ton *Petrel* was crafted at Gaultois in 1849 and registered in London in 1850, but the builder is unknown. This vessel was transferred from London to Newfoundland in 1899 and rebuilt at Gaultois in 1900, thus lasting for more than fifty years.

Only four shipbuilders were active in the 1850s. George Carter of Port aux Basques constructed the 16-ton *Dart* at Codroy River in 1850. This small vessel was lost at sea twenty-two years later. Benjamin Knee of Rose Blanche built the 30-ton *Lark* in 1852. James Bagg of Cape La Hune constructed the 21-ton *Electric* at Belleoram, Fortune Bay, in 1857. And Abraham Skinner of Hermitage Bay crafted the 23-ton *Emily* in 1858. Curiously, Skinner was still a resident of Hermitage Bay in 1866 when he built the 21-ton *Providence* at Fortune.

From this point onwards we will deal only with significant shipbuilders of the region, particularly those who have built four or more ships and those who can be considered as shipbuilding families. All other builders are listed in the Appendix to Chapter Five.

THE FARRELL FAMILY

The Farrells of La Poile Bay were the first family of shipbuilders to emerge in this area, and they probably represent three generations of builders from about 1877 to 1967.

What has seemed to be a mystery about the Farrell family may simply be a striking coincidence. They were living in the Bay du Nord area of Fortune Bay and building ships there from 1877 to 1907. Thomas Farrell built the 34-ton *Henrietta Clinton* at Bay du Nord in 1877. Joseph and William Farrell constructed the 46-ton *Mary Callopes* there in 1880. The inconsistency seems to be with Edward and Josiah Farrell who jointly built the 26-ton *Poppy M.* at Bay du Nord in 1907, but Josiah was at La Poile in 1906 to build the 9-ton *Mary S.* Perhaps "Josiah," in this record, should read "Joseph." That appears to be the only way to reconcile the inconsistency. Adding further to the mystery is that North Bay, La Poile, was also at some point in the past called Bay du Nord. It should be noted also that in 1902, at Bay du Nord, George Joseph Miles built a ship for Philip Farrell. Perhaps Philip stayed behind in Fortune Bay when the family moved to North Bay, La Poile.

Thomas Farrell of La Poile Bay may have been the progenitor of the family. After building the 34-ton *Henrietta Clinton* at Bay du Nord in 1877, he then constructed three ships at North Bay, La Poile Bay, between 1902 and 1916: the 8-ton *Doris* was built for a merchant at Rose Blanche, and the 10-ton *Catalogue* and the 11-ton *Lily Collins* were constructed for fishermen at Burnt Islands and Petites. The last ship was built at La Poile itself.

Josiah Farrell of North Bay, La Poile, may have been a younger brother of Thomas. He began his building career in 1906 at La Poile with the 9-ton *Mary S.* but did not build his second ship, the 12-ton *Topsail Girl*, until 1913. By 1916, with the 15-ton *Puzzle*, he had hit his productive stride, and over the next twenty-one years he constructed another fifty-two vessels and rebuilt two, an amazing record. He crafted four vessels in 1926, three in 1927, three in 1928, three in 1933, four in 1941, six in 1943, and three in 1945. By 1927 the ship registers accord him the occupation of shipbuilder. All but two of the vessels were constructed for fishermen; these two were built for merchants. His ships ranged in size from 9 to 25 tons. Practically all the ships carried personal names and were obviously named for the fishing families for whom they were built. Some of the more interesting names were the 22-ton *Jock Scott* of 1933, the 14-ton *La Poile* and the 14-ton *Carolina Moon* of 1934, and the 17-ton *Syabilla M.* of 1926 which was jointly owned by Abigail and John Horwood. The ship registers err in calling Abigail a fisherman; she was actually a merchant. Josiah's last ship was the 14-ton *Miss Margaree* built in 1947. All his ships were built at North Bay except the 11-ton *Annie J. Meade* of 1935, which was constructed at Bay du Nord. Is this an errant use of the old name, or did he return to Fortune Bay to build the ship? Most likely it is the former. After 1937 Josiah's place of residence was usually called North Arm rather than North Bay. His was a long and distinguished building career.

Joseph and Edward Farrell of North Arm, La Poile, were probably younger brothers of Thomas. Edward appears to have been at Bay du Nord assisting Joseph (rather than Josiah) in building the 26-ton *Poppy M.* in 1907. They jointly built three ships: the 13-ton *Everett* in 1916 for John Harvey, merchant at St. John's; the 13-ton *Annie J.* in 1917; and the 26-ton *Ralph & Blanche* in 1919. These last two were for fishermen. Joseph alone is the master builder of the last three ships between 1921 and 1923. They ranged in size from 11 to 16 tons and were all constructed for fishermen in the area. Then Joseph disappears from the records.

From 1929 to 1947 Edward becomes a master builder working on his own. His first ship is the 17-ton *Bennett Brothers*. During these years, he builds another eighteen ships and rebuilds one. His ships are also small, ranging in size between 11 and 24 tons, all of them fishing ships with engines being installed in them from about 1931 onwards. All of his ships carry personal names, usually a combination of a female and a male name and probably reflecting the names of a fisherman and his wife. Edward's last ship was the 24-ton *Phyllis & James* built in 1947.

Eugene Farrell of North Bay, La Poile, began his building career in 1938 with the 11-ton *Ada May* and concluded it in 1967 with the 7-ton *Katie Arlene*. During this period he constructed ten ships and rebuilt one. His place of building is usually given as North Bay, but some of the records state his place of residence as Bay du Nord; perhaps this was also the original name of the community. Eugene's largest ship was the 23-ton *Gloria Marie* of 1946, and his smallest ship was the 7-ton *Mary V. S.* These were all fishing ships, at least some of them one-masted. Eugene was probably a brother of Joseph and Edward.

John S. Farrell of North Bay may have been yet another brother. Between 1946 and 1964 he built eighteen ships, all at North Bay. The Farrells must have had a shipyard with several docks to facilitate so many projects. John started in 1946 with the 22-ton *Rita & Alma*. His largest ship was the 29-ton *Robbie & Brad* crafted in 1964, and his smallest ship was the *Margaree Duck* which was less than 5 tons and was also his last ship. Both his largest and smallest ships were built the same year. At least eleven of his ships were more than 20 tons, and the ship registers do not give the tonnage of two others. These were all fishing ships but were larger than other ships being built in the region. Some of the more interesting ship names were the 22-ton *Miss Rose Blanche*; the *Margaree Queen*, whose name was later changed to *El Toro*; the 9-ton *Incha*; the 21-ton *Atlantic Ranger II*; and the *Margaree Duck*.

William S. Farrell of North Bay constructed three fishing ships between 1960 and 1966. His largest ship was the 17-ton *Debbie & Clara* of 1964, and his smallest was his last ship, the *Donald & Edward*, which was less than 5 tons; yet it was more than twenty-three feet long. The last of the Farrell shipbuilders was Arthur Farrell of North Bay who built only one ship, the 16-ton *Marilyn & Marvin* in 1966.

Shipbuilding families such as the Farrells, the Kendells of Bay D'Espoir, the Stricklands of North Bay, and the Roberts of Bay D'Espoir provided by far most of the fishing ships needed in this area, and so we see a lessening of shipbuilding by other individuals. These shipbuilding families were constructing many ships from about 1920 to about 1985.

There were, however, several individual shipbuilders between 1889 and 1927 who are worthy of honorable mention here.

George Scott of Port aux Basques constructed his first ship at Burnt Islands in 1889: the 16-ton *Dora* for a local merchant. He then moved on to greater things and, between 1897 and 1924, built ten more ships and rebuilt three. Most of his vessels were small fishing ships, but he also built for merchants and mariners. His largest ship was his second: the 59-ton *Good Ship Jubilee* built in 1897 for master mariner William Carter of Channel. He also crafted three ships and rebuilt two for merchant Emmanuel Pike of Port aux Basques. The new ships were the 27-ton *Mildred* in 1907, the 35-ton *Sea Scout* in 1912, and the 12-ton *Hill Caribou* in 1916. The 9-ton *Winning Cup* was built at Grand Bay in 1917. All other ships except the first were built at Channel-Port aux Basques. His three rebuilts were of Nova Scotia-built vessels. And Scott's last vessel was the 49-ton *Julia A. Anderson* of 1924.

It is difficult to know where to place Matthew Nash. He is variously said to have been from St. Jacques, McCallum, and Trepassey, but we will consider him here because it was in this region that he did most of his shipbuilding. The only other Nash shipbuilder encountered in the records was Henry Nash of Bonne Bay, who in 1864 and 1875 built two ships in Fortune Bay. Perhaps he moved to Bonne Bay following this period. Peter W. Nash was a master mariner at Branch, St. Mary's Bay, in 1904. The 19-ton *Emily V.* was Matthew Nash's first ship, built at Belleoram in 1891 for a local fisherman. In 1896 he was at Trepassey where he constructed the 23-ton *E. J. Wilson*. Soon after this, he was attracted to Ramea where he became the master shipbuilder for the merchant firm of John & George Penny. There he built six or seven ships for Penny, including the 38-ton *Maris Stella* in 1896, the 23-ton *John Cabot* in 1897, the 25-ton *Venus* in 1899, the 31-ton *Izette* in 1900, the 51-ton *Shamrock* in 1903, and possibly the *Lilly Swift* in 1900. In 1907 he also rebuilt the *Venus*, which he initially constructed in 1899. At Ramea in 1898 he built the 22-ton *Rose* in June for a planter in Trepassey, and in 1904 at Little River he crafted the 21-ton *Florence S.* for a planter in Conne River. But it was as a builder for Robert Moulton of Burgeo that Nash achieved his greatest work. In 1900 he moved to Burgeo and began construction of the 152-ton, three-masted schooner *Duchess of Cornwall* for Robert Moulton. The vessel was completed and launched in 1901 and registered on December 9, 1901. She is described in the ship registers as having a V-stern and a scroll head. She had a forecastle, master's and mate's rooms, sail and bosun's stores. Her registry was transferred to Sydney, Nova Scotia, in 1916, but she remained in possession of the Moulton firm. After giving sixteen years of good service in the trade, the *Duchess of Cornwall* was torpedoed by a German submarine on December 18, 1916, on the way from Burgeo to Oporto, Portugal. The crew of six men became prisoners of war and were released when hostilities ended in 1918. In 1902 at Burgeo, Nash constructed the 82-ton *Albert Moulton*. He returned to Ramea to build his last vessel for the Penny firm and in 1905 was again back in Burgeo to build the 33-ton *Mollie Moulton* for Robert Moulton. His building career ended with the rebuilding of his own *Venus* in 1907 for two merchants at Rose Blanche—the end of a distinguished shipbuilding career.

John Davidge of Burgeo built his first vessel at Pushthrough in 1893, the 24-ton *R. G. W. C.*, for George Chambers, merchant at Pushthrough, so the initials probably stood for members of the Chambers family. The next year, Davidge constructed the 37-ton *Agnes M.* for Thomas and Robert Moulton, merchants at Burgeo. The *Colenso* was built in 1900, but no particulars could be found on this vessel. In 1908 Davidge crafted his masterpiece: the 136-ton, three-masted schooner *Chrissie C. Thomey* for Robert Moulton. The vessel had a scroll head, three bulkheads, forecastle and mess room, sail room and stores, and a turret or trunk. The newspaper *Free Press* of October 28, 1908, reported at her launch that she was "built of oak, most of which came out of the American schooner *Golden Rod* which was refloated last year." She was destined for the foreign trade. On January 12, 1909, Moulton sold half the shares in the ship to John C. Crosbie, so each man held thirty-two shares; then on May 25, 1910, they both sold the tern schooner to "His Majesty King George V as represented by Hon. Louis Phillipe Brodeur, His Majesty's Minister of Marine & Fisheries for the Dominion of Canada for the time being." The vessel was transferred to the Ottawa registry on July 26, 2010. Working for the Canadian government, the *Chrissie C. Thomey* made several voyages into Hudson's Bay and was lost "many years later" at the mouth of Rupert River in James Bay. William L. Davidge of Burgeo was very likely a brother of John and built the 81-ton *Pretty Mary* in 1911 for Robert Moulton; it was William's only ship. He would undoubtedly have been a shipwright in the building of the *Chrissie C. Thomey*.

James Matthews of Burgeo built two ships and rebuilt two others between 1897 and 1929. He began his building career in 1897 by rebuilding the 61-ton *Nina Pearl* which had been constructed at Essex, Massachusetts, in 1860. This vessel was registered de novo in 1909 and was lost at sea in 1913, having lasted for a remarkable fifty-three years. In 1900 Matthews built the 53-ton *Ladysmith* for Robert Moulton. Two years later he crafted the 17-ton Landseer for Rupert Matthews, a trader at Burgeo and probably his brother. There was a long pause of twenty-four years before Matthews constructed the 16-ton *Eva Billard* for the Burgeo & La Poile Export Co. Limited. He probably constructed other ships during this period, but no records could be found. Matthews completed his career with the rebuilding of the 22-ton *Joseph Earle* in 1929 for his own use. This vessel had been constructed in Nova Scotia in 1910.

Jonathan Rowsell of Pushthrough, Hermitage Bay, constructed the 35-ton *Sisters* in 1904. He had been a partner with George Rowsell in 1885 when George built the 30-ton *Mary Hannah* in Hermitage Bay, so George may have been an older brother of Jonathan. It was George's only ship and both men were planters. Jonathan's stated occupation in 1904 is that of merchant, and that appears to be an error in the ship registers. By 1915 Jonathan begins building for the Moulton merchant firm of Burgeo and St. John's. In 1915 he builds the 77-ton *Nellie Moulton* for R. Moulton Ltd. with its headquarters at St. John's; in 1916 it is the 32-ton *Ethel B. Dicks* for Moulton; in 1917 the 37-ton *Albert Sydney Moulton* for John T. Moulton of Burgeo; in 1918 the 36-ton *Cora B. Rose* for John T. Moulton; and in 1924 Rowsell rebuilds his last vessel and renames it *Arthena M.* All his building was done at Pushthrough except for the *Ethel B. Dicks* crafted at Burgeo.

There were three other Rowsell shipbuilders at Pushthrough. Edward Rowsell built the 24-ton *Two Sisters* in 1866, the 24-ton *Victoria* in 1871, and the 25-ton *Annie R.* in 1900. Edward was probably the progenitor of the family, and it is noteworthy that he was a trader/dealer for thirty-four years. Note the names of Jonathan's and Edward's first ships; that may confirm a family connection. Robert Rowsell was a mariner and built the 42-ton *Ferula* in 1908; his partner was mariner Henry Rowsell. Hedley Rowsell constructed the 7-ton *Ella Richards* in 1923 for the Burgeo & La Poile Export Co. Ltd. These three men were probably brothers of Jonathan.

The next two men are mentioned not because of any great shipbuilding feats but because of their possible connection with a merchant firm from the Jersey Islands. In fact, in the ship registers, Joseph C. Le Seelleur is accorded the status of merchant in 1899 when he builds the 25-ton *Pearl* somewhere in La Poile Bay. As we have seen, it was not uncommon for a merchant to be a shipbuilder if the building site was close to his business and he could supervise the daily construction. Thomas Le Seelleur of La Poile was also a merchant when in 1908 he built the 12-ton *Jersey Lass* at Little River Harbour. Note the ship name for a possible Jersey Islands connection. In 1927 Thomas expresses his sense of humor when he names his newly built 8-ton ship *Atta Boy*.

Frank M. Young of Grey River constructed the 13-ton *Lady of Safety* there in 1908, and this vessel was rebuilt in 1930 at Isle aux Morts, thus lasting twenty-two-plus years. At Little River in 1912, he constructed the 11-ton *Nico*, and in 1920 at Burgeo he built the 10-ton *Bridget M.* for Charles Munden, fisherman. In 1930 Young was back in Grey River where he built the 33-ton *Frank M. Young* (naming a ship after oneself was usually a sign that one had become successful in business). Young completed his building career in 1934 with the crafting of the 22-ton *Annie Young*. William and Ephraim Young of Grey River were very probably brothers of Frank. William built three ships there: the 20-ton *Alice Bowles* in 1913, the 13-ton *Lizzie Buffett*, and the 13-ton *Mabel Durnford*, with these last two in 1914. Two of his ships were rebuilt thirteen and sixteen years later to last several more years. Ephraim Young of Grey River built only one ship: the 10-ton, two-masted sloop *Netta A.* in 1917.

George Bagg crafted all five of his ships at Dog Cove, his place of residence. The 16-ton *Nahoma B.* and the 11-ton *Stanley Crew* were both built in 1911, not the usual way of beginning a building career. In 1913 Bagg built the 12-ton *Kathleen Sheaves*, and this vessel was rebuilt at Channel twenty-one years later. In 1914 it was the 12-ton *Wallace M.*, constructed for a merchant at Fox Roost. And in 1917 Bagg built his fifth ship: the 17-ton *Maria S. Bagg*. Four of the five vessels were built for fishermen.

It will require a keen genealogist to sort out the difference between Joseph Miles of Milltown (and later Fortune) and Joseph J. Miles, George Joseph Miles, and Jas. (or possibly Jos. Miles) of Pool's Cove and Little Bay. We know from the ship registers that Joseph Miles of Bay D'Espoir built the 148-ton, three-masted schooner *Helen Jean* at Milltown in 1920, and she was registered on May 16, 1921. The vessel was built for St. John's merchants Albert E. Hickman, William G. Gosling, and Harold MacPherson. The Helen Jean discharged her cargo of codfish in Brazil sometime in 1922 and stopped at Turks Island to load salt. She began to leak badly after a few days at sea and was towed back to Turks Island where she was condemned and sold. She was lost with all her crew in a Caribbean hurricane sometime in 1923.

We know that John E. Lake, merchant of Fortune, had constructed a sawmill at Milltown in 1894 and that eighteen men were employed there. Much of the lumber produced here was transported to Fortune for ship construction, and it is possible that John E. Lake had attracted Joseph Miles away from Pool's Cove as his master builder and that Miles constructed the *Helen Jean* for Lake to sell to the St. John's merchants. John P. Parker, in his book *Sails of the Maritimes*, gives J. Miles credit for building the 203-ton, three-masted schooner *John E. Lake* at Fortune in 1917, but the ship registers say that John E. Lake was the builder. Perhaps Lake supervised the construction and J. Miles (Joseph?) was the builder. We know also that Joseph Miles was in Fortune in 1929 to rebuild the 70-ton *Rose L.* which had been built in Essex, Massachussets, in 1876. George Joseph Miles of Pool's Cove will be considered in the chapter on Fortune Bay, but he had a good record of shipbuilding, having constructed three ships between 1902 and 1909, plus the three-masted schooner *Newton Stanley Lake* in 1919, two ships between 1927 and 1933, and rebuilding two other ships between 1928 and 1930.

Henry Anderson of Port aux Basques constructed four ships and rebuilt one between 1929 and 1949. In 1928 he constructed the *Dorothy Regis* which was less that 5 tons and was not registered until 1943, a delay not entirely unusual on the south coast. In 1929 Anderson crafted the 12-ton *Ethel M. Martin*, and in 1934 it was the 10-ton *Rosie Martin*. In 1942 he rebuilt the 13-ton *Doris W.* which had been built at Ramea in 1917 by Martin Keeping. And in 1949 at Channel, he concluded his shipbuilding with the 62-ton *Maud Matilda*.

All his vessels were fishing ships. Two other members of the Anderson family at Port aux Basques were shipbuilders. George Anderson rebuilt the 12-ton *Doubloon* in 1931 and built the 47-ton *Gladys & Doris* in 1941. And Edwin Anderson crafted the 128-ton *Sadie & Eva* in 1963. He and George Anderson were mariners and partners in this large cargo vessel.

George William Kettle of Grand Bay built four small fishing ships between 1931 and 1947. He began his shipbuilding with the 8-ton *Olive Gordon* and continued in 1942 with the 13-ton *Shelac*. In 1945 he fashioned the 7-ton *Dyke* and in 1947 the 19-ton *Sheila Kettle*. These were all fishing ships. There were three other Kettle shipbuilders at Grand Bay, and each built only one ship. John Thomas Kettle constructed the 9-ton fishing vessel *Gertie Marie* in 1936; Ernest Kettle built the 32-ton *Mary & Wes* in 1947; and in that same year Howard Kettle constructed the 13-ton *Millville*.

THE STRICKLAND FAMILY

Thomas Strickland of La Poile Bay built the 18-ton *Hero* at Codroy River in 1840. He was very probably the progenitor of the family of shipbuilders who followed him at La Poile Bay, and he may have been the grandfather of the clan. Frank Strickland crafted his first ship, the 12-ton *Malinda K.*, at La Poile Bay in 1910: his second ship, the 11-ton *Vera E. Blanche*, in 1911; and his third ship, the 12-ton *Derceto*, in 1912. In 1916 it was the 12-ton *Agnes R.* and in 1917 the 16-ton *Beatrice Emily*. In 1918 he constructed the 16-ton *Walter Stanley*. These were all constructed for fishermen in the region. Strickland must have moved to Boston, Massachusetts, sometime after 1919 since the records show that in 1931, at Boston, he built the 42-ton *Edith Dore*. He may, like many Newfoundlanders, have been working in the Boston Shipyards. He must have sailed this vessel home to La Poile Bay where in 1937 it was rebuilt by Josiah Farrell. It was owned at that time by Frank Absalom Strickland of West Medford, Massachusetts, carpenter. It is possible that this was Frank Jr.

Robert Strickland of West Point, La Poile, built his first ship there in 1912: the 12-ton *Violet H.* The record then falls silent for nineteen years; perhaps Robert constructed ships that were registered by the new owner without providing the name of the builder. Robert, in 1931, rebuilt the 11-ton *Vera E. Blanche* which had been built by Frank Strickland in 1911. In 1935 Robert rebuilt the 12-ton *Harvey Brothers* which had been constructed in Nova Scotia in 1917. And in 1940 at West Point, he built the *Bessie & Dona* which was slightly more than 5 tons. Robert is also given credit in one record for building the 12-ton *Harriet Bella* in 1911 at La Poile. Another record states that merchant Henry Strickland was the builder, but Robert is most probably the builder.

Other Strickland shipbuilders at La Poile Bay were Alexander, Wilfred, and Albert. Alexander Strickland of North Bay (sometimes called North Arm) built thirteen ships between 1930 and 1949. The first eight ships averaged about 14 tons each; the last five averaged about 25 tons. His first ship was the 14-ton *Heron Brothers*. His smallest ship was the 9-ton *Bessie & Jane* built at La Poile in 1937, and his largest was the 30-ton *Basques* crafted in 1944. In 1947 Alexander built the 21-ton *Strickland Brothers*, and one wonders if there was a connection with a shipbuilding firm by that name which existed at Harbour Breton from 1973 to 1977. Alexander had established an enviable record as a shipbuilder. Wilfred Strickland of West Point, La Poile, constructed only one ship: the 13-ton *Freddie & Allan* in 1938. Albert Strickland of North Bay, La Poile, built two ships: the 24-ton *Allan & Gilbert* in 1942 and the 8-ton *Meade Brothers* in 1943.

Garfield Strickland was an itinerant shipbuilder, constructing his four ships in four different locations: the 17-ton *W. E. Taker* at McCallum in 1946, the 17-ton cargo vessel *Judy Jean* at Little Bay in 1958, the 14-ton *Eleanor & Emmie* at Stone Valley in 1969, and the 15-ton *Robert & Jane* at Harbour Breton in 1975. It cannot be determined if Little Bay is in Fortune Bay or La Poile Bay, but it is probably the former. Garfield was probably one of the shipbuilders who formed Strickland Brothers at Harbour Breton and constructed four ships there between 1973 and 1977. These were small, one-masted fishing vessels averaging about 10 tons each. These were the *Norma Lee II*, the *Darrell & Paul*, the *Charlie & Wade*, and the 13-ton *Janice Marie*.

The other three Strickland builders were located at Port aux Basques and built only one ship each and are listed in the Appendix to Chapter Five.

THE KENDELL FAMILY

One of the most prolific shipbuilders on the south coast was John William Kendell of Morrisville, Bay D'Espoir. Kendell started slowly with the construction of the 11-ton *Annie K.* in 1914, the 41-ton *M. E. Kendell* in 1918, and the 38-ton *Victoria Kendell* in 1920. In 1921 he constructed the 93-ton schooner *Gladys E. Bullen*, and his partners were his brothers James R. Kendell and Albert E. Kendell. By 1923 there are references in the ship registers to the "Kendell Brothers," so all of them were shipwrights, but John is always given credit for being the master builder, except in the case of the *Victoria Kendell* which in 1922 was rebuilt or refurbished and restored to the ship registry with her named changed to *Annie F. Hartigan*.

In 1923 John built the 35-ton *Sentra* and the 17-ton *Della Belle* and in 1924 the 64-ton *Lizzie M. Kendell*. All three brothers are named as having been joint builders of the *Victoria Kendell* and the *Sentra*, but in all other cases John alone is stated to be the master builder.

From 1928 onwards, John crafted vessels practically every year and several vessels in some of these years: four in 1934, two in 1935, two in 1942, two in 1943, two in 1946, and three in 1947. Strangely, he built no ships between 1936 and 1941. He constructed a total of twenty-eight ships and rebuilt three in a period of thirty-four years, an enviable record indeed.

John's largest ships were the 93-ton *Gladys E. Bullen* and the 93-ton *A. L. Roy* built in 1933. Other ships of good size were the 64-ton *Lizzie M. Kendell*, the 57-ton *M. T. Collier* of 1929, the 52-ton *Bellegreve* of 1935, the 46-ton *Alice Jean* of 1944, and the 40-ton *Morris Ville* of 1935. Most of John's ships were crafted for fishermen and traders and ranged in size between 11 and 26 tons. John completed his shipbuilding feats in 1947 with three vessels: the 19-ton *Shirley Spicer*, the 32-ton *Olive & Cora*, and the 36-ton *N. E. Roy*.

Some of the more interesting names given to his ships were *Annie E. Laurie* of 1931, *Point May* of 1934, *Sfax* of 1942, and *Diamond Horseshoe* of 1946. John built the 23-ton *Margaret Brenton* in 1934 for Margaret Brenton of Burin who was a World War I bride from Scotland and whose husband, John, was a sea-going captain. Margaret sold the ship after ten years.

When John built his first ship in 1914, he was classified as a fisherman. From 1918 to 1923 he and his brothers were named non-marine tradesmen. From 1924 they were called merchants (actually, lumber merchants), and from 1935 to 1947 they were classified as shipbuilders. It is unusual to find such a variety of occupations in the registers.

John's two brothers were also master shipbuilders in their own right. James R. Kendell built the 40-ton *K. C. Gordon* in 1920 at Morrisville. He was then classified as a non-marine tradesman, as were his two partners John W. Kendell and Albert E. Kendell. In 1924 James constructed the 27-ton *Jean Dorothy* for a merchant at Jersey Harbour. Albert Kendell rebuilt the 38-ton *Wilfred L. Snow* at Ramea in 1931. This vessel had been built in Shelburne, Nova Scotia, in 1905. Presumably this is the Albert E. Kendell of Morrisville.

THE ROBERTS FAMILY

The Roberts family built their ships at Bay D'Espoir between 1899 and 1949, but it is not until 1927 that we find references specifically to the Head of Bay D'Espoir. It was possibly the same location referred to in the early 1800s as Great Jervais and the place where John Oxford, Thomas Power, and John Hurdle built large ships for the English and Jersey merchants.

Robert G. Roberts was very probably the father of both Wilson and Morgan Roberts, but it was Morgan who became the builder par excellence. Undoubtedly he was assisted by his brother Wilson through most of his years of building, 1917 to 1949.

When Robert G. Roberts built the 19-ton *Wilsie* in 1899 his partner was Morgan Roberts, and they were both trader/dealers. One wonders if the ship's name was an affectionate version of his other son's name.

Wilson Roberts constructed three ships at Bay D'Espoir: the 29-ton *Roberts Brothers* in 1913, the 60-ton *Alice Roberts* in 1916, and the 31-ton *J. Badcock* in 1933. For the first ship he is classified as a non-marine tradesman, for the second he is listed as a fisherman, and for the third he is called a shipbuilder. Wilson is known to have worked as a builder with his brother Morgan for many years.

Morgan Roberts is the builder par excellence of the south coast. In thirty-two years, from 1917 to 1949, he constructed forty-two ships, several of them large vessels, and two of them were three-masters. He began his illustrious shipbuilding career with the 29-ton *Meta M. Dibbon* which one year later was renamed *Nannuk* and sold to the Hudson's Bay Co. with its headquarters in London, England. The transition from a 29-ton vessel to a 117-ton vessel seems surprising, but he was responding to a need and rose to the occasion. This second vessel was a tern schooner, the 117-ton, three-masted *Tommie G.* crafted in 1918 for Wilson Garland, merchant at Gaultois, and Thomas Douglas, master mariner of Fortune. She was registered on September 19, 1918. The *Tommie G.* was abandoned at sea on the way to Oporto, Portugal, on April 11, 1921, and was set on fire before the crew left so she would not be a hazard in the shipping lanes. Morgan Roberts built two more small ships in the next two years and in 1921 constructed his second three-masted vessel, the 189-ton *Ronald M. Douglas*, also for Wilson Garland and Thomas Douglas, both of whom were now merchants at Gaultois. This vessel had a round stern, a cut-water head, and two bulkheads. It also had a forecastle, cabin, mate's cabin, sail room, master's room, and boatswain's room. The ship was registered on June 2, 1922. John P. Parker concedes that she had "good average passages on her voyages in the export fish trade," but states, "the usual fate overcame her." She was abandoned at sea in the North Atlantic on November 12, 1930, having lasted for almost nine years.

Roberts' next four ships were built for Wilson Garland, including the 18-ton *W. Garland* in 1924 and the 125-ton *Gaultois* in 1925. Throughout this period, Robert G. Roberts and Wilson Roberts are listed as partners with Morgan, but beginning in 1925 Morgan alone is mentioned as the builder. The amount of information recorded by the registrar of shipping had changed; perhaps the registration form had been revised. Undoubtedly, Robert and Wilson were still acting as shipwrights with Morgan.

It would be tedious to list all the ships that Morgan Roberts constructed, but so many of them were ships of substantial size that these are worthy of mention, such as the 52-ton *Thomas Garland* of 1928, the 64-ton *Alice & Kathleen Ryan* of 1926, the 67-ton *Alice Garland* of 1927, the 68-ton *Morgan Roberts* of 1928, the 69-ton *Minnie & Muriel* of 1930, the 69-ton *Jennie and Ada* of 1932, the 79-ton *Adolphe Roberts* of 1936, the 94-ton *Marlorita* of 1942, the 95-ton *Rita Carter* of 1940, the 97-ton *Denmo* of 1943, the 102-ton *Clarice Andrews* of 1942, the 124-ton *Saval* of 1944, the 126-ton *Mustang* of 1945, the 144-ton *Shirley Blanche* of 1949, the 150-ton *Joan Garland* of 1947, and the 196-ton *Dingo* of 1947. The *Dingo* was built for Fishery Products Ltd. of St. John's, and the *Shirley Blanche* was built for Thomas Garland Ltd. of Gaultois, as were many of the other vessels such as the 48-ton *Garland's Trader* of 1938. It was not possible to determine the fate of these vessels. Morgan Roberts constructed only two vessels under 20 tons: the 18-ton *W. Garland* of 1924 and the 19-ton *Geraldine G.* of 1919. All the others were vessels of substantial size.

Morgan Roberts is variously described in the ship registers as non-marine tradesman, shipbuilder, and merchant. However we describe him, he had a remarkable career as a shipbuilder supplying ships to fishermen, traders, merchants, and business firms. Certainly an enviable record.

There were several companies in this region which built ships, and there is no way to identify the individual shipbuilders. The first of these companies was the West Coast Export Co. Ltd., which rebuilt the 72-ton *Margaret Cavell* at Milltown in 1929. This vessel had been built at Grand Bank by Eli Harris in 1902 and had been named the *Sentinel.* It had already lasted for twenty-seven years and likely served for many more.

There was not another shipbuilding company in the area until Bay D'Espoir Enterprises Ltd. came into being at St. Alban's in 1973. This became a large operation as they constructed forty-two ships in seventeen years. The first thirty-three were wooden fishing vessels, and the last nine, constructed in 1988 and 1989, were steel fishing ships. Their wooden fishing ships were both one-masted and two-masted. These ranged in size between 7 and 52 tons. Their highliner years were 1987 (when they built four ships) and 1979, 1981, and 1989 (when they constructed six ships each year). Several of these ships were owned by the Fisheries Loan Board until they were sold to individual fishermen; it is possible that the entire operation was being financed by the Board.

Some of the more interesting ship names given by Bay D'Espoir Enterprises Ltd. were the 31-ton *Southern Brave* of 1974, the 23-ton *Island Mist* of 1975, the 30-ton *Atlantic Lady II* of 1979, the 30-ton *Silver Foam* of 1979, the 28-ton *Atlantic Mist* of 1979, the 28-ton *Atlantic Venture* of 1980, the 29-ton *North Queen* of 1980, the 25-ton *Strait's Star* of 1982, the 43-ton *Morning Rose* of 1985, the 26-ton *Rainbow Venture* of 1987, and their last wooden fishing ship, the 44-ton *Ocean's Joy*, of 1987 which was powered with a turbo-charged diesel engine.

In 1988 and 1989 Bay D'Espoir Enterprises produced nine steel fishing ships: the 52-ton *Cape Ryan*, the 53-ton Northern Enterprise, the 54-ton *Ocean Glidder*, the 55-ton *Atlantic Prince*, the 55-ton *Northern Voyager*, the 55-ton *Ashley & Brothers*, the 68-ton *Eastern Explorer*; the 74-ton *Miss Jacqueline IV*, and finally the 74-ton *Atlantic Sea Clipper*. The company must have folded after this, just three years before the imposition of the Cod Moratorium.

The T. J. Hardy Co. Ltd. of Port aux Basques, in 1978, rebuilt the 23-ton *Nina Maria* at Isle aux Morts. This vessel had been built in 1973 by Clarenville Dockyards & Shipbuilders Ltd. when it was registered at 28 tons.

Eric King's Fisheries Ltd. of Burnt Islands in 1986 rebuilt the 7-ton *Gloria & Junior II* at Isle aux Morts. This vessel had also been built by Clarenville Dockyards & Shipbuilders Ltd. in 1973.

And finally, Seacraft Ltd. of Hermitage built the 17-ton GRP-fishing vessel *Jamie & Sisters* in 1988. The name of the vessel was later changed to *Sea Venture.*

This ancient part of Newfoundland was comprised of settlers from England, Ireland, and France, the Mi"kmaq, and some residents of the nearby British maritime colonies, which made an interesting mix in population. Port aux Basques served as a kind of commercial hub both for this area and the west coast-southern section. The rich timber stands of the Bay D'Espoir area attracted the early French and English shipbuilders, but we know of their building feats only from about 1813. We can only speculate what may have been achieved earlier. The timber resources of La Poile Bay were fully exploited at later dates.

In this area we also see the emergence, in the late nineteenth and early twentieth centuries, of several shipbuilding families who supplied the needs of fishermen and merchants alike. During this period, the production of individual shipbuilders diminished sharply. The area also produced several men who crafted the famous three-masted vessels of the early twentieth century—men such as Matthew Nash, John Davidge, and Morgan Roberts. Merchants in this area also looked to the builders of Nova Scotia to supply many of their large cargo vessels, and the area produced some of the most amazing foreign-going captains of Newfoundland.

CHAPTER SIX

FORTUNE BAY

WHILE WE ARE FOLLOWING the somewhat arbitrary boundaries set by the Maritime Shipping Project at Memorial University in the 1950s, we will consider Fortune Bay to be that specific area from Coombe's Cove up into Fortune Bay and down to Point May on the Burin Peninsula. The *Encyclopedia of Newfoundland and Labrador* defines Fortune Bay somewhat differently as the fifty-six kilometre stretch from Point Crewe, on the Burin Peninsula, to Pass Island at the entrance to Hermitage Bay. Nevertheless, Fortune Bay is the first large discrete bay we have encountered since leaving White Bay in Chapter Two.

Basque and Portuguese fishermen may have been the first European visitors to Fortune Bay, and the name probably derived from the Portuguese word "fortuna" or a similar Basque word. The Basque fishing stations in this area were actually referred to as "Fortuna." "Y. Da fortuna" appeared on Pedro Reinel's map of 1505, and "Fortuna" appeared on Majollo's map of 1527. The rich fishing grounds off the south coast of Newfoundland soon attracted the French, Spanish, and English fishermen who all appear to have been frequenting the area from the 1500s or the 1600s. The earliest settlements were established by the French, and their census of 1687 shows Cap Negre with a population of seventy-two, Havre Bertrand with a population of thirty-six, Grand Banc (or Banq) with forty-five residents, and Baie de Fortune with seventy-two residents. The latter statistic may have included several tiny settlements in what we now know as Fortune Bay. What is now the town of Fortune was occupied by the Basques well before 1697.

By 1713 with the Treaty of Utrecht, the English were granted exclusive rights to the south coast, and since France was ceded sole rights to St. Pierre et Miquelon, the English settlers there moved to various places, mostly into Fortune Bay. When Capt. William Taverner concluded his survey of 1714 to 1718 he mentioned English settlers at Grand Bank, Fortune, Connaigre, and Corbin. When Capt. James Cook surveyed the south coast in the summers of 1763, 1765, and 1766 he mentioned settlers at Grand Bank and Fortune but also at St. Jacques, Harbour Breton, Boxey, Dawson's Cove, Pass Island, Lang de Surf, and Bande de la Rier (Belleoram). It was not until the conclusion of the Seven Year's War in 1763 that the English came in droves to the area, most of these from the West of England and the Channel Islands. Capt. Cook had also mentioned in his report that the Poole merchant firm of Clarke & Young had a branch in the area. Philip Nicolle & Co. had established a branch firm at Jersey Harbour about 1790, and Newman & Co. of London, which had a firm at St. Lawrence since about 1788, now expanded its operation into Harbour Breton by 1816 and into Gaultois by 1826. Other sources indicate that Newman & Co. had been established at Pushthrough as early as 1672 and by 1679 had expanded to Harbour Breton, Gaultois, and Hermitage.

The prosperous inshore fishery that developed during and after settlement led to the building of small ships called shallops which carried crews of two to five men. Note the small size of ships in the narrative that follows. An equally prosperous herring fishery developed in the second half of the nineteenth century and led to the lucrative sale of bait to both St. Pierre et Miquelon and to American fishermen. Many of these ships were less than 5 tons and many more less than 10 tons. While many open boats were being built for the fishery, only decked vessels were required to be registered.

The first reference found to the building of an open boat in Fortune Bay was in 1811. The first specific reference to a ship, a decked vessel, was in 1820 when John Wakely, planter of Grand Bank, built the 39-ton *Liberty* somewhere in Fortune Bay. In 1831 Wakely constructed the 22-ton *Branch* at Corbin, Fortune Bay (as opposed to Corbin Head, Placentia Bay). According to the records, he was also residing at Corbin. In 1838, when he constructed the 18-ton *Morning Star* somewhere in Fortune Bay, he was a merchant, but his place of residence is not given.

Records on other shipbuilding in Fortune Bay in the 1820s are sparse indeed.

John Gorman of Boxey built the 29-ton *Elizabeth* in 1820, and the vessel was lost at sea the next year. In 1820 also he "raised on" and decked the 27-ton *Thomas*, which had been built as an open boat somewhere in Fortune Bay in 1811. Gorman was a planter and master of this vessel.

John Patten of Fortune, in 1825, rebuilt and decked an open boat, which had been built at Fortune in 1816, and named it the *Indiana*; it was 23 tons. In 1825 this vessel was "transferred for debt to Charles Fox Bennett et al, merchants at St. John's." In 1829 this same vessel was owned by William Evans, merchant of Grand Bank and St. John's, "and was sold under a Deed of the Central Circuit Court of the Island." Patten bounced back from his indebtedness and in 1829 built the 17-ton *Annabella*, though he did not register it until 1832. In 1831 Patten bought the 26-ton *Alphaeus*, built in Hant's Harbour, Trinity Bay, in 1826. And in 1838 he was the builder of the 22-ton *Hero* which he sold to C. & T. Bennett of St. John's. Merchant and planter were again on good terms. Patten was very probably the rebuilder of the 38-ton *Rose* which had been built as an open boat in Fortune Bay in 1815 and "raised on and decked in the winter of 1826 at Fortune Bay." He probably also rebuilt the 32-ton *Vanguard* which had been "built as an open boat at Fortune Bay in 1814 and decked in 1828 and never before registered." This vessel also was rebuilt for William Evans.

There were several shipbuilders in this region in the 1830s, but most of them seem to have constructed only one or two ships. Jonathan Snook and James Hamlin of Fortune were co-builders of the 31-ton *Elizabeth* in 1830. Both men were planters. This vessel was lost at sea in 1843, but they appear not to have been owners of the vessel at that time. Snook alone had been the builder of the 24-ton *Exchange* in 1837. This vessel lasted for twenty-seven years. John B. Cox of Fortune built the 32-ton *Indian Lass* in 1833 and sold it to James MacBride, merchant at St. John's. Henry Nichols, planter at Grand Bank, crafted the 27-ton *Three Sisters* in 1833, and it was registered de novo in 1848. The 106-ton brigantine *Duck* was constructed somewhere in Fortune Bay in 1834, but it is impossible to determine the name of the builder or the building site. John Forsey, in 1834, was the builder of the 32-ton *Hester and Charlotte* somewhere in Fortune Bay, probably Grand Bank since he built other ships there later. Also in 1834 Joseph Bragg of Fortune Bay built the 27-ton *Thetis* for Robert Alsop Jr., merchant of St. John's. Samuel Cox, planter of Grand Bank, in 1835 decked an open boat which had been built in Fortune Bay in 1823. Wilson Hickman, also a planter at Grand Bank, built the 29-ton *Vigorous* there in 1835, and in 1837 he constructed the 23-ton *Charlotte*, which he sold the next year to a planter in Belleoram. James Porter Jr. of Bird Island constructed the 44-ton *Six Brothers* in 1836, and two of his partners were Thomas and William Porter. Benjamin Tibbo, planter of Fortune Bay, built the 21-ton *Owl* in 1836.

And in the 1840s, Nicodemus Crocker of Fortune constructed two ships: the 18-ton *Elizabeth* at Fortune in 1840 and the 17-ton *Three Brothers* in 1859. George Forsey of Grand Bank built the 29-ton *Aid* in 1842. George Henry Evans of Grand Bank fashioned the 40-ton *Terra Nova* in 1843, and his co-partner was Edward Evans. On May 1, 1848, Edward "transferred by Bill of Sale 32/64 shares to G. H. Evans." By this time George was a merchant at Lamaline and was master of the 48-ton *Sophia* which had been built at Lunenburg, Nova Scotia. Robert Lee of St. Jacques built the 22-ton *Mary Jane* in 1843, and when it was registered in 1846 it was owned by Charlotte Lee, probably Robert's widow, and Robert Kiddle was the master. At some point between 1846 and 1862 this small ship was involved in the seal fishery. And finally, in 1848 Andrew Bedford of Fortune "raised on" and decked the 16-ton *Kate* which had been built as an open boat at Placentia in 1842.

From this point onwards we will deal only with significant and prominent shipbuilders, primarily those who have constructed four or more ships. All others are listed in the Appendix to Chapter Six.

THE LAKE FAMILY

George Lake appears to have been the progenitor of the Lake family of Fortune. He was at Fortune in 1834 when he enlarged to 27 tons and decked an open boat which had been built at Burin in 1829 and named it *Cleopatra*. As a planter at Fortune in 1838, he constructed the 25-ton *John Lake*. This vessel was built upon and enlarged to 35 tons in 1848 and was lost at sea in 1872, having lasted for thirty-four years. In the same year that George Lake enlarged the *Cleopatra*, James Lake of Fortune crafted the 31-ton *Friendship*. George and James were very probably brothers, and they were fellow planters. This was very probably the James Lake who built the 17-ton *George Thomas* at Fortune in 1862.

George Lake Jr. constructed three ships at Fortune between 1853 and 1861. His first was the 25-ton *Sam Slick*. His second was the 20-ton *Friend* of 1860; and his last vessel was the 26-ton *Uncle Tom*. His partner was a fellow planter, William Lake.

George T. Lake (note the name of the ship *George Thomas* mentioned earlier) built at least three vessels at Fortune: the 15-ton *Mary Joyce* in 1876, the 48-ton *Grace Darling* in 1885, and the 33-ton *Nancy Jane* in 1893. George A. Lake was a partner with John E. Lake in the construction of the 39-ton *Ada* in 1885 and the 25-ton *Bessie Lake* in 1890, but George A. was the master builder in both cases. They were also partners in the construction of the 48-ton *Ethel May* in 1887, but this time John E. Lake was the builder. John E. would go on to become the most prominent of the Lake shipbuilders and businessmen. As early as 1885 John E. was a trader/dealer, and by 1890 he was a merchant.

John Lake Sr. was classified as a planter in 1858 when he crafted his first ship, the 35-ton *R. T. F.*, but when he built his second ship, the 42-ton *Britannia*, he was noted to be a merchant. His partner in this vessel was William P. Lake (almost certainly William Pittman Lake), whom we shall meet later. In 1874, when he built both the 35-ton *Charles* and the 24-ton *Philip*, John Sr. is again classified as a planter. In 1881 with the building of the 31-ton *Albert* and in 1884 with the building of the 58-ton *Sailors Home*, he is classified as a trader/dealer. It is impossible to explain these inconsistencies. The Customs' Returns state that John Lake was paid $171 of bounty.

Thomas E. Lake's 31-ton schooner *Sam Slick* of 1867 was named after George Lake Jr.'s vessel of the same name built in 1853. That vessel was broken up in 1865, so Thomas's vessel constructed two years later must have been named as a tribute to George who may have been his father. It was Thomas's only ship. Philip Lake may have been another son of John Lake Sr. since one of John's vessels had been named *Philip*. Philip built four vessels between 1867 and 1888. The first was the 23-ton *Wesley*, the second was the 36-ton *Lizzie A.* in 1871, the third was the 27-ton *Lizzie Lake* of 1874, and the last vessel was the 17-ton *Eliza*.

William Pittman Lake may have been yet another son of John Lake Sr. He was a partner with John Sr. in the 42-ton *Britannia* of 1868. It was not until 1873 that he struck out on his own and constructed his first of nine ships: the 17-ton *Glide*. His period of building lasted for at least twenty-three years, possibly twenty-eight years if he assisted his father in the construction of the *Britannia*. In 1874 William P. built two ships: the 24-ton *Sarah Jane* and the 20-ton *Clara*. This was followed in 1875 with the 19-ton *Clara* and the 16-ton *Maggie Lake* and in 1876 with the 22-ton *Mary*. William P. collected the government bounty of $117 on the three ships. There was a pause of eleven years before William built his next ship, but in the meantime

William became a trader/dealer along with Ann J. Tuck and John Tuck of Fortune who was the builder and master of the 75-ton *George A. Tuck* in 1886. Ann was very probably the wife of John Tuck, and the three would have been involved in coastal trading along the south coast through the 1880s and 1890s. Ann was probably a member of the Lake family. The vessel was lost at sea in 1895. William resumed building in 1887 with the 22-ton *Willie P. Lake*. In 1889 he constructed the 95-ton *Effie M. Lake* and completed his building career in 1895 with the 21-ton *Marion Lake*. William is variously described in the ship registers as planter, trader/dealer, merchant, and shipbuilder.

John E. Lake (mentioned earlier) became the most prominent shipbuilder in the Lake family and the preeminent builder and businessman of Fortune. John E. built his first ship in 1869—the 44-ton *Minnie A. Lake*. This was followed in 1873 by the 15-ton *Topsey*, in 1875 by the 28-ton *Bessie Steer*, in 1876 by the 16-ton *Caroline* and the 27-ton *Two Brothers*, in 1880 by the 19-ton *Eddie*, and in 1887 by the 48-ton *Ethel May*. Customs' Returns for 1875 and 1876 indicate that John E. collected the government bounty for the ships built in those years. During this period, John E. is described as a planter, a shipowner, a trader/dealer, and in 1887 as a merchant. There was then a pause for thirteen years, undoubtedly for the furtherance of his business interests, and in 1900 John E. rebuilt the 59-ton *May Belle* at Fortune; this vessel had been fashioned in 1878 by George Forsey Bell of Grand Bank. In the meantime, John E. had expanded his business interests to Bay D'Espoir when he started a sawmill in 1894 at Milltown. Lumber from this mill was being shipped to Fortune for shipbuilding and for other purposes. By 1907 the sawmill had been destroyed by fire twice but rebuilt and restarted. In 1908 John E., as a merchant, resumed shipbuilding with the 56-ton *Hubert Mack*, and in 1911 he built the small, 39-ton, three-masted *Dorothy Lake*, which had an elliptic stern, a straight-stem head, and two bulkheads. The vessel was also equipped with two gasoline motors which were British-built and supplied by the Bruce Stewart Co. of Charlottetown, Prince Edward Island. Fitted with a fifty-horse-power engine, the *Dorothy Lake* could make speeds of ten knots per hour. The vessel also carried a full set of sails. She was registered on October 11, 1911. After twelve years of service to the Lake firm, she was sold in 1923 to St. Pierre interests and was lost on the St. Pierre Banks later that same year.

John E. Lake's greatest shipbuilding feats were yet to come. In 1913 at Fortune he constructed the 171-ton, three-masted schooner *George Ewart*, which had an elliptic stern and a billet head. On September 12, 1917, the *George Ewart* was rammed by an iron ship while lying to in a severe storm off the coast of Gibraltar. The iron ship proceeded on its way. For three hours in the raging storm, the Newfoundland crew attempted to repair the damage but eventually had to abandon ship. Shortly afterwards, a German submarine surfaced nearby and determined that the vessel was sinking and so submerged again. Eleven hours later, the small open boat arrived on the Spanish coast and the crew learned that the submarine had torpedoed more than fourteen ships in the same area in the few preceding months. In 1917, John E. was the supervisor of construction for his masterpiece—the 203-ton, three-masted *John E.* or *John E. Lake* as she is called by both names in the records. She had a forecastle, store room, master's cabin, master's berth, officer's mess, mate's and steward's room, and pantry. She was registered on December 28, 1917. On March 19, 1918, twenty-two of the sixty-four shares were sold to G. M. Barr, merchant of St. John's, and three shares were sold to William Roberts, physician of St. John's. John P. Parker, in *Sails of the Maritimes*, asserts that J. Miles was the master builder of this vessel. We know that Joseph Miles was in Fortune in 1929 to rebuild the 70-ton *Rose L.* for John E. Lake, so it is likely that while John E. Lake was general supervisor of the construction, Joseph Miles was his master builder. The *John E.* was totally lost off the coast of Brazil, near Bahia (Salvador), on June 20, 1918, possibly carrying a load of salt.

John E. and George Lake (very probably George A. Lake) were of such stature that they employed other builders in Fortune to build ships for them. Some of these were Simon Noseworthy and Thomas Rogers in the 1880s, John Rogers in the 1890s, and John Tuck in the early 1900s.

James Major Lake built four vessels: two in 1875, the 34-ton *Mabel* and the 15-ton *Minnie Ella*, and two in 1876, the 19-ton *P. Rossier* and the 20-ton *Bertha*. He collected the government bounty of $147 on the last three vessels, and the bounty on the *Mabel* was paid to H. W. Le Messurier. William Edward Lake constructed only one ship, the 22-ton *Ellen* in 1880. This vessel must have been staunchly built since she lasted for forty-nine years. Philip E. Lake built two ships at Fortune, and they were ships of considerable size, very different from the small vessels constructed along the south coast. These were the 66-ton *Harry Lake* in 1889 and the 72-ton *Alice Lake* in 1896. Philip E. also was a merchant builder. Philip G. Lake of Fortune was a master mariner from Fortune who built only one ship, the 49-ton *Millie Lake* in 1908.

Jasper Lake of Fortune built the 26-ton *Lake George* in 1915 for merchant John E. Lake. His next two projects were enormous compared to this small vessel. He was the master builder for two large, three-masted schooners, and undoubtedly he was assisted in this venture by several of the Lake shipbuilders in Fortune. Otherwise it would be difficult to explain the transition from such a small ship to such large ships. The first of the three-masted vessels was the 150-ton *Russell Lake* in 1919, which was constructed for H. B. Clyde Lake and Harry Lake, merchants of Fortune. The vessel was registered on May 5, 1919. She lasted for ten years and was lost on March 16, 1929, when in gale force winds and driving snow she struck Small's Island near Burgeo. Five of her six crew members were lost. The second three-masted schooner for Jasper Lake was the 200-ton *Eileen Lake*, which must have been in the stocks at the same time as the *Russell Lake* because the construction date is given as 1919, but she was not registered until July 5, 1920. This vessel was also constructed for merchants H. B. Clyde Lake and Harry Lake. Author Robert C. Parsons gives a vivid description of her demise in January 1922. She was abandoned forty miles from Cape Race on a bitterly cold winter night. For four days and nights the crew in the ship's boat rowed towards land, one of the crew dying in the effort, the others cold, wet, and exhausted. On January 23, they were rescued by the Belgian steamer *Persian* and taken to Europe. Ben Lake of St. John's stated in 2009 that his grandfather, Jasper Lake, also built the 72-ton *Rameaux* at Milltown, Bay D'Espoir, in 1935, but the ship registers give the credit for that vessel to George Pevie of Milltown. It is probable that the two men were joint builders.

William Thomas Lake, son of Jasper Lake, was the last of the Lake shipbuilders of Fortune. His two ships were built at Milltown, Bay D'Espoir: the 89-ton *Tweedsmuir* in 1935 and the 87-ton *Howard & Cecil* in 1946. Named after his two sons, this last vessel was towed to Fortune and rigged there. In 1945 William Thomas Lake was at Fortune where he rebuilt the 144-ton *Mary Ruth* as a cargo vessel; this ship had been built in 1918 at Shelburne, Nova Scotia. In 1947 he was again at Fortune where he rebuilt the 108-ton schooner *Mary F. Hyde* which had been constructed at Allendale, Nova Scotia, in 1911.

Thus the 113-year reign of the Lake shipbuilders came to an end.

There were a number of prominent shipbuilders in the region from about 1834 to 1878, all of them worthy of mention.

Jasper Collier of Fortune constructed six ships between 1836 and 1868. Jasper was a planter, but he must have been building some of these ships for other planters and fishermen. They were mostly small ships, the smallest being the 15-ton *James* in 1867, and the largest was the 28-ton *Wanderer* in 1862. His first ship was the 19-ton *Resolution*, and his last ship was the 24-ton *Trial.*

William Henry Buffett was a planter from Grand Bank but built only two of his four ships there. The 25-ton *Alert* had been built as an open boat at Grand Bank in 1847, and William Henry rebuilt it there in 1853; he was very likely the original builder. Curiously he was living at Jersey Harbour in 1861 when he constructed the 34-ton *Flying Cloud.* In 1864 he was at Fortune and built the 50-ton *Friendship*; this ship lasted for twenty-one years. By 1876 William had returned to Grand Bank where he crafted the 26-ton *Idler* that year. For his efforts he collected the government bounty of $78.

THE CLUETT FAMILY

It is difficult to distinguish between John Cluett Sr. and John Cluett Jr. (John R. Cluett?) of Belleoram who together built fifteen ships between 1848 and 1911. John Cluett Sr. built his first ship in 1848—the 22-ton *Acorn.* John Cluett Jr. was master and owner of this vessel. John Cluett built the 34-ton *Ripple* in 1867, and his partners were Thomas and Aaron Cluett. He also built the 25-ton *Willie Ann Mary* in 1879, the 38-ton *Polly Dicks* in 1884, and the 34-ton *Rose of Sharon* in 1885. It is stated specifically in the records that John Sr. was the builder and his partners were John Cluett Jr., Isaac Cluett, Walter Cluett, and Alton Cluett. In 1886 John Cluett constructed the 40-ton *Winnie & Lillie.* Now here is a mystery. If John Jr. was old enough to be master and owner of the *Acorn* in 1848, he was about sixty years old in 1886 which means he may have been the builder of these last four ships and become the new John Sr. The new John Jr. would be John R. Cluett who begins building in 1897 and concludes in 1910.

Seven other Cluetts appear in the ship registers for Fortune Bay (once the name is spelled Clewett). Two of these are from the east side of Fortune Bay, three are given the general designator Fortune Bay, and three are noted to be from Belleoram. These three are Samuel Cluett who built the 27-ton *Phoebe L. Cluett* in 1884; Samuel's partner was William John Cluett, undoubtedly members of the same family. Also the Stephen V. Cluett who died at Belleoram on February 23, 1926, was very probably the Stephen Cluett who built the 29-ton *Arthur Levi* somewhere in Fortune Bay in 1871. All of the above built only one ship each. William L. H. Cluett of Belleoram was the builder of the 20-ton *Prima Donna* in 1884, and Sarah Cluett, his wife, became the new owner. She became a widow shortly after, and the vessel was broken up at Belleoram in 1915; presumably she was the owner for much of this period. Sarah must have been a noteworthy woman since another vessel owned by Arthur and Levi Cluett (her sons?) was given her name in the early 1900s.

John R. Cluett began his shipbuilding career with the modest 26-ton *Juanita*, and in 1899 he built the 80-ton *Grayling*. The next year he constructed the 55-ton *Bellona* for Mary Ann Brenton and Joseph Brenton of Belleoram. Joseph was a planter. Mary Ann's husband was Charles Brenton. Mary Ann held thirty-two of the sixty-four shares in the ship. I learned from interviews in Belleoram in 1993 that Mary Ann was very involved in the business end of the fishing venture; she and Charles were the parents of Rev. Jacob Brenton of St. John's. Also in 1900 John R. Cluett was the master builder of the 64-ton *Sparling*. In 1901 he constructed the 70-ton *Elector* for the Hollett family, merchants at Burin. Then in 1906 it was the 44-ton *Sir Douglas Haig* and in 1908 the 19-ton *Arkadian K.* Sometime in 1906 John R. took time off to travel to Grand Beach and built a small schooner (name unknown) for Thomas Foote of Grand Bank. The *Free Press* of June 23, 1907, writes, "Thomas Foote of Grand Bank has a fine schooner being built here by John Cluett of Belleoram…it is of 29 tons…the first built here. There is only enough water in the Gut to float a 30-ton schooner."

Then came John R. Cluett's masterpiece in 1909—the 132-ton tern schooner *John Harvey* for Charles J. Kearley, merchant at Belleoram, and George Kearley, master mariner, for whom John R. had built most of his ships. This vessel had an elliptic stern and two bulkheads, crew space in the forecastle, master's and mate's accommodations, ship's stores, bosun's locker, and chain locker. The vessel was registered on May 8, 1909, and the mortgage was held by John Harvey, merchant of St. John's. In 1912 at Quirpon the *John Harvey* was badly damaged but repaired to sail again; then she was totally lost in a severe winter storm in January 1917 while on the way home from Gloucester, Massachusetts. She was attempting to remain close to the Nova Scotia coast in order to avoid the Eastern Banks when she grounded near Gabarus, Cape Breton, and stuck fast. The crew was saved, but two crew members later died from exposure. This vessel is remembered in a well-known Newfoundland ballad, "Loss of the John Harvey." In 1910 John

R. Cluett concluded his shipbuilding career with the 52-ton *Lucy Kemp* for Hugh and Michael Reddy, merchants of Marystown.

Shipbuilding by the Cluetts of Belleoram appears to have been done through three generations by three different John Cluetts.

Arnold Cluett of Belleoram may have been a younger brother of John R. Cluett, but he was somewhat of an itinerant builder at the beginning and at the end. In 1903 at Stone's Cove he constructed the 41-ton *Columbine* for two fishermen. Then in 1908 at Harbour Breton he built the 25-ton *Mary Hearn* for John Smith, merchant of Harbour Breton. In 1909 and 1910 Arnold was at St. Jacques where he crafted the curiously-named, 48-ton *Armenia N'y* for merchant and master mariner George and Charles Kearley of Belleoram; this vessel was lost at sea in 1933, thus lasting twenty-four years. Also at St. Jacques, he constructed the 59-ton *Norman O.* for a local planter. And then he returned to Belleoram where in 1910 he built the 92-ton *Lillian O.* for the Kearleys.

In 1916 Arnold Cluett was at Summerside, Bay of Islands, where he began construction of the enormous 510-ton, three-masted schooner *Arnish*. And here the records become somewhat confusing. It appears that Arnold Cluett may have been working under the supervision of J. Herbert Carter, who very probably had a contract to construct the large vessel for merchants Flett & Tulk. Joseph Flett was a merchant at both St. George's and Curling, specializing in catching and curing herring. Tulk appears to have been a merchant at St. George's, though he may have had an earlier connection with Harbour Buffett. The vessel was completed in 1917 but was not registered until September 11, 1919. There were extreme difficulties involved in the launching of the vessel, and it was not until the second or third attempt that success was achieved. The *Arnish* was tragically lost near Fogo less than two months later on November 2, 1919.

THE FORSEY FAMILY

There were seven Forsey shipbuilders in Grand Bank between 1834 and 1883, but it is difficult to make connections between them. Most of these appear in the Appendix to this chapter as builders of two or three ships each. John Forsey of Fortune Bay, later located in Grand Bank, built the 34-ton *Hester and Charlotte* in 1834. George and Robert Forsey of Grand Bank were his partners when George constructed the 29-ton *Aid* in 1842. Robert and John Forsey were partners in 1862 when Robert built the 32-ton *Amelia*. This vessel was rebuilt at Grand Bank in 1878, but its final fate is unknown. And when Joshua Hickman Forsey crafted the 46-ton *Selina Forsey*, in 1883, his partners were John Forsey and John Hickman Forsey. For the *Selina Forsey*, Joshua collected a bounty of $138.

A best guess concludes the John Forsey who built the *Hester and Charlotte* in 1834 is the progenitor of the Forsey clan. He may have been the builder of the 23-ton *Union* in 1844 for Robert Forsey, the 18-ton *Welcome Return* in 1859, and the 32-ton *Amelia* in 1862, when again Robert Forsey is his partner, or this could have been a new John Forsey, perhaps John Jr. If so, then he may well be the John Forsey who is the builder of the 39-ton *Pointer* in 1874 and of the 32-ton *Sarah Joseph* in 1879. We know that John Forsey was a partner with John Hickman Forsey and Joshua Hickman Forsey who was the builder of the 46-ton *Selina Forsey* in 1883.

It may also be that John Forsey Jr. is the father of both John H. Forsey (H. for Hickman?) and James Forsey, whose claim to fame at Marystown was the building of six large, three-masted schooners from 1918 to 1920.

John H. Forsey was a builder of note before he constructed his first tern schooner. He built six substantial-sized ships and repaired one between 1902 and 1911. These were the 79-ton *Tubal Cain* in 1902, the 82-ton *Prospector* in 1905, the 96-ton *George Rose* in 1906, the 88-ton *Linda Tibbo* in 1907, the 117-ton *Grace Tibbo* in 1910, and the 108-ton *Lucy House* in 1911. In 1907 he went to Lamaline and repaired the *Hispianola*. Four of these ships were constructed for Simeon M. Tibbo and one for Charles Forward, merchants at Grand Bank. So Forsey was ready when the call came to begin the construction of three large, three-masted schooners for Aaron F. Buffett, merchant of Grand Bank. The construction of all three vessels was done at Stapleton's Point, Marystown, rather than at Grand Bank. This area of Marystown was used from at least 1910 to 1935 for construction of several bankers and the large tern schooners. G. & A. Buffett of Grand Bank had been operating out of Marystown from about 1912, exporting fish to Europe and South America. John Forsey's first ship was the 228-ton *Jean & Mary* in 1918. The records of construction are so similar to those followed by Eli Harris of Grand Bank that they were undoubtedly following very similar plans. This vessel was registered on September 9, 1918. She was lost on December 22, 1921, while being towed to Twillingate, heavily laden with coal, where she would pick up a load of fish for transport to Europe. In a sudden blinding snowstorm, she was detached from the tug and was "beat to pieces" on the northeast point of South Penguin Island. Construction of the 205-ton *Violet Buffett* must have begun immediately after the *Jean & Mary* as the new vessel was registered on September 13, 1919. She was returning from her maiden voyage to Cadiz, Spain, on February 27, 1920, undoubtedly laden with salt, when she drove ashore at Mortier Point near Marystown. Thankfully, the crew was rescued. John H. Forsey's last tern schooner was the 190-ton *Ria* which was registered on September 28, 1920. It would have taken at least nine or ten months to complete the construction of such large vessels. The move to Marystown was probably undertaken due to the limited suitable shore space at Grand Bank for the building of such large vessels at a time when Eli Harris was constructing large tern schooners for Samuel Harris Limited. For eleven years, the *Ria* fought Atlantic storms in many crossings, but in late September 1931, she left Cadiz, Spain, with a load of salt, and for fifty-four days fought the fury of Atlantic storms until all her canvas was stripped away and her planking was strained to the point where she began to leak. Supplies of food and water were soon exhausted and the crew began desperately burning whatever they could find, including their clothes, to attract the attention of vessels that may have been passing. Not until November 9 were they rescued, and then it was the SS *Aztec* on the way from England to Honduras. Each of the six crew members had been shipwrecked at least once before this harrowing experience.

What is most curious about James Forsey is he has no prior record of shipbuilding. He may have had considerable experience as a shipwright in the Grand Bank shipyards, probably with his brother John H. Forsey and possibly with Eli Harris in building the 195-ton, three-masted schooner *Roberta Ray* in 1917. He was now building at Marystown, so in concert with his brother—and very probably experienced shipwrights from Grand Bank, Garnish, and Marystown—he built three large tern schooners in 1918, 1919, and 1920. They were all built for the Marystown Trading Co. Ltd., which was owned by Samuel Harris Ltd. of Grand Bank, and they were all "Generals." First there was the 232-ton *General Byng* in 1918, and the specifications are again almost identical with those of his brother's ships. This vessel was registered on September 14, 1918. Because of uncertain "trade conditions," this vessel was lying up for two years and had a difficult voyage after that long period, but she recovered. Caught in heavy seas and high winds, she came to her end on March 9, 1928, on her way back from Grand Turk in the West Indies with a load of salt after lasting for ten years. The 188-ton *General Knox* must have been started as soon as the first ship was completed since she was registered on September 6, 1919. In a raging storm in the North Atlantic on her maiden voyage on October 14, 1919, her bow was split open, her masts were jarred, and she was entirely disabled. One crew member was washed overboard, and the others were picked up by the SS *Toronto* and taken to New York. The 184-ton *General Rawlinson* followed in 1920 and was registered on November 5 of that year. In January 1922 at Leixoes, near Oporto, Portugal, while a local tug was attaching towropes to tow the vessel upstream for the discharge of her cargo, a sudden storm with cross winds sprang up, and the vessel had to be moored quickly in an exposed area. Then a gale from the west-north-west struck, and the vessel was driven onto the rocks, the crew having no choice but to abandon her as she sank. For six months she lay in that position, and in July the Newfoundland crew raised her, and she was surveyed and condemned. Samuel Harris then sold her to Portuguese interests, and she was renamed *Pacos de Brando*; she then became one of the Great White Fleet which regularly visited Newfoundland. Capt. James Harris went aboard the vessel on the Grand Banks in the summer of 1949, twenty-nine years after she had been built. Her final fate cannot be determined. In the first record for James Forsey, it is stated that he was from Grand Bank; in the other two records, he is said to be a resident of Marystown. There seems to be little doubt that he was a son of John Forsey Jr.

Edward George Bennett of Fortune constructed four ships between 1856 and 1879 in a building career of twenty-four years. First there was the 23-ton *Olive Branch*; then the 33-ton *Fleetwing* in 1864, which was rebuilt at Musgravetown in 1880 and lasted well into the early 1900s; and then the 48-ton *Charles R. Ayre* in 1875. Customs' Returns for 1875 indicate that Bennett collected a government bounty of $96 for this vessel. Bennett concluded his building with the 29-ton *Hyacinth*.

Charles Bennett of Fortune was undoubtedly a brother of Edward George. His building career spanned the years 1855 to 1880. The 21-ton *United Brothers* was constructed at Fortune in 1855 and was lost on the Labrador coast in 1876, thus lasting for twenty-one years. His second ship was the 23-ton *Charles Gaetz* in 1863, and his third was the 16-ton *Minnie* in 1874. In 1880 Charles launched the 21-ton Dora E. and sold it to Benjamin and William Snelgrove, merchants of Catalina. This little vessel must have been sturdily-built since it was registered de novo in 1906 to last for several more years.

Morgan and George Foote of Grand Bank were undoubtedly brothers and may be considered together here. Note the name of George Foote's first ship, the 33-ton *Two Brothers* in 1858. Morgan was his partner and a fellow planter. George then built the 34-ton *Jane* in 1862. Morgan now becomes the master builder producing four ships between 1867 and 1884: first the 35-ton *J. B. Foote* and then the 56-ton *Jemy S. Foote* in 1873. This last vessel was lost at sea at Great Brehat in 1907, thus lasting twenty-four years. Then Morgan built the 15-ton *Smuggler* in 1880 and finished his building with the 62-ton *Clarence T. Foote.*

Thomas A. Hickman Sr. of Grand Bank crafted five ships between 1868 and 1885, all of them at Grand Bank. Thomas was a planter, but in one of the records he is called a fisherman. He began his building career with the 28-ton *Crystal Wave* and continued with the 39-ton *Annie Laurie* in 1870. In 1878 he built the 56-ton *Earnest J. S. Simms*, but Thomas was the sole owner of all three ships. Perhaps the last ship name was a tribute to a friend or a member of his wife's family. When Thomas constructed the 43-ton *Chester*, in 1881, his partners were James William Hickman and Joshua Hickman, and all three were classified as fishermen. This vessel was rebuilt at Grand Bank in 1898 by the famous George Forsey Bell to last several more years. Thomas concluded his career with the construction of the 79-ton *Bertha Iuni Hickman* in 1885.

Samuel Kelly Bell was a partner with his brother George Forsey Bell when they together built the 18-ton *Ortolan* at Grand Bank in 1873. Shortly after this, Samuel moved to St. John's and, according to the *Encyclopedia of Newfoundland and Labrador*, became "the leading shipwright in Newfoundland until his retirement" in 1917. George remained in Grand Bank and became a shipbuilder of note in the years from 1875 to 1911. He built a total of twenty-two ships and rebuilt one. His first solo effort was the 43-ton *Irene* built in 1875; the government bounty on this vessel was paid to R. Inkpen, the new owner. George's second ship was the 56-ton *May Belle* constructed in 1878 and rebuilt at Fortune by John E. Lake in 1900. His first of eight ships built for Samuel Harris Ltd. of Grand Bank was the 69-ton *Kitchener* in 1881. Others were the 71-ton *Mary F. Harris* in 1887, the 63-ton *Nellie* of 1902, the 73-ton *Garfield* of 1903, the 77-ton *Nellie Harris* of 1905, the 83-ton *Ruby* of 1906, the 87-ton *Blanche Forsey* of 1907, the 80-ton *Castle Carey* of 1911, and the 48-ton *Chester* rebuilt for Harris in 1898. George Bell also built for other merchant firms: for Thomas Foote of Grand Bank in 1886, the 78-ton *George Foote* and in 1909 the 24-ton *Maude Foote*; for George R. Forsey and Charles P. Forsey, the 69-ton *Grandbanker* in

1886; for John B. Foote, the 68-ton *Cora* in 1902; and for George A. Buffett, the 69-ton *Sunbeam* in1886, the 65-ton *Occident* in 1900, the 65-ton *Orion* in 1901, and the 74-ton *Pleiades* in 1903. Practically all his ships were of substantial size, the largest being 87 tons, and the smallest was his first, the 18-ton *Ortolan*. Many of the Grand Bank shipwrights learned their trade under the tutelage of this eminent shipbuilder.

ELI HARRIS OF GRAND BANK

Perhaps the preeminent shipbuilder of Grand Bank was the talented Eli Harris, brother of merchant Samuel Harris. It is not the number of ships that impress but the size of these vessels, particularly the tern schooners. Eli built his first vessel for his brother in 1885, and he did not begin small. This was the 71-ton *Emily M. Harris*, which lasted for thirty-four years and was broken up at Burin in 1919. Curiously, there was a pause of fifteen years before Eli's next project: the rebuilding and enlarging of the 73-ton *Kitchener* which had been built by George Forsey Bell at Grand Bank in 1881. Also in 1900 Eli built the 75-ton *Passport* for Thomas Foote, merchant at Grand Bank. In 1901 he rebuilt and enlarged the 66-ton *John B. Patten* which had been constructed in the United States in 1866. The 67-ton *Sentinel* came off the stocks in 1902 for Thomas Foote. This vessel was rebuilt at Milltown, Bay D'Espoir, in 1929 and registered de novo in 1930, having already lasted for twenty-eight years. The 94-ton *Bessie MacDonald* was built in 1909 for George C. Harris and the 60-ton *Wallie G.* in 1910 for his brother Samuel. When Eli visited St. John's in May 1912, the *Free Press* dubbed him "the well-known dory builder," so it must have been during this short pause in building that he developed and excelled at his new business.

Five years later Eli took up the mammoth challenge of constructing four large, three-masted schooners for Samuel Harris Ltd. in a span of four years. In 1917 it was the 195-ton *Roberta Ray*. It had an elliptical stern, two bulkheads, forecastle, cabin, captain's room, officer's mess room, water closet, and store room. It was registered on June 14, 1917, and the mortgage was secured by the Bank of Nova Scotia in Grand Bank. The *Roberta Ray* lasted for four years and was crushed in ice somewhere in the mid-Atlantic on March 12, 1921, but all crew members were rescued. In 1918 Eli Harris constructed the first of three "Generals," named after prominent military figures of World War I. The 195-ton *General Currie* appears to have been built from the exact plans of the *Roberta Ray*, but it had as additions a flag room, a pantry, and a lazarette. It was registered on September 13, 1918, and again the mortgage was secured by the Bank of Nova Scotia. After four years of carrying fish to European markets, this vessel drove ashore and was totally lost at Dog Island, St. Pierre, on March 30, 1922. The 177-ton *General Allenby* was crafted in 1919 and registered on September 12, 1919. The only apparent change from the others was the addition of a chain locker and the slightly reduced size of the vessel. On a stormy night in June 1922, she drove ashore near Ville de Conde while approaching Oporto, Portugal; the crew was rescued. The last of Eli's great vessels was the 202-ton *General Ironsides* of 1920 which was registered on September 24, 1920. Again the vessel seemed to be built on the same plans as the others, but this time additional crew space was provided. In 1920 the distinguished career of Eli Harris came to its conclusion after thirty-five years. The Harris firm was declared bankrupt in 1924, and the *General Ironsides* was sold by liquidators to Samuel Shaw, master mariner of Dartmouth, Nova Scotia. It was later sold to Portuguese interests, and her name was changed to *Nossa Senora Dos Anjos*.

THE 177-TON, THREE-MASTED SCHOONER *GENERAL ALLENBY* BEING LAUNCHED AT GRAND BANK ON AUGUST 20, 1919. THE MASTER BUILDER WAS ELI HARRIS.
(Photo used by permission of the Maritime History Archive, Memorial University of Newfoundland.)

There were four Tuck shipbuilders at Fortune between 1866 and 1905. They must surely have been of the same family. George Tuck, a planter, was probably the father of the clan and built two ships and rebuilt one: the 50-ton *Hiram* in 1872, and the 33-ton *Fred* in 1875, and the rebuilt and enlarged 37-ton *Hero* in 1880. Customs' Returns for 1876 indicate that George was paid a government bounty of $64 for the vessel *Fred*. In 1898 Fred Tuck, probably the son after whom George's third ship was named, built the 18-ton *Caroline* and sold it to Thomas Garland, merchant at Pushthrough. William Tuck, probably another son, built the 54-ton *Agro* in 1895. But it is John Tuck who excels in the shipbuilding trade. Between 1886 and 1903 he constructed eight ships and rebuilt one, several of them of substantial size. Curiously, his first ship was his largest, the 75-ton *George A. Tuck*, and probably a tribute to his father. Another curiosity about this ship is that John had two partners who are designated as trader/dealers: Ann J. Tuck, presumably his wife, and William P. Lake. This is undoubtedly William Pittman Lake, and it is quite possible that Ann was a member of the Lake family. As trader/dealers, they would have been doing coastal trading along the south coast, and Ann's job on board ship was very probably taking and handling the money. Ann had very likely continued this trade for nine years until the ship was lost at sea in 1895. In 1892 John constructed the 54-ton *Winnie F. Tuck* for Fred Tuck, fisherman and probably his brother. This vessel was lost at sea on the Labrador coast in 1919, thus lasting for twenty-seven years. After building the 47-ton *A. B. Morine* in 1899 for two mariners at Grand Bank, John Tuck began building for the Lake family of Fortune. In 1901 it was the 66-ton *Mack Lake* for John E. Lake; in 1902 it was the 70-ton *Stanley Mack Lake* for John E. and George Lake; and in 1903 it was the 46-ton *Bessie C. Lake* for Lake & Lake Bros. of Fortune. Thus John's shipbuilding career came to an end.

Wilson Grandy of Garnish constructed eight ships, five of these at Garnish and one each at Jacques Fontaine, Bay L'Argent, and Bay du Nord. For John B. Foote of Grand Bank, he built the 31-ton *Carrie Evelyn* in 1912. And for Samuel Harris of Grand Bank, he constructed the 42-ton *Millie Frances* in 1917, the 37-ton *Beatrice P.* in 1922, and the 36-ton *Maggie & Lucy* in 1923. In 1908 at Bay du Nord, he crafted the 40-ton *Chesley Lamb* for Denis and Thomas Burke, merchants at St. Jacques. He had constructed his first ship in 1886, the 26-ton *Hound*, when he was a fisherman, and his partner was

Thomas Grandy. His last ship, built in 1935, was his largest, the 50-ton *Andawaka*. His building career had spanned forty-nine years.

It is difficult to sort out the Miles family at the Head of Fortune Bay. William A. Miles built the 20-ton *Lizzie* somewhere in Fortune Bay in 1884 for the Burke family, merchants at St. Jacques. This little vessel was lost in 1917 near Grand Bank, so it lasted for thirty-three years. William's place of residence is not stated. In 1885 he constructed the 22-ton *Antelope* for the Burkes, but again only the general designator of Fortune Bay is given. When he built the 15-ton *Clyte* in 1893, his residence is stated as Little Bay. When William rebuilt the 27-ton *Clara* in 1897 at Little Bay East, Anna Vale McKenzie, married woman of St. John's, was the owner. This little vessel lasted for a remarkable thirty-six-plus years. Also in 1897 William constructed the 13-ton *Janet*. When he built the 19-ton *B. Hooke* in 1901, he was living at Little Bay, and his two partners were Joseph J. Miles and Thomas A. Miles, also of Little Bay, so it appears this had become their permanent home. The 28-ton *Kathleen Burke* was constructed at Terrenceville in 1908. William's last ship was his largest, the 38-ton *Morning Bloom*. Over a period of twenty-six years, he had constructed nine ships.

James Miles may have been a brother of William. The ship registers give him credit for only one ship: the 25-ton *Mary Ann*, which he built in 1887. He and his partner, Henry Loring, were fishermen, but their specific location in Fortune Bay is not given. Their little vessel was broken up in 1907 at Brig Bay on the Northern Peninsula, which suggests it was probably a Labrador fishing vessel. Abraham Miles of Fortune Bay built the 25-ton *Virginia* somewhere in Fortune Bay in 1901, and his partner was a trader at Rencontre. In 1906 Abraham constructed the 24-ton *Ada B. M.* at Terrenceville for St. John's merchant R. G. Rendell. We are not sure of Abraham's place of residence. John Miles of the "Head, Fortune Bay," built the 18-ton *Winona* at Bay du Nord in 1902. This vessel was rebuilt and enlarged in 1927, thus lasting for twenty-five-plus years.

The genealogical connection between the Miles family of the eastern side of Fortune Bay and the Pool's Cove area is uncertain, but both John Miles and George Joseph Miles built vessels at Bay du Nord in 1902. Were they the first residents of the family settled in this area? George Joseph Miles built the 25-ton *Preceptor* at Bay du Nord for Philip Farrell, fisherman of Bay du Nord (see the Farrell family of North Bay, La Poile Bay, in Chapter Five). Miles builds his next three ships at Pool's Cove: the 24-ton *Olive Daisy* in

1908, the 44-ton *T.J. Layman* in 1909, and then the 122-ton, three-masted schooner *Newton Stanley Lake* in 1919. This last vessel was constructed for John E. Lake, merchant of Fortune. Lake must have been using the same plans because this vessel too had an elliptic stern. She was registered on July 5, 1920. The *Newton Stanley Lake* was leaving Lisbon, Portugal, on January 6, 1921, undoubtedly with a load of salt, when she ran into a severe winter storm and began to leak badly. She was abandoned on January 19 after herculean pumping efforts failed. Her crew was picked up by the SS *Campbella*.

George Joseph Miles was living at Cinque Isles Bay in 1922 when he built the 6-ton *John Cunningham* for the Congregational Home Missionary Society Inc. of St. John's, which had established a very active church community at Pool's Cove. This little vessel was lost at Pool's Cove in 1950. In 1928 George Miles of Pool's Cove (undoubtedly the same man) rebuilt and enlarged to 33 tons the *Kathleen Burke* originally built by William A. Miles at Terrenceville in 1908 (another possible family connection?), and in 1929 he rebuilt the 23-ton, Nova Scotia-built vessel *Sadie Shirley*, and again his place of residence (place of building?) is given as Cinque Isles Bay. In 1933 Miles concluded his building career with the 41-ton *Joyce E. Shirley*. Here also his name is given in the record as George Miles.

And yet another mystery: Were George Joseph Miles and Joseph Miles the same man? One record states that Joseph Miles was a resident of Milltown, Bay D'Espoir, at some point. Was he simply there working for John E. Lake and his burgeoning timber industry? John P. Parker suggests, in *Sails of the Maritimes*, that J. Miles was the master builder of the 203-ton tern schooner *John E. Lake* at Fortune in 1917, in which case John E. Lake the merchant would have been the construction supervisor. At Milltown in 1920 Joseph Miles constructed the 148-ton tern schooner *Helen Jean* for three St. John's merchants. She may have been built under contract with John E. Lake for the new owners. We know for sure that Joseph Miles rebuilt the 70-ton *Rose L.* for Lake at Fortune in 1929. Perhaps a genealogist can eventually sort out the mystery.

George Brown built the first of five, possibly six, ships at Coombe's Cove in 1889: the 21-ton *Extenuate* for a fisherman of that place. His next five ships were constructed at Pool's Cove, so this was undoubtedly his place of residence. He built the 28-ton *Mary E.* in 1903. The St. John's newspaper *Free Press* on March 31, 1908, mentions that George Brown had "launched a schooner for Mr. Burdock and is putting another one up." One of these must have been the 35-ton *Edna Carter* which Brown launched sometime in 1908 for Ernest J. Burdock, merchant of Belleoram. Brown built his third ship for Mr. Burbock, the 23-ton *Gwennie Burdock*, also in 1908. In 1927 the *Mary E.* was enlarged to 31 tons and the name changed to *Calvin Lloyd*, but it cannot be determined if Brown did this work.

The shipbuilding career of Joseph Grandy of Garnish spanned thirty-two years, from 1897 to 1919. All his building was done at Garnish. He started with the modest 12-ton *Vera C.*, and did not build his second ship until 1907: this was the 25-ton *Garnishee* constructed for Samuel Harris, merchant of Grand Bank. All his subsequent ships were built for Harris, including the 51-ton *Barbara Dunford* of 1908, the 28-ton *Margaret Bartlett* also in 1908, the 49-ton *L. C. Norman* of 1909, the 55-ton *Jessie Grandy* of 1910, and the 33-ton *Elnor & Marion* of 1919. After twenty years of use, this last vessel was rebuilt and had a motor installed.

Joseph E. West of Garnish built five ships between 1898 and 1919 and rebuilt one in 1926. His first ship was the 24-ton *Lizzie Jane*, but he did not build another until 1911: the 27-ton *Nellie E.* for Grand Bank merchants Charles Forward and Felix Tibbo. This vessel was rebuilt in 1928 to last for several more years. His third vessel, the 39-ton *Lily B.*, was also constructed for Forward & Tibbo, and the date was 1916. In 1918 he built the 46-ton *Ethel & Nellie* for the Marsh family of Garnish, six of them fishermen. The 118-ton *Queenie B.* was his masterpiece, and his last ship was built in 1919 for George C. Harris, merchant of Grand Bank. West must have come out of retirement in 1926 to rebuild the 22-ton *Centurion*.

There were several Grandy shipbuilders at Garnish, but Cephas was chief among them. Cephas Grandy built eleven ships and rebuilt two others in the period 1928 to 1954. He began his building career by rebuilding two Nova Scotia-built ships: the 31-ton *Alice M.* in 1928 and the 23-ton *Pearl Marie* in 1929. The latter ship had been built at Tancook and was formerly called the *Petawawa*. Also in 1929 Grandy crafted his first ship: the 28-ton *Mary Solonge*. The 30-ton *Eva King* was constructed in 1934. In 1935 he also built two ships, but these were much larger: the 76-ton *Beatrice & Grace* and the 103-ton *Jean & Mona*. This latter ship was not registered until 1936, so the two vessels must have been built one after the other rather than in tandem. Grandy continued with the construction of large schooners, but the ship registers do not reveal for whom they were built. In 1939 he built the

118-ton *Harold Guy*. In 1941 he rebuilt the 152-ton *Josie & Phebe*, which had been constructed at Essex, Massachusetts. In 1943 it was the 144-ton *Garnish Queen*, and in 1946 it was the 177-ton *Daphne & Phyllis*, which was his last large vessel. This vessel had originally been schooner-rigged but was at some point changed to ketch-rigged. The others built from 1944 to 1954 ranged in size between 14 tons and 50 tons. His last ship constructed in 1954 was the 50-ton *Fortune Breeze*. All his building was done at Garnish. His vessels were so highly regarded that his clients came to him. The 14-ton *Eva Grace*, which Grandy constructed in 1936, was rebuilt and enlarged to 15 tons in 1960, thus lasting twenty-four-plus years.

William Rose of Belleoram constructed nine ships in twelve years, 1898 to 1909. His first ship was the 36-ton *Lizzie Nash*, and his second, in 1899, was the 45-ton *Marconi*. This vessel was fashioned for Caroline Critchell, widow of Matthew, and her two sons Uriah and James, planters of Belleoram. Caroline owned sixteen of the sixty-four shares. The vessel was lost at sea in the Strait of Belle Isle in 1921, which means it was very probably engaged in the Labrador fishery; it had lasted for twenty-two years. In 1902 William Rose built the 15-ton *Nyanza* for Josiah Rose, merchant, and Allan and Francis Rose, trader/dealers. The *Free Press* of February 12, 1907, states that William Rose was at Belleoram constructing a 50-ton schooner for Kearley Brothers. This is yet another indication that shipbuilders did not always receive the credit in the ship registers. William's last ship, the 89-ton *Allan F. Rose* was also built for Josiah. Josiah himself had built the 38-ton *Maggie* at Belleoram when he was a mariner, so Josiah and William Rose were probably brothers. The *Allan F. Rose* was acquired by George Penny of Ramea in 1920, and she was lost at sea in the North Atlantic in 1928, so she must have been used as a fish-carrier in the later years. Another of William's long-lasting ships was the 27-ton *Finance* constructed in 1905 and rebuilt in 1928 to last for several more years. William also built the 52-ton *Hilda & Elsie K.* in 1907 for Kearley Bros. at Belleoram and the 38-ton *Angela Marie* in 1908 for the Burke brothers, merchants at St. Jacques.

Considering the Grandy Bros. of Grand Bank and Fortune will be a fitting conclusion to this chapter as their accomplishments were considerable in the shipbuilding trade. The father of the clan was Stephen Leonard Grandy who took over dory building from Eli Harris, probably in the 1920s, and established a factory for the construction of dories. It is estimated that he and his sons built about 3000 of these for the Bank fishery and for other purposes.

The sons who took over the business were probably Roy and Leonard Grandy. They operated from 1947 to 1954 under the title of Grandy Brothers. In 1947 they rebuilt the 148-ton *Ronald George* as a cargo/fishing vessel. It had been built in Lunenburg in 1928. In 1949 they built the small, 8-ton cargo vessel *Gray*. This was followed in 1950 by the rebuilding of the 54-ton *Palfrey* originally constructed by the famous Thomas Palfrey at Placentia in 1924. This ship now became a passenger vessel and was renamed *Spencer II*. Then in 1951 they rebuilt the 149-ton *Harriet & Vivian* which had been built at Lunenburg in 1928. This now became a cargo vessel. The 39-ton *Mercedes* was constructed in 1952 for a mariner at English Harbour West and carried a Mortgage B of $20,135 and a Mortgage C of $7,000 with the Fisheries Loan Board. The next year it was the 46-ton fishing vessel *Fortuneday*, and in 1954 it was the 60-ton *Joyce & Doreen* for a mariner at Grand Bank. This vessel carried a Mortgage B of $17,800 and Mortgage C of $9,955.

The next nine ships appear in the ship registers under the personal names of the builders, Roy and Leonard Grandy, between 1956 and 1962. The 63-ton *Jean & Edith* was built in 1956, and the mortgage, which was taken on May 8, 1956, was discharged on January 2, 1958. These were prosperous fishing days. The Grandys built moderate-sized fishing vessels during this period—the 28-ton *Shirley Madonna* in 1957 and the 29-ton *Wayne Rover* of 1958—but they also built small fishing ships: the 11-ton *Lydia & Gordon* in 1961, the 17-ton *Satori* in 1961, and the 16-ton *Elaine & Gwendolyn* in 1962, all crafted at Fortune. There was also the 63-ton *Dorothea Reeves* built in 1959. In 1958 they constructed the 13-ton yacht *Pollylou*. And in 1959 they rebuilt and enlarged from 34 to 38 tons the *St. Barbe* constructed by Henry William Stone at Monroe, Trinity Bay, in 1937. This now became a patrol vessel.

The final phase of the Grandy business went under the title R. & L. Grandy Ltd. between 1964 and 1978. In 1962 they had made a permanent move to Fortune, and all the ships built up to 1978 were constructed at the new site. In 1964 they constructed the 246-ton cargo vessel *Frederick L. Blair* for the Island Shipping Co. Limited. From 1965 onward they constructed only wooden fishing vessels of small to moderate size. These were one-masted and two-masted vessels. Three ships were built in 1965: the 19-ton *Margie G.*, the 43-ton *Agnes & Brendan H.*, and the 19-ton *Phyllis Irene*. There were also three vessels built in 1966: the 14-ton *Loretta B.*, the 20-ton *Randy & Roddy*, and the 73-ton *Oderin*. Then followed two vessels with the unimaginative titles *F. L. B. 451* and *F. L. B. 452*, obviously constructed for the Fisheries Loan

Board but as yet without owners. Over the next eleven years, they built one or two ships per year, mostly of the small type. The 53-ton *Olga F. Deborah* was crafted in 1971, and their last ship, constructed in 1978, was the 12-ton *Brenda Lori.*

By way of summary, what is true of Fortune Bay is true of the entire south coast: the small size of so many of their fishing ships. In the early days, the favoured ship was the shallop for the inshore or near-shore fishery, and the popularity of the small decked vessel continued throughout this period. But in Grand Bank itself, even by the 1880s, the size of many ships increased to 71, 73, and 74 tons. Shipbuilders from Grand Bank, Fortune, and Garnish were also going to the head of Fortune Bay to build their ships rather than transporting the timber to their home communities. Shipbuilders at Garnish in particular were building ships for planters and fishermen at St. Jacques, Jacques Fontaine, Belleoram, and other communities. There was very little building of ships for St. John's merchants, just a few in the 1890s or in the early 1900s. It seems that Fortune Bay men preferred to do business with local merchants. It also was not uncommon along the south coast for fishermen not to register their small ships until ten, fifteen, even thirty-two years after they were built. Registration was required by the early 1800s, but south coast men took a relaxed attitude toward government regulations, and the government was obviously not breathing down their necks.

There was also an obvious decrease in shipbuilding by individual fishermen and planters after the early 1900s in this region. It is difficult to understand why. Perhaps planters and fishermen were buying their vessels from the professional shipbuilders of La Poile Bay and Bay D'Espoir: the Farrell family, the Kendall family, the Roberts family, the Strickland family, and closer to home, the Grandys of Garnish and the Cluetts of Belleoram.

CHAPTER SEVEN

PLACENTIA BAY

THIS "PLEASANT" BAY, IF indeed the origin of the name is the French *plaisance*, became one of the major shipbuilding regions of Newfoundland from the very beginning. But the Basques were here first. A map of 1504 titles Placentia Bay as "Insulace Corte Realis" and Kallard's map of 1547 shows "Isle de Plazienca," which means a harbour within a womb of hills. Placentia was visited by Sylvester Wyet in 1594, and he counted sixty vessels in the harbour.

Samuel de Champlain had suggested as early as 1603 that Plaisance should be established as a French colony, but it was not until 1632 that the English acknowledged French fishing rights in the area. All that was now needed was the compliance of the weak King Charles II of England, who was in effect a vassal of France, and he surrendered what some would call the best part of Newfoundland to the French, leaving the area from Cape Race to Cape Bonavista for the English. The town of Plaisance became the French capital of Newfoundland, and the first French settlers, about eighty in number, arrived with their new governor in 1662. Most of these settlers were apparently Basques or from St. Malo. Soon there were hundreds of soldiers and many more settlers, and the town was strongly fortified. D. W. Prowse asserts that "Placentia was the Gibraltar of North America," easily defended against intruders and never captured by the English. Its magnificent beaches were ideal for the drying of fish; it was practically free of ice every spring, so they could get their products to market more quickly; the surrounding sea provided abundant spring herring for bait; and its splendid harbour could accommodate many anchored ships. Baron Lahontan, in 1693, described the harbour as "the largest, the best and the most commodious, for it is surrounded by mountains, the anchorage marvellous, and in that...one could easily draw up eight hundred ships which the smallest cable would be sufficient to hold in any storm that could occur." The English Capt. Wheler reported in 1684 that the French at Placentia had only one ruined fort and very little ammunition, that the French fished mostly on the Banks, and that foreigners, including the English, could fish in the area "without disagreeing." Wheler also reported that in 1678 there had been "60 great ships" involved in the fishery, but that by 1684 there were only about thirty vessels and that some of the large ships carried as many as thirty-six guns. Undoubtedly many of these ships would have been built in Newfoundland.

The French were better at defense and military strategy than they were at fishing and building a prosperous trade and supply business. Complicating matters further was their dependence on faraway France for the bulk of their food and supplies, and settlers chafed under the arbitrary rule of their governors. In 1697 and again in 1705, the French brought in reinforcements to attack English settlements as far north as Trinity, and a year before the conclusion of the Seven Years' War, in 1762, they captured St. John's, which was soon taken back by English forces.

Burin harbour was being used by the Biscayans well before 1697. By the Treaty of Utrecht in 1713, Britain acquired Placentia and the southwest coast, and the French settlers at Placentia were transported to Cape Breton Island or Isle Royale as it was then known. After 1713, Britain appointed Capt. William Taverner of Trinity and Poole to do a survey of the south coast, which he concluded in 1718. The English then began to institute a successful trade and supply business which the French were never able to accomplish. A period of great prosperity followed. Prowse states that the Parliamentary Report of 1718 indicates that nearly all the Poole vessels engaged in the trade had been built in Newfoundland. This would have included other areas of the island such as Trinity, Harbour Grace, and Carbonear.

William Spurrier Sr., merchant of Poole, established his business on the west side of Placentia Bay probably as early as the 1750s and immediately began a shipbuilding enterprise at Ship Cove, Burin, as well as at Ship Cove, Oderin Island, and at St. Lawrence. Included amongst Spurrier's ships were several barques and brigs as well as smaller fishing vessels. One of these was the 320-ton *Upton*, but the date and place of building are unknown; it is known the firm had at least ten other ocean-going vessels. The business expanded to include operations at Mortier (today known as Marystown), St. Mary's, Isle Valen, and Bar Haven Island. In 1773 Spurrier was appointed Naval Officer for these areas. In 1800, Spurrier's son, William Jr., died, and William Sr. died in 1809, leaving the business to his son Christopher, who then appointed his nephew, William Jubber Spurrier, and his uncle, Peter Joliffe, to run the Newfoundland operation. Christopher's extravagant lifestyle and a few bad years in the Newfoundland fishery led to the bankruptcy of the firm in 1830.

Winterhousing was a common practice in coastal Newfoundland from the very beginning and up until at least the early 1900s, so it is instructive to read the comments of Rev. William Wilson, the Wesleyan missionary to Burin in 1827:

> The practice of going into the woods in the fall of the year, and continuing until the spring, for the purpose of getting firewood, building fishing boats, etc. is common in most parts of Newfoundland, but in Burin is carried to an extent that I have not seen in any other harbour in the Island.

He then mentions that this migration occurred in November, lasted for about five months, and involved about 300 people in winter quarters. So few people remained in Burin proper that the winter people built a tilt for the missionary and his family. Their winter quarters were "The Western Shore, about forty leagues distant Maltier Bay [Mortier?], about nine miles distant, and Freshwater Pond, about seven miles distant." Rev. Julian Morton, in Bonavista Bay in the early 1850s, stated their winter purpose as "to fell and square timbers, saw boards, cleave coopers' staves, make birch hoops for casks, or build boats."

On the other side of the Bay, at Placentia, and probably about the same time as William Spurrier located at Burin, Richard Welsh of New Ross, Ireland, set up his business and soon became one of the most prominent Newfoundland merchants of the eighteenth century. Little is known about Welsh, but much is known about his business successors. When Welsh and his son died, the business passed to his three daughters and their husbands: William Saunders, Peter Farrell, and Roger Sweetman. Saunders already had the experience of being a clerk under Richard Welsh and managed the

Placentia business, building it by 1786 into a firm with 50,000 pounds sterling invested in the fishery. Farrell already had extensive experience in the Newfoundland trade. The business soon expanded to include Paradise, Mortier (Marystown), Point Roche, and Point Verde. Saunders did not depend solely on the Old Country for supplies but traded with merchants in Quebec and New England. Roger Sweetman's son, Pierce, was by 1785 an assistant agent in the Placentia business, and his boss was Thomas Saunders, brother of William. Pierce Sweetman must have been a quick learner since by 1788 he was in charge of the Placentia business, sending crews out to cut timber, and during that winter he personally supervised the building of a large ocean-going vessel and the beginning of another ship. In the spring of 1789 Sweetman sent out nineteen shallops to the fishing grounds, each with a four or five man crew. The business focussed on shipments of dried cod to Spain, Portugal, and Italy, and in 1789 Sweetman sailed on one of his ships to Cadiz to improve relations with the firm's agents there. During this period, many Irish settlers were brought to Placentia and the surrounding area because Saunders especially was convinced that Irish labourers were much more productive than their English counterparts. When William Saunders died in 1788, the firm became known as Saunders & Sweetman, with Thomas Saunders as senior partner and director. Pierce Sweetman left Newfoundland in 1803, and his brother, Michael, was appointed to supervise the Placentia operation. Thomas Saunders died in 1808, and in 1813 Pierce's son, Roger Forstall Sweetman, was sent to Placentia to revitalize the trade, and he remained in Newfoundland until his death in 1862.

The Spurriers and the Sweetmans were heavily involved in the shipbuilding trade, but all of their ships would have been registered in England or Ireland before 1800. They did register ships in Newfoundland when registration was made mandatory about the turn of the century. Even then, however, registration was sporadic, and it is not until about 1818 that complete and fulsome records are found. By 1825 the records are quite accurate and reliable.

The earliest reference in the ship registers to a boat built in Placentia Bay was in 1804. It was built as an open boat at Burin in that year, and in 1819 it was repaired and decked there by George Lock "Ship Builder." It was named the *Hope* and was registered at 42 tons. In 1826 Edward Appleby was master of this vessel. George Lock was presumably the shipbuilder for the Spurrier merchant firm since, in 1820, he decked the 45-ton *Nancy* which had been built as an open boat at Burin in 1814. The owners of this vessel were Christopher Spurrier, William Jubber Spurrier, and Peter Joliffe, merchants of Poole. This is almost certainly the George Pitt Locke who in 1833 was master of the 75-ton *Brazilian Patriot* built at Petit de Grat, Nova Scotia, in 1827 and in 1829 was acquired by Nathaniel Woodley, merchant of St. John's. Nathaniel died that same year, and his extensive business was carried on until 1857 by his wife Elizabeth Woodley who owned four vessels during this period, including the *Brazilian Patriot*. The records show she loaned money, borrowed money, bought land, rented her properties, paid insurance on two houses, bought sails, rope, anchors and tarpaulins for her ships, paid for "curing fish," and exported fish cargoes on at least three foreign-going vessels.

The 42-ton *Rob Roy* was built as an open boat at Mortier Bay in 1808 and decked at St. John's in 1819. Neither the name of the builder nor the new owner is known. Joseph Pico, planter at Burin, in 1823 rebuilt the 28-ton *Swallow* which had been constructed as an open boat somewhere in Fortune Bay. In 1840 at Burin, Pico built the 47-ton *Amelia Jane* for Edward P. MacKay, merchant of Burin, and in 1850 it was transferred to Montreal where its new owner was Alexander McDonald, grocer, which reveals how far some ships travelled.

George Butler, at Mortier Bay in 1825, rebuilt and decked the *Jersey* which had been built in 1814; the new owner was John Marshall, planter of Burin. In 1827 Butler repaired and decked at Burin the 33-ton, curiously-named *Ate* which had been built as an open boat at Mortier Bay in 1815. As a planter at Burin, Butler was the owner of this vessel. The builder of the 48-ton *Hope* "of Cape Broyles" cannot be determined, nor is the name of the rebuilder in 1815 at Little Bay known. It was undoubtedly built many years before this date.

John Samstead of Placentia was almost certainly the shipbuilder for Roger Forstall Sweetman when in 1818 he constructed the 40-ton schooner *Hope* and in 1819 the 102-ton brig *Placentia* "of Waterford." Between 1819 and 1837, John Murphy of Burin crafted five ships at Burin and Merasheen. In 1819 he altered and decked at Burin the 61-ton *Susan* which had been constructed at Burin in 1814. He then went to Merasheen where in 1829 he built the 102-ton brig *Micromagus* for Sam Kough, a local merchant. He stayed in Merasheen and built the 55-ton *Isabella* for Kough in 1831. Returning to Burin, he constructed the 58-ton *Mary Jessie* in 1836 for Alexander Chambers, merchant, and in 1837 the 36-ton *Union* for Thomas

Adams, planter. Murphy had very probably been a builder for the Spurrier merchant firm. In fact, in 1819 he is accorded the formal title of "Ship Builder."

In 1825 at "Mortier Harbour," Walter Mullowney decked and rebuilt an open boat which had been constructed in Bay D'Espoir in 1820 and enlarged it to 50 tons. He named it *Billow*, and the new owner was Edward Morris, merchant of Burin.

James Stevens, in 1820 at Little Placentia (later Argentia), was the builder of the 53-ton *Priscilla* "of Poole," and the owners were George Neave and Richard Penney, merchants of Poole, and Thomas H. Brooking of St. John's, undoubtedly their local agent. It is difficult to know where to place John Rose since he was an itinerant shipbuilder who built only three ships in a thirty-seven-year period; the ship registers are not always complete. In 1820 at Mortier Bay, Rose constructed the 38-ton *Wimbourne* for Richard Daw, planter at Rock Harbour. This shows Rose's or Daw's connection to England. In 1832 Rose rebuilt at Barrier Island, Placentia Bay, the 64-ton *Orion* which had in 1814 been crafted as an open boat. It appears from the record that he may have been the original builder. And in 1851 at Placentia, Rose constructed for Roger F. Sweetman the 35-ton *Capelin*.

Henry and John Brown, planters at Oderin, built the 31-ton *Brothers* in 1822 but did not register the ship until 1829, an action not uncommon on the south coast. Also in 1822 Thomas Goddard Sr., planter of Burin, repaired and decked the 34-ton *Success* which had been built as an open boat in 1816. The fulsome record states that the ship was built "under the hand of Thos. Goddard, builder, planter, owner and master." Michael Brennan of Placentia built the 56-ton *Ceres* in 1823 for Roger F. Sweetman, merchant of Waterford and, of course, Placentia. This is now the third shipbuilder we have encountered for Sweetman in these early years.

Other occasional shipbuilders found in the records in the 1820s are the following: Thomas Connors of Mortier Bay, who in 1824 crafted the 35-ton *Cottage Maid*; James Rolls of Black River, who in 1826 built the 45-ton *Mary Ann*; Thomas Kinslaw of Merasheen, who in 1829 constructed the 35-ton *Fairy Queen* for St. John's merchants Bland, Kough & Henderson; and Thomas Leonard of Southern Harbour, who built the 26-ton *Freedom* in 1829 for his own work as a planter. The builder of the 40-ton *Martha* in 1826 at Argentia cannot be determined, but it is known that the ship was originally registered at Poole, England, and re-registered at St. John's in 1832.

The fourth shipbuilder for the Sweetmans encountered in the ship registers was Thomas Miller Senior. During the twenty years between 1826 and 1845, Miller built twelve ships; eight of these were for the Sweetmans, one for Timothy Hogan, merchant of St. John's, and two were owned jointly by Hogan and Sweetman. Sweetman was assigned two addresses: Placentia and Waterford, Ireland. In 1826 Miller constructed the 70-ton *Alert*; this was followed in 1827 by two vessels: the 75-ton *Leonard* and the 42-ton *Messenger*; in 1828 it was the 49-ton *Juliet* and in 1831 the 32-ton *Gleaner*, which in 1835 was sold to Michael Kirwan, planter at Burin. Miller's first four vessels were registered in the names of Pierce and Roger Sweetman; Pierce died in 1841. In 1832 Miller constructed the 132-ton brig *O'Connell* and in 1833 both the 69-ton *Erin* for Sweetman and the 32-ton *Mary* for Hogan. Then came Miller's largest vessel, the 164-ton brig *Juliet* for Sweetman in 1840. There had been a seven-year pause in his building career. In 1843 Miller fashioned the 13-ton *Midge* for F. L. Bradshaw, a professional at Placentia; it was very probably a pleasure boat. Miller completed his building career with the 37-ton *Reindeer* in 1844 and the 30-ton *Zephyr*, both ships jointly owned by Hogan and Sweetman. In 1847 Thomas Miller Sr. curiously went to the Bras d'Or Lakes in Nova Scotia and built the 49-ton *Rover*; he owned the ship jointly with his sons Patrick and Thomas Jr., who are noted in the record as shipbuilders. The vessel was registered at St. John's, and James Manuel II was master of the vessel in 1848. This is a curious situation indeed. Had the Millers moved permanently to Nova Scotia but retained their connection with Newfoundland through their ship? This cannot be known with certainty.

Practically all the shipbuilders of the 1830s in Placentia Bay have only one ship to their credit, so these are listed in the Appendix to Chapter Seven. We will deal here only with those who built two or more ships in this early period and also a few which are of particular interest.

William Jarvis of Flat Islands curiously built his first two ships at Salmonier, St. Mary's Bay: the 30-ton *Venus* in 1831 and the 36-ton *Greyhound* in 1834. Perhaps he was in the process of moving permanently to Placentia Bay. By 1841 he was settled at Flat Islands where he built his last ship: the 27-ton *Mary Ann*. Jarvis was a planter. Patrick Ennis of Merasheen built two ships there: the 22-ton *Liberty* in 1832 and the 22-ton *Fancy* in 1835. Patrick's brother, James, is credited with being the co-builder of the second ship. Isaac King Moore was a merchant builder who constructed two ships in the 1830s: first the 131-ton brig *John Stuart* in 1833 at Barren Island (Bar Haven) and then the 33-ton *African* in 1837 at Isle Valen. The *John Stuart* was registered de novo in 1834 and disappears from the record, so she was probably sold to a foreign owner. It is quite possible that Moore had been a shipbuilder for the Spurrier firm and remained in Newfoundland to become a merchant after the Spurriers went bankrupt in 1830. Both Bar Haven and Isle Valen had large establishments owned by the Spurrier firm.

John Hollett and Thomas Gilbert of Sound Island co-built the 33-ton *Friends* in 1834. This vessel was rebuilt and enlarged to 74 tons at Placentia by John's son Josiah in 1840. Father and son become partners from this date, and Josiah's building extends to 1871. It seems best to deal with his ships here. In 1843 Josiah builds the 33-ton *Rainbow*, and father and son are still partners. There is a pause in building and then in 1863 Josiah builds the 37-ton *Chase*; in 1869 the 18-ton *Brilliant*; and in 1871 the 19-ton *Fair Play*. In 1869 Josiah is called a merchant but in 1871 his status returns to that of planter.

In 1834 William, John, and Joseph Lockyer of Isle Valen "built upon and decked" the 35-ton *Three Brothers* which had been built as an open boat at Merasheen in 1826. They also gave the vessel its new name. In 1844 William Lockyer alone constructed the 20-ton *John*. The three brothers were planters. John and Daniel Corbin of Placentia co-built the 19-ton *Ellen* in 1837; as planters they shared the task of being masters of the vessel. In 1842 John Corbin alone built the 24-ton *Margaret* for William Corbin, fisherman at Placentia. The name Corbin originates from Guernsey in the Channel Islands. Was this the family that gave the name to Corbin on the Burin Peninsula?

There are three other vessels from the 1830s that are worthy of mention. Henry Benest of Burin, in 1835, "built upon and decked" an open boat, which had been crafted at Oderin in 1825, and gave it the awesome name *Spes Ultima*. The 59-ton *Mary Jessie* was built somewhere in Placentia Bay in 1836, but the name of the builder cannot be determined; a brief mention in the *Public Ledger* of 1842 is all the data we have. The third instance is of special interest: Catherine Brown, widow of Burin, owned sixteen of sixty-four shares in the 19-ton ship *Catherine* when it was built in 1837. Richard Brown, the shipbuilder, owned the other forty-eight shares. Richard had to take a mortgage on his shares; Catherine did not. They still owned the vessel in 1847.

There are a number of notable shipbuilders from this area during the 1840s. John Butcher of Long Island built the 28-ton *Brothers* in 1841 for his own use as a planter. When he constructed the 22-ton *Ring Dove* in 1853, his partners were fellow planters George and Thomas Butcher. When John built the 26-ton *Hope* in 1859, his partner was Jonathan Butcher. This vessel was wrecked at Trepassey in 1886, having lasted for twenty-seven years. It must be remembered that shipbuilders' names were omitted from the ship registers from 1854 to 1877, so we are now entering a period when we cannot know the full production of most shipbuilders.

Patrick Collins of Lamaline built two ships in the 1840s: the 24-ton *Mary* in 1841 and the 17-ton *Mary* in 1849. The first ship was probably lost and the same name given to the second ship (see John Collins later in this chapter). Thomas Rielly of Placentia built the 25-ton *Industry* there in 1841. In 1870 Thomas Rielly crafted the 27-ton *Mary Joseph*. Was this the same person? And if so, how many ships had he built between 1854 and 1869? The situation is similar with Herbert Whiffen of Harbour Buffett. As a mariner in 1841, he constructed the 28-ton *Ann*, and in 1873 as a trader/dealer he built the 43-ton *Walter*.

John Hodder of Rock Harbour rebuilt the 25-ton *William* in 1846, and later that same year at Mortier Bay, he built the 22-ton *Three Sisters* for John Stuart, merchant of St. John's. We see nothing more of Hodder's production until 1875 when he builds the 23-ton *Grand Master*. He probably fashioned another six or eight ships during that period.

John Collins of Lamaline was very probably a prolific shipbuilder, but the ship registers give him credit for only three ships. He constructed the 16-ton *Shamrock* in 1849, and the registers next credit him with the 34-ton *E. M. Collins* in 1879 when his partners are Patrick, Michael, David, and Thomas Collins, all of them fishermen and all given the status of shipbuilders. In fact, the ship register attributes the building to the "Collins Bros." and John Collins was master of the vessel. In 1900 John Collins built the 25-ton *Albatross* at Placentia. If this is the same man, his building career spanned fifty-two years, and he would undoubtedly have crafted many more ships than these.

For the 1850s we will deal in this narrative section only with those who have built three or more ships or builders who are of particular interest. For example, Edward Doran of Placentia was the fifth shipbuilder engaged by

Roger F. Sweetman, and Doran built the 21-ton *Fly* for Sweetman in 1853; Doran had also crafted the 31-ton *Martha* in 1851 at Great Barrisway. There are other examples of the notorious gap in the records: Richard Collett of Harbour Buffett built the 26-ton *Brothers* in 1850 and is not given credit for another until 1879 when he builds the 31-ton *Annie Laurie*; Thomas Dunphy of Placentia builds the 20-ton *Ranger* in 1856, and his next ship is the 23-ton *Mary* in 1873; Richard Purchase of Lamaline builds the 18-ton *Comet* in 1856, the 21-ton *Dove* in 1861, and the 33-ton *Wave* in 1870; and Richard Quirk of St. Lawrence builds the 30-ton *Anastine* in 1856 and the 59-ton *Saint John* in 1892. We can only guess at what their real production might have been.

The Haley brothers of Lamaline were builders from 1851 to 1883. James and Thomas Haley co-built the 22-ton *Priscilla Adelaide* in 1851 and then branched out on their own. Thomas Haley constructed the 20-ton *Diamond of the Deep* in 1861, the 27-ton *Uncle Con* in 1867, and the 26-ton *Resistance* in 1882 for Robert Haley, fisherman. James Haley is not given credit for any ships between 1852 and 1879 which almost exactly matches the period when shipbuilders' names were omitted from the registers. Then in 1880 he builds the 20-ton *Bessie* for Patrick Haley, fisherman, and in 1883 builds his largest vessel, the 44-ton *Louisa*, and his partner is Albert Haley, fisherman. Throughout the records, James is called a planter. Saul Bonnell of Lamaline starts his career in 1852 with the rebuilding of the 18-ton *Harriet* constructed as an open boat at Lamaline in 1844. His second ship, constructed in 1857, was the 18-ton *Margaret Ann*. By 1859 he had moved westward to La Poile where he built the 20-ton *Onward*.

There were few significant shipbuilders in the 1870s in Placentia Bay. One who is worthy of mention is Charles Tulk of Harbour Buffett who built the 41-ton *Garland* in 1877. Little is known about him, but he may have been a merchant at St. George's by 1917 and a partner with merchant Joseph Flett, both of whom are given credit in the ship registers for the construction of the three-masted vessel *Arnish* at Summerside in 1917. They may have simply been the owners while the actual construction was supervised by J. Herbert Carter of Curling, with the master builder being Arnold Cluett of Belleoram.

The Reeves family of St. Lawrence began their distinguished building career in 1877 when Thomas Reeves crafted the 19-ton *Challenge*. It was his only ship. In 1879 Robert Reeves built his first ship, the 22-ton *M. S. Brothers*, and his partners were fellow planters James, Giles, and Thomas Reeves. They were very probably brothers. Over a thirty-five-year period Robert built eight ships: the 26-ton *Contest* in 1883, the 30-ton *U & I* in 1888, the 30-ton *P. K. Jacobs* in 1900, the 37-ton *Swan* in 1903 at Epworth, the 18-ton *Alice Mack* in 1911, the 13-ton *F. E. Pike* in 1912, and the 59-ton *Creusa S. Giovannini* in 1914. Seven of his eight ships were built at St. Lawrence. Perhaps even more noteworthy than Robert's building production is the construction of the small 25-ton, three-masted vessel *Hilda G. Reeves* by younger brother Giles Reeves in 1916. Why such a small vessel was built with three masts is curious, yet John E. Lake of Fortune had built the 39-ton, three-masted *Dorothy Lake* in 1911; and the three-masted *Maid of the Grove*, built in Western Bay in 1817, was only 32 tons. After twenty years of service, the *Hilda G. Reeves* was blown out to sea and cast away in 1936 but salved and rebuilt that year by George King at Creston, converted to a two-masted vessel, and restored to the ship registry; the vessel was registered de novo in 1940 but cannot be traced beyond that date. It is possible the vessel was renamed. George King was not a prominent shipbuilder—he had constructed only one ship: the 17-ton *Maggie Dorcas* in 1910, but he did have related experience such as the rebuilding of the 33-ton *Nellie E.* in 1928 and the rebuilding of the 20-ton *Woodrow Wilson* in 1935. His work on rebuilding and restoring the three-masted *Hilda G. Reeves* after it was cast away and blown out to sea is worthy of mention.

Patrick Murphy appears to have begun his shipbuilding career at Little Placentia in 1872 with the 41-ton *Morning Star*. He built the 25-ton *St. Joseph* in 1883 at Placentia and the 26-ton *Willie A. M.* there in 1897. By 1908 Murphy was a merchant at Argentia where he constructed the 29-ton *Little Hudson*. He was one of many merchant shipbuilders.

There were four significant shipbuilders in Placentia Bay whose building began in the 1880s. Gabriel Gilbert was somewhat of an itinerant builder. His first ship, the 29-ton *Stella Maris*, was built at Oderin in 1880. It cannot be determined where the 29-ton *Katie Bloomer* was built in 1885, but the new owner was a planter at Trepassey, so Gilbert may have done the construction there. The 27-ton *Flora* was fashioned at Flat Islands in 1886, the *May Power* was built in 1889 in Placentia Sound, and the 20-ton *Lily Albert* of 1891 was probably constructed at Flat Islands. Another noteworthy builder during this period was Benjamin Foote. The records on his production are incomplete and confusing. He began his building career in 1888 by building the 31-ton *Village Belle* at Ragged Islands. He may have built a second vessel that same year which was rebuilt in 1931 and lasted for an amazing sixty-seven years. In 1890 Foote built the 33-ton *Katie May* at Red Island. In 1900 he was living at Tack's Beach and built a 25-ton vessel which was rebuilt in 1924 and lasted for forty-four-plus years. In 1903 he was at Isle Valen where he built the 24-ton *King Edward VII*, and in 1911 at Ragged Islands he crafted the 29-ton *Albert C. Best*. The ship registers in 1931 state that Foote was living at Harbour Buffett. He had been a true itinerant shipbuilder. As was John Dunphy who constructed five ships in four different places between 1882 and 1903. His building career began at Placentia with the 25-ton *Mary Joseph*, and in 1889 Dunphy was at Paradise to construct the 22-ton *Minnie*; in 1895 he was at Petit Forte to build the 27-ton *Mary Nagle* which had an engine installed forty-two years later to last for several more years. And in 1898 Dunphy went to Little Placentia to build the 27-ton *J. K. Dunphy*. He concluded his building career in 1903 at Paradise where he constructed the 21-ton *Susie & Lizzie*. The only way to explain the mystery of the fourth noteworthy builder is to assume there were two men, father and son, with similar names. James Brown built the 23-ton *Royal Arch* at Ragged Islands in 1889, and his partner was Samuel Brown, probably his son. Samuel James Brown is the builder of the 31-ton *Lottie M. Dunford* in 1923, the 26-ton *Bertha Kirby* at Harbour Buffett in 1926, the rebuilder of the 23-ton *Martha E.* at Tack's Beach in 1926, the rebuilder of the 32-ton *Adele* at Kingwell in 1929, and the builder of the 66-ton *Cyril & Frank* at Tack's Beach in 1935.

The first significant shipbuilder of the twentieth century was John Drake of Oderin. Drake built four ships between 1900 and 1923. He first built the 21-ton *Pioneer* at Oderin, then the 38-ton *Western Annie* in 1913 at Rushoon, and the 28-ton *A. B. Flynn* in 1914 at Petit Forte; his last ship was the 24-ton *Lucy M. Drake* constructed at Oderin in 1923. The *Western Annie* was rebuilt after lasting sixteen years and the *Lucy M. Drake*, which was co-owned with Clement Drake, was condemned in 1951, presumably after twenty-eight years of use as a fishing vessel.

THOMAS PALFREY

Early twentieth century shipbuilding in Placentia Bay belonged to Thomas Palfrey. His distinguished career lasted from 1899 to 1936, and during this period he constructed twenty-three ships and rebuilt two others. In the 1940s he served at Clarenville as one of the master builders of the Splinter Fleet.

His career began in 1899 with the construction of the 25-ton *Francis L. Power* at Placentia. This ship was lost at sea after twenty-eight years of use. In 1901 Palfrey crafted the 26-ton *Jubilee*, also at Placentia. In 1907 he was at Marystown to build the 40-ton *Mary*, and this vessel was rebuilt in 1930 to last for several more years, testimony to the skill of the builder. The next year, Palfrey journeyed to Ramea where he constructed three vessels for George Penny, merchant of that place: the 41-ton *Little Jewel* in 1907, the 57-ton *Vignette* in 1908, and the 35-ton *Maple* in 1909. As he completed his efforts in Ramea, a local correspondent to the St. John's newspaper said of Palfrey that he was "credited with being one of the most successful builders in Newfoundland." In 1911 he returned to Marystown where he rebuilt the 71-ton *Edith V. Gretta* which had been built in 1888 at Grand Bank by James Belbin, and later that same year Palfrey journeyed to Burgeo where he constructed he 59-ton *Lucid* for George Penny. Staying in the area, Palfrey built the 34-ton *Anita C.* in 1914 at Grand Bruit for John P. Chetwynd, merchant of that place, and the same year, at Ramea, the 42-ton *Maris P.* for George Penny.

Palfrey had built nine ships and rebuilt one, ships ranging in size between 25 and 71 tons, before he began construction of the large ships and particularly the three-masted (tern) schooners. His first was the three-masted, 296-ton *Elizabeth Fearn* in 1917 at Placentia for George C. Fearn, merchant of Placentia and St. John's and owner of the Fearn Co. Shipyard at Placentia. This vessel easily passed the British Lloyd's requirements at the time of her construction and was at that time valued at $60,000. On a return voyage from Bahia, she lost most of her canvas and drove ashore at Quidi Vidi, near St. John's, on February 12, 1921. She carried $40,000 insurance. All attempts to rescue her were in vain, but some of her canvas, rigging, and spars were saved before she sank, as well as the captain's log, charts, and sextant. Palfrey, in 1918, constructed the two-masted, 103-ton *Cecil Fearn* and the three-masted, 364-ton *Herbert Fearn* in 1919. An American steamer collided with the *Herbert Fearn* in late October 1919 in the English Channel, and the American captain admitted fault; the schooner was badly damaged but was repaired at Plymouth. Her name was changed to *Jean F. McCrae*, when she was bought by R. D. McCrae of Harbour Grace, and then to *Mildred Pauline*, in 1940, when she was purchased by the Sainthill merchant firm of North Sydney; she was then transferred to the Nova Scotia registry. The vessel disappeared while on the way from Barbados to Nova Scotia in 1942, and it is believed she was the victim of a German submarine. She had lasted for twenty-three years. In 1920 Palfrey constructed the three-masted, 130-ton *Mollie Fearn*. This vessel also had a long life of thirty years. Her name was changed to *Tishy* in 1936 when she was sold to John Quinton of Red Cliff. She was at that time converted to a two-masted ship and fitted with an engine. In 1950 she was wrecked at Shambler's Cove.

From 1922 onwards, Palfrey was building at Placentia for local merchants Patrick, James, and John Kemp and for merchants of St. John's. In 1922 he constructed the 34-ton *Brian & Anne* and the 22-ton *Magdalene Kemp* for the Kemps, and in 1923 and 1924 he built the 45-ton *Anna-Agatha* and the 54-ton *Palfrey* for W. S. Monroe of St. John's. In 1926 it was the 32-ton *Harold M. Flynn* for James Baird Ltd. of St. John's. Also in 1926 he rebuilt the 33-ton *Samoset* which had been built in 1898 at Gloucester, Massachusetts. The year 1935 was a banner period for Palfrey as he built five ships: the 76-ton *Alice & Adelaide*, the 38-ton *Minnie Tobin*, the 22-ton *Annie Hayes*, the 92-ton *Lindy C. Barbour*, and the 25-ton *Nellie Murphy*. The *Lindy C. Barbour* was constructed at Harbour Buffett.

From 1944 to 1947 Thomas Palfrey was one of the master carpenters in the construction of the Splinter Fleet at Clarenville. These were ten wooden vessels of 500 tons each which were commissioned by the Department of Natural Resources. These are dealt with in detail in Chapter Three of Volume One. Thus came to an end the remarkable building career of Thomas Palfrey.

☸

Thomas P. Kemp of Jerseyside, Placentia Bay, was the grandson of Patrick Kemp who in 1850 had begun a ferry service across the Placentia Gut in a boat called the *Black Punt*, which he had probably built himself. Thomas was born in 1880 and also became a shipbuilder. When the merchant George C. Fearn returned to England, Kemp managed the operation and later changed the name to T. P. Kemp & Co., and his three brothers—Patrick, James, and John Kemp—were his partners. When the Kemp business failed sometime in the 1920s, Kemp once again became a shipbuilder. He is given credit in the ship registers for only three vessels: the 36-ton *Alice Brydle* built in 1921 but not registered until 1925; the 64-ton *Queen May* built in 1923; and the 42-ton *Mary Kemp* built in 1935. John P. Parker gives T. Kemp credit for building, in 1917, the three-masted, 296-ton *Elizabeth Fearn*, which as we have seen already was attributed to Thomas Palfrey. Since Thomas Kemp may have been involved at this point in managing the Fearn firm, he and Palfrey very probably collaborated on more than one of these vessels.

There were several members of the Hodder family of Marystown-Creston who were shipbuilders; the two most prominent of these were James and Thomas J. Hodder. James Hodder began building in 1902 with the 20-ton *A. B. Francis*. He was then living at Fox Harbour and built the ship at Fortune. In 1913 he constructed the 18-ton *Ida Pearl* at Mortier Bay. In 1926 he rebuilt the 12-ton *Stanley Eugene* at Creston. James and William Hodder built the 134-ton *Beatrice Vivian* at Burin in 1935, and in 1937 James built the 25-ton *Elsie and Susie* at Creston. It was not uncommon for a building career to span thirty-five years, but the fact that, for this last ship, the builder's name is given as James C. Hodder may mean that two men are involved here, perhaps father and son, and the last two ships may be the work of the son.

Thomas J. Hodder of Marystown constructed twelve ships and rebuilt four others between 1899 and 1953, a building career spanning fifty-four years. The 18-ton *Winnie Elizabeth* was crafted at Marystown as was the 23-ton *J. R. Rogers* in 1910. By 1925 Thomas was settled at Creston and rebuilt there the 20-ton *Gordon Stanley* in 1925. He then constructed two ships for the Hayden family of fishermen at Petit Forte, and went to Great Burin in 1927 to fashion the 21-ton *Zipalong*. At Port au Bras in 1928, he rebuilt the 32-ton Finance and, in 1933, built three 19-ton ships with the unromantic names *Customs no. 1*, *no. 2*, and *no. 3*. His building and rebuilding continued throughout the 1930s and 1940s, and in 1949 Hodder rebuilt the 101-ton *Retlas* which had been built in Dayspring, Nova Scotia, in 1939, and he renamed it the *Thomas J. Hodder*. Also in 1949 Hodder built the 235-ton schooner *Alberto Wareham* for Freeman Wareham of Alberto Fisheries Ltd. of Spencer's Cove. Freeman Wareham purchased much of the material for his new vessel from a ship that had been wrecked near St. Shott's. After interviewing one of the men who was a shipwright on the *Alberto Wareham*, Robert C. Parsons explains that the schooner "was over-built...was 26 inches deeper than it should have been...[and] any fault in construction came from an overzealous owner, not the master shipwright." This was said by one source to be the last Newfoundland schooner to be built and also to be "the largest wooden fishing schooner ever to be constructed on the Atlantic seaboard." She was constructed for the Banks fishery but was used primarily in the coastal trade. Hodder completed his building career in 1953 with the 63-ton *Veteran Explorer*.

William Wakely of Haystack is credited in the ship registers for building only one ship, but the *Free Press* of June 1907 reported that he had "constructed several small schooners." In fact, the newspaper gave a full description of Wakely's *Pandora*, which he had just sailed into St. John's:

> The ketch schooner *Pandora* built at Haystack by William Wakely, her owner, is one of the prettiest schooners to come from Placentia Bay. She is of Mr. Wakely's own design (and) is a departure from the old model. One prominent feature is the shape of the hull aft; she is hollowed on each side so as not to cause so much suction from 'dead water' as the ordinary craft, a fact that adds considerably to her sailing power. The builder has constructed several small schooners of the same rig, all of which have been proven to be excellent sailers and staunch sea boats. The *Pandora* is fitted with Angel's Patent pump, wheel and steering gear, which worked splendid on the trial trip. She measures something over 40 tons.

Thomas Wakely, merchant of Haystack, is given credit for building the 27-ton *Regiment* in 1915, but it could be that William was the builder of this one and that Thomas was his brother.

George V. Peavie of St. Joseph's was an itinerant shipbuilder and constructed twelve ships between 1909 and 1947 in seven different places. He is not to be confused with George Pevie of Milltown, Bay D'Espoir. Peavie began his building career at Marystown with the 48-ton *Western Queen* and the next year rebuilt a small 17-ton ship. In 1911 he was at St. Joseph's to craft the 21-ton *H. M. Dibben*, and in 1917 he went to Rock Harbour to construct the 28-ton *H. A. Brown*. There followed the 33-ton *Jessie Power* in 1925 at Harbour Buffett, the rebuilding of the 24-ton *A. A. Kelly* at Marystown the same year, and the 32-ton *M. & J. Hayden* at St. Joseph's in 1926. In 1933 Peavie was at Fox Harbour where he built the 35-ton *E. & Mary King*, and in 1934 he was at Tack's Beach to construct the 38-ton *Ada & Maud Best*. He returned to St. Joseph's in 1946 to build the 13-ton *Ian Maxwell* and concluded his building career in 1947 at Burnt Island with the 21-ton *Eric & Beatrice*.

Edward Mitchell constructed seven ships and rebuilt one between1911 and 1928, and all his building was done at Marystown. His first ship was the 24-ton *Grace Bell*, and this was followed in 1916 with the construction of two ships: the 23-ton *Bridie Withers* for the Marystown Trading Co. and the 29-ton *Anna M. Walsh* for George A. Buffett, merchant at Grand Bank. In 1918 Mitchell built his second ship for the Marystown Trading Co.—the 48-ton *Catherine B.* He constructed two more ships and rebuilt another, finishing up with the 30-ton *Gonzalo* in 1928.

William Williams of Tack's Beach built only two ships: the 26-ton *Willie S.* in 1911 and the 19-ton *Ella C. Travers* at Brewley in 1941, but in between these two dates he rebuilt four others: the 20-ton *Evelyn* in 1927, the 13-ton *Mary Williams* in 1930, the 15-ton *Bella Blanche* also in 1930, and the 32-ton *Mary V. Brown* in 1934. There were many builders who specialized in rebuilding, and Williams was one of these.

Edward Spencer of Marystown began his building career with the 19-ton *Woodrow Wilson* in 1912. Like William Williams, he became more of a rebuilder than a builder as evidenced by his next three ships: rebuilding the 21-ton *Celestina* in 1914, the 23-ton *Margaret R. Power* in 1917 at Mooring Cove, Mortier Bay, and the 32-ton *Bellaventure* in 1925. In 1926 at Creston, Spencer built his last ship, the 38-ton *Ruby Wiscombe*, for merchant James W. Wiscombe.

Joseph Matterface, fisherman of Boat Harbour, was probably the son of Charles who is listed in the *Lovell Directory* of 1871 at Boat Harbour. Joseph crafted five ships at Boat Harbour between 1915 and 1932. He began with the 19-ton *Joseph M.* which lasted for a remarkable thirty-seven years and was lost at sea in Fortune Bay in 1952. Joseph's next ship was the 27-ton *E. W. C. Lockyer* which was built in 1921 for a local planter. There followed the 30-ton *Lily and Jessie* in 1926, the 13-ton *Myrtle and Gerald* in 1928, and his last ship, the 25-ton *George and Nelson*, in 1932. The *Myrtle and Gerald* lasted for twenty-two years and was condemned at Jean de Bay in 1950. Joseph constructed small, sturdy vessels.

William Brown of Marystown and Creston was an itinerant builder. He began his career with the construction of the 17-ton *Mayor's Pride* for the Marystown Trading Co. in 1915. The next year he rebuilt the 34-ton *Harvey & Maud*. This vessel was for a brief time in 1928 owned by Mary Ann Bennett, widow of Port au Bras. In 1917 Brown built the 35-ton *B. C. McGrath*, in 1920 the 26-ton *Annie Gover*, and in 1926 at Burin he built the 37-ton *James Young*. He returned to Burin in 1928 to rebuild the 21-ton *Ida Pearl* and went to Boat Harbour later that year to fashion the 15-ton *J. W. Brown*. After a pause of fifteen years, Brown was in Brookside (Bay de L'Eau) where he constructed the 38-ton *Ernest Baxter*. In 1959 he was living at Tack's Beach but went to Woody Island and rebuilt the 27-ton *James & Lucy*. In a building career spanning forty-five years, Brown had built eight ships and rebuilt two.

It was to Stapleton's Point in Marystown that the Forsey brothers of Grand Bank came in 1918 to begin construction of six large tern schooners for Grand Bank merchants. John H. Forsey built the 228-ton *Jean and Mary* in 1918, the 205-ton *Violet Buffett* in 1919, and the 190-ton *Ria* in 1920—all for G. & A. Buffett. James Forsey constructed three terns for the Marystown Trading Co. owned by Samuel Harris Ltd. of Grand Bank: the 232-ton *General Byng* in 1919, the 188-ton *General Rawlinson* in 1920, and the 184-ton *General Ironsides* in 1920. This was very probably a cooperative effort between the brothers with a bit of competition on the side.

Patrick Norman of Long Harbour, Placentia Bay, constructed four ships, and rebuilt one other, in the years between 1926 and 1942. All his building was done at Long Harbour. His first ship was the 33-ton *Catherine Bruce* constructed for Alberto Wareham, merchant at Harbour Buffett. In 1928 he rebuilt, and undoubtedly renamed, the 33-ton *Lizzie M. Bruce* for his own use. There followed the 32-ton *Imelda & Walter* in 1931, the 35-ton *Mary & Catherine Bruce* in 1935, and the 24-ton *E. F. J. Power* in 1942.

John Wareham of Kingwell constructed two ships and rebuilt four others between 1926 and 1941. He began by rebuilding the 37-ton *Village Bride* in 1926 for Alberto Wareham, merchant of Harbour Buffett. In 1927 he rebuilt the 31-ton *Mary E.* at Sound Island and renamed it *Calvin Lloyd*. In 1928 he built the 17-ton *Walter T.* at Kingwell. In 1930 and 1932 he rebuilt at Kingwell the 48-ton *Mistletoe* and the 16-ton *Gimbal* respectively. Both of these vessels lasted for well over thirty years. In 1941 Wareham concluded his building career by constructing the 27-ton *Ellen & Bernard* at Red Island.

Thomas Duke and Jeremiah Duke of Fox Harbour were undoubtedly brothers. Thomas constructed four ships and rebuilt one in the years between 1926 and 1935. His building career began with the 35-ton *Catherine Mary Hann* which was crafted at Merasheen for Wilfred W. Wareham, merchant of Harbour Buffett. There followed at Fox Harbour, in 1928 and 1930 respectively, the 19-ton *Henry Healey* and the 35-ton *Ellenora Spurvey*. In 1931 Thomas rebuilt the 12-ton *Bride & Annie*, which lasted for more than thirty years. The last ship for Thomas was the 68-ton *Gladys Wiscombe* which he constructed at Argentia in 1935 for Anthony Smith, merchant at Argentia. This is not to be confused with the 98-ton *Gladys*

Wiscombe which was constructed in 1938 by Emmanuel Stone of Monroe under the name *Trinity North* and later acquired by the Wiscombe firm. Jeremiah Duke of Fox Harbour had a short building career: in 1928 he rebuilt the 28-ton *Lena Jean*, and in 1931 he rebuilt the 28-ton *Mary Spurvey*. Not only were Thomas and Jeremiah building ships for the Spurvey family, but they built their last ships together at Argentia in 1935. Jeremiah's last ship was the 26-ton *Margaret Ann Smith*.

Likewise, we consider John J. Hann and James B. Hann as brothers because they both had connections with Petit Forte. John was probably the elder brother as he began his building career in 1927 by rebuilding the 21-ton *Blanche M. Stevens* which had been built at Tancook, Nova Scotia, in 1918. This was followed by the rebuilding of the 14-ton *Mary A. Picco* in 1928 and the rebuilding of the 38-ton *Western Annie* at Rushoon in 1929. In 1930 John rebuilt the 17-ton *Madeline Culleton* at Bar Haven, and in 1932 he rebuilt the 28-ton *Guadina* at Baine Harbour. When he rebuilt his last ship at Fox Harbour in 1935, the 32-ton *Nellie Healey*, the record states John was a resident of Petit Forte. He had come home. James B. Hann appears to have remained at Petit Forte, but he was also an itinerant builder, beginning his building career in 1930 with the 12-ton *Lucy and M. Hann* which lasted for twenty-six years. This was followed with the 14-ton *Elpida* in 1933 at Baine Harbour, the 47-ton *G. E. M. Battcock* at St. Mary's, St. Mary's Bay, in 1935, and the 34-ton *Maggie Walsh* at Fermeuse in 1940. For his next three ships, he was at home in Petit Forte: the 28-ton *Ernie Loretta* in 1942, the 43-ton *Glider* in 1944, and the 42-ton *Marion M. Bruce* in 1947. This was his last ship, and it was registered de novo in 1971, having already lasted for twenty-four years.

Frederick William Gosling of Flat Islands, Placentia Bay, built five ships between 1930 and 1942. His first ship was the 27-ton *Elsie Maud Parsons*. Most of his ships were of small size, the smallest being the 12-ton *Myra Kathleen* also constructed in 1930, but in 1934 he built the 70-ton *Margaret M. Riggs*. His last ship was the 19-ton *Okak*; it was built as a patrol vessel for the Minister of Education. All of Gosling's ships were built at Flat Islands.

George Brown of Creston is worthy of an honorable mention not because of the number of ships he constructed, but because of the large size of his two vessels. In 1935 he went to Burin and built the 106-ton *Calvin & Pauline*. The name of the new owner is not given in the ship registers, but it was very probably built for Hollett's Fisheries Limited. Then in 1948 at Marystown, he constructed the 131-ton *J. T. Murley* for Murley's Vessels Ltd. of Marystown.

John Pomeroy of Paradise began his building career with the 23-ton *Regina & Lottie* at Great Paradise in 1939. This was followed by the 53-ton *Laura & Norah* at Paradise in 1942 and the 54-ton *Bertha Joyce* in the same place in 1947. He finished his building career with a flourish by constructing the 137-ton *Violet Dicks* at Harbour Buffett for Alberto Wareham & Sons Ltd., local merchants.

Henry Philip Pardy of Burnt Island, Placentia Bay, built three ships and rebuilt one between 1943 and 1958. He started with the 25-ton *Dixie Lee* and two years later constructed the 16-ton *Evette*. At Port Anne in 1956 he built the 26-ton fishing vessel *Rita M. Wareham*, which was probably constructed for the Wareham merchant firm at Harbour Buffett. He went to Tack's beach in 1958 to rebuild the 51-ton *Anna V. Fagan* as a cargo and fishing vessel. This ship was already twenty-three years old and would last for several more years.

James Francis Vaters crafted the 28-ton *David & Kevin* at Rushoon in 1947 and probably used it as his own fishing vessel for the following sixteen years because it was not until 1963 that he returned to the art of shipbuilding; then it was to rebuild the 22-ton *Gailtyre* at Spencer's Cove in 1963. This ship had been built at Bar Haven in 1947. From 1981 to 1984 it was owned by an Ontario woman, so it must have lasted for more than thirty-seven years. At Harbour Buffett in 1964, Vaters rebuilt one of Henry William Stone's vessels. This ship, the 52-ton *Invasion*, had been built at Monroe as a minesweeper and was now converted by Vaters into a cargo vessel. Vaters completed his building career by rebuilding the 28-ton *Doris & Annie* at Arnold's Cove in 1965; this also was converted to a cargo vessel.

There were two shipbuilding companies functioning at Argentia from 1981 to 1990, and it seems fitting to consider them as one because there may have been only a small name change in 1989. Beginning in 1981, the Neldo Marine Development Co. Ltd. produced thirteen small fishing ships, most of them about 10 or 11 tons and one of these even less than 7 tons. These were all GRP (Glass or Fiberglass Reinforced Plastic) ships, and the last two were described as "moulded." The trend towards smaller ships for the inshore fishery had now become prevalent throughout Newfoundland and Labrador, and these ships were undoubtedly constructed to supply the needs of fishermen in Placentia Bay. The company's first ship was the 11-ton *Esther Jane*. Eight of these vessels were produced in the first year, including *Castor South*, *Midnight Rider*, and *Miss Island Cove*. Most of the ships carried personal names and were probably built for or sold to specific fishing families. Activity dropped off after the first year, and one ship was constructed in each of their four last years, 1987 to 1990. Their second last vessel was the 10-ton *Sea Miss*. Modern Marine Industries Ltd. at Argentia built only two ships: the 70-ton *Sea Voyager II* and the 33-ton *Avalon Voyager*, both constructed in 1989 and both GRP fishing vessels.

THE MARYSTOWN SHIPYARD

It seems most appropriate to deal with the Marystown Shipyard last in this chapter because of its interesting history and its continuing contribution to the economy of the Burin Peninsula and to the province in general.

Marystown is situated in Mortier Bay, which was in fact known simply as Mortier until 1909. Dr Leslie Harris, in the *Encyclopedia of Newfoundland and Labrador*, writes of Mortier Bay as "one of the finest harbours on the Atlantic coast of North America, capacious and, like all of Placentia Bay, free of ice." It was an ideal location for a shipyard. William Spurrier Sr. had expanded his business to include Mortier Bay in the 1700s, and since he had shipbuilding operations at both Burin and Oderin, it is possible that some of his large brigs and barques may have been built at Mortier Bay. We have already noted references in this chapter to boatbuilding and shipbuilding as early as 1718 and 1808, and undoubtedly the Basques and the French had used the timber resources of the area for their own ship construction. Practically all of the ships built before 1818 would have been registered in European home ports.

The Marystown Shipyard was first established by the Commission of Government about the beginning of World War II, at the same time the Clarenville Shipyard was being established. The Department of Natural Resources managed the Marystown operation. The shipyard produced four minesweepers during this time, but the shipyard facilities were destroyed by a fire in 1941 or 1942. The names of the four vessels were *Jude*, *Marticot*, *Merasheen*, and *Oderin*—all named after islands in Placentia Bay. A careful search of the ship registers from 1939 to 1945 could not find any of these names. One source affirms these vessels were the first and only Newfoundland-built war ships. That may very well be, but Henry William Stone at

Monroe was also building minesweepers for the war effort during this period (see Volume One). It is likely that the names of these four ships were changed as the vessels were quickly prepared for service and sent to England to engage in the war effort.

Andrew Horwood has stated that the "*H.M.S. Emly* was built in a Newfoundland ship yard." This cannot be confirmed from the ship registers under *Emly*, *Emily*, or *H.M.S. Emly*. This ship may have been constructed in the Marystown Shipyard and subsequently registered in England. According to Horwood, the vessel travelled in a convoy from Newfoundland to England (no dates given). Enemy ships or submarines destroyed three of the larger vessels in the convoy, but the *Emly* escaped during a gale which sprang up, and under Capt. Isaac Thornhill the vessel made it into the English Channel and from there to the Royal Navy site on the Humber River. The fact that the ship was captained by a Grand Bank skipper may lend credence to the fact that she was a product of the Marystown Shipyard.

The Encyclopedia of Newfoundland and Labrador also states that in 1949 the government set up a facility for building longliners at The Beach in Marystown, and that fifty longliners were constructed between 1959 and 1966. The ship registers do not confirm these statements exactly. An entity called the Nfld. Fisheries Development Authority managed the Marystown Shipyard between 1960 and 1964 and constructed only nineteen vessels during this period. Their first vessel was the 63-ton *Cape La Hune*, and in the same year they produced the 62-ton *Cape Anguille*. Four ships were constructed in 1961, including the 56-ton *Cape Ballard* and the 16-ton *Cape Broyle*. Only one ship came off the stocks in 1962—the 14-ton *Killinek*. And four 17-ton vessels were built in 1963, including the *Cape Harrison*. Their last ship was named *Seals Nest*, one of the three vessels built in 1964. All the other ship names were personal or family names. The only other large vessel the company produced was the 66-ton *Sandra & Carolann* in 1961.

This company was succeeded by another named Nfld. Marine Works Ltd., and it operated under that name from 1967 to 1973. It constructed two large, steel fishing ships in 1969: the three-masted, 624-ton *Atlantic Carol* (the first steel hull constructed there) and the three-masted, 624-ton stern-trawler *Atlantic Margaret*. Both ships were constructed for Atlantic Sugar Refineries Co. Ltd. of Montreal, which had moved into Marystown and established a fish plant at Mooring Cove in 1967. During this period,

Nfld. Marine Works Ltd. employed more than 200 workers. They were also involved in servicing the Grand Banks trawler fishing fleet at a second facility in Marystown.

The name of the company was changed to Marystown Shipping Enterprises (1971) Ltd. and operated under this name from 1973 to 1978. The only ship constructed during this period was in 1973: the 750-ton, steel fishing vessel *Cape Verde*. This vessel was rebuilt in 1986 by Ferguson Industries at Pictou, Nova Scotia, and reduced in size to 459 tons and re-acquired by Marystown Shipyard in 1988.

The Marystown Shipyard Ltd. came into being as a separate entity in 1973 and was managed by John Rannie with the operation being stabilized and many of its operating losses being reduced. A time of relative stability ensued. In 1973, its first year of operation, two steel fishing vessels were constructed: the 751-ton *Cape La Have* and the 750-ton *Cape Wrath II*. Three vessels came off the stocks in 1974, all of them two-masted and each 661 tons: *Atlantic Lindsay*, *Atlantic Clare*, and *Atlantic Elizabeth*. In that same year, the Shipyard rebuilt the 384-ton twin ships *Harmon* and *Harmon II*, both of which had been built in Norway in 1961 and 1962. Seven vessels were constructed in 1975: the 94-ton *Sand Launce*, the 661-ton *Atlantic Olga*, the 93-ton *Blue Hake*, the 93-ton *Barracudina*, the 661-ton *Atlantic Dorothy*, the 748-ton *Cape D'Or*, and the 748-ton *Cape Hunter*. Only one ship was constructed in each of the years 1976, 1977, 1979, 1980, and 1981: the 338-ton *Pennyhope*, the 338-ton *Cape Sambro*, the 659-ton offshore supply boat *Offshore Trader*, the 1269-ton *Sable Sea*, and the 377-ton *Zandvort*. This last ship carried a Mortgage A for $7 million plus interest. Two ships were produced in 1982 and one in 1983: the 377-ton *Zandberg*, the 673-ton steel-supply tug *Mortier*, and its twin the *Beau Bois*. The 632-ton steel-tanker *Erin T.* was rebuilt at Marystown in 1982; it had been built in Leith, Scotland, in 1964. The *Offshore Hunter* was purchased from Norway in 1984, and it appears alterations were made to the vessel at the Marystown Shipyard.

Only the 476-ton, steel Ro-Ro-Ferry *Beaumont Hamel* was built in 1985. The 330-ton passenger-auto steel-ferry *Gallipoli* and the 15-ton steel-workboat *Mark Bolt* were constructed in 1986. Two ships were produced in each of the years 1987 and 1988, and they were all steel fishing vessels: the twin ships, each of 241 tons, *Funk Island Banker* and *Belle Island Banker*, and the twin ships, each of 360 tons, *Newfoundland Alert* and

Newfoundland Arrow. The five ships produced in 1989 also were steel fishing vessels. Three of them of were 436 tons: *Newfoundland Bounty*, *Newfoundland Breaker*, and *Newfoundland Breeze*. The other two were of 242 tons and were named *Makkovik Banker* and *Nain Banker*. The last ship found in the ship registers up to 1992 was the 577-ton *Flanders*, which was described as a steel Ro-Ro-Ferry.

It is passing strange that an Internet source on the Marystown Shipyard, with pictures, shows additional ships built at Marystown: the *Cape Brule* (possibly 1973), the workboat *Captain Ed* (1976), the *Normand Rock* (1978?), the *Normand Rough* (1979?), the *Normand Trader* (1979?), the *Balder Hudson* (1979), the *Balder Baffin* (1981), the *Hull 35 COGS Mary Hickens* (1983), and the *Sea Rose* (2004). A plausible explanation may be that most of these vessels were registered outside Newfoundland, or never registered (for example, the workboat *Captain Ed*). And my check of the ship registers stopped at 1992, so the *Sea Rose* would not have been found. The Internet source also mentions a Coast Guard ship *Montmorency*, which was the first ship to be taken up on the new synchrolift; perhaps it was in for refit or repairs.

While the names of the owners of these ships is not usually stated, it should be noted that most of their large ships, up to and including 1975, were built for or sold to Tele-Direct, Montreal. Following 1975, some ships were built for the Lake Group and National Sea Products, and most were listed as owned by Her Majesty the Queen until they were sold. The tugs were constructed for the Norwegian oil industry, and one of their ships was built as a Canadian fisheries patrol vessel. The ferries were constructed for the Newfoundland government. In the mid-1990s the Shipyard obtained contracts for steel construction in connection with the Hibernia platform, such as pontoon barges, drilling modules, and temporary access towers.

The reader should note in the Appendix to Chapter Seven the high number of rebuilds in Placentia Bay during the 1920s and early 1930s. Perhaps there was a scarcity of timber in some areas, or it is possible that so many older ships were available that it was considerably less expensive to refurbish these. It hardly seems possible that there had been a downturn in the fishery, because new ships were being built at the same time.

In Volume One Chapter Three, it was suggested that Trinity Bay might well deserve the title of "that Far Greater Bay" because of the emergence of several prominent shipbuilding families spanning several generations in each family. However, the title rightly belongs to Placentia Bay because of the many magnificent harbours supporting significant shipbuilding over hundreds of years and because of the great timber stands, especially at the head of the bay. The existence of so many suitable building sites bearing the names Ship Cove and Ship Harbour (such as at Burin and Oderin) bears testimony to the pervasiveness of ship construction in the region. The largest vessels ever constructed in Newfoundland were crafted at the Marystown Shipyard, vessels up to 750 tons each and carrying mortgages of more than $7 million. While most of the old docks in Newfoundland have disappeared, except from the memories of our elders, Marystown is one of the few that remains, and it continues to stimulate the economy of the province, and hopefully will do so for many years to come.

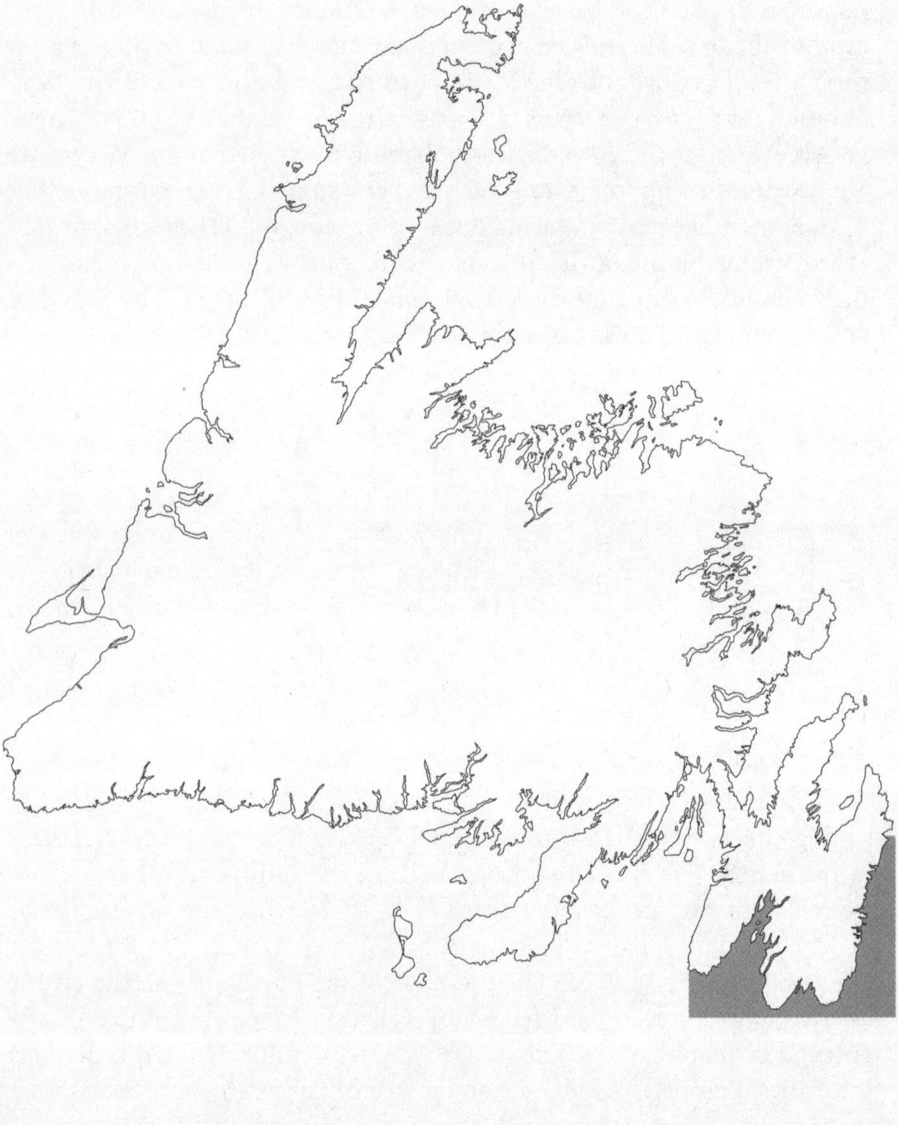

CHAPTER EIGHT

SOUTH AND SOUTHEAST AVALON PENINSULA

THIS AREA INCLUDES St. Mary's Bay and Trepassey Bay and extends from Cape St. Mary's in the west to Cape Race in the east and north along the southeast Avalon to Petty Harbour. From earliest times, the region was frequented by the Basques, the French, the Spanish, the Portuguese, and the English. Exploration of the peninsula and exploitation of the abundant fisheries dates from the sixteenth century.

The English preferred the east coast of Newfoundland and focussed their fishing efforts on the area from Cape Bonavista in the north to Trepassey in the south. The French concentrated on the south coast, particularly from Placentia Bay westward to the Gulf of St. Lawrence, though Jean Denys of Harfleur had left his "boats and barks" to overwinter at Rougnoust (Renews) as early as 1506. The presence of the Portuguese in the area is attested to by the fact that what is now Calvert was recorded on very early Portuguese maps as "R[io] das patas" (goose or auk river) and is perhaps the earliest European-named site on the island. The name Fermeuse appears on early Portuguese maps as "R. fermosa," "Rio fremosa," and "Formosa" at least as early as 1519; it was a fishing station and a site for ship repair and related activities for the Portuguese from the early 1500s. It was also mentioned in Sir Henry Cary's proposals for setting up a plantation in the early 1600s.

After John Guy's colony was established at Cuper's Cove (Cupids) in 1610, the next land grant made by England in the Avalon Peninsula area was to William Vaughan in 1616 and consisted of "the southern part of the Harbour of Caplin [later Calvert] as far as the Gulf of Placentia." Some of this land came into the hands of Sir George Calvert, later Lord Baltimore, and some was acquired by Sir Henry Cary, First Viscount Falkland, including the Renews-Cappahayden area. Attempts at settlement were made from about 1613, and certainly from 1621, but most of these efforts failed, and it was not until Sir David Kirke arrived at Ferryland with 100 colonists in 1638 that organized settlement began to flourish. Kirke was a polarizing figure, particularly in his aggressive attitude towards the French and other settlers outside his colony, and he was eventually recalled to England and probably never allowed to return. Curiously it was Lady Sara Kirke and her sister (or sister-in-law), Lady Frances Hopkins, who became the mainstays of settlement in the region, though at one time Lady Kirke sent a petition to the King stating she and her children were starving. The Kirkes were a sturdy family, however, and it may be concluded from census evidence and other historical data that these two women were plantation owners and boat owners, and possibly ship owners, and pursued an inshore fishery for about forty years, which Lady Kirke's sons carried on after her death.

The English migratory fishery was being pursued from Renews during the sixteenth century and expanded greatly after about 1550. Some sources affirm that John Cull was a fisherman at Ferryland in 1612 and Thomas Cruse fished at Ferryland before 1617. About 1616 William Vaughan sent the first of his colonists to Aquaforte, but these were soon moved to Renews. Fishermen from Barnstaple and Bideford focussed on this area at least for the period 1610 to 1630, but the English Civil War of 1642 to 1646 interrupted this activity. Aquaforte appears on maps as early as 1519 as "R da aguea" and by 1544 was known as "la baya de l'Islet." By 1670, if not well before that date, Aquaforte was being used as a fishing station by migratory fishermen from north Devon, England. Ferryland (the name was probably derived from the French word Forillon) began to appear on maps as early as 1547, and there were many variations of the name on other maps from the sixteenth century onwards. It was a very early and very important fishing station and settlement, used by French, Spanish, Portuguese, and English fishers. One of its early attractions was the heavily-forested areas that surrounded the harbour, holding timber which was suitable for boatbuilding and shipbuilding. It is asserted that Sir Humphrey Gilbert timed his arrival in August 1583 so he could meet with ships of several nations which would be departing for home at that time and trade with them for supplies. He expected to find Spanish, Portuguese, and English ships in the harbours of Renews, Fermeuse, and Ferryland. When the Bristol ship *Grace* visited Ferryland in 1593, she reported there were twenty-two large fishing ships in the harbour. And during the 1700s, Ferryland was the Newfoundland headquarters of the fishing ships of Teignmouth and Dartmouth.

From dispositions taken at Ferryland in 1652, we learn from Anne Love, who had been a planter there from 1628 to 1638, that Sir George Calvert (Lord Baltimore) had "built a shippe called the *Anne* and divers boates... and also built divers stages for making and drying the fish...all at his own expense." Since Anne Love was also listed as a planter in 1661, it may be assumed she had been a planter for at least thirty-three years. From these same dispositions we learn that Amie Taylor, a Ferryland planter, claimed that Calvert had spent 1700 pounds sterling on improvements in the town and that "he built 150 fishing boats as well as stages." John Staughton of "Capelinge bay" bought and built boats and stages and used thirty-two boats in the fishery; he also affirmed that Calvert had not spent more than 1800 pounds sterling on improvements. And Nicholas Neville testified that he had lost thirty boats when they were burned during an attack by the Dutch in 1673. These testimonies give us some idea what life and work were like in the 1600s in this area.

We may safely assume that shipbuilding on a larger scale began in this area in the 1700s. Since the Parliamentary Report of 1718 noted that almost all of the Poole vessels engaged in the trade had been built in Newfoundland, we may conclude that Ferryland, Caplin Bay (Calvert), Renews, Fermeuse, and Aquaforte were engaged in the art of shipbuilding early in the eighteenth century. However, the first hard data we have about early shipbuilding, apart from the earlier reference to Calvert's *Anne*, is D. W. Prowse's list of ships constructed in Newfoundland in 1804. The only ships listed by Prowse for this area are the 31-ton sloop *Capelin Bay*, which was crafted at Capelin Bay (Calvert), and the 52-ton schooner *Trepassey*, which was constructed at Trepassey. The only other vessels listed for the south coast are the 94-ton schooner *Fanny* built at "Bay Despair," the 54-ton schooner *Victor* constructed at Audierne (Oderin), and the 232-ton "ship" *Alicia* built at Great Placentia. We know now that Prowse's list is incomplete and that he missed at least seven ships constructed that year in Conception Bay. He may have missed others on the south coast.

We need to be reminded yet again that the ship registers are incomplete and unreliable until about 1818. There is a little reporting for 1813 and a few references throughout the records to ships built as early as 1804. Ships constructed in Newfoundland until about 1818 were routinely registered in European ports, and many even had been registered there after that date.

The first reference in the ship registers to a ship constructed in this area is the 40-ton *Henry* which was crafted at Trepassey in 1810. The name of the builder is unknown. The first registration of this ship was in 1828 when it was owned by three merchants at Bonavista; it had undoubtedly been used by its owner/builder for the previous eighteen years as a fishing vessel. Tracing its history through five subsequent registrations we discover the ship was owned in 1830 by a merchant at Trinity, in 1837 by two trader/dealers at St. John's, in 1840 by a merchant at St. John's, in 1844 by two St. John's shipbuilders (Nicholas Power and Nathaniel Knight), and in 1848 by a trader/dealer at St. John's. When the vessel was registered in 1848 its tonnage had dropped from 40 to 32 tons, so it was probably rebuilt by Power and Knight. The sturdy vessel was lost at sea in 1872, having lasted for a remarkable sixty-two years.

The 55-ton *Savanna* was built at Brigus South in 1811, registered that same year, and then "altered in her dimensions" and her tonnage increased to 59 in 1820 at the same place. She had previously been owned by Adam Jack, merchant of St. John's, but by 1820 she belonged to merchants Stuart & Rennie of Greenock, Scotland. Adam Jack may have been their Newfoundland agent. The name of the builder remains unknown.

The 30-ton *Speculator* was fashioned at Renews in 1811, but the name of the builder cannot be determined; this vessel was rebuilt at Bonavista in 1829 by Robert Brown, planter, master, and owner.

Nor do we know the name of the builder of the 33-ton *Betsey* at St. Mary's in 1818. Actually she was built as an open boat at St. Mary's in 1818, and in 1820 was "raised on and decked" at the same place. Richard Waterman was master of this vessel from 1821-23, and the owners were John and Robert Brine, merchants of St. John's.

The name of the first shipbuilder in the area is that of William Deady of Renews who in 1818 built the 49-ton schooner *Capelin* at Renews. The owners were Thomas Stabb of Torquay, Devon, and John Preston, both merchants. George Stabb was master of the vessel. William Jeans, in 1818, constructed the 60-ton schooner *William Jewell* at St. Mary's for William Phipard of the same place, and Garrett Curtis was the master. This is almost certainly the "Garret" Curtis of Salmonier, so he would have done this just before moving to the Bay of Exploits to be the master shipbuilder for John Peyton. Curtis is quoted by James P. Howley as saying that he "left St. Mary's in 1819" to go to the Bay of Exploits. John Piercey of Brigus South, in 1818, built the 47-ton *Hope* for planter Edward Power of Brigus South. William Marsh was the master of the vessel.

Thomas Rossiter of Ferryland is the first prominent shipbuilder we encounter in the area, and his building career spans the years 1818 to 1833. Family researchers claim he fought with Lord Nelson in either the *H. M. S. Victory* or the *H. M. S. Conqueror* at the Battle of Trafalgar and came to Newfoundland shortly after 1805, settling at Caplin Bay (Calvert). He married there and had at least four children. He may have been the Thomas Rossiter who was baptized in Wexford, Ireland, in 1784. He may well have been the father of Richard Rositer, who was in Ferryland in 1841, and of Anne Roseter (note the variations in spelling), who was at Caplin Bay in 1849. At Ferryland in 1818, Thomas built the 32-ton, one-masted sloop *Collector* for Robert Carter and James Howe Carter of Ferryland and Elias Rendell of Devon. At Caplin Bay in 1820, Rossiter crafted the 86-ton *Iris* for two Sweetland men (one of whom was Benjamin Sweetland) and Matthew Morey, all local merchants. Still at Caplin Bay, in 1822 he decked an open boat which had been built there in 1816 and enlarged it to 54 tons and named it *Eclipse*. The register notes the certificate of rebuilding was signed by Rossiter. This ship was also owned by the same merchants. In 1831 at Caplin Bay he decked, "raised on," and enlarged the 39-ton *Snipe Fish* which had been built as an open boat at Caplin Bay in 1825. It had been registered previously, but a careful search of the records did not find that registration; perhaps Rossiter had done other alterations to the vessel in 1829. The new owners were Benjamin Sweetland and Matthew Morey, both in 1829 and 1831. Rossiter's last ship was the 132-ton brig *Waterlily* constructed in 1833 at Ferryland for Thomas Wright, merchant of Ferryland.

This vessel was offered for sale in April 1840, and it was stated that she was about 100 tons New Measurement (N.M.) which would equal about 125 to 135 Old Measurement (O.M.); the advertisement stated that the ship could carry 2300 quintals of fish in bulk, i.e., twenty-three quintals per ton.

Since the publication of Volume One, Anna Kearney Guigne, Folklorist and Adjunct Professor of Music at Memorial University, has supplied both additional and corrective information about the Kearneys of Ferryland. From this family came the preeminent shipbuilder Michael Kearney. Actually, he was Michael Kearney Jr. since his father also bore that name. The John Kearney who constructed at Bay Bulls in 1820 the 84-ton *Messenger* for Michael Mulcahy, planter, was almost certainly Michael Sr.'s brother, John Kearney I. Michael Kearney Jr.'s name does not appear in the ship registers as a builder until 1833 when he constructs the 110-ton brig *Angerona* at Ferryland; he was then just twenty-two years old. In 1837 the John Kearney II who crafts the 85-ton brig *Harmony* at Ferryland is very probably Michael Jr.'s brother; the joint owners of this vessel are John and Michael Kearney, so Michael undoubtedly assisted his brother in the construction. And Michael built the 125-ton *Scotch Lass* at Ferryland in 1838, and John II was a co-owner of this vessel. During the 1830s, Michael is said to have served apprenticeships in two shipyards in Ireland. My guess is he returned home in 1833 to build the *Angerona* and went back to Ireland for the second apprenticeship sometime before 1838. For a fuller treatment of perhaps the greatest individual shipbuilder that Newfoundland ever produced, see Michael Kearney in Chapter One of Volume One.

William Radmore was the builder of the 73-ton brigantine *Avalon* at Ferryland in 1820. The vessel was constructed for Arthur Hunt Carter, merchant of Ferryland. It is the only vessel for which Radmore is given credit in the ship registers. Carter employed a second shipbuilder in 1823 in the person of Valentine Keefe who "raised on" and decked the 53-ton *Ferryland Packet* which had originally been built as an open boat. Keefe apparently rebuilt this vessel again in 1827 for Robert Job, merchant of St. John's. In 1825, also for Arthur H. Carter, Keefe rebuilt the 36-ton *Favourite* which had been built as an open boat somewhere in Fortune Bay, but the original date is unknown. For another merchant at Ferryland, James Morrison, Keefe crafted the 52-ton *Tweeds* in 1831. And thus his building career ended. Robert Saunders rebuilt the 40-ton *Aginoria* at Fermeuse in

1824 for Prowse, Preston & Congden, merchants at Torquay, Devon. This vessel also had been built originally as an open boat.

We turn our attention now to St. Mary's Bay and Trepassey Bay to look at shipbuilders in the 1820s. John Doody of St. Mary's Bay constructed the 21-ton *Sally* on Colinet Island in 1825. Doody was a planter and used the vessel for his own purposes. It was lost at sea in 1869, having lasted for a remarkable forty-four years. In 1842 Doody built the 31-ton *Brothers* for John Stuart, merchant of St. John's. At Trepassey in 1826 Patrick Fitzpatrick constructed the 63-ton *Sir Thomas Cochrane* for Brine & McNeil, merchants of St. John's and Trepassey. Fitzpatrick may have worked for them at the fishery. Also at Trepassey in 1826, George Sutton built the 73-ton *Liberty* for Bland & Henderson, merchants of St. John's, and in 1831 he constructed his second ship, the 86-ton *George Sutton*, for Robert Brine, St. John's merchant. Naming a ship after oneself was often a sign that one had achieved a significant level of success or standing, so it is curious that there are no further references to Sutton in the registers. It is possible that Fitzpatrick or Sutton may have constructed the 40-ton *Henry* at Trepassey, a vessel referred to earlier in this chapter. John Bridgeman of St. Mary's decked and rebuilt the 27-ton *Flora* in 1828 for Wood & Lush, merchants of St. John's and St. Mary's. It was Bridgeman's only building venture.

William Sanders of Ferryland was a planter and fashioned two ships in the 1830s. In 1831 it was the 92-ton *Coquette*, and in 1836 he co-built with John Sanders the 41-ton *Cousins*. The latter ship was briefly owned from 1844 to 1845 by Mary O'Neill, widow of Fermeuse, and Cornelius O'Neill was master of the vessel. Perhaps Cornelius was Mary's son or brother-in-law; in 1845 Mary sold the vessel to Dugald Markellar, merchant of St. John's. William Saunders of Ferryland is probably the same as William Sanders above. Saunders constructed the 125-ton brig *Malvina* at Ferryland in 1832, and the owner was Jeremiah Callahan, planter of St. John's.

The Winsers of Aquaforte were merchants and mariners of great stature. And Peter Winser was a merchant shipbuilder. He constructed the 117-ton *Pelter* in 1831 at Aquaforte, and Henry Winser, mariner, was his partner. In 1844 Caroline Winser, married woman, held shares in this ship as did her sister-in-law Jane Winser. It is of special interest that Caroline Winser held these shares twenty-two years before the Married Women's Property Act became law in Newfoundland. She was either flaunting or ignoring the law. When Peter Winser built his second ship, the

108-ton *Aquafort* in 1837, his partners were Henry Winser and George Jones, both of them mariners.

Robert Furey constructed the 100-ton brigantine *Henry & Mary Ann* at Witless Bay in 1833, and the owners were Jacob Chafe and Richard Allen, planters at Petty Harbour. It was Furey's only ship. In that same year, Matthew Hudson, a planter at Blackhead, built the 32-ton *Three Sisters*. It was lost at sea in Conception Bay in 1869, having lasted for thirty-six years. Nicholas Coady of Bay Bulls built the 26-ton *Margaret* in 1836. The new owner was Robert Alsop, merchant of St. John's, and since Coady was master of the vessel, it is likely he was working for Alsop. Also, the Swain family of Calvert had arrived in a wave of Irish immigrants in 1805 and by the 1830s had become well known as boatbuilders; their names do not appear in the ship registers, so these must have been undecked boats rather than decked vessels.

GARRETT CURTIS

Garrett Curtis of St. Mary's Bay, whom we mentioned earlier as a ship's master in 1818, went in 1819 to the Bay of Exploits to become a master shipbuilder with John Peyton. He was then thirty years of age. For a full treatment of Curtis see Chapter One. He succeeded John Fudge who had been Peyton's shipbuilder up to 1820. Since Curtis was at the Bay of Exploits during the fiercest conflict with the Beothuk, James P. Howley was able to elicit from Curtis— through Rev. J. St. John, parish priest of Salmonier— the story of what happened during the conflict, and this is recorded in Howley's book *The Beothucks or Red Indians*. Curtis was at that time "a very old inhabitant of that place." Between 1823 and 1833 Curtis had crafted seven ships for Peyton, and these ranged in size between the 34-ton *Joseph* and the 118-ton brig *Worcester*. When Curtis returned to the southeast coast, he was engaged by Alan Goodridge, merchant at Renews, to build three ships. These were all constructed at Renews: the 131-ton brig *Amanda* in 1838, the 190-ton brig *Gratia* in 1838, and the 45-ton schooner *Avalon* in 1840. The *Newfoundlander* of December 5, 1839, mentions that the keel of the Gratia was "laid about this time last year…in the building-yard of Mr. Goodridge." The *Public Ledger* gives the tonnage of the vessel as 189 (N.M.) and says the vessel was "built of juniper and witchazel, "and measured eighty-six feet long, nineteen feet wide, and fourteen feet "deep of hold." When Curtis had completed these three ships, he returned to

St. Mary's Bay and in 1844 constructed the 154-ton brig *Michael Anthony Fleming* for John and James Kent, merchants of St. John's and Waterford, Ireland. He was at Salmonier for the construction of his next two vessels: the 33-ton *St. Patrick* in 1846 for John Stuart, St. John's merchant, and the 25-ton *Fairy* in 1847 for John Antle, mariner of Brigus, Conception Bay. Two years later, in 1849, Curtis built the 29-ton *Snake* for Smith McKay who in 1854 would discover the copper deposit at Tilt Cove, Notre Dame Bay. Curtis built his last three vessels at home in Salmonier for St. John's merchants: the 45-ton *Blanche* in 1859 for J. B. Sawyer, the 131-ton brigantine *Clio* in 1851 for D. J. Henderson, and the 27-ton *Kate* in 1852 for W. L. Anthony. On March 28, 1851, the *Public Ledger* made this comment about the *Clio*: "a light, airy craft, sitting the water with elegance, at the same time that she has an appearance of strength, which it is confirmed upon a close inspection." And so with the *Kate* the distinguished building career of Garrett Curtis came to an end. Over a twenty-nine year period, he had constructed sixteen ships, five of these over 100 tons. It is possible he built ships beyond 1852, but we cannot be certain because from 1854 to 1877 the names of shipbuilders are omitted from the ship registers. He would have been the builder of the *Snake* which he owned in 1849, and he was almost certainly the builder of the 77-ton *Phoca* at Salmonier in 1855. Curtis died at Salmonier in 1882 at age ninety-three. His mother, Anne (Dillon) Curtis had died in 1848 at Salmonier at age eighty-four, and her headstone reveals that she was a native of County Waterford, Ireland.

William Curtiss of Salmonier (despite the spelling of the surname) was the son of Garrett Curtis and constructed the 15-ton *Teresa* in 1878 and the *Madora* in 1887. Garrett had ten children, and his five sons were all likely involved in the enterprise that the 1877 Rochfort Business Directory calls Garrett Curtis & Sons. It is intriguing to speculate that Michael Ryan at St. Mary's, Michael Dennis at Salmonier, Michael Dinn at St. Mary's, and Andrew and Thomas Nowlan at Salmonier may well have received their shipwright training in the Curtis shipyard since they all became shipbuilders after Curtis returned to St. Mary's Bay.

It is curious that so few vessels were built in this region in the 1830s and 1840s. In fact, only the 21-ton *Liberty*, constructed by Michael Fagan of St. Mary's in 1839, was found in the ship registers for the 30s; the new owners were Wood & Lush, merchants of St. John's and St. Mary's. And only three ships were constructed in this large region in the 1840s. Most of the fishing must now have been undertaken in small boats. Michael Shea, at Renews, built the 139-ton brig *Viola* in 1843 for Alan and John Goodridge, local merchants. Shea had now replaced Garrett Curtis who had moved on to Salmonier. Shea had undoubtedly been brought in for that specific purpose since this is the only time his name appears in the ship registers. Michael Ryan, at St. Mary's, built the 24-ton *Brothers* in 1845 for Peter Brennan, St. John's merchant. And Michael Dennis, at Salmonier in 1849, constructed the 46-ton *Susan* for Philip Duggan, merchant of St. John's.

THE NOWLAN FAMILY

Thomas Nowlan built three ships and rebuilt one at Salmonier between 1851 and 1882. His first ship was the 22-ton *Mary*. Then occurs the notorious gap of 1854 to 1877 when the names of shipbuilders were omitted from the registers. In 1882 Nowlan builds the 32-ton *Annie G.* for James Fox, merchant of St. John's. This vessel was wrecked in 1889 but rebuilt, probably by Nowlan, and restored to the ship registry in 1890 to last for a total of thirty-eight years. In 1883 Nowlan built the 45-ton *Isabel*, also for Fox. During his building career, Nowlan most likely built ten or twelve ships. He was very probably a worthy successor to Garrett Curtis. Andrew Nowlan of Salmonier, who constructed the 27-ton *Anastatia* in 1853, was very probably a brother of Thomas. Also to be considered as younger brothers or possibly sons of Thomas are two others. Michael Nowlan of Salmonier built two ships: the 28-ton *Zepho* in 1885 and the 21-ton *Reporter* in 1891. James Nowlan built the 34-ton *Nimble* in 1888 at Salmonier. How many more ships these men built cannot be determined.

Also to be considered as brothers are M. Battcock and John Battcock of Brigus South. M. Battcock (first name not given) built three ships at Brigus South for the merchant firm of Goodridge of St. John's: the 21-ton *Mary* in 1875, the 23-ton *Star of the Sea* in 1884, and the 23-ton *Mary Jane* in 1886. It is a curiosity often encountered in the ship registers that Battcock did not register his first ship until twenty-three years after it was built, the second ship until fourteen years later, and the third ship until twelve years later. John Battcock constructed two ships: the 23-ton *Star of the Sea* in 1878 and the 23-ton *Shamrock* in 1883, both for St. John's merchants. John registered both ships in the years they were built. Both brothers must have been working from the same ship designs.

William Crockwell of Bay Bulls built three ships between 1878 and 1890. His first ship was the 31-ton *Eliza*, his second the 26-ton *Village Belle* in 1884, and his third the 29-ton *Veronica*. All three ships were fashioned at Bay Bulls, the first for Peter and Lewis Tessier, merchants of St. John's, and the other two for the Goodridge merchant firm; most of the ships built in this area during this period were built for the Goodridge firm. There was a William Crockwell at Upper Island Cove, Conception Bay, in 1882 where he built the 31-ton *Susanna* for a planter of that place; it is not likely the same person, but sometimes a shipbuilder went where a job needed to be done or as a favour for a friend.

William Power of Tors Cove constructed three ships there and one at Bay Bulls. Three of his ships were built for the Goodridge merchant firm and one for Peter Tessier. In 1885 Power built the 24-ton *Gordon*, in 1888 it was the 34-ton *Annie May*, in 1889 it was the 37-ton *Ruby* at Bay Bulls, and in 1900 it was the 32-ton *Mary Ettie*.

THE POWER FAMILY OF SAINT MARY'S BAY

David Power was from Holyrood Beach, Salmonier. There in 1889 he built his first ship: the 24-ton *Ann Joseph* for William Job, St. John's merchant. He was probably related to John Joseph Power who built the 29-ton *Rolling Wave* at Branch in 1887; John Joseph's partner was Ambrose Power. Power is absent from the registers from 1890 to 1917, but in 1918 he emerges with the 217-ton, three-masted *Carl R. Tibbo* whose construction he supervised at Grand Bank for Simeon M. Tibbo and George E. Tibbo, Grand Bank merchants. The *Carl R. Tibbo* was totally lost at Seldom Come By, Fogo Island, on December 19, 1919; no other details could be found.

We hear nothing more from David Power of St. Mary's Bay until 1926 when he builds the 12-ton *Rita Madeline Power* at Regina, Salmonier. This was followed by the 16-ton *E. M. Alison* in 1933 at New Bridge, Salmonier, and in 1936 by the 24-ton *Margaret J. Doody* at St. Joseph's, St. Mary's Bay. If this is the same David Power who constructed the large tern schooner, no doubt he would have been ably assisted by several Grand Bank shipwrights and may have taken along with him several relatives from St. Mary's Bay, including the shipbuilders John Joseph Power, Joseph Power, Leo Power, and Stephen Power, who were all building ships in the 1920s and 1930s.

Michael and Paul Power of North Harbour, St. Mary's Bay, may have been of the same family. In 1944 Michael built the 22-ton *Rose Murphy* as a fishing vessel. But he co-built the 30-ton *Joan & Arthur* in 1950 with Thomas Power II, probably his brother. This vessel was sold in 1954 to Alberto Wareham Ltd. at Harbour Buffett. In 1953 Michael constructed the 34-ton *Donald & Dianne* and sold it to Michael Richard Power, fisherman at Portugal Cove, Trepassey. All Michael's building was done at North Harbour. Paul Power of North Harbour built two ships there in 1950 and 1952: the 16-ton *Madonna Mary* and the curiously-named, 30-ton *E. C. F. no. 1*. The ship register gives his name, in 1952, as Peter Paul Power.

There was a burst of shipbuilding activity in St. Mary's Bay, most of it concentrated at Admiral's Beach, beginning in the early 1960s and continuing to 1981. Several individual shipbuilders were involved, most producing only one ship each (see the Appendix to this chapter). The boom was led by the Power family who may have been descendants of David Power. Leonard J. Power of O'Donnells was the first of the family builders, beginning in 1964 with the 22-ton *Bridget A.* and continuing in 1965 with the 22-ton *Bridget A. II*. Both ships were constructed at Riverhead. But in 1967 Leonard was at Admiral's Beach where he crafted the 22-ton *Catherine Ellen*. In the meantime, Walter Patrick Power constructed the 16-ton *Joan & Janice* at Admiral's Beach in 1967. Curiously we hear nothing more from Walter Power until 1972 when he builds the 26-ton *Bickford*. This is followed in 1973 with the 18-ton *Laurie & Lloyd*. In 1981 Walter constructs three ships, each of them just under 7 tons: the *Anita Ann*, the *Wanda Marie*, and the *Deborah & Perry*. Other members of the family were John and Joseph Power who in 1979 co-built the 12-ton *Priscilla & Jane*. The company which built the 13-ton *Paula & Jordan* at Admiral's Beach in 1980 must surely have been connected with the same family as is evident from its name—More Power Construction Ltd.

It is possible that the Powers of St. Mary's Bay were descendants of Thomas Power I who was building large ships at Bay D'Espoir for English merchant firms in the 1820s and 30s; the records show that he built his last ship at Burin in 1838 for the Morris merchant family. It would have been a short move from there to St. Mary's Bay.

Patrick Sutton of Trepassey crafted the 33-ton *Forget-me-Not* in 1904 for James Baird, merchant of St. John's. Sutton was very probably the grandson of George Sutton, a shipbuilder at Trepassey in the 1820s and 1830s. After twenty-four years of use, this vessel was rebuilt by William March at Haystack, Placentia Bay, in 1928 and renamed *Norman Wareham*. The vessel was now owned by merchant Wilfred W. Wareham. It was lost at sea somewhere in Fortune Bay in 1935, having given good service for thirty-one years.

Patrick J. Pittman and Cornelius Pittman of Renews were probably brothers. Patrick built in 1948 what is probably the smallest ship registered at St. John's: the 4.30-ton *Kathleen K.* It was a fishing vessel and measured twenty-eight-point-two feet long. Between 1945 and 1957 Cornelius built three ships: the 6-ton *Lizzie L.*, the 12-ton *Betty S. L.* in 1950, and the 16-ton *Rita Marie.* All ships were constructed at Renews.

John F. Barron of O'Donnells constructed four ships in St. Mary's Bay between 1963 and 1966. In 1963 he built two small fishing ships: the 17-ton *Little Sisters* at St. Joseph's and the 16-ton *Brendan H.* at O'Donnells. The next year it was the 17-ton *Joan & Kevin* at Mount Carmel. Barron completed his short building career in 1966 at O'Donnells with the 22-ton *Anita Christine.*

Augustus Leo Dalton constructed four ships in three different locations in St. Mary's Bay. These were all small fishing ships, but it was an impressive feat since the first three were built in three separate communities in 1965: the 21-ton *C. Brothers* at St. Joseph's, the 16-ton *Denise C.* at Mall Bay, and the 22-ton *Margaret Gertrude* at Admiral's Beach. Dalton remained at Admiral's Beach to construct the 25-ton *Daley Bread* in 1967. That ship must surely have been built for the Daley family. Dalton started his building career so admirably that one would have expected a longer period of building.

The company Nfld. Quick Freeze constructed four one-masted fishing vessels at Witless Bay in 1973. These were ships of substantial size, the first three ships being of 54 tons each: the *Avalon Rover*, the *Avalon Mist*, and the *Kathy Michelle.* The fourth ship was slightly larger at 56 tons: the *Avalon Challenge.* This venture bears the marks of a government program then withdrawn.

The same may be true of the Richard Gibbons Co. Ltd. of St. Vincent's, St. Mary's Bay, which built five ships between 1979 and 1982. These were all small wooden fishing vessels between 10 and 15 tons each. In 1979 it was the *Nancy Luann*, in 1980 *The Lady Harvester*, in 1981 the *Jenny & Trevor*, and in 1982 the *Lady Dolphin II* and the *Deanna Dean*.

It is worthy of note that the 6.15-ton wood yacht *Scademia* was constructed at Riverhead, St. Mary's Bay, in 1981 by Edward Allison. The vessel was not registered until 1986 (only three new vessels were registered that year) and was then noted to be an auxiliary motor screw. The *Scademia* has become well-known as a tourist vessel in the St. John's area.

We alluded earlier in this chapter to the Swain family of Calvert who were recognized in the 1830s as exceptional boatbuilders, and both the narrative and appendix to this chapter name several shipbuilders at Caplin Bay, the early name for the town of Calvert. In 1980 Canada Manpower and the College of Fisheries cooperated in establishing at Calvert a boat shop which employed ten men and built two boats while teaching shipwright skills to a number of people. It is not known how long this program lasted, but it was undoubtedly an extension of the activity which the College of Fisheries had established at the Bulley & Job premises on the St. John's waterfront in 1966 and which included a plate-fitting and boatbuilding shop.

The English Shore, stretching from Cape Bonavista in the north to Trepassey in the south, was the area preferred by the English fishers from the early sixteenth century at least. Other nations fished along this coast at the same time. There are frequent references in the literature to the great timber stands, particularly around Ferryland, and ship repair was taking place along this coast as early as 1519. Sir George Calvert, Lord Baltimore, had a ship constructed at Ferryland in the 1650s, and by the 1660s he had built at least 150 fishing boats. And arguably the greatest individual shipbuilder in Newfoundland history, Michael Kearney, may have originated from this area. And while the southern coast of the Avalon Peninsula is important to the history of shipbuilding on the island, the area has also gained a dangerous reputation as a place where ships end their careers; there have been many ship groundings and losses over the years. More than fifty shipwrecks have been reported in the Mistaken Point area alone, one of the many graveyards of the Atlantic coast.

CHAPTER NINE

WERE THE NEWFOUNDLAND TERN SCHOONERS INFERIOR IN CONSTRUCTION? A CHALLENGE TO JOHN P. PARKER'S *SAILS OF THE MARITIMES*

THE SCHOONER WAS a vessel-type developed originally for cod-fishing in the general area from New England to Newfoundland and the St. Lawrence River and may be traced back to Gloucester, Massachusetts, in 1713. For many years it was a two-masted, fore-and-aft rigged vessel, but in the latter half of the nineteenth century, vessels with three, four, and even seven masts were constructed, mostly as cargo vessels. Sixty-six three-masted schooners were constructed in Newfoundland between 1900 and 1929. In fact, fifty-seven of these were built in a four-year period, from 1917 to 1920, and were all known as tern schooners. "Tern" was an American term; Canadian ships of the same type were designated as three-masted vessels. The three masts were of the same height and were extended by three topmasts of equal height, and the sail rig was characterized as fore-and-aft.

Newfoundland shipbuilders, from at least the early 1700s, were producing great ships, both small and large. Large three-masted barques were being constructed here at least by the latter half of the 1700s and possibly earlier and reached 320 tons in size, often lasting many years beyond the average life expectancy of such vessels. With such a long and distinguished history of shipbuilding on the island, it is disconcerting to discover that some

Newfoundland writers have simply accepted the assertions of the Nova Scotia writer John P. Parker that the Newfoundland tern schooners of the early nineteenth century were "not a success" and that they were inferior in construction. Parker was a highly respected maritime writer, a recipient of the M.B.E., a former master of a tern schooner, and was for several years Superintendent of Pilots for Sydney Harbour and the Bras D'Or Lakes. In his 1960 book, *Sails of the Maritimes*, he was not at all kind in his judgments of the Newfoundland tern schooners. He declared they were not a success and not of good quality. He also insisted the Newfoundland tern schooners were built by men who were expert only at building smaller craft, built hurriedly with unseasoned timber of poor grade, lightly designed, and that most of them were built without great capital investment. Parker's books are well researched, well written, and documented as carefully as was possible at the time, so his conclusions should be considered seriously. As far as is known, Parker's assertions regarding the Newfoundland tern schooners have never been challenged; although, in my judgment, they require at least an attempt at refutation.

THREE-MASTED BARQUES OF NEWFOUNDLAND

Parker implied that Newfoundland shipbuilders were not accustomed to building large ships and were instead focussed on the construction of small vessels for the local fishery. "Large" and "small" are relative terms, and we must consider what evidence there is, bearing in mind that very little solid documentation exists from the 1700s. Parker stated that, up until 1900, Newfoundland men "had built some small square-rigged vessels" (92) for exporting fish and that "They built all their small craft themselves, so they well knew what they had to work with" (181). Actually, between the 1720s and 1857, the Newfoundland barques ranged in size between 106 tons to 320 tons. The 320-ton *Upton*, built for the Spurriers in Placentia Bay probably in the 1760s, was undoubtedly a barque. These sizes may not compare well with the enormous vessels produced at a later period in Nova Scotia and New Brunswick, some as large as 1800 tons, but Newfoundland's square-rigged vessels were not small.

Parker also wrote, "The Newfoundland fish exporters had depended up to this time [about 1900] on chartering outside vessels for their export trade" (92). This is only partially true. Contrary to what Parker asserted elsewhere, ships from the Maritime colonies were less expensive to buy, and there are many instances in the St. John's newspapers noting how these ships arrived at port, were unloaded of their cargo, and then immediately put up for sale, usually selling for less than it would have cost to build in Newfoundland. This could be done because the governments of the other colonies subsidized shipbuilding materials, but the government of Newfoundland either would not or stated they could not afford to do so. In November 1917, for example, three Nova Scotia-built vessels sold in St. John's for $12,000, $19,000, and $40,000. The bidding wars on freight rates by Scandinavian and British vessels were also attractive to the Newfoundland exporters, and high insurance rates also resulted in hiring "foreign-built sails." So Newfoundland exporters did not turn away from buying Newfoundland ships because they were inferior in quality; they purchased vessels built elsewhere simply because those foreign-built vessels were cheaper, or they hired foreign ships as a means of saving money. And, as a footnote, it should be noted that mariners and merchants from the maritime colonies also bought Newfoundland-built ships, encouraging one to believe they were not inferior to vessels built in other colonies.

The evidence shows that scores of 100-plus and 200-plus-ton brigs, brigantines, barques, and schooners were constructed in various parts of Newfoundland, and these are all listed and described in the narrative of this two volume set. The skills honed in the shipyards of Michael Kearney, the Newhook family, the Rowe family, the Pittman family, the Gulliford family, the Manuel family, and many others were husbanded through many generations, and Newfoundlanders produced many superb vessels for the foreign trade and for trips "across the pond" to Europe and the Mediterranean, south to "the Brazils," and even across the Atlantic from ports in South America.

THREE-MASTED SCHOONERS OF 1817 TO 1916

The tern schooner originated somewhat earlier and in an entirely different place than Parker suggested when he wrote that "The first authentic tern was launched in the United States in 1849" (47). Unfortunately, he neglected to provide the vessel's name, tonnage, place of building, or the name of her builder. He also stated that the 98-ton *Bonita* was the first Canadian-recorded tern he was able to find and that she was owned by Nelson Hammond in Yarmouth, Nova Scotia, in 1857. Again the builder's name cannot be found. The first authentic Canadian tern, he wrote, was the 108-ton *Lady Mulgrave* built at Arichat, Nova Scotia, by Hypolite Marmaud in 1858.

Despite Parker's claims, however, historical documentation reveals that Newfoundland holds the distinction of producing the first two authentic tern schooners in the world, but we must decline the distinction accorded by the *Canadian Encyclopedia* which states that the *Jenny* of Harbour Grace was "the first recorded tern schooner in the world." According to Newfoundland historian Alan D. Cass, the *Jenny* was built in 1783 at Harbour Grace as a 50-ton, two-masted schooner. In 1791 the vessel was lengthened, enlarged to 78 tons, and converted to a three-masted vessel, thus becoming a tern schooner, but that work was done in Bristol, England, not in Newfoundland.

In 1817, twenty years after the *Jenny* was lost, James Howard and John Evans of Western Bay, Conception Bay, built the 32-ton, three-masted schooner *Maid of the Grove*. When she was registered de novo in 1837, she was owned by John Stuart, merchant of St. John's, and her master was James McDonald. She was registered again on November 25, 1841, and the last information available on this ship is that Denis Prendergast was appointed her captain on May 14, 1844; the *Maid of the Grove*, then, lasted for a remarkable twenty-seven-plus years.

The second authentic tern schooner in the world was the 98-ton *Resolution* built at Brigus in 1825 by Henry Norman; this vessel went missing at sea in 1829. Curiously, it was the only vessel constructed by Norman, and we have to assume the ship registers are correct, though owners at the time of registration are sometimes considered builders. The vessel may have been built for Norman by George Martin or William Cole or some other prominent builder in Conception Bay with Norman supervising the construction.

Jonas Newell Newhook was almost certainly the builder of two tern schooners at Hall's Bay: the 82-ton *Prince Alfred* in 1867 (which was wrecked off Fogo Island in 1869) and the 79-ton *Stour* in 1870 (which was registered de novo in 1876 at Falmouth, England, so its final fate is unknown). Other builders of tern schooners during this early period were James Gulliford of Hant's Harbour who fashioned the 140-ton *Lottie* there in 1882, Thomas French of Tizzard's Harbour who crafted the 261-ton *Nellie M.* at Burnt Bay in 1900, Matthew Nash who built the 152-ton *Duchess of Cornwall* at Burgeo in 1901, Job Manuel who constructed the 120-ton *Nina L.* at Northern Arm in 1907, John Davidge who built the 136-ton *Chrissie C. Thomey* at Burgeo in 1908, John R. Cluett who crafted the 132-ton *John Harvey* at Belleoram in 1909, John E. Lake who built the 39-ton *Dorothy*

Lake at Fortune in 1911 and the 171-ton *George Ewart* in 1913, and Giles Reeves who built the 28-ton *Hilda G. Reeves* at St. Lawrence in 1916.

Gulliford's *Lottie* of 1882 was stranded and lost off Pictou, Nova Scotia, in 1883 but salved and restored to the Pictou registry in 1884 and registered de novo at St. John's in 1891. She was converted to a two-masted vessel by her original builder, but her final fate is unknown. About the *Nellie M.* of 1900, Andrew Horwood wrote, "Her performance gave the lie to the rumor that Newfoundland-built vessels were inferior to those built abroad of soft-wood construction" (*Newfoundland Ships and Men*, 72). A newspaper report of January 6, 1917, extolled her amazing record of service for sixteen years, of her success "as a good carrier, a smart sailer and an able sea-boat...in construction and hull she is thoroughly seaworthy." The report commented on her many successful trips, to Brazil especially. Horwood wrote again that under her three captains she "carried more than a quarter of a million quintals of fish to Brazil, lasting out more than the expected life of a softwood vessel" (*The Book of Newfoundland*, Volume Four, 82). When her registry was transferred to Bridgetown, Barbados, in 1917 she had already served for seventeen years. The *Nina L.* of 1907 had a comparatively short life of about four years. Horwood commented, "The vessel was a beautiful little thing but was plagued from the very beginning." (*Newfoundland Ships and Men*, 51). Capt. Charlie Moore was sent out from St. John's to inspect her for Crosbie & Co. and to supervise the rigging. During the process of rigging the vessel, a man fell to his death. The ship was later caught in a severe storm and thrown over on her side and the cargo had to be jettisoned. While approaching a harbour in Notre Dame Bay, she was caught in the dense smoke of a raging forest fire and the crew were almost totally overcome by the smoke and barely survived. An unrelenting westerly gale kept her imprisoned for fifty days in the Mediterranean just inside the Straits of Gibraltar. And she was finally abandoned in the mid-Atlantic during a severe storm on December 12, 1911.

By way of summarizing the fate of these thirteen early Newfoundland tern schooners, one of them lasted for two years; three for four years (one of these was rammed by an iron ship and sank); one for six-plus years (it was transferred to another registry); one for eight years; one for nine-plus years; one for twelve-plus years; one for fifteen years (it was torpedoed); one for seventeen-plus years (it was transferred); one for twenty-four-plus years; one for twenty-seven-plus years; and one was lost "many years later," possibly lasting for more than twenty years. The sheer range of lifespan and the sea-going longevity a number of these ships enjoyed should be enough to prevent inaccurate generalizations regarding the quality of the earliest Newfoundland three-masted schooners.

THE TERN SCHOONERS OF 1917 TO 1929

A total of fifty-eight tern schooners were constructed in Newfoundland between 1917 and 1929. Parker had records for only forty-nine of these fifty-eight vessels. The tern schooners he missed are the 372-ton *Attainment*, the 136-ton *Fisherman*, the 117-ton *Tommie G.*, the 504-ton *Bella Scott*, the 498-ton *J. O.* (or *Jayo*), the 582-ton *Sordello*, the 351-ton *Kinsman*, the 180-ton *Port Union*, and the 159-ton *Workman*. These and all of the fifty-eight Newfoundland tern schooners are discussed in the narrative sections of *Master Shipbuilders* Volume One and Two.

Aside from having an incomplete list, Parker presented several inaccuracies about the terns. About the 417-ton *Ruth Hickman* of George W. Clarke at Springdale, he said she was built in 1918, rather than 1917, and that she was lost on the coast of Ireland on February 1, 1920. In fact, she was torpedoed in the North Atlantic on May 30, 1918, and the crew landed safely at Angra in the Azores. About the 203-ton *John E.* of John E. Lake at Fortune, Parker stated she was built in 1919, rather than 1917, and that she did not even complete her maiden voyage when, in actuality, she was lost off the coast of Brazil on June 20, 1918. Parker incorrectly surmised that the 428-ton *Marie Louise H*, constructed at Charlottetown by Archibald Chaulk in 1919, may have been built in Nova Scotia; he also wrote of a tern called the *Louise Hickman*, which he thought may have been built in Nova Scotia. That was, actually, the *M. L. Hickman* which was indeed built in Nova Scotia for the Hickman firm of St. John's. About the 169-ton *Rose M.* of Job Manuel at Norris Arm, Parker stated she was lost in the Azores on January 14, 1919, but it was in 1922. Parker specified that the 127-ton *Monchy* of Jacob Evans at Harbour Grace was built in 1920 rather than 1919, and he spelled her name *Monchey*. He called the 122-ton *Newton Stanley Lake* of George J. Miles at Pool's Cove the *Newton Lake* and stated she was built in 1920 rather than the correct date of 1919.

EXAMINING JOHN P. PARKER'S ASSERTIONS

Parker specifically claimed that the Newfoundland tern schooners were "not a success" (140), and he continued, "They were constructed by men who were expert only at building smaller craft. In the haste of producing the schooners it was general that the wood was not of good quality" (140). He elaborated further on the vessels of 1919:

> The schooners constructed during this period in Newfoundland were not of good quality and with a few exceptions did not last long. To repeat a few of the faults—they were built of unseasoned timber of poor grade, were too light in design and were insecurely fastened. On the other hand quite a few were lost as a result of stranding, but this was the fault of the navigators and not the construction of the vessel. (179)

And further, he wrote:

> It must be remembered that our vessels were built of softwoods.... In addition they were built hurriedly, and most of them without great capital investment. There is no doubt that in service the majority were overloaded, especially in the bulk salt trade, and were badly strained soon after launching. To have a vessel in those days meant she could be loaded until the sheerstrake was in the water amidships, the load-line requirements not affecting vessels of this class. (181)

He also suggested the pumping was "primitive" in that many of the terns had only wood pumps.

These are serious allegations by an experienced shipowner and operator, master mariner and maritime historian. Parker asserted that the Newfoundland tern schooners "with a few exceptions did not last long" (179). He further added, "To many readers it may seem that practically all these little ships came to a violent end.... Very few of this great fleet ended their days by rotting away on a beach" (180-181).

It is true that thirty-eight of the sixty-six tern schooners produced between 1900 and 1929 were lost in the first four years. That may seem like a terrible record until one examines the facts. About twenty-three of these were lost in severe, terrible storms in the Atlantic—mostly the North Atlantic and along the Newfoundland coast—in the period between November and March, the most unpredictable and treacherous time of year in the North Atlantic. Two of the terns were torpedoed, two were lost by fires on board, one was run down by another ship, one foundered at sea in a severe storm, and three were caught in heavy ice. While nine were abandoned at sea (the reasons are not given in the records), the "demon salt," in Dr. Harry Roberts' words, was likely the cause for some of these losses. Four of the terns drove ashore in terrible storms, and one was lost in a Caribbean hurricane. There is some overlapping here since sometimes there were dual causes for the loss of a ship. Some of those lost at sea or abandoned at sea, particularly in the North Atlantic, may have struck German mines left over from World War I that still remained floating in the shipping lanes until at least 1921. H. Gordon Green, in his book *Don't Have Your Baby in the Dory: A Biography of Myra Bennett*, wrote that ships even during this period "had to proceed with extreme caution, particularly when in coastal waters, because the sea was infested with mines" (23). Yet the Newfoundland terns continued to take their cargoes of codfish to European and South American ports. As soon as a ship was launched, rigged, and provisioned it was off "across the pond."

One of the greatest causes of these ships' early demise was the recklessness or negligence of merchant owners who put ships and crews in constant peril in their haste to deliver cargo. A Newfoundland crew in those days would seldom question the judgment of the owner, even if they knew their lives were in immediate danger. Newfoundland sailors had an acceptance of risk, danger, possible shipwreck, and even death at sea, but a similarly buoyant hope that if shipwrecked they would most likely be rescued; in fact, most crews were rescued. Andrew Horwood wrote, "But no vessel was ever tied up for the want of a captain and crew in any Newfoundland port" (*The Book of Newfoundland*, Volume Four, 82). Parker also paid tribute to Newfoundland sailors: "The men were tough and had absolutely no fear of the sea" (181). Sir Winston Churchill paid Newfoundlanders the high compliment that they were the best small boatmen in the world. And yet there were many losses of life at sea.

There are numerous examples of merchant recklessness, but two stories will suffice. The *Monchy* was sent north from Harbour Grace to Port Union in late January 1920 to take a load of codfish to Europe, spending three days in damaging coastal ice before she could get free of shore with her load. She then encountered a severe winter storm with strong winds, and the ship lasted for twenty-five continuous days before having to be abandoned. The recklessness in this example is exposed by the date of the event. In 1976, Frank Saunders of Carbonear was quoted in a newspaper article:

> Newfoundland captains were fully aware that they should not make a northern passage in winter. If done the ship would be running into heavy gales of adverse winds, sea and cold atmospheric

> conditions. They preferred to make a southern passage, where they would meet fair winds and calmer seas, above all, warmer weather.

See also his 1981 book *Sailing Vessels and Crews of Carbonear* (63, 97).

The attempt at a late-January northern crossing guaranteed the *Monchy*'s fate. And, in a second example, the *Jean & Mary*, heavily laden with coal in December 1921, was towed by tug, from St. John's, north towards Twillingate because there was an opportunity to pick up a load of codfish from Earle & Sons and transport it to Europe. The original captain, who had brought the ship from North Sydney, refused the owner's orders and left the ship at St. John's, where a new captain was then engaged. Both ships were caught in a blinding snow storm when the wind shifted to the southeast between Cat Island Harbour and Penguin Island. During the night, the tug "grounded on the breakers" and the *Jean & Mary* was "beat to pieces" on the northwest point of South Penguin Island. The crew of the tug barely made it to shore by means of a breeches buoy. The crew members of the *Jean & Mary*, all from Grand Bank, were lost. That was the kind of madness that resulted in the loss of too many vessels and too many precious lives.

Despite the unpredictability of storms and the avarice of merchants, fourteen of these tern schooners lasted between six and twelve years. The average life of a wooden ship was estimated by some to be about nine years; others have estimated the average life to be about fifteen years when the vessel is properly maintained and regularly refurbished. But even if properly maintained, a ship could fall victim to a sudden storm. Most ships engaged in the fishery around Newfoundland and Labrador were anchored for the winter. Those who dared to remain at Labrador beyond October ran the risk of severe fall storms, loss of the ship and cargo, and loss of life. The island of Newfoundland has over 6,000 miles of deeply indented coastline, and the coast of Labrador can be treacherous even in the balmy summer period when storms can emerge with great suddenness. Parker recognized this when he wrote, "The seas bounding Newfoundland are cruel. There are periods of ice, others of fog, and always the threat of a storm blowing up on the steep rocky shore" (181). I. C. Morris, a local historian, wrote in a St. John's newspaper in January 1923, "it was not unusual to see a large ship enter port with her top gallant masts and her top masts and her jib-boom carried away and having nothing left but her lower masts... [and other ships] with bulwarks and rails carried away also." There were many times when parts of the cargo had to be jettisoned in order to save the ship and her crew. During the stormy season of the year, ships arriving in Newfoundland would often stop at Trepassey or Aquaforte and telegraph St. John's requesting a tug to tow them to the city. They would not trust themselves to sails alone in rough, changeable weather.

In 1918, Capt. L. Blandford tried to bring the new, Nova Scotia-built vessel *Jean Campbell* to St. John's from Halifax, and they were caught in a series of terrible storms that once drove them 500 miles to sea and a second time 800 miles to sea from Cape Race. They made the Cape several times but were forced away by southeast winds which then turned to northwest winds. The situation was further complicated by the presence of heavy ice. They left Halifax on February 13th and arrived in St. John's on April 18th. Many other vessels approaching Newfoundland at various times had to heave to in the storm and let their vessel find its head, often drifting hundreds of miles to sea and even across the entire Atlantic, recovering only when the storm abated. A hurricane on the Labrador coast in late July 1908, "the second real hurricane which I have ever seen," in the words of Dr. Wilfred Grenfell, littered the entire coast north of Indian Harbour, and Dr. Grenfell counted fifty-eight wrecks in just two coves as he headed north to assist with the rescue. A storm on October 28, 1921, saw more than forty vessels ashore and wrecked throughout Notre Dame Bay. Andrew Horwood maked a fitting comment on the storms: "Every day was a challenge. Every storm called forth the best that is in Newfoundland seamen. The widows and orphans may best tell of the tragedies" (*The Book of Newfoundland*, Volume Four, 83).

The United States Navy Department measured Atlantic waves in 1921 and drew these conclusions: the normal average wave was thirty feet high; in rough weather, this increased to forty to forty-eight feet. During storms, waves could be 500 to 600 feet long and endure for ten to eleven seconds; the longest measured wave was half a mile long and spent itself in twenty-three seconds.

There was also the danger of colliding with derelict vessels left drifting in the ocean. It was estimated in 1921 that an average of eight vessels per year were lost in the North Atlantic because of collisions with derelict ships. It was further estimated that at least thirty derelicts were floating in that part of the ocean at any given time.

Ice was also a constant menace to ships, as the mighty *Titanic* discovered on April 14, 1912. *The New York Fishing Gazette* of July 11, 1914, reported, "The greatest ice blockade in the recent history of the Atlantic fisheries will be associated with the spring of 1914 for a long time to come no doubt." On June 1, 1918, the lighthouse keeper at Long Point, Twillingate, counted more than 200 icebergs from his vantage point. Later in June, several icebergs between Groais Island and Bonavista were standing more than 200 feet out of the water. The year 1919 is a good case in point. In early January it was estimated that seventy-five miles of ice had passed through the Strait of Belle Isle in the two weeks prior. Even at the end of May 1919 ice was filling Green Bay, and Arctic ice was almost up to Cape St. Francis. And in mid-June, the Strait was filled with ice east of Red Bay. More than 200 icebergs were counted on June 23rd at Tilting Harbour and Fogo, and a correspondent noted, "Never was such an ice jam seen before as at Fogo and Tilting." On July 15th the Strait of Belle Isle was still blocked with ice. Even in November an iceberg was seen that was estimated to be 650 feet long and 200 feet high. And in October 1923 an iceberg measuring 900 feet long and 200 feet high was seen on the Grand Banks. Running a ship in ice-infested waters was always a daunting task.

During World War I the presence of German submarines was an even greater menace. It seems quite irresponsible that it was not until January 1917 that the publication of the movements of all foreign-going ships was discontinued at St. John's. Newspapers of 1917 seemed to be publishing reports of "sunk by the Huns" every week. Shipowners stated matter-of-factly that they had great faith that the Royal Navy would provide all the protection needed. Even the Mediterranean was not a safe zone. In January 1917, Baine-Johnston & Co. lost its 99-ton schooner *Roma* there when twenty-five shells were fired at it from a German submarine. Sinkings were also reported on the east coast of South America. More than 100 Newfoundland fish carriers were lost in 1917 alone. At one point in 1918 the local newspaper noted that forty-three locally owned vessels and steamers engaged in the foreign trade had either been lost or sunk by submarines. Sometime during the war there were fourteen Newfoundland crews at Gibraltar waiting for transportation home, all the victims of German attacks on the high seas. Yet the traffic across the Atlantic did not cease. Apparently all the foreign-going ships during this period carried "war risk insurance"; this was only a reassurance to the merchant owners, not to the vulnerable crews. In August 1918 the Germans were creating havoc on the Grand Banks after they seized a large Newfoundland trawler, the *Triumph*, and used it as a raider. One of its captors exclaimed, "We don't want your food or your lives; we want your ships." Shortly after the capture, it was estimated that seventy banking fishermen whose vessels had been sunk by the raider during the past few days were making for land in their dories, some of them having to row 180 miles. It is nothing short of miraculous that so many vessels engaged in the trade were able to elude the German submarines during the four years of World War I.

The remaining tern schooners were those which were transferred to other registries or sold outside Newfoundland or whose end came in some other way. Several of these lasted for many years. The 491-ton *Kathleen* built by Job Manuel was sold to Greek owners after two years, and the 430-ton *Armorel* built by Jacob Evans was sold to French owners after three years. Likewise, the 344-ton *Dobbie* constructed by Daniel Pelley was sold to a St. Pierre firm after five years, and the 202-ton *General Ironsides* crafted by Eli Harris was damaged and sold to Portuguese interests after eight years. The 152-ton *Duchess of Cornwall* fashioned by Matthew Nash was transferred to Sydney, Nova Scotia, after fifteen years of use in 1916, but continued to be owned by the J. T. Moulton Company. Andrew Horwood wrote of the *Duchess of Cornwall* that "she took all the Atlantic had to give trading back and forth to and from Europe from 1901 to December 1916" (*The Book of Newfoundland*, Volume Four, 83). She was destroyed by a German submarine on December 8, 1916, in the mid-Atlantic. The 582-ton *Sordello* built by Adam Chalk was used for fifteen years and then became a storage hulk in Twillingate harbour. The 261-ton *Nellie M.* fashioned by Thomas French was transferred to Bridgetown, Barbados, after sixteen years of use, and Parker wrote that she was abandoned many years later. The 136-ton *Chrissie C. Thomey* built by John Davidge was transferred to Ottawa after two years, and Parker stated that she was lost at Rupert River, James Bay, many years later. The 364-ton *Herbert Fearn* constructed by Thomas Palfrey was transferred to Sydney, Nova Scotia, after twenty-four years of use, in 1940, and was torpedoed and sunk in 1942. The 25-ton *Hilda G. Reeves* crafted by Giles Reeves lasted for more than twenty-four years since she was registered de novo at St. John's in 1940, but her final fate cannot be determined. Thomas Palfrey's 130-ton *Mollie Fearn* (later renamed *Tishy*) lasted for thirty years before she was wrecked in 1950. The 184-ton *General Rawlinson* crafted by James Forsey was damaged in a storm in Portugal in 1922 and sold to Portuguese interests where after repair she became part of the Great White Fleet and was still fishing on the Grand Banks in 1949. And finally, the 152-ton *Bessie Marie* fashioned by Eleazer K. Mills was in active use for more than thirty-five years and possibly as many as forty-eight years.

JAMES FORSEY'S 232-TON, TERN SCHOONER *GENERAL BYNG* UNDER CONSTRUCTION AT STAPLETON'S POINT, MARYSTOWN, IN 1918.
(Courtesy of The Marystown Heritage Museum.)

A few missing details about the fate of the tern schooners listed in Volume One of this set are supplied here in order to give a more complete picture of these large ships. First, we will discuss the tern schooners of Bonavista Bay. Four of these were constructed by Archibald Chaulk at Charlottetown. His 332-ton *Joan Hickman* was struck by a sudden gale of wind within a short distance of the Spanish port, where she would discharge her load of codfish, and blown ashore and wrecked between Bonanza and Huelva on February 18, 1920; the 182-ton *Florence Swyers*, after seven years of service, was lost while carrying a load of salt in a severe storm 45 miles S.S.E. of Cadiz on May 30, 1925, after having just loaded. Andrew Horwood described the *Florence Swyers* as "an ugly looking schooner but a great sailer" (*Newfoundland Ships and Men*, 61); the 428-ton *Marie Louise H.* was overwhelmed by a major storm in the North Atlantic and was abandoned "in a sinking condition" on February 10, 1920; and the 159-ton *Workman* was lost on the way to Seville, Spain, in February 1923 when the *S.S. Maryland* carrying 10,000 tons of coal collided with the *Workman* cutting into her side and destroying the cabin house. The quick-witted Newfoundland crew jumped into the rigging and then onto the deck of the Maryland. Andrew Horwood described the

Workman as "one of the most beautiful schooners" (*Newfoundland Ships and Men*, 60) to come from the Chaulk shipyard. The 351-ton *Kinsman*, fashioned by Ernest Chaulk, lasted only two years and was abandoned at sea near Horta in the Azores on December 4, 1921. Three terns were built by Daniel Pelley at Port Blandford: the *Dobbie*, with its Bureau Veritas status, has already been noted; the 212-ton *Imprimus* was wrecked in a hurricane with winds of more than 100 miles per hour about 300 miles south of Bermuda while on the way from Turks Island with a load of salt on October 7, 1921; and the 431-ton *Pelleen* was caught in a terrible December storm with high northwest gales and was driven toward St. Pierre et Miquelon and was totally lost at Cape Piercly, Miquelon, on December 9, 1924. And finally, the 130-ton *Optimist*, crafted by Baxter Burry at Glovertown, spent her short life engaged in the trade to Oporto, Portugal. She was abandoned at sea in the North Atlantic on January 28, 1922.

As for the tern schooners of Trinity Bay, their careers and ends often seem part of a now familiar story. For the Port Union Shipbuilding Co., James Jones constructed six tern schooners. The 136-ton *Fisherman* was on her way to Spain on July 16, 1918, when she was becalmed about 400 miles from the Portuguese coastline. A German submarine surfaced nearby. The crew of the *Fisherman* were taken off the ship and given a hearty meal onboard the sub while the Germans removed foodstuffs and other valuables and then attached explosives to the schooner and watched it sink with its cargo. In a humane gesture, they towed the Newfoundland crew in their boat for two hours towards the Portuguese coast and let them row the remainder of the way. After rowing for six days, the crew arrived safely in Portugal. The fate of the 402-ton *Nina L. C.* is dealt with later in this chapter, as are the 125-ton *Mintie* and the 180-ton *C. Bryant*. The 304-ton *President Coaker* was on her way back to Port Union from Pernambuco when she was wrecked at Shoe Cove near Cape Race in early February 1924; all six crew members were lost. It is believed the vessel drove ashore in heavy weather and broke up. Debris from the wreck was later found near Cape Ballard. The 180-ton *Port Union* was totally destroyed by fire as it was moored in Port Union harbour on December 28, 1922. George Allan Gulliford's 264-ton *Barbara Barr* of 1918, crafted at Britannia, Trinity Bay, was abandoned in heavy ice near Colinet Island on March 12, 1921. The crew returned to the vessel the next day, but nothing could be done to save her, and she sank on March 19th. Gulliford also designed the 273-ton *Union Jack* for Emmanuel and Henry W. Stone, but the vessel was built by Josiah Frampton. This vessel was transporting a cargo of

200,000 feet of lumber and a deck load of logs (intended for use as telegraph poles) from Seldom Come By to Bay Roberts when she encountered gale-force winds from the southwest and struck rocks at the northeast side of North Penguin Island on November 28, 1926, and was lost; the crew, fortunately, was saved. The 172-ton *Humorist* was fashioned by Josiah Frampton for Henry W. Stone in 1921. John P. Parker conceded that she was "one of the better ones built in Newfoundland" (196). On one of her voyages back from the Caribbean, she was close enough to the Newfoundland coast to signal Cape Race and then was blown away by a punishing wind and eighteen days later arrived at Barbados with much damage including a broken rudder. After giving twelve years of excellent service, she ran ashore at the entrance to Argentia, Placentia Bay, on December 20, 1933, and became a total loss.

The only other tern schooner from Volume One of this set whose fate needs further description is the 203-ton *Over the Top*, which was constructed at Birchy Bay by William G. French in 1919. She was used as a fish carrier for four years, very probably paying for herself in that period, and was sold for less than $10,000 in July 1923 to Capt. James H. MacKinnon of Sydney, Nova Scotia, and her name was changed to *Sunner*. In August 1927 she left St. John's with a load of fish for Pernambuco and with Capt. Harry Thomasen of Grand Bank taking his wife and two young sons along for what might be a leisurely trip. Robert C. Parsons interviewed the captain many years later and discovered that the storm was so severe on the way south that Capt. Thomasen had to lash himself to the wheel. During the storm, the foremast was damaged. No replacement could be found either at Pernambuco or Maceio, so the crew repaired the mast as best they could. Encountering another severe storm on the way north from Turks Island in February 1928 with a load of salt for Lunenburg, the foremast broke again, this time plunging through the deck into the bottom planking, and the ship began to take on water. As they were loading their crew into the lifeboat, including Mrs. Thomasen and their two sons, the distressed ship was spotted by a Nova Scotia banker, the *Palitana*, which was fortunately way off course, and the *Sunner*'s crew was rescued. The vessel sank on March 9, 1928, having given nine years of good service.

When one examines the foreign-built ships which were owned in Newfoundland, whether they were British-built, American-built, or constructed in the Maritime colonies, a similar pattern of short lives ended at sea is evident. Dr. Harry Roberts, in his book *The Newfoundland Fish Boxes*, provides numerous reasons for the losses of Newfoundland-owned, foreign-built vessels: “total loss in a storm”, “suffered heavily from the ravages of the sea”, “crushed in the ice”, “run down by a steamer”, “missing and presumed lost”, “abandoned in the North Atlantic”, “too much salt and stormy seas”, “driven ashore in a gale”, “came to her end at the hands of the sea”, “caught fire while at anchor”, “caught in the ice and sank”, “torpedoed by an enemy submarine,” “a strong sea claimed her”, “ran into heavy weather, lost a rudder, was dismasted”, “snow storm and gale...another major storm...disabled”, “went quietly to her grave off the coast of Brazil”, “ran into heavy seas and soon became waterlogged”, “suffered from heavy seas and commenced leaking.” In short, foreign-built vessels, like Newfoundland-built vessels, were subject to powers beyond their control.

This overview helps us to have a clearer understanding of the lives of these sixty-six tern schooners of Newfoundland as we continue to examine John P. Parker’s assertions.

Parker pointed to the navigators as being part of the problem with ship losses, particularly by stranding, but the historical record shows only one case where a Newfoundland captain was both inexperienced and negligent. The captain of the 169-ton *Rose M.* held no certificate of competency or service when he lost the ship at Horta in the Azores on January 14, 1919, and though the mate was an experienced sailor, he too was found to be negligent. Incidentally, the term *stranding* is almost never used in the Newfoundland ship registers.

Though Parker paid high tribute to Newfoundlanders as daring, fearless men on the sea, tough and accustomed to a hard life afloat, he asserted that “The masters of most of the vessels were not certificated, and their knowledge of celestial navigation was very rudimentary” (182). While it is true that many, if not most, of the men who sailed around the coast and took their ships to the Labrador probably did not hold certificates of any kind, this was not at all true of the men who sailed across the Atlantic or south to the Caribbean and South America. The case above was a notable exception. Certificated masters and mates were not required for vessels travelling from Newfoundland to Canada or the United States. As early as 1788, Capt. William Pittman, retired master mariner at Trinity, was teaching navigation there, even to the sons of George Garland Sr. after 1798. From the early 1800s until about 1875, William John Youden (also known under the name of Thomas), a retired British naval officer, was teaching navigation at Bull Cove, near Brigus. Youden’s night classes and private lessons were largely responsible for the town’s reputation for producing master mariners, especially the Normans, the Bartletts, and the Wilcoxes, among others. Alexander O'Donovan at Carbonear taught navigation from 1843 to 1864. James Campbell came to Trinity from Ireland about 1840 to teach navigation, and the writer of an early article on Trinity characterized him as "the best navigator in a land of navigators." James Campbell and Henry Roche taught navigation at St. John's in the 1850s and 1860s, and Francis J. Doyle succeeded Campbell in 1863, setting up a formal Nautical School, and he is credited with graduating more than 100 masters as well as mates, among whom were the illustrious Robert Abram Bartlett (Captain Bob) and Abram Kean. Before the 1850s many mariners went to Boston, Halifax, and England for formal training in navigation. By about 1875 all foreign-going captains of vessels were required to hold formal certificates of competency. It was little wonder that H. F. Shortis and I. C. Morris, local historians, boasted in their columns about the great feats of the captains of Harbour Grace, Carbonear, and St. John's in their square-rigged ships, the splendid condition of these ships when they entered the home harbours after some amazingly fast trips "across the pond" or from "south in the Brazils." Someone should write a book about these amazing masters of Newfoundland vessels.

Furthermore, examination of the facts shows no justification for Parker's dismissive statement that the terns were "built hurriedly." To this he added, "In the older European countries the shipwrights took more time and used better materials to build their vessels" (181). Two examples may serve to refute Parker's statements. Job Manuel of Northern Arm built the 120-ton tern schooner *Nina L.* in 1907. This job was not done "in haste." By this time Manuel had already constructed eight ships including the 102-ton schooner *Dictator* and the 83-ton *Drummer's Tax* which lasted for twenty-one years. The Manuels were the most prolific family of shipbuilders in the history of Newfoundland. Through at least four generations they produced thirty-three master builders. Over a period of 150 years they produced over 200 ships. A ship of average size was begun in mid-fall and the crew worked at it until the launch in May or June of the following year. A larger ship, such as a tern schooner, would require an even longer period of building. I also have the testimony of my father-in-law, Gordon Locke, who as a fifteen-year old boy went to Thwart Island with his father, Alexander Locke, in the fall of 1916 to join Robert Evans and his shipbuilding crew for the construction of the 372-ton tern schooner *Attainment*. Apart from a short Christmas break, they worked continuously at the ship until it was launched in September 1917.

Based on interviews with master shipbuilders, shipwrights, and ship's carpenters and a thorough search of newspapers, the average time for the construction of a moderately-sized ship (say 40 to 60 tons) would be about six months, starting usually in November and launching the ship in May. The fisherman/planter who was also the builder would have been doing other things during this period by way of preparing for the coming season's fishery, but if he was using seasoned timber already pit-sawn, the six months would have been a good average time. Construction of the tern schooners required a much longer time. The 372-ton *Attainment* at Thwart Island, for example, required eleven months from start to launch. The 504-ton *Bella Scott* at Botwood in 1918 required more than a year for construction.

Michael Kearney would start construction of a vessel at any time of the year, even in May, and the Newhook family of Trinity and New Harbour even launched ships in January and February. Several instances were found of keels being laid in August, October, and November and launches taking place the following June or July. That was the norm. Men of the stature of Kearney, the Newhooks, and the Rowes could vary their start times because they were professional shipbuilders who were generally not restricted by the cycle of the annual fishery as were the fishermen and planters who built ships in the period from late fall until late spring.

Parker was also critical of the quality of the wood used in ship construction. It is true that Newfoundland lacked oak, but in the early days it had plentiful supplies of witchhazel (yellow birch) even up to the time of the construction of the tern schooners, and through all these years, much juniper (tamarack), birch, black spruce, and pine. The keel was made of witchhazel when it was available or birch or imported oak. The bottom planking consisted of birch because it was most durable under water. The frame and ribs were made of juniper or alternating juniper, birch, and spruce. Decks were often made of white pine. Black spruce might be used for topside planking. Spars were of pine or spruce, but many of these were imported in the later years. In fact, much of the wood for the tern schooners was imported.

The account books of the Horwood Lumber Co. offer many specifics for both the tern schooners *Attainment* and *Nancy Lee*. When William F. Horwood hired Robert Evans to construct the *Attainment*, he arranged for Robert to visit St. John's, gave him the blueprints for the ship, and sent him down to the harbour to examine some of the tern schooners anchored there. The whole venture was undertaken with the greatest care and seriousness. The Grand

Bank Museum has a posted blueprint entitled "Midship Section of 3-masted schooner to be built for Gander Stores Ltd." (This was the Horwood Lumber Co.'s store at Campbellton, their headquarters in the north). This latter would most likely have pertained to the building of the *Attainment*. The details specify the woods to be used:

> Hard pine rail 4 ½" x 12". Bulwark plank 2" thick spruce or pine. Bulwark stanchions 6" x 7" juniper or black spruce. Deck planking 4" thick soft pine. Deck beams 60" centres 12" x 12" juniper or pine. Beam shelf 7" thick hard pine. Stern post, rudder post, apron stem, all oak, elm or juniper. Breast hook juniper. Oak or juniper trenails for plank fastening. Planks over 7" wide to have 2 trenails in each timber. Hold stanchions 5" x 10" juniper on every second beam. Keel 12" x 12" oak. False keel 12" x 6" birch. Keelson 14" x 14" pitch pine. Rider Keelson 14" x 14" pitch pine (on top of keelson). Sister-keelsons 10" x 10" pitch pine (on each side of keelson). Garboard 6" thick x 10" wide, bolted (each side of keel as first plank). Note: No bolts to be nearer than 5' 0" to each other and 2 butt bolts and 1 rivet bolt through each butt. Frames not more than 5" apart. Floor timber 9" square juniper double. Straps 3" x 2 ½" iron, 8 each side. Deck beams 60" centres. Top timber 8" square juniper or spruce.

Complementing this are the Horwood Lumber Co.'s account books at the Newfoundland Public Archives. The accounts from 1915 to 1921 have been carefully examined, and there are many details about both the *Attainment* and the *Nancy Lee*. There are references to cutting bomb plates for the bow, to 1908 feet of ship's oak being delivered to the shipbuilding site, to 12" x 12" x 30' pieces of oak, of 12" x 14" pieces of pitch pine for the ship's keel and keelson, to 125,815 feet of pitch pine boards, to 83,246 feet of spruce deals being delivered from St. Mary's, of oak timber and pitch pine plank being delivered from Harbour Grace, to ship's iron being delivered from Lunenburg, Nova Scotia, to 1048 oak trenails, to hundreds of yards of duck of #1, #2, and #7 grades for the sails, to manila bolts, spectacle clews, grommets, port lights, wire, paint, tallow, etc. These facts go a long way in refuting Parker's contentions that the tern schooners were built in haste with wood of poor quality.

An example of the care which was taken in the construction of the *Attainment* may be seen in the testimony of my father-in-law, Gordon Locke, who stated that Mr. William F. Horwood arranged to have three or four caulkers sent out from St. John's to complete and supervise the caulking of the vessel. Two of these men were "Nicky Chislett" and "Old Man Boone." These were probably George Chislett and Joseph Boone, two prominent shipwrights of St. John's whose names appear in Volume One, Chapter One of this set. Gordon remarked that their work was superb. They would "expertly finger the oakum in front of the caulking iron." The planks were slightly beveled to hold the oakum more securely. The vessel was "under insurance" and it was required that the caulking be first class. Pitch or white lead was placed in the seams after the caulking was completed. "One old man went along after the caulking was done and made sure it was up to standard." Gordon also said the pumps were made of wood and galvanized iron which would not rust. "There were two pumps," he said, "They were connected. One with the handle on the top would bring the water up. The other would shut it off so the water could be brought up and flushed out from the deck." Parker had asserted that many of the ships' pumps were made of wood only. Even as early as 1907, William Wakely of Haystack was installing Angel's Patent Pump, wheel, and steering gear in his schooners, so it should be expected that ten years later the large schooners would have the latest equipment installed.

Total cost of construction of the 372-ton *Attainment* was $55,584.68. This was rounded out to $60,000 as "cost to construct and commission." Horwood collected a government bounty of $5,952 for the ship, charged freight on lumber from Campbellton of $1,465.06, collected a rebate duty of $2,003.15, and then sold the ship to the St. John's merchant firm of Campbell & McKay for $69,420.21. Today this amount would equal over $1,322,000, so Parker's contention that the tern schooners were constructed "without great capital investment" appears untrue. Total cost of construction of Horwood's other tern, the 149-ton *Nancy Lee*, was $41,392.30. Very little data is available on costs of other ships, but we know that in 1918 total construction costs of the 182-ton *Florence Swyers* was $75,000, that the 296-ton *Elizabeth Fearn* constructed in 1917 was valued at $60,000, and that the 491-ton *Kathleen* of 1918 carried a mortgage of $70,000. These figures indicate significant capital investment, but owners knew they could recoup their costs in a few years of successful voyages. Parker also stated that "the Newfoundland yards were able to pay much lower rates and thus produce a cheaper vessel" (179). The wages of shipwrights at St. John's in 1917 were $3.50 per hour for an eight-hour day, and in that same year local shipwrights were being recruited by Nova Scotia shipyards for $165 per month plus board. By way of comparison, Newfoundland seamen were routinely paid higher wages than those of Denmark, Norway, and Canada. The Board of Trade new schedule of wages for 1920 was as follows: certified captains $150 per month, non-certified captains $120, certified mates $85, non-certified mates $75, cooks $75, boatswains $65 and able seamen $60. So not only were the Newfoundland tern schooners built with great capital investment, but Newfoundland builders were paid very well.

How John P. Parker drew the conclusion that the Newfoundland terns were built in haste and with inferior woods is passing strange. He owned and operated a tern schooner himself and held conversations with some of the Newfoundland captains during this period, but it is implausible that these men furnished him with such assessments. He may have read some of Dr. Wilfred Grenfell's romantic and casual remarks about the Newfoundland shipbuilders' use of softwoods such as spruce and fir to build fishing schooners and make them appear as if by magic each spring at the mouth of a river. Dr. Grenfell was not always accurate in his portrayal of the trade. Parker may have gathered some information from the St. John's *Evening Telegram* which featured several articles on local shipping versus foreign shipping, ships of the Maritime Provinces and trade, and a debate between a "Mr. D," Capt. Abram Kean, and local historian H. F. Shortis between 1918 and 1923.

This interesting and unresolved dialogue was printed in the *Evening Telegram* in January and February 1922. It was initiated by a "Mr. D" who argued that "while we continue to employ fore and aft rigged craft during the Fall and Winter seasons in our transatlantic fish trade that our losses must continue to be heavy." He, like H. F. Shortis, was a champion of the square-rigged vessel. He continued:

> The thrust of the spars in the square-rigged—or some square-rigged-vessels is largely fore and aft—the direction in which the hull is structurally strongest, but in the fore and aft rigged vessel the thrust of the spars is largely lateral, the direction in which the hull structurally offers the least resistance.

Mr. D admitted it had been fifty years since he went to sea ("before the mast") and that he had not a high level of knowledge in naval architecture, but he argued forcefully that "there is something inapplicable in fore and aft rigged vessels to the fitting of them to successfully make winter Western ocean voyages." The editor of the *Telegram* then attempted to corroborate Mr. D's findings by musing about "weakness in the construction of shipping", "haste in building", "rushing contracts", "that ships rushed to completion should be structurally defective", etc. This language was so different from the flaming rhetoric that greeted every new vessel which arrived spanking new in St. John's harbour from all parts of Newfoundland in the preceding years. The editor did make the point that insurance costs for local shipowners were so "prohibitive and excessive" that it caused many of them to hire "foreign built sails" while "many of our local carriers are rotting at their moorings."

Capt. Abram Kean then entered the dialogue, offering his contribution of "some plain common sense." He boldly asserted that "no vessel was lost by the fact that she was a fore and aft rig rather than square-rigged." He had sailed in both and knew them well. Kean then introduced a new idea why some of these vessels may have been lost at sea. He suggested that "We have had more vessels abandoned this past 10 years on account of their rudders than any 10 years in our foreign trade in the last 50 years." He recounted other reasons for losses: contact with the rocks, several burnt, some abandoned because they lost their canvas. He quoted two theories about the rudders: "One is the patent steering gear, which does not in my opinion give the rudders so much play as the wheel chains. The other is the rake of the sternpost today compared to the sternpost of 30 years ago." He then commented, "And I want to say right here that if all our vessels were built out of the same class of wood and fastened in the same way as our English vessels are, you would hear of no foundering at sea regardless of whether they were rigged fore and aft or square-rigged." This is where Parker may have gotten his idea that the Newfoundland terns were not a success and that they were built with wood of poor quality.

The nostalgic H. F. Shortis entered the dialogue at this point. Ever the champion of the square-rigged vessels "with their skysail yards and studding sails," he poked fun at the tern schooner which he called the "three-legged" schooner, and he harked back to the great captains Joyce, Nichols, Wakeham, Vine, Gosse, Coward, English, and others. Kean replied to "the incorrigible Shortis," and accused him of having "a large spread of canvas" and reminded him that he (Kean) served at sea in the square-riggers for twelve years and that the fore-and-aft tern schooners are an improvement on the old ships. He opined that every shipyard in Canada, the United States, and Newfoundland were working overtime to cope with the great loss of ships through the submarine menace, and further that "Some shipyards on account of a scanty supply of timber may have turned out worse ships than others." Kean further reminded Mr. Shortis that steamers are finding the same fate at sea.

Back came Mr. Shortis with the contention that the captains of the fore-and-afters would be looked upon as landlubbers by the deep-sea veterans of the square-riggers. He then made a suggestion that the Nova Scotians and Prince Edward Islanders will not appreciate: "The strength, durability and sailing qualities of the square-riggers that were built in Nova Scotia and Prince Edward Island may be attributed to the natural genius of the Newfoundland skippers and shipwrights...because it was they who planned and saw carried out, the improvements necessary, not alone for the vessels to battle with the ice-floes but to battle with the wind and waves of the Atlantic during mid-winter." It is true that merchant owners sometimes sent their best captains and shipwrights to the colonies to attend and supervise construction of certain vessels for specific purposes. For example, Bowring Bros. sent Capt. Mark Burke of Carbonear to Liverpool, Nova Scotia, in 1916 to supervise construction of their new vessel, the *J. S. Gardiner*. We have also seen that Charles Newhook V of Trinity both built ships in Prince Edward Island and was called back on at least one occasion to supervise the completion and launch of a large vessel. Mr. Shortis, however, sometimes got carried away with his own rhetoric, and this was one such occasion. Capt. Kean then gave a non-reply to Mr. Shortis in an article that focuses entirely on the seal fishery and the government's silly and useless laws. He concluded with the contention that we ought to build more ships of the *Adventure* type that will be useful for summer trade as well as for spring time. No mention of winter voyages.

At this point, Mr. D re-entered the dialogue. He returned to his initial argument of the athwart-ship straining a ship was subject to in the fore-and-after rig during transatlantic crossings, and wrote:

> Only a competent naval architect is qualified to offer an acceptable opinion thereon. To enable even the most competent naval architect to decide this would call for his making a series of careful tests of the tortional and crushing strengths of the timber employed… Perhaps Insurance Associations or other proper authorities could procure an expert decision on which rig is better.

He then dismissed Capt. Kean's contention that the rudder and the rake of the stem may have caused some ships to founder. Capt. Kean and Mr. Shortis must have tired of the dialogue by this time, and the fitting conclusion to the issue was furnished by a public debate at the prestigious Methodist College Literary Institute, which tried to resolve the issue of whether "the products of Newfoundland should not be exported in foreign bottoms…and that

Newfoundland should have her own mercantile marine in which to export her products." The affirmative won by one vote. "It was clearly the opinion of the Institute that as a matter of abstract principle Newfoundland should have her own mercantile marine in which to export her products—a marine suitable and adequate." The negative side expressed the opinion that the Newfoundland fish carriers were too big but had already paid for themselves and now the Danish ships were of a more appropriate size for shipping Newfoundland products. Capt. Abram Kean was a member of the winning side, and Joseph R. Smallwood made comments from the floor.

R. J. Cunningham and K. R. Mabee, in their book *Tall Ships and Master Mariners*, echoed the criticisms of Parker when they wrote, "Owing to a shortage of suitable timber handy to her ports, Newfoundland was not part of the great shipbuilding endeavour." Cunningham and Mabee may have drawn their unwarranted conclusions from the fact that the Newfoundland government in 1905 expressed its concern about "obtaining suitable timber for ship building, within reasonable distance of the settlements" and "reserving under more stringent regulations what remains ungranted of this valuable colonial asset for the purposes of Marine Architecture," but this was due to the onslaught that large lumber mills and the burgeoning pulp-and-paper industry were making on available timber stocks.

Dr. Harry Roberts asserted that the "demon salt" was the cause of many ship losses in the North Atlantic and on return trips from Turks Island and Grand Turk. In speaking of the loss of the British-built top-sail schooner *Muriel*, he wrote:

> On December 10, 1892, she sailed from Alicante for St. John's with a cargo of salt and was never heard from again. Perhaps it should be noted here why many of these vessels were lost while travelling westward with cargoes of salt. Salt was the most dangerous of the many products carried on these ships because it plugged the pumps and rendered them inoperable after heavy seas caused leaks in the wooden framework. Consequently, salt, which was necessary for the curing of fish, was ironically the ogre in the days of wooden ships and manually operated pumps.

Salt, more than poor quality wood and inferior workmanship, was the likely cause of many ship losses which have remained unexplained so far. Dr. Roberts listed the many ships who were victims of the "demon salt" as they plied the North Atlantic or brought their fatal cargoes from the Caribbean Ocean.

It is known for certain that at least eight of the Newfoundland tern schooners were lost while carrying loads of the "demon salt": the *Nina L. C.* in 1919 with a load of salt from somewhere in the Caribbean; the *Imprimus* in 1921 with a load of salt from Turks Island; the *Helen Jean* in 1921 with a load of salt from Turks Island; the *Norma B. Strong* in 1922 with a load of salt from Cadiz; the *Florence Swyers* in 1925 with a load of salt from Cadiz; the *General Byng* in 1928 with a load of salt from Grand Turk; the *Sunner*, also in 1928, with a load of salt from Turks Island; and the *Ria* in 1931 with a load of salt from Cadiz and fighting fierce storms in the North Atlantic for fifty-four days.

It is possible that eleven of the other terns were lost under similar conditions, but it is impossible to be certain since reports do not always indicate whether these vessels were coming or going and do not always state the cargo. The *John E.* was totally lost off the coast of Brazil near Bahia (Salvador) on June 20, 1918. The *Pauline Martin* was abandoned in the North Atlantic on December 9, 1918. The *Mabel Davis* fell victim to the North Atlantic when she was totally lost on May 10, 1919. The *General Knox* was lost in a raging storm in the North Atlantic on October 14, 1919, when her bow was split open, her masts were jarred, and she was entirely disabled. Overwhelmed by a major storm in the North Atlantic, the *Marie Louise H.* was abandoned "in a sinking condition" on February 10, 1920. The *Violet Buffett* was lost on Mortier Point on February 27, 1920, on the way back to Marystown from Cadiz, almost certainly with a load of salt. On a return trip from Portugal, the *Newton Stanley Lake* ran into a severe winter storm on January 6, 1921, and began to leak badly—the crew abandoned ship on January 19th after herculean pumping efforts failed. The *Mintie* was abandoned in the North Atlantic on January 10, 1921. The *Optimist* spent her short life of three years engaged in the trade to and from Oporto and was abandoned at sea in the North Atlantic on January 28, 1922. The *C. Bryant* was abandoned at sea thirty-six miles northeast of Bermuda Island on March 26, 1928, again almost certainly with a load of salt. And the *Ronald M. Douglas* was abandoned at sea in the North Atlantic on November 12, 1930. Parker conceded that this last vessel had "good average passages on her voyages in the export fish trade" (195) but stated that "the usual fate overcame her" (195). She was then nine years old.

There is an interesting case reported in the *Evening Telegram* of October 17, 18, and 24, 1919. When the Newfoundland crew of the British-built *Onita* was rescued in a midnight storm in the Atlantic on the way from Oporto to a Newfoundland port with its load of salt, the captain of the rescuing vessel did not believe the crew's story that the cargo of salt had shifted, crushing to death Capt. Brushett and his brother Ernest. The four members of the crew were locked up and held for mutiny and murder, but one week later they were exonerated of the charges by the British Consul in Philadelphia. Such were the risks that carrying salt entailed.

Were the tern schooners overloaded, as Parker implied? The merchant owners of these large ships may have regarded them as almost invincible or at least as the means of making quick money, shipping at all seasons of the year, since it is known that a busy tern could pay for itself in very few years with successful trips. Parker asserted that overloading was a significant cause of losses: "There is no doubt that in service the majority were overloaded, especially in the bulk salt trade, and were badly strained soon after launching" (181). That is a rather sweeping statement offered with no supporting statistics. I have read Newfoundland newspapers on microfilm from 1917 to 1925 to determine the facts. In that nine year period, there are more than thirty-five instances in which the size of the cargo was stated, the starting point of the voyage, the stated destination, etc. This includes the Newfoundland tern schooners, terns from the Maritime Provinces, British-built ships, other foreign ships, and two or three steamships.

What, in fact, was the carrying capacity of a wooden vessel? In newspaper accounts in the *Public Ledger* and the *Newfoundlander* between 1839 and 1869, there are at least fourteen instances where the carrying capacity of schooners and brigs is clearly stated. The estimates range from about 20 quintals per ton to about 26 quintals per ton. For example, the 100-ton brig *Waterlilly*, built at Ferryland by Thomas Rossiter, was offered for sale in April 1840, and it was stated the vessel could carry 2300 quintals of fish in bulk (i.e., 23 quintals per ton). The 100 tons was said to be New Measurement, so by the Old Measurement the vessel would have measured about 125 tons.

Another factor also needs to be taken into account. There were three different measurements for tonnage: gross tonnage, net tonnage, and registered tonnage. Adam Chalk's tern *Sordello* had gross tonnage of 582 and net tonnage of 486, but her registered tonnage was 440. This was due to extra additions such as space for propelling power and a variety of other spaces such as chart room, boat store, and sails room, etc. consisting of 142 tons. The tern schooners had several additions that might not have been in the earlier brigs such as officers' mess rooms, steward's room, bathrooms (usually called water closets), lazarette (for quarantine purposes or to hold extra provisions), excess of hatchways, chain lockers, various deck houses, cook room, pantry, etc.

For our purposes, carrying capacity of the tern schooners will be calculated by registered tonnage only and not by gross tonnage or net tonnage, and the calculations are based on the average of 22 quintals per ton. And a few examples reveal striking results.

The 402-ton *Nina L. C.* had a registered tonnage of 325, so her carrying capacity would be about 7150 quintals, and she was cleared from Port Union on January 14, 1919, with 6682½ quintals. She was loaded almost to her maximum and sailed at a most dangerous time of year. She had been rejected for Crosbie & Co. at the time of building because the inspector felt her fastenings were poor. This deficiency may have been corrected as a result of the inspection. She was abandoned in the North Atlantic on her maiden voyage, January 25, 1919.

The 430-ton *Armorel* had a registered tonnage of 379 and thus a carrying capacity of about 8400 quintals. She left St. John's on January 3, 1919, with 8000 quintals and was bound for Italy. She continued to carry cargoes of codfish, but her voyages are difficult to trace, and in 1921 she was sold to new owners in France.

The 127-ton *Monchy* had a registered tonnage of 109 and therefore a carrying capacity of 2398 quintals, and she had met the demanding requirements of Lloyd's surveyors. On her maiden voyage from Port Union on January 20, 1920, she was overloaded with 4000 quintals of codfish. She was caught in punishing ice for three days before she could get free of the coast and then encountered a severe winter storm with heavy winds which lasted for several days. She was abandoned on January 28th.

The 149-ton *Nancy Lee* had a registered tonnage of 114 and a carrying capacity of 2508 quintals, but she sailed from Little Bay Islands for Malaga on November 19, 1923, with 5000 quintals of Labrador fish from James Strong Ltd. She left St. John's on February 23, 1925, for Pernambuco with 1645 drums and 3290 half-drums containing 3760 quintals of fish for the Monroe Export Co., and her next trip was on October 1, 1925, from Horse Harbour, Labrador, with 5515 quintals of codfish in bulk for Seville, and the shipper was Lazo & Co. In all three cases, the *Nancy Lee* was seriously overloaded. During the last trip bound for Seville, she was lost on October 25th in the mid-Atlantic during a severe storm characterized as "a torment of fury."

The 130-ton *Mollie Fearn* had a registered tonnage of 118. Her carrying capacity was 2596 quintals, but on May 31, 1920, she loaded 4320 quintals of codfish from T. P. Kemp & Co. of Placentia for Halifax. She was overloaded but survived the trip. On August 10, 1920, she cleared for Porto Rico with a more reasonable load of 2142 quintals of codfish and 143 quintals of haddock from Job Bros. & Co. We know of only one specific load that the 296-ton *Elizabeth Fearn* carried; she loaded from Bowring Bros. on September 15, 1920, for Bahia, and we do not know how many quintals she was carrying (her capacity would have been about 5412 quintals since her registered tonnage was 246), but on November 4th it was reported that, in order to save the ship in stormy weather, Capt. Vatcher had to jettison several hundred packages of fish.

The 180-ton *C. Bryant*, with a registered tonnage of 141 and with a carrying capacity of about 3100 quintals, loaded 3850 quintals for Oporto on October 15, 1921, at Port Union. And finally, the 99-ton *Vickers-Vimy* would have had a carrying capacity of about 1900 quintals, but on December 22, 1921, she was loaded at Brigus with 2000 quintals of casked codfish for export; the destination is not given, but she must have completed that trip because she lasted for seventeen years.

The situation was similar with foreign-built ships owned by or chartered by Newfoundland merchants. The 147-ton *Clintonia* owned by Campbell & McKay had a registered tonnage of only 99 and a carrying capacity of about 2200 quintals, but she was wrecked in early November 1921 on the way to Oporto with 3445 quintals aboard. The 108-ton *Mary F. Hyde* had a registered tonnage of 79 and a carrying capacity of less than 1800 quintals but carried 2200 quintals in June 1918 shipped by N. & M. Smith from "the Ancient Colony." The 109-ton *Defender* carried 2960 quintals of codfish from Burin to Lisbon on January 29, 1919, more than 760 quintals of an overload; on February 3rd she put back to Burin in a leaky condition. Presumably this was fixed, and she proceeded later, but no follow-up reference could be found for that particular trip. She was wrecked in 1932. The 110-ton *Nina Lee* sailed for Oporto in late March 1921 carrying more than 550 quintals of an overload from A. E. Hickman & Co., and again in September of that year with more than 700 extra quintals, and again from A. E. Hickman & Co. She was abandoned at sea in the Mediterranean later that year. When overloading occurred on trips to Europe and South America, it was the fault of the merchant owners and does not reflect on the skill of the shipbuilders, the staunchness of the vessels, or the navigational skills of the captains.

Parker stated that one of the reasons the Newfoundland tern schooners were "not a success" was that they were "constructed by men who were expert only at building smaller craft." A thorough check of the Newfoundland ship registers was done for the period 1803 to 1935, and the results of this research are quite interesting.

Newfoundland shipbuilders during this period constructed 416 ships ranging in size from 100 to 613 tons, and 328 of these were built before the 1917 to 1921 period, which is the focus of Parker's criticism. Twenty-two were built after 1921. In the period 1815 to 1935, our shipbuilders also constructed 355 ships measuring between 80 and 99 tons. "Large" is a relative term in this context, and, granted, these sizes do not compare with some of the enormous ships constructed in Nova Scotia and New Brunswick, but it is a fitting description of the brigs, brigantines, barques, and tern schooners built in Newfoundland and many of the tern schooners built in the Maritime provinces. The sixty-six Newfoundland tern schooners ranged in size between 117 tons and 582 tons.

There was a measure of concentration on building large ships in the early years, roughly from 1800 to the 1880s, and then occasional activity in the 1890s, then a particular focus on smaller ships for the Labrador fishery and the Banks fishery, and then came a resurgence in the building of large fish carriers in the period 1917 to 1921. Small ships had always been constructed to pursue the inshore and near-shore fishery, and during the period when the Labrador fishery was being vigorously pursued (roughly the 1860s to the early 1900s) medium-sized ships were being built; most of the Labrador ships were probably between 35 and 65 tons, though many were smaller still. The Grand Banks fishery saw the construction of many very small ships, some of them no larger than 5 or 7 tons, but most of these were decked and thus required to be registered.

Newfoundlanders were expert builders of both large and small vessels, but the size of the ship does not guarantee a long life. The large ships of the Maritime Provinces also had trouble with the elements, winter storms, and contrary seas. These ships were also stranded, wrecked, abandoned, blown out to sea, cast away, dismasted, burned and destroyed, and sometimes within a year or two of being constructed. The men of New Brunswick and Nova Scotia may have been builders of larger ships, but no ship was immune to the ravages of the sea. Though Parker indicated in both of his books the fate of many Nova Scotia vessels, he never made a comment about their having been built hurriedly or with inferior woods or by inexperienced shipbuilders. Nor did he point out the short lives of many of these vessels.

It was grossly unfair of Parker to state that the Newfoundland shipbuilder lacked the knowledge and skills to construct the tern schooners properly. Some of the men who built these or supervised their construction had sailed tern schooners from Britain, the Maritime Provinces, and the United States, or had even supervised the construction of ships in Nova Scotia and Prince Edward Island for their Newfoundland merchant-owner bosses in order to assure these vessels were staunchly constructed to deal with the ice, wave, and wind conditions of the cruel Newfoundland coasts and the North Atlantic. There was an innate knowledge and skill in the hands and heads of the Newfoundland shipbuilders that resulted in well-built ships. The skills honed in the early years of shipbuilding, and particularly under the tutelage of English and Irish master builders, many of whom stayed and produced generations of new shipbuilders, were not lost but husbanded into a particular love of wood with skills to match. The Newfoundland shipbuilder had control over the quality of the ships he constructed but had no control over the elements, the recklessness or poor judgment of merchant owners, or the navigational skills of the captains.

Most of the Newfoundland shipbuilders were men of considerable experience, usually belonging to shipbuilding families who had pursued the trade for several generations. A total of twenty-nine master builders constructed fifty-eight tern schooners.

Several of the builders of the tern schooners were of the third or fourth generation of shipbuilding families—men like Henry William Stone (probably best considered as the supervisor of two of the terns, rather than the builder), Josiah Frampton, Job Manuel, John E. Lake, Jasper Lake, Robert Evans, Jacob Evans, John H. Forsey, James Forsey, Baxter Burry, William G. French, and Eleazer K. Mills—and others were certainly at least second generation builders—men like Morgan Roberts, James Jones, Archibald Chaulk, Ernest Chaulk, Job Wiseman, and Arnold Cluett. Others are more difficult to place generationally, but no one would argue with the record or the skills of men such as Thomas Palfrey, Adam Chalk, Eli Harris, George Allan Gulliford, George W. Clarke, Joseph Miles, and George J. Miles. We lack detailed information about men such as Robert White, John J. Norris, Theophilus Wells, and David Power, but all of them seem to be from at least the second generation of shipbuilders; these last three may be considered as anomalies unless further information comes to light. Daniel Pelley is best considered as a manager of operations, but it should be noted that one of his three tern schooners was awarded Bureau Veritas status, as was the *Kathleen* of Job Manuel. By way of summary, the facts assembled here about the vast majority of the builders of the Newfoundland tern schooners of the early 1900s call into serious doubt several of the assertions of John P. Parker.

The detailed descriptions of the tern schooners recorded in the original registration documents suggest they all must have been built from very similar blueprints. References to gross tonnage were followed by a catalogue of "less...as per contra," defining the deductions for captain's cabin, mate's cabin, steward's pantry, bosn's locker, forecastle, etc. in order to calculate the net tonnage. Use of blueprints was an innovation for some of these shipbuilders because they had been accustomed to building by the rounded or layered model rather than by formal blueprints. Where did A. E. Hickman & Co., Horwood Lumber Co., Campbell & McKay, the Port Union Shipbuilding Co., Newfoundland Shipbuilding Co., etc. obtain their blueprints? Newfoundland's connection with the New England states was much stronger in those years than with the Canadian Maritime Provinces, so it is most likely that this is where the blueprints were acquired. The Grand Bank builders and owners favored the American-style schooner because of its sailing qualities, and the influence of the Newfoundland Shipbuilding Co. at Harbour Grace would have come from two sources: America, which was the headquarters of the Norwegian financiers who were funding this operation, and Norway and Sweden from which many of their staff, including the manager and chief engineer, came. In view of this, Parker's comment about the Newfoundland terns being "too light in design" is questionable.

SUMMARY

It may be of interest to note which merchant firms were having these tern schooners built. The A. E. Hickman Co. had ten of them constructed for their own purposes. Samuel Harris Ltd. of Grand Bank had seven. John E. Lake and the Lake Bros. of Fortune had four. The Monroe Export Co., G. & A. Buffett, and J. O. & Arthur Williams each had three. And the others were constructed by shipbuilding companies or individual master builders for other merchant firms or business firms.

After careful consideration of the facts put forward in this chapter, I would give the causes of ship losses in the following order: the severe winter storms of the North Atlantic, the reckless demands of merchant owners, the "demon salt" and its effects on ships' pumps and timbers especially when the salt became wet from storms, the enemy submarines and floating mines during and following World War I, the overloading of fish cargoes, the insufficiency of ballast when a ship was not carrying regular cargo, and then a variety of causes mostly relating to collisions, heavy ice, wind, snow storms, waves, fog, fire, etc.

What is truly disconcerting is that some Newfoundland writers and speakers have, over the years, simply accepted the conclusions drawn by Parker about the Newfoundland tern schooners without examining the facts. I hope this study will discount some if not all of Parker's conclusions and give the benefit of the doubt to the Newfoundland master builders.

There is another fact which ought to be considered. If the Newfoundland tern schooners were inferior in construction, why were foreign nationals, the Canadian government, Nova Scotia merchant firms, and master mariners regularly purchasing them? These facts speak for themselves.

The Newfoundland tern schooners of the early 1900s were not built too hurriedly; they were built too late. The boom was over before the ships of 1921 were launched, possibly also the ships of 1919 and 1920. The steamship had arrived and was supplanting the large wooden fish carrier in getting cargoes to Europe and South America. It had long been contended that codfish carried in steamships would be contaminated by the fumes of oil and gas, but this proved not to be so. The enormous loss of ships during the early years of World War I led to a spate of shipbuilding in Newfoundland but not haste in building. The building of a ship was undertaken with the greatest seriousness because the builder knew his ship would be surveyed and inspected either on the building site or at St. John's and then recommended for the bounty. Teams of expert caulkers were on occasion sent to the building site to inspect and perfect the work of local tradesmen. There was a decided drop in the building of large ships in the Maritime Provinces well before the large "fish boxes" began to emerge in Newfoundland. It appears that by the time these vessels had paid for themselves their merchant owners simply abandoned them. Both the government of Newfoundland and merchant owners were too late in building and too inaccurate in forecasting the future.

EPILOGUE

WHAT MORE CAN WE say about the master shipbuilders of Newfoundland and Labrador?

Men who were skilled at crafting ships through the hundreds of years of our history turned their attention now and then to the construction of public buildings: churches, schools, lodges, houses, and the shops and stores of merchant firms. The term "builder" appears occasionally in the directories or census records, and it can have a double meaning—either shipbuilder or building contractor. As there was a Shipwright's Society in St. John's, there was also a Master Builders Association. The distinction between the two trades was a fluid one. When the shipbuilder constructed public buildings, he used many of the same methods as in shipbuilding, thus transferring his skills from sea to land. The use of ship's knees to support an upper storey or to strengthen the connection between upper wall and roof was common. These are plainly visible in the Rorke Store in Carbonear and in the United Church building at Cottrell's Cove constructed as a Methodist church in 1906. The joining of large timbers through a process called scarfing extended the length of a timber as the shipbuilder lengthened the keel of his ship. The use of wooden trennels rather than bolts, both in scarfing and in joining timbers at various angles, is clearly evident in the church at Cottrell's Cove. As the shipbuilder used oakum to seal spaces between the ship's planks, so the house builder used oakum the same way, as in the Lester-Garland house at Newhook's Point in New Harbour with its "barrelled" ceiling.

AN EXAMPLE OF HOW TIMBERS WERE "SCARFED" TO EXTEND THE LENGTH OF A VESSEL'S KEEL. NOTE THE TRENNELS (TREENAILS) WHICH FASTEN THE PIECES SOLIDLY TOGETHER. (Author's Collection)

Few of these churches still exist, and those that do should be preserved for their unique features. The church at Cottrell's Cove was constructed by shipbuilder Matthew Dalton Jr. in 1906. In 1907 his colleague Jonas John Newhook, son of the famous Jonas Newell Newhook, built the Roman Catholic church at Fortune Harbour with its beautiful flying buttresses. Charles Newhook II was the "Architect" of the Anglican church in New Harbour in 1815. William Newhook II helped build the Anglican church at Catalina and was also a house carpenter in his later years. After Charles Newhook V finished his amazing shipbuilding career, he worked as a carpenter for several years at Trinity with his colleagues Charles Granger and David B. Grant. Robert Horwood of Carbonear was the master builder of the Anglican church at Heart's Content in 1878. James J. Mackey of St. Brendan's, Bonavista Bay, following a twenty-year career of shipbuilding in the early 1900s, turned his attention to the construction of churches and schools. Mackey had a reputation for being a fine "finished" carpenter and cabinet maker. And the list goes on and on.

The Methodist church at Grand Bank was constructed in 1876. I was living there in 1965 when it was demolished and its hand-carved florets and screens and rails carried off to the mainland. After ninety years of enduring wind and wear, it was still "as solid as the church." The coloured memorial windows of the church at Northern Arm were salvaged in 1995 and placed in the new chapel ninety years after the old building had been erected. In both cases, I learned that much cursing was done by the contractors as they struggled to separate timbers which had been so firmly and securely fastened by the original builders.

The lives of Newfoundlanders have always been governed by the sea. It has provided our livelihood and our transportation for centuries. In the words of Edward A. Whitcomb, Newfoundland is "the only Canadian province where the sea has been more important than the land in shaping its history... the history of Newfoundland and Labrador centres on the exploitation of sea resources." Historian David Alexander writes of "a depressing tendency to neglect the province's most obvious natural resource—the sea" (Hillier and Neary, 18). The sea as both friend and enemy has been portrayed in Tom Cahill's adapted parody from the 1960s: "The sea, oh the sea, the wonderful sea, long may it roll between people and me." The key to understanding the song is in the double meaning of the word "wonderful." In traditional Newfoundland thinking, wonderful can mean either glorious or terrible. The sea gave us a feeling of splendid isolation, of wonder, that regularly fed the soul.

An accurate picture of the Newfoundland man's traditional relationship with the sea can be portrayed by three statements laid side by side and pondered. First, the sea surrounding Newfoundland was regarded by Britain from earliest times as a nursery where men were rigorously trained and shaped for the formidable Royal Navy. Second, in the words of Sir Winston Churchill, Newfoundland men were "the best small boatmen in the world." And third, when the tern schooner *Ria* was shipwrecked in the North Atlantic in November 1931, after fighting the fury of an unrelenting storm for fifty-four consecutive days, the newspaper of the day noted that each of the six crew members had been shipwrecked at least once before this harrowing experience. To say the sea is in their blood is no exaggeration. There is only one thing Newfoundlanders have not done with the sea, and that is walk on it.

It is almost sixty years since I first began to gather information about my family's shipbuilding exploits. My search in the intervening years has been uneven, sometimes postponed and often interrupted, but in the past five years it has been clearly focussed. This undertaking has required twenty-five to thirty years to gather all the material, another year to organize it, and two years to write these two volumes. To say this has been a labour of love is to understate the commitment. A common maxim states that the secret of good writing is in the re-writing. These books have been re-written many times, and the polishing continues until the editorial process is complete. I am happy to commend them to you, the reader, as at least good and worthwhile books, filling a largely forgotten chapter in our history, honouring men whose achievements were inestimable, even if my craft of writing pales in comparison to the craft of our master builders.

UPDATE ON THE CULTURE OF OUTPORTS PROJECT

LESSONS FROM THE OUTPORTS

PHILIP EVANS

WHEN THE CULTURE OF OUTPORTS program began in 2010, we were observers keenly interested in the cultural heritage of Newfoundland's outport communities. Over the span of four years, we feel we're no longer visitors: we've developed a unique understanding of these communities, and the influence of the people and places of Newfoundland can be seen in the broader heritage work we do.

We've learned a great deal from the rural Newfoundland cultural landscape, and the next step will be to apply these lessons on a wider scale. With the help of our partners—TD Canada Trust, the Canada Arts Council, and the Province of Newfoundland and Labrador—we are closer to understanding the future of the outport community and rural Canada on a larger scale. We see the words "outport" and "rural" as interchangeable, especially as we enter a period of transition from resource-driven economies to the possibilities of a culturally driven process of reinvigorated settlement.

We know that outport and rural communities are valuable. New residents still join the rural environment even without the resource-driven opportunities that created these communities, as this environment offers the opportunity to explore alternative lifestyles. The rural can be a flexible place, a place of experimentation, a workshop or design studio to craft a pleasing setting for many. This is an important space, place, and activity for Canada and Canadians. More than just old buildings, historic and distinct traditions, the outport and rural environment can offer various lifestyles, by land or by sea. The components of the Culture of Outports program are growing to include a variety of services to the rural environment.

Over the last four years, we've documented dozens of outports, speaking with residents, local businesses, public sector agencies, politicians, potential investors, students, and educators. We've studied the outport settlement, growth and decline patterns. We've examined various scales and groupings of outports and observed outport types. We've explored tangible and intangible cultural heritage, mapped patterns of growth. We've explored numerous private ventures and public-private opportunities, and we've been intrigued by other community initiatives and models for growth and adaptation.

The Culture of Outports model is ideally a cycle: Select a location, research it, study it, analyze our findings, test our ideas, learn from the experience, and share the information we discover. We don't have an expectation of a grand master plan or answers to heavy questions such as what is the future for outport communities and rural Newfoundland.

Our initiative works with community members to gather information on the community in the form of historic pictures and records, audio recordings, maps, our own site photography, and other records of the community's development. Taking a holistic approach to communities, we explore what we consider to be the original creative industries and creative economies of North America. Based on this research, our Community Cultural Economic Plans address the opportunities intrinsic within cultural heritage. The Plans propose a Cultural Heritage Development Framework for the town to consider in preparing future planning: its values, its vision, and its priorities. The Plans identify a planning context, outline a planning process, and provide benefits and guidelines for the preparation of an official town plan based on the incorporation of its cultural heritage resources.

The next step is a community build. In partnership with the community and graduate architectural students, we design and build a small-scale permanent installation on the site. We document the design/build project, such that it may be used by the community for future fundraising purposes, or by neighbouring communities to imagine the potential in their own context.

The heritage value and adaptive reuse potential of existing buildings, as well as local cultural practices, rituals, and intangible heritage traditions, inform the siting, design, and construction of the installation.

In addition to the design-build, related community engagement activities are undertaken to communicate the reasoning behind the project and celebrate the local heritage which will be highlighted through the installation. In this way, community builds serve as forums for transmitting knowledge and skills about tangible and intangible heritage.

These activities are all aligned with our program's key principles:

LIVABLE COMMUNITIES FIRST: A vision that prioritizes the needs of the year-round community first, helps to create a vibrant place that will inevitably attract visitors in a way that a singular usage approach cannot. Investing in the town's cultural resources, as part of its future growth, will have economic returns and social benefits for all.

REGIONAL PERSPECTIVE: A regional approach which considers both the needs and values of local communities and the larger region while encouraging long-term investment and commitment from a wide range of stakeholders, ensuring continued success.

NEW USES FOR EXISTING PLACES: The best way to build a sustainable community is to work with existing resources. Culture of Outports will complete an inventory of these resources and produce strategies for the best way to use, maintain, and preserve them as part of the community's future management.

CROSS GENERATIONAL ENGAGEMENT: Where prior to 1992 the culture of Newfoundland and Labrador was defined by the traditions and economy of fishing, Culture of Outports provides a unique opportunity to build connections between two distinct demographics in an effort to establish the future of Newfoundland's identity.

PLACE-BASED ECONOMIES: Many small and mid-sized towns throughout North America are working to redefine their identities through new creative economies. Culture of Outports examines how similar communities are developing sustainable economies and will generate strategies.

INCREMENTAL GROWTH: As an approach to sustainable development, incremental growth allows for small, manageable investments. These changes can also provide opportunities to test and refine ideas for future investment and growth potential.

COMMUNITY VALUES: Culture of Outports embraces the values and priorities of the community. As a first step in realizing the potential of the community, the team will design a temporary installation, which helps to gain momentum for the community build and inspires the community to dream big.

Initially, Culture of Outports (CoO) developed these principles in order to guide community approach and discussions with the outport. Now we've taken these principles two steps further. First, we've developed a typology of outport communities to better communicate the opportunities we see available for future growth in these locations. Second, we've collected a number of lessons, which we would like to share with other outports and rural communities across Canada. We hope this can help bring the knowledge inherent in these communities to other areas experiencing the same challenges and strengthen our responses to the evolving rural cultural landscape.

OUTPORT/RURAL TYPOLOGY

Surprisingly, we haven't encountered much literature on the nature of outport communities, their variety, types, and roles. This is a crucial oversight that we've only recently recognized. In qualifying subtle differences and unique characteristics in hundreds of outport communities, we can focus strategies and opportunities to develop specific approaches and connect new partners.

Our typology begins with "Origin Outports," which we see as the foundational types of outport communities. Of course, there are no set boundaries for these types of outports. Many are a combination of two or more types, or are in a process of evolution from one type to another.

RESOURCE OUTPORTS were probably the most common and developed through necessity to accommodate resource-driven economic opportunities such as fishing, shipbuilding, mining, logging, sawmilling, etc. Initially they were seasonal, or established only as locations to build or fish from, leading to cultural heritage characteristics defined by their origins as "unofficial" settlements. Some Resource Outports still exist today, but they are certainly fewer in number.

WINTER OUTPORTS were year round settlements, often connected to the railways, and hosted permanent residents who would have worked in various Resource Outports throughout the area, clustered around the winter outport.

TRADING OUTPORTS were larger centers of trade. These include larger communities. Many communities within proximity to a trading outport certainly depended on services and goods from the trading outport. The trading outport likely had a direct connection to distribution and shipping channels across the island and back to England or Portugal.

Today, the origin outports are still evident. As mentioned, the Resource Outport is slowly disappearing as resources across the island are depleted. In many cases, resource extraction had become concentrated in fewer communities, particularly as fewer resources were available and government regulation or policy evolved.

"Growth Centres" or Service Outports, which are often connected with the TransCanada Highway, have replaced Winter Outports. Many Growth Centres were located inland, such as Gander, a transition stewarded by Joey Smallwood beginning in the 1950s.

Trading Outports have moved beyond their origins of rural typology and include cities like St.John's and Corner Brook. For generations, St. John's has had constant investment as the dominant port of trade. Even over the last five years, it's clearly growing and experiencing "good times" as spin-off investment and activity from new resource oil extraction is conducted.

However, this growth can pose the risk of diluting the original character of St. John's. While it's a pleasure to see a "real-life" working port by the water's edge, as one of Canada's oldest cities, its cultural built heritage is an enormous asset. This is not to suggest the city shouldn't grow, but that it simply needs to manage its growth while protecting its original character.

We should also acknowledge that our definition of "origin" is limited and, unfortunately, exclusionary. We have not yet been able to properly study the heritage of First Nations settlements, which of course have origins well before the communities we have had the pleasure of studying. The influence of the First Peoples of Newfoundland—and, more broadly, Canada—is found within the cultural heritage of all settlements.

APPLYING THE TYPOLOGY TO THE PROCESS OF ADAPTION

This typology allows us to accomplish two things. First, we can better understand our relationship with the communities we work with, and second, we can select future partners through our understanding of how these outports evolve and how we can best strategize for future growth and change.

Variations of these typologies can be applied to the communities we've partnered with through the program. These variations come from economic strategies unique to the post-resource-driven communities now found throughout the province:

THE DESTINATION OUTPORT offers an experience or adventure. Fogo Island functions as a kind of retreat for artists. These communities often try to introduce a business case that leverages the cultural values within the community.

Example of a Culture of Outports partner community: Burlington

As with many outport towns, Burlington has a long history of both fishing and shipbuilding. This 2011 project drew upon traditional building technology and local materials to design and construct a new waterfront destination that would serve as a gathering place, lookout, performance stage, fire pit, campsite, and local landmark.

THE "STAGED" OUTPORT is often focused on tourism and keeping the community as close to an authentic experience as possible. Often a restoration approach is taken. A great example is Trinity.

Example of a Culture of Outports partner community: Brigus

Our 2012 project built a bright red deck-like structure on a historic lighthouse trail that had become underused. The design is meant as a destination point, a gathering place, a lookout, and a visual flag for the trail itself. Its design plays off local wood construction such as docks, boardwalks, and piers, and incorporates the use of traditional drystone walls. With this project, we were able to bring more awareness to the trail, encourage its use, and stimulate local and tourist engagement in an important cultural resource

THE BOUTIQUE OUTPORT is often driven by place-based economies. These are communities that are open to altering their performance and terrain.

Example of a Culture of Outports partner community: Port Union

Founded in 1916, Port Union was long the headquarters of the Fishermen's Protective Union and is North America's only union-built town. Our project, known as Foundation Square, was sited at the central waterfront location in town and is intended as a landmark, meeting place, picnic area, and playground. The Square includes a new boardwalk connection to the existing shoreline walk, an arch framing the view of the ocean, seating for rest and dining, and a fire pit to gather around at night. All materials were locally salvaged, and community members of Trinity Bay North (including residents of Catalina, Little Catalina, and Melrose) were fully engaged in the entire design-build process.

THE SERVICE OUTPORT communities are those that have maintained enough infrastructure investment over the years to have solidly established their regional importance. The majority are connected to a major highway (if not the TransCanada). In many cases, the outports in close proximity to the TransCanada often establish a modern copy of their town, as opposed to adapting their historic versions.

Example of a Culture of Outports partner community: Botwood

Botwood, a town of 3000, was a significant settlement for the Beothuk people, and became a major point of settlement for Europeans. The site has served as a major port of trade (both air and ocean), and was an important base for the RCAF during WWII. The Culture of Outports project here was the "Viewfinder," a wood-frame, open-plank pavilion that serves as a shade structure, windbreak, and a frame for significant heritage views of the locale. It is intended as a focal point for community engagement, a landmark to stimulate activity in the community, and a stepping stone toward the cultivation of future cultural and economic opportunities.

THE BEDROOM OUTPORT is often smallish, mainly residential, and dependent on larger or clusters of outports. Usually located within an hour of a larger community, you go there to sleep, retire, and enjoy recreation. We have yet to engage this type of community, but we look forward to the opportunity.

THE PHOENIX (RE-LOCATED) OUTPORTS are those that, as the Resource Outports disappear, out of the ashes will rise again and join neighbouring communities in Newfoundland or across Canada. As a community driven initiative toward "Relocation," many outport residents have joined together and come forward to leave their communities, relocating to other areas with greater economic viability. We have yet to engage this type of community but look forward to the opportunity.

We've developed loose criteria to select outport communities. At first, the selection process was somewhat random, and the majority of the communities came to us through our research on the master shipbuilders. In the last couple of years, as we observe distinct outport types, we are able to evaluate applications as opportunities within a broader context and explore settings or situations that we might learn from.

As a cultural heritage architect, I like to think of the work we do with historic sites as being similar to a mechanic working on old cars. The range of approaches may include everything from restoration, preservation, rehabilitation, stabilization, and documentation.

Each conservation approach to an outport community would accommodate a particular lifestyle, the condition and state of buildings and cultural landscape, the features within the community, the abilities and everyday performance. It's a delicate balance of community expectations as they consider the ideal conservation approach. Admittedly, it can be difficult to have these conversations, but it can be just as equally exciting.

Today's outport finds itself in a time of great experimentation. As many of us realize, there are only so many museums, parks, interpretation centers, demonstrations sites, and tourist destinations that the outport and rural Newfoundland can support. More than tourism, Newfoundlanders, and indeed people across the nation, want outports and rural settlements to be livable communities.

It's obviously impossible to predict what our outports will be in 100 years. During our time in these communities, we've enjoyed discussing the possibilities with residents, but the majority of these conversations end with residents preferring not to guess. I suspect they're afraid of "jinxing" their futures.

LESSONS LEARNED

We started our work in outport communities with the idea that we were developing tools or articulating opportunities for the communities we partnered with. As it turned out, we were often the ones on the receiving end of this knowledge transfer. We've learned a lot from the many conversations we've had, and we've been able to distill some key changes, challenges, and shifts in thinking that we've seen along the way. These lessons will form the foundation of our future work and our articulation of the common threads that we're beginning to uncover in rural research across the country, and beyond.

LESSON 1: OUTPORTS ARE MIGRATORY.

Since the outports were settled as migratory fishing sites, they have evolved with a migratory workforce. In other words, people go where the work is, and this is one of their most resilient qualities to forge a future, whatever form it might be.

Certainly not all residents of outport communities show the resilience towards a migratory way of life. Sandwiched between youth and seniors, the working class is more willing to migrate in search of employment. We have anecdotally found that, in many outports, anywhere from 10 to 30 percent of residents "work away" during parts of the year.

As far as entire families are concerned, we have noted migration across the island to existing and new outports or inland communites. In other cases, residents have moved into the city of St. John's in search of opportunities.

LESSON 2: A CONTINENTAL MIGRATION IS UNDERWAY.

From centuries of fishing and shipbuilding, Newfoundlanders are sharing their migration tendencies with the mainland and building communities exported from their place of origin.

In some way, the migratory behavior of many Newfoundlanders may in fact be foreshadowing the fate of many rural resource communities. For Canadians, it's important we learn from the 400 years of investment in our outports because it offers models to transition in and out of communities.

Newfoundlanders have been resettling to parts of the mainland continent for some time. In the 60s, 70s, and 80s many Newfoundlanders were migrating to Ontario. Now, in many ways, Fort McMurray and its satellite "resource communities" are representative of a similar settlement pattern that Newfoundlanders had been using for years to fish and build ships, carrying their culture and skill sets into new areas.

A cultural geographer, Sara Beth Keough, in her paper "Examining the Cultural Imprint of Newfoundlanders in Fort McMurray, Alberta," noted the "cultural markers left by Newfoundlanders on the landscape with the sense of attachment felt…toward their province of origin." With a long history of migration, a Newfoundland diaspora now extends across the nation.

LESSON 3: CULTURAL VALUE OVER FUTURE.

Rather than concerning ourselves with the future of outport and rural places, it's important to focus on the present tense and attempt to understand their current value and evaluate their potential.

It's virtually impossible to predict the future of a particular outport. However, we can identify features within existing outports and rural communities that would lend themselves as likely candidates for renewed investments. The details of who can stay and what they might do requires a larger framework for which they could contribute.

The most effective studies and cultural economic plans for the outport and rural places are those that inventory the assets, suggest a conservation approach, and describe a number of potential opportunities which can be tested, either in the form of community builds or individual business plans.

LESSON 4: AN INVESTMENT IN CONTROLLED EXPERIMENTATION IS PARAMOUNT.

Economic remodeling isn't for the faint of heart. The first Newfoundland settlements were led by wealthy English merchants who risked investment with support from the government of England. This model can still be useful to evaluate investments in the outport and rural setting and seems to support recent language around "public and private partnerships."

Although we are huge advocates for adapting and restoring buildings, investments without primary focus on the individuals and their business models, it's very easy to get distracted by fixing up an old building. A successful economic driver, like the former cod fishery, will generate the ability to build, maintain, and manage, and it's vital that we assess and identify potential economic drivers.

We've developed ways for testing our cultural economic studies and plans. The community build component of the CoO programming affirms our research and provides an extremely focused opportunity to engage.

Community building has something for everyone across a variety of demographics: from seniors to youth, from the working class to families, from private businesses to civic management.

LESSON 5: OUTSIDERS ARE WELCOMED.

Some pretty amazing examples of new economic drivers are coming from away, from outside the province, as immigrants, foreign business ventures, and prodigal children who migrated not too long ago to the mainland create new opportunities. Zita Cobb's Shorefast (in Fogo Island and Change Islands) and Ken Sooley's Cape Race (focused on the Avalon and Bonavista peninsulas) and Shaun Majumder's The Gathering (in Burlington) all present unique ways of engaging with outport communities.

LESSON 6: INVEST AND EXPAND OUR OUTPORT VOCABULARY.

Further to our earlier discussion, in order to speak about outport and rural communities, we need to appreciate their variety, evolution, and type, otherwise we risk limiting community engagement to a one-size-fits-all approach, which oversimplifies our approach and quickly becomes unproductive.

We seem to make a trip every few months to connect with residents, visit their communities, and speak with investors. At each opportunity we're touring the coastal roads, wandering through each town, enjoying their food, staying in the lodgings, and sparking random conversations with folks on their way down the road. We've only scratched the surface in our travels. This engagement at the grass-roots level uncovers the complexity of each individual community and creates an opportunity for ground-up thinking rather than top-down approaches which fail to understand or even acknowledge the differences that exist between communities.

Classifying outports and rural communities is key. Without knowing their candidacy for rural conservation approaches and opportunities, we're comparable to a master shipbuilder who's only seen a few coves in a single bay while searching for the perfect site.

LESSON 7: CONNECT OUTPORT AND RURAL COMMUNITIES ACROSS CANADA AND THE UNITED STATES.

Alternative futures discussions for our outport and rural economies would benefit greatly if people are given the opportunity to share their struggles and gains: agricultural farmers in southern Ontario struggling with the ever-expanding suburb; logging communities in western Canada; mining communities in northern Ontario; wheat farmers in the Prairies; and oil-sand towns in northern Alberta. We're all part of a disconnected community that warrants larger discussion and connection to each other.

I've recently enjoyed an extremely productive conversation with Frank and Deborah Popper regarding their "Buffalo Commons" project. In response to the devastating farming practices of middle America, the Buffalo Commons suggests ideas to avoid the excesses of boom-bust cycles. Their work connects with the National Centre for Frontier Communities in New Mexico. As a national organization, they believe the frontier (or rural) areas are a vital, integral, and significant component of the national fabric. It isn't difficult to imagine that our Newfoundland outports and Canada's rural communities could be of similar value.

WHAT'S NEXT?

Master shipbuilders have been building communities for centuries. We've seen the influence of their creativity, skill, and adaptability in every rural community we've visited as part of our program. That wasn't surprising.

What *has* been surprising is our discovery that the outport community characteristics we've studied in Newfoundland can also be found in rural communities across North America.

The Culture of Outports program is growing into a true Newfoundland export. As we start to look at logging communities in Northern BC, mining communities in Quebec, and the new wave of *outports* clustered around Alberta's oil sands, we're beginning to apply the models we've developed in Newfoundland to a wide range of interest in rural study.

We feel there is a shift toward a revitalized ruralization in North America, one that would adapt these nationwide outport communities from their settlement origins. Our focus is to now study this bigger picture over the next two to three years.

As planners and architects, we constantly ask ourselves about the role of sustainability in community building. Over the last fifty years, Canadians have slowly moved away from the outports and rural areas for many reasons: depletion of resources, innovation in agricultural practice, changing economies. We don't have the reasons, or possibly the resources, to occupy these areas in the ways in which they'd been settled. So now we look at the new resources available in rural areas. Can rural communities offer features that accommodate various lifestyle preferences? Is this sustainable? Many of us have been lured to cities as a manageable and responsible way to mitigate our impact on the natural environment, following the "work where you live" method of reducing our footprint. Could outport and rural communities offer a new model for sustainable, livable communities? The answer to these and other questions are on the horizon, and like the master shipbuilders, we are heading out into uncharted territory to seek the answers.

Despite benefits in consolidating and managing our growing population in cities and the promise of urbanization, we still have a need to connect with our rural heritage. We feel this heritage could potentially shape a major demographic shift in the coming decades. This shift is not about hobby farming and second homes, but about a new wave of culturally driven renewed settlement. So these are exciting times, and we're looking forward to visiting and learning from many more communities as we continue our exploration of Canada's rural cultural landscape.

THE 33-TON SCHOONER *NORMAN WAREHAM* BEING REBUILT AND ENLARGED BY WILLIAM MARCH AT HAYSTACK, PLACENTIA BAY, IN 1928. CURIOUSLY, IT APPEARS THE VESSEL WOULD BE LAUNCHED SIDEWAYS AT HIGH TIDE.
(Photo used by permission of the Maritime History Archive, Memorial University of Newfoundland.)

ACKNOWLEDGEMENTS

HOW DOES ONE THANK the countless people who have contributed to this two-volume set as I have worked on it over the past twenty-five or thirty years? A simple thank you does not seem to be enough, but hopefully when said with deep gratitude and appreciation, it will suffice for the moment. I have lost track of some of them, but there are others who need to be mentioned.

Three of these were my colleagues at Memorial University of Newfoundland: Retired Professor Gordon Handcock of the Department of Geography; Professor Lewis Fischer of the Department of History; and Heather Wareham, Archivist of the Maritime History Archive. They have offered advice, guidance, support, and stimulating ideas over several years. Gordon Handcock provided a valuable critique of the introduction in Volume One of this set and offered several suggestions for the improvement of the Preface in Volume Two.

Staff members at several institutions are deserving of thanks as well, particularly those at the Centre for Newfoundland Studies at Memorial University, the Memorial University Archives, the Reference Department of the Newfoundland Public Libraries in the St. John's Arts & Culture Centre, the Newfoundland Provincial Archives (now The Rooms), the National Archives in Ottawa, the McGill University Libraries, and the various museums and public libraries throughout Newfoundland. Special thanks are due to Betty Williams, Registrar of Shipping in St. John's, and her colleague, Madonna Lavers.

My grandson Philip and I have visited more than thirty communities in Newfoundland during the summers of 2010, 2011, 2012, and 2013, and I have visited many others in prior years, and we are indebted to so many people who welcomed us into their homes for interviews or who provided information during more informal chats or who offered impromptu tours of communities. We thank in particular Alan D. Cass, William Gilbert, Henry and Wayne Vokey, Retired Judge Chester Stone, Wayne Stone, Alec and Sadie Rowe, Jim Miller,

Vernon Petten, Barney Dooley, Ethel Reta Dooley, Clayton Newhook, Larry Spracklin, Bernice Spracklin, Gordon Goulding, Beverly Warford, Jill Marshall, Everett Elliott, Harold Manuel, Gilda Parsons, Cindy Tedstone, Murley Berkshire, and Anna Kearney Guigne. Special thanks also to the staff at the Winterton Boatbuilding Museum during our many visits: Beverly King, Stephanie Piercey, Jennifer Gushue, Howard Cooper, and Jerome Canning. It has also been such a privilege to be able to work with my grandson on this project.

From replies to a letter to the editor printed in the Evening Telegram, I received much valuable information about shipbuilders. Thanks to Darren Scott, Don Scurlock, Dan Porter, Clarence Snook, Douglas Benson, Ben Lake, Dean Penton, Maurice Devine, Herb Davis, Joe Jennings, Don Blackmore, Hilary Dickson, and Donald Newhook. A special mention is made of Alonzo Saunders of Burlington, Green Bay, for the supply of much valuable information about the shipbuilders of Green Bay, and for access to his extensive picture collection and his personally-crafted community museum. And more recently, I am indebted to Don Collins of Gambo who unearthed the valuable Customs' Returns and Bounty Payments for the years between 1875 and 1910; those for 1875 and 1876 supplied the names of shipbuilders which are missing from the ship registers because of a revised form which did not collect these names for a twenty-four year period—1854 to 1877. Archivist Melanie Tucker of The Rooms and information specialist Andrea Hyde of the Legislative Library in St. John's helped with searches for additional data. Unless there are more such records buried in Colonial or Departmental archives, we have pretty well exhausted the sources for additional information.

Special thanks also to the staff at Breakwater Books for taking on this enormous project and seeing it through in a very thorough and professional manner, and in particular to James Langer, editor.

I owe a major debt of gratitude to my wife, Goldie, for her patience and support as I have laboured through this seemingly endless project. Perhaps there are quieter days ahead.

To all who helped in any way, I express my heartfelt gratitude and deep appreciation.

APPENDICES

GENERAL NOTE

If an Appendix states that a builder constructed only one or two ships, this does not necessarily mean that this number was his total production. Sometimes ships were not registered at all. Sometimes vessels were lost before being registered. Sometimes ships were registered many years after construction. Sometimes vessels were registered in another country. And sometimes they were registered in the name of the owner with no attribution to the builder. It is also possible that some of these one-time builders were brought from England or Ireland to build a particular ship for a merchant, or the builder may have been a mariner or trader/dealer and more interested in going to sea or doing business than in building ships, so the building of a particular ship may have been incidental to the man's main profession. Additionally, some of the builders may have died young, likely lost at sea, after building one or two ships. Again, we must take into account the infamous gap from 1854 to 1877 when the registration forms were changed and shipbuilders' names were omitted.

Shipbuilders who constructed four or more ships appear in the narrative section of each chapter. Those who built three or fewer are listed in the Appendices.

Note the general and imprecise designators of where some ships were built (e.g., Green Bay, Bay of Exploits, etc.). Often, only the name of these larger regional designators is provided in the ship registers.

ABBREVIATIONS

b	built
BB	Bonavista Bay
BD'Es	Bay D' Espoir
BofE	Bay of Exploits
BofIsls	Bay of Islands
Brk	Brook
CB	Conception Bay
Cv	Cove
E	East
FB	Fortune Bay
GB	Green Bay
Hbr	Harbour
Isl	Island
Isls	Islands
N	North
NB	New Brunswick
NDB	Notre Dame Bay
NS	Nova Scotia
NWI	New World Island
PEI	Prince Edward Island
PB	Placentia Bay
Pt	Point
r	rebuilt
s	ship
S	South
SGB	St. George's Bay
SMB	St. Mary's Bay
Snd	Sound
TB	Trinity Bay
W	West
WB	White Bay

APPENDIX TO CHAPTER ONE: NOTRE DAME BAY INCLUDING BAY OF EXPLOITS, HALL'S BAY, AND GREEN BAY

SHIPBUILDER, RESIDENCE, PLACE(S) BUILT, NO. OF SHIPS, YEAR(S)

Abbott, William. GB, s:2, 1862-68

Andrews, Henry Levi. French Shore, s:1, 1869

Anstey, Alexander. Little Bay Isls, s:1, 1909

Anstey, Henry. Seal Bay, s:1, 1907

Antle, Thomas Jr. Northern Arm, BofE, Griquet, s:2, 1881-89

Ball, Solomon. Scissors Cv, s:1, 1896

Barrett, John. Burnt Bay, s:1, 1877

Bartlett, John R. South West Arm, GB, s:1, 1911

Bartlett, William. North East Arm, Middle Arm, GB, s:1, 1875

Batstone, Alexander R. Nipper's Hbr, s:1, 1966

Batstone, Charles. Nipper's Hbr, s:2, 1900-08

Batstone, James W. Silverdale, r:1, 1928

Batstone, Thomas. Nipper's Hbr, s:2, 1881-90

Batstone, William. GB, s:1, 1861

Batt, James. GB, s:1, 1835

Blunden, Thomas. Lewisporte, s:1, 1947

Boone, Edward. Cottrell's Cv, New Bay, s:2, 1900-20

Boone, John W. Cottrell's Cv, s:1, 1979

Boone, Samuel. Cottrell's Cv, s:1, 1902

Bowers, Job. Nipper's Hbr, s:3, 1900-02

Bowers, Stewart. Nipper's Hbr, s:1, 1973

Bowers, William. GB, s:1, 1834

Boyles, Benjamin T. NDB, s:1, 1904

Bridger, Pleman. Brighton, s:1, 1963

Brien, Daniel. GB, s:1, 1860

Brimsell, John. Hall's Bay, s:1, 1840

Brine, John. Fortune Hbr, s:1, 1879

Brown, Amos. Laurenceton, s:2, 1905-09

Brown, George. Kite Cv (Laurenceton), s:1, 1883

Budgell, Allan. Cottrell's Cv, s:1, 1981

Budgell, Fred. Cottrell's Cv, s:1, 1981

Burge, Owen. Pilley's Island, Long Tickle NDB, s:3, 1883-1903

Burnt, Samuel & John. GB, s:1, 1852

Burt, Henry. Long Tickle, s:2, 1884

Burt, Thomas. South West Arm, GB, s:1, 1898

Burton, Edward Randolph. Beaumont, s:1, 1969

Burton, George. Ward's Hbr, s:1, 1881

Burton, James & John. GB, s:1, 1863

Burton, Timotheus. South Brk, s:1, 1964
Butler, William Alfred. Burnt Arm, s:1, 1908
Byrne, Michael & Patrick. NDB, s:1, 1871
Campbell, Daniel. GB, s:1, 1856
Caravan, Wesley Norman. Lushes Bight, s:2, 1967-74
Card, William. Jackson's Cv, s:2, 1902-10
Carroll, William. Fortune Hbr, BofE, s:1, 1878
Clarke, Leslie Leo. Cottrell's Cv, s:2, 1971-74
Clements, John. GB, r:1, 1851
Coffin, Samuel. Bear Cv, Robert's Arm, s:1, 1898
Coish, Samson. Indian Isls, s:1, 1904
Colbourne, Robert. Robert's Arm, Leading Tickles, s:1, 1974
Collins, Richard. Indian Isls, s:1, 1879
Collins, William. Indian Isls, s:3, 1879-93
Cooper, John. GB, s:1, 1880
Crewe, Samuel. King's Pt, s:1, 1984
Croucher, Clyde George. Beaumont, s:2, 1969-81
Croucher, James. GB, Hall's Bay, s:1, 1860
Croucher, Raymond Stafford. Beaumont, s:1, 1969
Cutler, Charles. GB, s:1, 1863
David (Baevid?), James. Nipper's Hbr, s:1, 1891
Dinney, John. Sop's Arm, s:1, 1906
Dorey, John. GB, s:1, 1867
Dorey, William. GB, s:1, 1874
Dower, Thomas B. Grand Falls, Botwood, s:2, 1959-62
Dwyer, Edward. Exploits, s:1, 1880
Dwyer, Patrick. GB, s:1, 1870
Dwyer, Thomas. Burlington, s:1, 1934
Elliott, Ben. Fogo, Burnt Arm, s:1-plus, 1921
Elliott, John. Exploits, GB, s:2, 1871-97
Elliott, Wilfred. Lock's Cv, s:1, 1956
Ellsworth, James. GB, Gander Bay, s:1, 1881
Freake, Charles. Joe Batt's Arm, Birchy Bay, Norris Arm, s:2, 1889-1910
Freake, James. Burnt Bay, s:1, 1879
Freake, Uriah. Lewisporte, s:2, 1910
French, Samuel. Laurenceton, s:1, 1910
Fudge, Bruce D. Brighton, s:1, 1980
Gates, John. Burnt Bay, s:1, 1890
Ginn, Thomas. GB, s:1, 1852
Glavine, Matthew. Fortune Hbr, s:1, 1880
Gray, James & Thomas Welshman, GB, s:1, 1867
Green, James. Exploits Hbr, GB, s:2, 1883-1905

Green, John. GB, s:1, 1847
Greenham, Frank & Gordon Pittman, Newstead, s:1, 1981
Guppy, George. Indian Arm, s:1, 1877
Haines (Hynes?), Richard. Indian Isls, s:1, 1882
Hall, Basil. Burnt Bay, s:1, 1879
Harris, Richard. Indian Isls, s:1, 1879
Hawkins, Harvey Edison. Beaumont, s:1, 1949
Head, Albert. Birchy Cv, s:1, 1884
Heath, Henry. Robert's Arm, s:1, 1947
Henniffant, Patrick. Black Isl, s:1, 1872
Hewlett, Ford. King's Pt, Port Anson, s:1, 1952
Hewlett, Hubert. Port Anson, s:1, 1966
Hewlett, Israel. Robert's Arm, s:1, 1904
Hewlett, John. Robert's Arm, s:1, 1897
Hicks, Alfred. Western Arm, s:1, 1900
Hicks, Ernest. Western Arm, s:1, 1906
Hicks, James. North West Arm, s:1, 1885
Hicks, Philip. Western Arm, s:1, 1896
Hill, Henry & Thomas. Black Isl, Burnt Bay, s:1, 1874
Hill, Henry & William Martin, NDB, s:1, 1869
Hill, Percy John. Little Burnt Bay, s:1, 1970
Hoddinott, James. Indian Isls, r:1, 1904
Hoddinott, John A. Indian Isls, s:1, 1884
Hoddinott, Samuel. Indian Isls, s:1, 1902
Hodinott, John. GB, s:1, 1853
Hollett, George. Norris Arm, s:1, 1948
Hull, Andrew. Lewisporte, Hughes Brk, BofIsls, s:1, 1936
Hull, Samuel. Robert's Arm, Lushes Bight, s:1, 1940
Hutchings, Alfred W. Botwood, Northern Arm, s:1, 1902
Hutchings, George. Kite Cv, s:1, 1891
Hutchings, Hollett. Pt of Bay, Pt Leamington, s:1, 1966
Hyde, John. BofE, s:1, 1875
Hynes, Lionel. Muddy Hole, s:2, 1891-97
James, Frederick. Little Bay Isls, s:1, 1951
Jerrett, Frederick. Exploits, Kite Cv, s:1, 1883
Jure, Jabez. Kite Cv (Laurenceton), s:1, 1894
Jure, John. Exploits, s:1, 1837
Jure, John. Kite Cv, s:1, 1889
Kennedy, Patrick. Leading Tickles, NDB, s:2, 1873-75
Kidgell, James. Exploits, s:1, 1835
Kough, Martin & Daniel. GB, s:1, 1867
Lacey, Richard. Exploits Isls, BofE, s:2, 1876-82

Lannon, James. Fortune Hbr, s:2, 1891-92
Lannon, John. Fortune Hbr, s:1, 1893
Larmen, Matthew. North West Arm, s:1, 1877
LeDrew, Charles S. Burnt Arm, s:1, 1907
LeDrew, Solomon. Burnt Arm, s:2, 1892-1908
Lidstone, Isaac. Burnt Bay, s:1, 1887
Locke, Clement. Little Bay Isls, s:1, 1944
Locke, Harvey. Miles Cv, s:1, 1964
Locke, James. Little Bay Isls, s:1, 1934
Luff, Francis. Exploits Isls, BofE, s:2, 1875-77
Luscomb, Thomas. Loon Bay, s:1, 1897
Lyver, James. GB, BofE, s:2, 1848-79
Maddocks, Patrick. GB, s:1, 1870
March, Joseph. New Bay, s:1, 1883
Martin, Frederick. North West Arm, Burnt Bay, s:1, 1875
Martin, William & George. BofE, NDB, s:1, 1874
Mews, John. Bird Isls NDB, Comfort Cv, s:1, 1884
Miles, Francis. GB, s:1, 1876
Moore, Edmund. New Bay, GB, s:3, 1868-76
Moore, Edward. New Bay, GB, s:1-plus, 1858-71
Moore, James. New Bay, s:1, 1898
Moore, John Thomas. Boat Hbr, New Bay, s:1, 1909
Moores, Samuel C. Burnt Bay, s:1, 1879
Morey, Clifford. Miles Cv, NDB, s:1, 1962
Morey, Jacob. Sunday Cove Isl, s:1, 1905
Morey, Theophilus. Miles Cv, s:1, 1920
Morgan, George. GB, s:1, 1847
Mursell, Charles. GB, s:1, 1863
Mursell, William. NDB, s:2, 1869-75
Newman, John. GB, s:1, 1840
Nippard, Nathan. Embree, s:1, 1980
Noble, George & James. GB, s:1, 1857
Noble, John T. Little Bay, s:1, 1917
Noble, Lorenzo. Nipper's Hbr, s:1, 1973
Normore, Darius. Sunday Cv Isl, s:2, 1880-1902
Northcote, Joseph. Burnt Bay, s:1, 1892
Oake, James. BofE, s:1, 1884
Oxford, Francis. Hall's Bay, Sunday Cv Isl, s:3, 1879-84
Oxford, Henry. Little Bay Isls, s:1, 1880
Oxford, John Robert. Little Bay Isls, s:1, 1966
Parmiter, Wesley. Pt Leamington, s:1, 1950
Parsons, Duncan A. Springdale, s:1, 1923

Parsons, Eli. Seal Bay, s:1, 1902
Parsons, Job. Lushes Bight, r:3, 1913-26
Parsons, Peter. Long Isl, s:1, 1938
Parsons, Peter. Lushes Bight, s:1, 1905
Parsons, Samuel. Lushes Bight, s:1, 1903
Pearce, Andrew Sr., Exploits Isls, Birchy Bay, Burnt Bay, b:2, r:1, 1876-81
Penny, Albert. Pilley's Isl, s:1, 1900
Perry, Philip. Indian Isls, Rocky Bay, s:1, 1880
Perry, William John. Indian Isls, s:2, 1941-48
Perry, William. Nipper's Hbr, s:1, 1974
Perry, William. North West Arm, Western Arm, s:2, 1883-85
Peyton, Thomas & Elias. Exploits, BofE, s:1, 1854
Philpott, John. Hall's Bay, GB, s:2, 1853-66
Philpott, Joseph. Loon Bay, Chapel's Isl NDB, s:2, 1876-80
Philpott, Stanley. Pt of Bay, Botwood, s:3, 1939-45
Philpott, Wesley. Botwood, s:1, 1946
Pilley, Edmund. Thwart Isl, s:1, 1927
Pilley, Temple. Harry's Hbr, s:1, 1927
Powell, Stephen. New Bay, s:1, 1881
Power, James. Nipper's Hbr, North West Arm, b:1, r:1, 1880-89
Power, Patrick. Exploits, s:1, 1831
Purchase, Josiah. Exploits, s:1, 1906
Reddick, Eli. Robert's Arm, s:1, 1889
Redman, Leonard. Harry's Hbr, Marshallville, s:1, 1913
Rendell, Samuel. GB, s:1, 1863
Rice, George. Dark Tickle, Pilley's Isl, s:2, 1906-08
Rice, Jonas. South West Arm, Flurry's Bight, Indian Pt, b:2, r:1, 1904-48
Rice, Joseph Jr., NDB, s:1, 1872
Rice, Meshach. GB, s:1, 1843
Rideout, Alwin. Robert's Arm, s:1, 1983
Rideout, Daniel. Exploits Isls, s:1, 1883
Rideout, George Arthur. Springdale, s:2, 1964-66
Rideout, George. Western Head, s:1, 1881
Rideout, John. Three Arms, r:1, 1927
Rideout, Joseph. Beaumont, s:1, 1901
Rideout, Joshua. Pilley's Isl, s:1, 1900
Rideout, Pearce. Beaumont, s:1, 1972
Rideout, Reuben. Western Head, s:1, 1883
Rideout, Simon. Western Head, s:1, 1881
Rideout, Thomas. Cantwell Arm, GB, s:1, 1879
Ridout, Frederick. GB, s:1, 1868
Ridout, Gilbert. Rogues Hbr, s:1, 1876

Robbins, William & Joseph. Southwest Arm, GB, s:1, c1860
Robinson, Boyce. Middle Arm, GB, s:1, 1980
Rolls, John. GB, s:1, 1860
Rose, Samuel. Laurenceton, s:1, 1895
Russell, Samson. Western Arm, s:1, 1893
Shea, William. Little Bay Isls, s:1, 1882
Sheppard, Eli. Indian Isls, s:1, 1899
Short, Edwin C. Beaumont, s:1, 1966
Short, Samuel. Hall's Bay, s:1, 1884
Short, William. GB, s:2, 1836-64
Simmons, John. Triton NDB, s:1, 1892
Simms, Archibald. Great Triton Hbr, NDB, s:1, 1900
Skinner, John. GB, s:2, 1850-66
Slade, Frederick. Loon Bay, s:1, 1882
Snow, John. Norris Arm, Exploits, s:2, 1892-1905
Snow, Thomas. GB, s:1, 1850
Somigithe (?), Henry. Birchy Bay, s:1, 1839
Squires, James. Burlington, Englee, s:1, 1979
Squires, John. GB, s:1, 1868
Squires, Thomas Henry. Smith's Hbr, GB, s:2, 1932-51
Stark, David. GB, s:1, 1854
Starks, William. Nipper's Hbr, North West Arm, s:1, 1880
Steele, William. Western Arm, s:1, 1900
Stride, James. Chance Hbr, s:2, 1907-08
Stuckless, Aaron. New Bay, s:1-plus,1870-71
Studley, Thomas & Absalom. GB, s:1, 1854
Taylor, Edward. Burnt Bay, s:1, 1878
Taylor, Edwin. Burnt Bay, s:1, 1880
Taylor, Simeon. New Bay, r:1, 1908
Tetford, John. Laurenceton, s:2, 1902-07
Thistle, Thomas. Little Bay Isls, Sunday Cv Isl, s:1, 1900
Thomas, John. Middle Arm, GB, s:2, 1933-36
Tilley, Ross Robert Ronald. King's Pt, GB, 1933
Turner, Charles. Fort Hbr Bay, New Bay, s:1, 1878
Turner, Nathaniel. Burnt Bay, s:1, 1889
Upwards, John. Harry's Hbr, s:1, 1905
Vincent, William Pearce. Triton West, r:1, 1949
Wall, Samuel J. Chance Hbr, s:2, 1902-09
Warford, Henry. French Shore, New Bay, s:2, 1879-95
Warford, William H. New Bay, s:1, 1902
Warren, John. GB, s:1, 1851
Watkins, Isaac. Woodford's Arm, Norris Arm, s:2, 1877-78

Wellman, Charles. Sunday Cove Isl, s:3, 1898-1904
Wellman, William. Port Anson, s:1, 1919
Wells, Francis. BofE, s:1, 1877
Wells, Henry. Exploits Isls, BofE, s:2, 1875-85
Wells, James. Exploits, s:1, 1838
Wells, John. GB, s:1, 1842
Wells, Samuel. BofE, s:1, 1879
Wells, William. Burnt Bay, s:1, 1880
Wells, Zephaniah. Swan Hbr, Samson Isl, s:2, 1897-1912
Wheeler, Elisha. Virgin Arm, Chapel Isl, Chanceport, s:3, 1922-38
Wheeler, John. Jones Cv, Chance Hbr, s:2, 1900-07
White, James. GB, s:2, 1854-60
White, James. Little Bay Isls, s:1, 1930
White, James. Little Bay, s:1, 1893
White, Levi. Indian Burial Place, s:1, 1880
Whiteway, John Jr., GB, s:1, 1850
Whiteway, Robert & John. GB, s:2, 1846-66
Williams, Dexter John. Triton, r:2, 1951
Williams, George. Pilley's Isl, s:1, 1895
Windsor, George. GB, s:2, 1834-40
Winsor, Robert. NDB, Fogo, Triton NDB, s:2, 1870-74
Winsor, Solomon. Round Hbr, GB, s:1, 1836
Woolfrey, Josiah. Burnt Bay, s:1, 1891
Woolfrey, T. Lewisporte, s:1, 1909
Woolfreys, Josiah. GB, s:1, 1864
Yates, Lloyd Wilson. Cottrell's Cv, s:1, 1964
Yates, Otto Colin. Cottrell's Cv, s:1, 1959
Yates, Otto. Springdale, s:1, 1980

APPENDIX TO CHAPTER TWO: WHITE BAY AND THE NORTHERN PENINSULA

SHIPBUILDER, RESIDENCE, PLACE(S) BUILT, NO. OF SHIPS, YEAR(S)

Adams, John Ross. Cape Onion, s:1, 1949
Aylward, John. Fishot Isls, s:1, 1965
Aylward, Leo. Fishot Isls, s:1, 1965
Bromley, Edward Francis. Fishot Isls, s:1, 1965
Bromley, Vincent. Fishot Isls, s:1, 1965
Burton, Donald. Baie Verte, s:1, 1979

Burton, Joseph. La Scie, s:1, 1903
Burton, Reginald Stephen. La Scie, s:1, 1957
Caines, Alonzo A. Bartlett's Hbr, s:1, 1968
Caines, Sidney Joseph. Bartlett's Hbr, s:1, 1967
Carroll, George. Lock's Cv, s:1, 1963
Cassell, Edward. Great Hbr Deep, s:1, 1979
Chaytor, Albert James. Croque, s:1, 1968
Combden, Joseph. Jackson's Arm, Western Arm, s:1, 1906
Compton, George Jr. Hooping Hbr, Englee, Canada Bay, s:2, 1880-93
Curtis, Joseph. Horse Isls, s:1, 1883
Decker, Abel. Sacred Bay, s:1, 1876
Dempsey, Irwin. Englee, s:1, 1977
Dempsey, Ronald. Fleur de Lys, s:1, 1975
Edenson, Jacob. Noddy Bay, s:1, 1879
Elliott, Benjamin. Hare Bay, s:1, 1881
Elliott, Simeon Lester. Raleigh, s:1, 1947
Elliott, Wilfred Thomas. Lock's Cv, St. Anthony, s:2, 1963-66
Elliott, William. Hooping Hbr, s:1, 1873
Fitzpatrick, James Michael. Roddickton, s:1, 1963
Foley, Benedict. Conche, Torbay, s:1, 1987
Ford, Job. Jackson's Arm, s:1, 1880
Genge, Calvin. Flower's Cv, Anchor Pt, s:1, 1964
Genge, Henry. Flower's Cv, s:1, 1928
Gibbons, Abraham. Currant Isl, s:1, 1903
Gillard, Enos. Roddickton, s:1, 1979
Gillard, Robert. Englee, s:1, 1875
Gillingham, George. Jackson's Arm, s:1, 1989
Gould, Alfred Joseph. Port au Choix, s:1, 1968
Guy, John. Quirpon, Sacred Bay, s:1, 1875
Hancock, Stanley. Roddickton, s:2, 1968
Hillier, James. BofE, Port Saunders, s:1, 1880
Hughes, John. Green Island Brk, s:1, 1963
Hynes, John Jr. Port au Choix, s:1, 1968
Jacobs, James. Westport, s:1, 1980
John Reeves Ltd., Englee, r:1, 1958
Kean, John C. Flower's Cv, s:1, 1883
Kearney, Francis & Jerome. Conche, s:1, 1981
Kearney, Ronald P. Croque, s:1, 1963
Kearney, Vincent Francis. Conche, s:1, 1967
Kennedy, Michael. Bird Cv, St. Margaret's Bay, s:1, 1960
Kennedy, Sylvester. Bird Cv, North East Arm St. Margaret's Bay, s:1, 1953
Lane, Roland Whitfield. Englee, s:1, 1968

Lane, Woodrow & Roland. Englee, s:1, 1979
Lavalle, Joseph Adolph. Port Saunders, s:1, 1967
LeDrew, Henry George. Big Brehat, Pistolet Bay, s:1, 1879
LeDrew, Philip. Ha Ha Bay, s:1, 1877
Lewis, George Sr. & Jr., Michael, John & Frederick Lewis, WB, s:1, 1870
McCormack, John. Coachman's Cv, s:1, 1903
McGrath, Timothy. St. Julien's, s:1, 1975
McLean, William. Searston, r:1, 1928
Norman, Herbert. Pacquet, s:1, 1935
Noseworthy, Henry. Green Island Brk, s:1, 1963
O'Keefe, Ralph Leo. Port au Choix, s:1, 1964
Ollerhead, George. St. Anthony, s:1, 1950
Ollerhead, Stanley. Main Brk Hare Bay, s:1, 1958
Pardy, John. Pacquet, s:1, 1926
Payne, Samuel. Parson's Pond, s:1, 1934
Pelly, John. WB, r:1, 1910
Pilgrim, Herman. Main Brk, s:1, 1981
Pittman, Chesley. Hbr Deep, s:1, 1967
Plowman, Joseph Walter. Port au Choix, s:1, 1964
Pollard, Maxwell. Hbr Deep, s:1, 1980
Pynn, William Charles. Raleigh, s:1, 1951
Randell, Cecil. Williamsport, s:1, 1967
Randell, Fred Charles. Williamsport, s:1, 1967
Randell, Fred. Englee, Great Hbr Deep, s:2, 1977-79
Randell, Jesse. Bide Arm, s:1, 1976
Randell, Kenneth. Hooping Hbr, Bide Arm, s:2, 1969-77
Randell, Naaman. Bide Arm, s:1, 1982
Randell, Oliver. Hooping Hbr, s:1, 1967
Randell, Robert. Great Hbr Deep, s:1, 1979
Randell, Stewart. Hooping Hbr, s:1, 1967
Ropson, Chesley. Hbr Deep, s:1, 1979
Rose, Albert S. Flower's Cv, s:1, 1929
Rumbolt, John Henry. New Ferolle, Castors River, s:1, 1938
Rumbolt, Patrick. Port au Choix, s:1, 1968
Sansford, Henry Stephen. St. Anthony, s:2, 1934-54
Saunders, Donald. Griquet, s:1, 1956
Saunders, Frederick. St. Lunaire, s:1, 1960
Saunders, Sherwin. St. Lunaire, s:1, 1985
Shelley, James Patrick. Fleur de Lys, s:1, 1973
Sheppard, Norman Ely. Brig Bay, s:1, 1963
Sheppard, Thomas K. Brig Bay, s:1, 1900
Sheppard, William. Ha Ha Bay, St. George's, b:1, r:1, 1885-1915

Skinner, Patrick. Hbr Round, s:1, 1979
Small, Allan. Wild Cv, s:1, 1975
Smith, Clarence Samuel. Roddickton, s:2, 1963-66
Snow, Francis & Martin. Griquet, s:1, 1980
Suley, John. St. Anthony, s:1, 1901
Tucker, Harris. Reefs Hbr, s:1, 1979
Tucker, Noah. Bartlett's Hbr, Reefs Hbr, s:1, 1979
Walsh, John & Thomas. Fleur de Lys, s:2, 1875-76
Whiteway, Ignatius. St. Julien's, s:2, 1967-76

APPENDIX TO CHAPTER THREE: LABRADOR

SHIPBUILDER, RESIDENCE, PLACE(S) BUILT, NO. OF SHIPS, YEAR(S)

Campbell, Stanley. Pinsent's Arm, s:1, 1971
Hicks, Lloyd. Port Hope Simpson, s:2, 1973-85
Kippenhuck, John Charles. Square Isls, s:1, 1964
Kippenhuck, Paul. Square Isls, s:1, 1967
Letto, George & Roger. L'Anse au Clair, s:1, 1978
MacKean Fisheries Outfitting Ltd., Rixon Cv, s:1, 1973
Penney, Alex. Port Hope Simpson, s:1, 1973
Poole, Eldred. St. Lewis, s:1, 1980
Powell, Benjamin Windsor. Square Isls, s:1, 1960
Rowe, Benjamin James. Port Hope Simpson, s:1, 1970
Russell, Freeman Samuel. Williams Hbr, Port Hope Simpson, s:2, 1969-71
Strugnell, Simon. Port Hope Simpson, s:1, 1969
Turnbull, Alexander G. Triangle, s:1, 1968
Williams, Henry John. Cartwright, s:1, 1965

APPENDIX TO CHAPTER FOUR: WEST COAST – SOUTHERN SECTION

SHIPBUILDER, RESIDENCE, PLACE(S) BUILT, NO. OF SHIPS, YEAR(S)

Anderson, Edward. Bonne Bay, s:1, 1913
Anderson, William. Bonne Bay, s:2, 1881-83
Antle, William J. Codroy, s:1, 1883
Barter, John. Codroy, s:1, 1895
Blanchard, John. Grand River, s:1, 1890

Blanchard, William. Big River, Codroy, s:1, 1875
Boyer, Kevin. West Bay Centre, Port au Port Bay, s:1, 1966
Brake, Hayward. Meadows, BofIsls, s:1, 1931
Brake, Joseph. Trout River, s:1, 1990
Burden, Joshua T. Shoal Brk, Bonne Bay, s:1, 1959
Burggraef, Klaus. Corner Brk, s:1, 1982
Butt, Leslie Dean. Heatherton, s:1, 1944
Butt, Nathaniel. SGB, s:1, 1898
Butt, Samuel. SGB, s:1, 1906
Caines, John. Birchy Head, Bonne Bay, s:1, 1891
Campbell, Archibald. Campbell's Cv, s:2, 1877-84
Carnell, Bernard. Bonne Bay, r:1, 1926
Carter, Edward. Searston, s:1, 1914
Childs, Edward. Lark Hbr, s:1, 1983
Coleman, George. Birchy Head, Bonne Bay, s:1, 1891
Collier, William. Codroy, s:1, 1890
Cormier, William & Hugh McInnis, Grand River, s:1, 1881
Crocker, James Henry. Woody Pt, Bonne Bay, s:1, 1950
Crocker, Thomas Francis. Trout River, s:1, 1977
Cutler, William. SGB, s:1, 1875
Dean, John Willis. Bonne Bay, s:3, 1879-82
Dean, Loyal. Bonne Bay, s:1, 1878
Dohman, Thomas. Humber Snd, s:1, 1881
Ellsworth, Ashley. Corner Brk, s:1, 1971
Fall, John. SGB, s:1, 1898
Farrell, Charles P. BofIsls, s:1, 1881
Farrell, Reuben. Curling, s:1, 1914
Fogarty, William. Bonne Bay, s:2, 1897-1916
Fudge, Pierce. Humbermouth, s:1, 1934
Furlong, Richard. Humber Snd, s:1, 1885
Gallant, Alfred. Halfway Pt, BofIsls, s:1, 1933
Gallop, Benjamin. Codroy, s:1, 1878
Galpin, John. Codroy, s:1, 1889
Gillis, John & Angus. Codroy, s:1, 1876
Gillis, Roderick. Big River, Codroy, s:1, 1876
Gosse, Samuel. Seal Cv, Bonne Bay, s:1, 1880
Gullage, Hezekiah. Corner Brk, s:1, 1957
Halfyard, Henry. Birchy Head, Bonne Bay, s:1, 1890
Halfyard, James. Bonne Bay, s:1, 1886
Halfyard, Mason McKenzie. Bonne Bay, s:1, 1889
Hall, John. Codroy, Grand River, s:1, 1907
Hall, Joseph. Middle Arm, BofIsls, s:1, 1940

Hann, Herbert Chesley. Summerside, s:1, 1945
Hann, Jacob. Bonne Bay, s:1, 1910
Hann, Jesse. Bonne Bay, s:1, 1898
Hawkins, Samuel. Bonne Bay, s:1, 1874
Hellard, Robert Joseph. Humber Snd, s:1, 1882
Hinds, William. Humber Snd, BofIsls, s:1, 1880
Hooper, John Sr. SGB, s:1, 1875
Hounsell, Herman. Pasadena, Jackson's Arm WB, s:1, 1955
House, Abraham. Bonne Bay, s:1, 1877
Hutchens, George. Birchy Head, Bonne Bay, s:1, 1895
Hynes, Henry Joseph. Fox Isl River, Port au Port Bay, s:1, 1968
Hynes, Joseph. Fox Isl River, Picadilly, s:1, 1980
Jesso, Edward. Sheaves Cv, Port au Port Peninsula, s:1, 1955
Joyce, Robert. Lark Hbr, s:1, 1888
Kendle, Samuel. Codroy, s:2, 1878-80
Legge, Philip. SGB, s:1, 1884
LeRoux, Edward. SGB, s:2, 1881-90
LeRoux, Walter. SGB, r:1, 1909
Major, George. Bonne Bay, s:1, 1890
Marley, John. BofIsls, s:1, 1900
Marshall, Edward. Bonne Bay, s:1, 1892
Martin, James. Picadilly, s:1, 1981
Matthews, William John. Corner Brk, Humbermouth, Curling, s:2, 1936-41
McIsaac, Alexander & Alexander Gillis, Codroy River, s:1, 1876
McKenzie, Hugh. Bonne Bay, s:1, 1888
McNeil, Bernard. BofIsls, s:1, 1893
Mitchell, Isaac. Bonne Bay, s:1, 1910
Moor, William. SGB, s:1, 1881
Moors, Stephen C. Shoal Brk, Bonne Bay, s:1, 1888
Morris, Charles. SGB, s:1, 1882
Murphy, James. Codroy River, s:1, 1876
Murphy, Michael. Bonne Bay, s:1, 1877
Murrin, Ira Raymond. Lark Hbr, s:1, 1973
Nash, Henry. Bonne Bay, FB, s:1, 1875
Neville, William. Bonne Bay, s:1, 1906
Nicolle, John Alexander. Rocky Hbr, s:1, 1966
O'Brien, Thomas. Humber Snd, s:1, 1890
Osmond, Benjamin. Silver Pt, Bonne Bay, s:2, 1879-95
Park, Fred. Curling, r:1, 1959
Park, Robert Jonathan. Lark Hbr, s:2, 1956-59
Parsons, Alexander Almond. Rocky Hbr, s:1, 1945
Parsons, Charles E. Jr. Humber Snd, s:1, 1896

Parsons, John Sheppard. Meadows, BofIsls, s:1, 1944

Parsons, Nicholas. Bonne Bay, s:1, 1878

Parsons, Taylor. Trout River, s:1, 1956

Parsons, William. Curzon Village, Woody Pt, Bonne Bay, s:1, 1935

Payne, John A. Cox's Cv, s:1, 1962

Penny, Archibald. Humber Snd, s:1, 1895

Power, Ernest F. Stephenville, s:1, 1979

Pynn, George. BofIsls, s:1, 1885

Roberts, Samuel Charles. Woody Pt, Bonne Bay, s:1, 1879

Roberts, Stephen. Deer Lake, s:1, 1956

Rolls, John. Codroy River, s:1, 1883

Ronald Gale, West Bay Centre, Port au Port Bay, s:1, 1956

Routledge, James. Port au Port, s:1, 1889

Ryan, William T. Norris Pt, Bonne Bay, s:3, 1929-44

Sams, James. Codroy, s:1, 1880

Scott, Lambert. BofIsls, s:1, 1908

Shepherd, William. SGB, b:1, r:1, 1892-1915

Sheppard, Austin William. Lark Hbr, s:1, 1968

Sheppard, George Jr. Lark Hbr, s:1, 1944

Sheppard, Isaac Jr. Lark Hbr, s:1, 1955

Sheppard, Isaac Sr. Lark Hbr, s:1, 1896

Sheppard, Richard Freeman. York Hbr, s:1, 1966

Simon, Millage. De Grau, Port au Port Peninsula, s:2, 1980-81

Strong, Alexander. Bonne Bay, r:2, 1929-30

Swyer, Samuel Jr. Sandy Pt, SGB, s:1, 1909

Thorne, Ronald Gordon. Corner Brk, s:1, 1976

Tuck, John. Codroy, s:1, 1905

Wells, James. Cox's Cv, s:1, 1974

Wells, Terry Gerald. Cox's Cv, s:1, 1973

Wheeler, Noah. Cox's Cv, Middle Arm, s:1, 1937

Wheler, Peter. Silver Pt, Bonne Bay, s:3, 1879-82

White, Anthony. St. George's, s:1, 1967

White, Eli. Rocky Hbr, s:1, 1939

Wight, Eunice C. Rocky Hbr, s:1, 1965

Winser, David. Western Arm, Bonne Bay, s:1, 1876

Young, James. Codroy, s:1, 1878

APPENDIX TO CHAPTER FIVE: SOUTHWEST COAST AND SOUTH COAST

SHIPBUILDER, RESIDENCE, PLACE(S) BUILT, NO. OF SHIPS, YEAR(S)

Anderson, Ephraim. West Pt, La Poile, b:1, r:1, 1929-32
Anderson, George. Otter's Pt, Burgeo, s:1, 1914
Anderson, John Ethelbert. Rose Blanche, s:1, 1963
Anderson, William. La Poile, s:2, 1913-14
Ashford, Joseph. Hbr Breton, s:1, 1944
Augot, John. Morrisville, s:1, 1984
Barnes, William Sr. Bay D'Espoir, s:1, 1888
Bennett, Thomas W. Burnt Isls, Channel, s:2, 1890-91
Billard, Martin. Margaree, s:1, 1940
Bowdridge, George William R. Burgeo, s:1, 1876
Bragg, Emanuel. Channel, s:1, 1919
Bragg, Gower Bruce. Channel, s:1, 1930
Bragg, Richard. Channel, s:1, 1932
Buckland, Thomas Horwood. Hbr Le Cou, s:1, 1963
Buffett, Thomas. Burgeo, s:1, 1914
Buffett, William. Margaree, s:1, 1940
Caines, Eliel. Burnt Isls, s:1, 1928
Caines, Snook. Great Jervais, s:1, 1885
Camp, Joseph. Pushthrough, s:1, 1906
Carter, William. Port aux Basques, s:1, 1869
Caswell, William. Burgeo, Little River, s:2, 1898-1900
Chambers, George. Pushthrough, Fortune, s:1, 1877
Collier, Matthew. Ship Cv, Bay D'Espoir, s:3, 1880-1909
Collier, Michael. Conne River, Ship Cv, s:2, 1867-86
Collier, Samuel Robert. Otter's Pt, s:1, 1912
Collier, Samuel. Hermitage Bay, Conne River, s:2, 1869-81
Collins, Henry. Petites, s:1, 1963
Coly, Thomas. Fox Isl Burgeo, s:1, 1916
Coombes, Jonathan. Piccaire Hermitage Bay, b:1, r:1, 1936-40
Courtney, Charles. Burnt Isls, b:1, r:1, 1898-1914
Courtney, James T. Otter's Pt, s:1, 1916
Courtney, Thomas. Burnt Isls, s:1, 1906
Currie, George & J. M. Port aux Basques, s:1, 1921
Currie, William & James M. & Isaac. Port aux Basques, s:1, 1911
Cutler, John. Ramea, b:1, r:1, 1920-31
Davis, Robert. Bay D'Espoir, Ship Cv, s:2, 1884-98
Davis, William. Channel, r:1, 1901
Dolimont, George. Hbr Breton, English Hbr Fortune Bay, s:1, 1884

Dominie, Cecil. Little Bay, Hermitage Bay, s:2, 1945-48
Dowden, Samuel. Hermitage Bay, s:1, 1911
Durnford, Benjamin R. Francois, r:1, 1927
Durnford, George W. Francois, s:1, 1930
Durnford, James. Francois, r:1, 1927
Durnford, Robert. Francois, s:1, 1912
Durnford, Ruben. Francois, s:1, 1926
Engram, George William. Burgeo, s:1, 1962
Engram, George. Piccaire Hermitage Bay, s:1, 1927
Engram, James. Little Bay, Hermitage Bay, s:1, 1947
Engram, John. Hermitage, Milltown, s:1, 1938
Engram, Thomas. Hermitage Bay, Bay D'Espoir, s:1, 1940
Frampton, William. Otter's Pt, Port aux Basques, Grand Bay, b:2, r:2, 1917-34
Francis, William. Hermitage Bay, s:1, 1911
Fudge, Benjamin. Gaultois, b:2, r:1, 1937-43
Fudge, James. Gaultois, s:1, 1945
Giles, Morgan. Ramea, s:1, 1930
Grant, Nicholas. Ship Cv, s:1, 1884
Hare, John K. Burgeo, s:1, 1899
Hayman, George. Fox Isl, s:1, 1927
Hayman, Hugh. Fox Isl, s:3, 1911-29
Henderson, William. Burgeo, s:1, 1915
Herridge, John. Hbr Le Cou, s:2, 1904-11
Herridge, William. Hbr Le Cou, La Poile Bay, s:2, 1911-13
Hoben, William. Burnt Isls, r:1, 1925
Hodder, Alexander. Margaree, s:1, 1947
Horwood, James. Hbr Le Cou, s:1, 1905
Horwood, Thomas. Hbr Le Cou, s:2, 1886-1916
Keeping, Angus. Burnt Isls, r:1, 1989
Keeping, Benjamin. Burnt Isls, s:1, 1942
Keeping, Harold Wendell. Burnt Isls, s:1, 1940
Keeping, Isaac. Ramea, r:2, 1929-30
Keeping, John. Burnt Isls, Ramea, s:3, 1922-33
Keeping, Martin. Ramea, s:2, 1917-22
Kendell, Clarence. McCallum, r:1, 1968
Laurence, Edward. Burnt Isls, b:1, r:1, 1911-33
Lawrence, Thomas. Burnt Isls, s:1, 1932
Lee, John. Bonne Bay Hermitage Bay, s:1, 1873
Lee, Matthew. McCallum, s:1, 1913
Leechman, Thomas. Grey River, s:1, 1919
Lidstone, Henry. Gaultois, r:1, 1900
Lomond, Gilbert. Mouse Isl, s:1, 1939
Mauger, Elias. Petites, s:1, 1896

McCourt, Philip. Port aux Basques, Garia Bay, s:1, 1869
McDermott, Keltie Lloyd. West Pt, La Poile Bay, s:1, 1966
Meade, Freeman. Isle aux Morts, s:1, 1930
Moores, Moses. Pushthrough, s:2, 1907-15
Munden, Joseph. La Poile, s:1, 1863
Musseau, James Earle. Mouse Isl, s:1, 1943
Musseau, Samuel. Mouse Isl, s:3, 1933-46
Neil, Archibald. Grand Bruit, s:2, 1939-47
Organ, David. Hbr Gully, Hermitage Bay, s:1, 1892
Organ, John. Ship Cv, Bay D'Espoir, s:3, 1882-1903
Organ, Samuel. Hermitage Bay, Ship Cv, s:2, 1867-87
Organ, William. Hbr Gully, Bay D'Espoir, s:1, 1906
Osborne, John T. Grand Bay, s:1, 1933
Osmond, Jeremiah. Margaree, s:1, 1926
Osmond, Thomas. Margaree, s:1, 1928
Parsons, William. Burgeo, s:2, 1891-1905
Penel, John. Burgeo, b:1, r:1, 1910-31
Perry, William K. Ship Cv Bay D'Espoir, s:1, 1898
Pevie, George. Milltown, s:1, 1935
Pinel, John. Burgeo, r:1, 1931
Power, Edward. Ship Cv, s:1, 1900
Rendell, John. Gaultois, s:1, 1884
Rodgers, Henry. Channel, Marystown, s:2, 1903-14
Skinner, Arthur. Isle aux Morts, Mouse Isl, r:2, 1929-30
Spencer, Hartley Nathan. Cul de Sac, Hermitage Bay, s:1, 1945
Stone, George Clarence. West Pt, La Poile, s:1, 1969
Stone, Pliny Lewis. West Pt, La Poile, s:2, 1929-48
Strickland, Henry. Petites, s:1, 1937
Strickland, Henry. Rose Blanche, r:1, 1925
Strickland, Norman. Port aux Basques, s:1, 1953
Strickland, Randell. Petites, s:1, 1943
Tailor, Edward. Margaree, s:1, 1919
Tibbo, William. Hbr Breton, s:1, 1939
Vallis, Joseph. Ramea, r:1, 1928
Vatcher, John. Burgeo, s:2, 1893-1903
Vickers, Walter. La Plante, s:1, 1911
Walters, John William. Port aux Basques, s:1, 1935
Warren, Albert. Fox Isl, s:2, 1913-27
Warren, Frank. Burgeo, s:1, 1965
Warren, James. Fox Isl, s:2, 1912-16
Wells, John. Pushthrough, Hermitage Bay, s:1, 1948
White, Thomas. Jersey Hbr, s:1, 1900

APPENDIX TO CHAPTER SIX: FORTUNE BAY

SHIPBUILDER, RESIDENCE, PLACE(S) BUILT, NO. OF SHIPS, YEAR(S)

Ansty, Charles W. Garnish, s:2, 1901-02

Ansty, William. Garnish, s:1, 1902

Antle, Thomas. Fox Cv, Fortune, r:1, 1926

Baker, Edward. Bay de L'Eau Isl, s:1, 1902

Baker, James. Hbr Mille, s:1, 1898

Baker, William. Rencontre, s:1, 1887

Banfield, George M. Garnish, s:1, 1898

Banfield, George Sr. FB, s:1, 1869

Banfield, James. Bay L'Argent, s:1 1889

Banfield, Samuel. Garnish, FB, s:1, 1864

Banfield, Thomas. Bay L'Argent, s:2, 1898-1902

Banfield, Thomas. FB, s:1, 1869

Barnes, Charles. FB, s:1, 1861

Barnes, Jacob. Hbr Mille, s:1, 1892

Barnes, John. Hbr Mille, s:1, 1899

Barnes, Samuel Sr. Hbr Mille, s:1, 1884

Bartlett, Thomas. Fortune, s:1, 1857

Bearnes, Abraham. Hbr Mille, s:1, 1904

Bearnes, Ambrose. Hbr Mille, s:1, 1904

Bearnes, Matthew. Jacques Fontaine, s:1, 1902

Bearns, John. Hbr Mille, r:1, 1928

Belbin, James. Grand Bank, s:1, 1888

Bennett, Aaron. Fortune, r:1, 1931

Bennett, Benjamin. Grand Bank, s:1, 1886

Bennett, Thomas Fox. Fortune, s:2, 1884-1909

Bennett, Thomas Sr. Fortune, s:2, 1859-72

Bennett, William. Fortune, s:2, 1852-67

Berkshire, William. Mose Ambrose, s:1, 1882

Bond, Thomas. Frenchman's Cv, s:1, 1873

Bond, William. Grand Bank, FB, r:1, 1870

Brenton, John. Bay du Nord, s:2, 1881-82

Brushett, George R. Jacques Fontaine, r:1, 1959

Brushett, John James. Jacques Fontaine, s:1, 1955

Brushett, John. Fortune, s:1, 1908

Buffett, Benjamin Robert. Grand Bank, FB, s:1, 1871

Buffett, George Abraham. Grand Bank, s:1, 1880

Buffett, William. Fortune, s:1, 1882

Bullen, John Thomas. Bay de L'Eau Isl, r:1, 1926

Bullen, Joseph. Bay de L'Eau, r:1, 1929
Bullen, Leo. English Hbr W., r:1, 1960
Burke, William & Patrick. St. Jacques, Bay L'Argent, b:2, r:1, 1867-74
Burton, Jonathan. Fortune, s:2, 1867-83
Burton, William. Bay de L'Eau Isl, Fortune, s:3, 1877-1911
Camp, John. Grand Bank, r:1, 1878
Clarke, John S. Little Bay E., s:1, 1931
Clewett, Thomas. Garnish, s:1, 1898
Clinch, David. Fortune, s:1, 1855
Cluett, George. Frenchman's Cv, s:1, 1886
Cluett, William & Owen. FB, s:1, 1861
Collier, Jacob. Fortune, FB, s:1, 1909
Collier, John. Fortune, FB, s:2, 1874-75
Collier, William. Fortune, s:1, 1862
Comtemy, Robert. Grand Bank, s:1, 1873
Congdon, Samuel. St. John's Isl, FB, s:1, 1878
Courtney, William George. Grand Bank, r:1, 1898
Cox, Philip & Daniel. Grand Bank, s:2, 1865-76
Cox, Philip. Grand Bank, s:2, 1886-96
Crocker, Luke. Fortune, s:2, 1877-82
Day, Thomas. Bay de L'Eau Isl, s:1, 1902
Dodge, George & Thomas. English Hbr, s:1, 1867
Drake, William. Lally Cv, FB, s:1, 1890
Elford, George Philip. Fortune, s:1, 1873
Evans, Chesley. English Hbr E., s:1, 1966
Evans, Henry. Grand Bank, Fortune, b:1, r:1, 1874-79
Evans, James. Little Bay E., s:1, 1903
Evans, Jonathan. Grand Bank, s:2, 1884-89
Evans, Joseph. Grand Bank, s:2, 1864-84
Evans, William George. Grand Bank, s:1, 1866
Fiander, Aaron. English Hbr W., Lally Cv, s:1, 1906
Fiander, George. Coombe's Cv, s:1, 1903
Fiander, Samuel. Coombe's Cv, s:1, 1885
Fiander, Stephen. Coombe's Cv, s:1, 1888
Foote, John. Belleoram, s:1, 1901
Foote, Thomas. Grand Bank, Grand Beach, s:2, 1906-07
Forsey, Aaron. Grand Bank, s:2, 1851-71
Forsey, George Robert & Charles Patten. Grand Bank, s:2, 1869-76
Forsey, Joseph. Grand Bank, s:2, 1858-59
Forsey, Robert. Grand Bank, s:3, 1852-62
Forward, Ambrose. Grand Bank, s:1, 1861
Forward, Edward. Grand Bank, s:1, 1880

Forward, George. Grand Bank, s:1, 1886

Forward, Robert. Grand Bank, s:1, 1858

Fudge, Silas. Belleoram, BofIsls, s:1, 1901

Gillard, George. Fortune, s:1, 1873

Giovanninni, Henry. Rencontre, s:1, 1882

Glaveen, David. FB, s:1, 1899

Good, Samuel. Bay L'Argent, Little Bay, s:2, 1876-1902

Gorman, Joseph. FB, Fortune, s:1, 1866

Grandy, Aaron. Grand Bank, s:2, 1886-91

Grandy, Abraham. Garnish, s:1, 1899

Grandy, Charles M. Garnish, s:1, 1900

Grandy, George. FB, s:1, 1871

Grandy, James H. Garnish, s:1, 1916

Grandy, John. Garnish, s:3, 1888-1900

Grandy, Maxwell. Grand Bank, r:1, 1949

Grandy, Samuel. Garnish, FB, s:1, 1865

Grandy, Stephen. Garnish, s:1, 1888

Grandy, Thomas B. Garnish, s:2, 1926-35

Grandy, Thomas H. Garnish, s:1, 1899

Grandy, Thomas Wilson. Garnish, s:1, 1913

Grandy, William. Garnish, Burin, Bay L'Argent, s:3, 1879-84

Grandy, Wilson. Garnish, s:1, 1899

Green, Thomas & Edward. Little Bay, s:1, 1870

Hackett, John. English Hbr E., s:1, 1899

Hackett, Joseph. English Hbr, s:1, 1903

Harris, Thomas. Grand Bank, s:1, 1860

Hickey, Andrew. Bay du Nord Brk, FB, s:1, 1886

Hickey, Daniel. Fortune, FB, s:2, 1869-85

Hickey, James. Terrenceville, Bay L'Argent, b:2, r:2, 1906-29

Hickey, Owen. Great Barrow, FB, s:2, 1872-86

Hickey, Thomas Patrick. Terrenceville, s:1, 1946

Hickey, Thomas. FB, s:1, 1885

Hickman, George A. Grand Bank, FB, s:2, 1872-74

Hickman, Henry John. Grand Bank, s:3, 1851-75

Hickman, John Morgan. FB, s:1, 1871

Hickman, Jonathan. Grand Bank, s:3, 1859-78

Hickman, Robert & John Henry. Grand Bank, r:1, 1867

Hickman, Samuel. Grand Bank, s:1, 1880

Hillier, Charles. Fortune, s:1, 1909

Hillier, Edward. Fortune, s:2, 1860-69

Hines, John. Jacques Fontaine, s:1, 1901

Hines, Joseph & Patrick. English Hbr, s:2, 1869-85

Hines, Thomas. Bay L'Argent, English Hbr, s:2, 1879-88
Hiscock, John. Grand Bank, s:1, 1876
Hodge, John. Fortune, s:1, 1851
Hyde, Ambrose. Grand Bank, s:1, 1868
Johnson, Philip. St. Bernard's, r:1, 1934
Keeping, Edwin. English Hbr W., s:1, 1982
Keeping, George. Fortune, s:3, 1855-81
Kerby, James. Belleoram, s:2, 1878-83
Kettle, George. Grand Bank, Grand Beach, s:1, 1931
Lake, Henry. Bay de L'Eau Isl, s:1, 1908
Lamb, Adam. Bay du Nord, FB, s:1, 1884
Laurence, Benjamin. FB, s:1, 1868
Legg, John. Garnish, s:1, 1883
Loring, James. St. Jacques, s:1, 1882
Lovell, Wilson. Grand Bank, s:2, 1857-61
Mager, Elias. Fortune, FB, s:2, 1858-65
Marsh, Thomas. Garnish, s:3, 1874-1901
Mayo, James. Fortune, s:1, 1876
McCarthy, Daniel. FB, s:1, 1887
McCarthy, Patrick. St. Jacques, s:1, 1883
McDaniel, Henry. FB, s:1, 1863
McKay, Hugh Colin. Grand Bank, s:1, 1935
Mitchell, John. Terrenceville, s:1, 1907
Mitchell, Michael. Terrenceville, s:1, 1904
Mitchell, William. Terrenceville, s:1, 1938
Moulton, Abel H. Loon's Cv, FB, s:1, 1934
Moulton, James. Garnish, s:1, 1902
Moulton, John. Garnish, s:1, 1898
Moulton, Thomas. Garnish, b:1, r:1, 1886-98
Murley, George. Frenchman's Cv, s:1, 1989
Myles, George R. Terrenceville, s:1, 1951
Noseworthy, Simon. Fortune, s:1, 1882
Osborne, William J. Little Bay, s:1, 1902
Ott, John. English Hbr, s:1, 1895
Pardy, Charles. Grand Bank, s:1, 1892
Parrott, John F. St. Bernard's, FB, s:1, 1923
Patten, Charles. Grand Bank, s:1, 1865
Patten, Edward. Grand Bank, FB, s:2, 1857-69
Penny, John. Fortune, s:2, 1873-79
Penwill, William. Grand Bank, s:1, 1866
Percey, John. Fortune, s:1, 1866
Perrott, John J. Fox Cv, FB, s:2, 1891-1902

Petite, William & Jeremiah. FB, s:1, 1865
Pinchard, Thomas. Fortune, s:1, 1859
Poole, John. Belleoram, s:1, 1885
Pope, Albert. Stone's Cv, FB, s:1, 1897
Pope, Ambrose. Stone's Cv, s:1, 1885
Pope, Edward. Stone's Cv, s:1, 1886
Pope, William & George. FB, b:1, r:1, 1863-66
Purchase, Albert & Thomas. Fortune, Grand Bank, s:1, 1880
Purchase, John. Fortune, r:1, 1890
Purchase, Thomas. Fortune, s:1, 1870
Ramsey, John. Fortune, s:1, 1877
Reeves, George. Garnish, s:2, 1887-1910
Riggs, Thomas. Grand Bank, s:1, 1865
Rogers, John. Fortune, s:2, 1896-97
Rogers, Thomas. Fortune, b:3, r:1, 1864-90
Rose, Charles. Grand Bank, s:1, 1885
Rose, James. Grand Bank, s:1, 1887
Rose, Jeremiah. Little Bay, Fortune, s:1, 1861
Rose, Jonathan. Grand Bank, s:1, 1867
Rose, Robert. Grand Bank, s:2, 1852-63
Rose, Samuel. Grand Bank, s:1, 1885
Rose, W. Belleoram, s:1, 1907
Rumsey, Thomas. Fortune, s:1, 1879
Scott, George. FB, s:1, 1862
Scott, Henry. FB, s:1, 1862
Scott, Jacob. Little Hbr, FB, r:1, 1927
Scott, William. Little Hbr, s:1, 1902
Skinner, Thomas. Fortune, s:1, 1867
Smith, Albert. Belleoram, Lally Cv, s:1, 1975
Smith, John. Grand Bank, s:1, 1851
Snook, Jabez. Fortune, s:2, 1882-87
Snook, Morgan. Fortune, s:1, 1874
Spencer, Charles Bennett. Fortune, s:3, 1890-1902
Spencer, John Hickman. Fortune, s:1, 1872
Spencer, John. Fortune, s:3, 1856-73
Spencer, William M. Fortune, s:2, 1889-1900
Stoodley, George. Grand Bank, FB, s:1, 1864
Strickland, Bertram. Little Bay, FB, r:1, 1962
Symes, George & Thomas. Grand Bank, s:1, 1866
Thornhill, James. Little Bay E., Little Bay, s:3, 1870-99
Tibbo, George. Grand Bank, s:3, 1856-74
Tibbo, James. Stone's Cv, Belleoram, s:1, 1893

Tibbo, John. Hare Hbr, s:1, 1887

Tibbo, Jonathan. Grand Bank, s:1, 1881

Tibbo, Samuel. Grand Bank, s:2, 1874-87

Tibbo, Simeon. Grand Bank, s:1, 1881

Tibbo, Thomas. Grand Bank, s:1, 1865

Tibbo, Wilson. Grand Bank, s:3, 1860-1901

Toms, Joseph. FB, s:1, 1865

Turner, Robert. FB, s:1, 1863

Vallis, John. Coombe's Cv, s:2, 1886-1906

Vallis, William H. Coombe's Cv, s:1, 1886

Vigus, Benjamin. Belleoram, s:1, 1901

West, Joseph. FB, s:1, 1866

West, Richard. Bay L'Argent, s:2, 1872-87

West, Thomas. Bay L'Argent, s:1, 1890

Wetherell, Jonathan. Fortune, Little Bay, s:2, 1898-1900

Williams, Isaac A. Pool's Cv, s:3, 1902-1907

Williams, Samuel. Pool's Cv, FB, s:2, 1880-91

Yarn, James. Mose Ambrose, s:1, 1903

Yarn, William. Mose Ambrose, s:1, 1879

Young, Hubert. St. Jacques, FB, s:1, 1872

APPENDIX TO CHAPTER SEVEN: PLACENTIA BAY

SHIPBUILDER, RESIDENCE, PLACE(S) BUILT, NO. OF SHIPS, YEAR(S)

Adams, Stephen. PB, s:1, 1873

Antle, Thomas. Fox Cv, r:1, 1926

Antle, Vincent. Mortier, Burin E., s:1, 1929

Appleby, David. Burin, s:1, 1925

Appleby, Edward (2nd). Burin, s:1, 1901

Appleby, Frederick. Burin, r:1, 1926

Bailey, Ignatius. Little Hbr W., PB, s:1, 1944

Bailey, John D. Oderin, s:1, 1927

Baker, John. Mortier Bay, s:1, 1838

Baker, Joseph. Marystown, s:1, 1902

Barron, John. St. Joseph's, r:1, 1926

Barron, Peter. Gallows Hbr, s:1, 1891

Barry, Laurence. Red Isl, s:1, 1884

Barry, Maurice. Red Isl, s:1, 1885

Beazley, John. Burin, s:1, 1926

Beazley, Joseph. Burin, Port au Bras, s:1, 1936
Beazley, Thomas William. Burin Bay Arm, s:2, 1899-1902
Bennett, Ambrose. Burin, s:1, 1867
Bennett, Patrick. Indian Hbr, PB, s:1, 1900
Bennett, Samuel. Burin, s:2, 1873-85
Best, Charles. Merasheen, s:1, 1877
Best, Josiah H. Oderin, s:1, 1906
Bishop, Edward. Salmonier, PB, s:1, 1926
Bolt, John H. Tack's Beach, s:1, 1912
Bolt, William. Tack's Beach, Haystack, s:1, 1940
Boucher, William. Burin, r:1, 1830
Bradley, George. Burin, r:1, 1848
Bradshaw, John Power. PB, s:1, 1873
Bradshaw, William George. Placentia, s:1, 1875
Brake, John. Marystown, Mortier Bay, s:2, 1895-1910
Braway, Richard. Baine Hbr, s:1, 1883
Brennan, Edward. Ship Cv, PB, s:1, 1909
Brennan, Patrick Joseph. Placentia, s:2, 1935-40
Brinston, Charles W. Bar Haven, r:1, 1931
Brown, Benjamin. Tack's Beach, s:1, 1935
Brown, Henry. Rock Hbr, s:1, 1895
Brown, John H. Tack's Beach, b:1, r:1, 1907-30
Brown, John H. Tack's Beach, r:1, 1930
Brown, John Joseph. St. Joseph's, PB, s:1, 1946
Brown, John. Tack's Beach, s:1, 1907
Brown, Patrick. Sound Isl, s:1, 1888
Brown, Peter. Sound Isl, s:2, 1873-76
Brown, Philip. Sound Isl, s:2, 1869-76
Brown, Uriah. Burin, s:2, 1877-85
Brown, William Henry. Burin, s:1, 1935
Brown, William J. Hbr Buffett, r:1, 1965
Brown, William. Paradise, PB, s:1, 1880
Brown, William. Tack's Beach, Woody Isl, r:1, 1959
Browne, John. Great Paradise, s:1, 1939
Bruce, Matthew. Ram's Isl, PB, s:1, 1889
Brushett, George R. Jacques Fontaine, r:1, 1959
Brushett, James. Rushoon, s:1, 1889
Brushett, Richard. Burin, s:1, 1880
Brushett, Samuel. Marystown, s:1, 1908
Bugden, John. Burin, s:1, 1880
Bugden, Reuben. Burin, r:1, 1917
Bugden, William F. Mortier Bay, s:1, 1912

Burfitt, William. Burin, s:1, 1877
Burgess, Elias. Burin, s:1, 1912
Burgess, William T. Epworth, s:1, 1914
Burton, Thomas. PB, s:1, 1913
Burton, William P. Little Hbr W., s:1, 1951
Burton, William. Little Hbr W., PB, s:1, 1929
Butcher, Jonathan. Arnold's Cv, s:1, 1882
Butcher, Josiah. Mussel Hbr Arm, PB, s:1, 1907
Butcher, Llewelyn James. Kingwell, s:1, 1965
Butcher, Samuel. Kingwell, PB, s:1, 1940
Butcher, William F. Kingwell, r:1, 1926
Butler, Thomas. Flat Isls, PB, s:2, 1945-46
Butler, Victor. Hbr Buffett, s:1, 1934
Byrne, Douglas Joseph. Paradise, PB, s:1, 1942
Cake, George. Lamaline, s:1, 1851
Canning, Peter. Merasheen, s:1, 1933
Chambers, John H. PB, s:1, 1846
Cheeseman, Charles. Rushoon, s:1, 1901
Cheeseman, Michael. Rushoon, b:1, r:1, 1902-24
Clark, Thomas & Joseph Lake, Port au Bras, s:1, 1835
Clarke, John (1st). Gallows Hbr, s:2, 1888-1905
Clarke, John (2nd). Flat Isls, PB, b:1, r:1, 1929-30
Clarke, Thomas. Baine Hbr, s:1, 1889
Cleal, William. Marystown, s:1, 1948
Coady, Joseph. Bar Haven, s:1, 1942
Coady, Richard. Spanish Room, PB, s:1, 1916
Coffin, George. PB, s:1, 1868
Coffin, Henry. Haystack, PB, r:1, 1868
Coffin, William. Haystack, s:1, 1885
Collett, Thomas. Hbr Buffett, s:1, 1886
Collins, Albert. Flat Isls, PB, s:1, 1905
Collins, Austin. Placentia, s:1, 1899
Collins, Cletus. Southern Hbr, s:1, 1974
Collins, Edward. Flat Isl, PB, s:2, 1872-90
Collins, Gabriel. Flat Isls, PB, s:3, 1886-1903
Collins, James Patrick. St. Anne's, PB, s:1, 1947
Collins, Joseph. Placentia, Ragged Isls, s:2, 1899-1922
Collins, Joseph. Placentia, s:1, 1839
Connor, Michael. PB, s:1, 1852
Connor, Peter. Lawn, s:1, 1843
Connors, Peter. Clattice Hbr, Arnold's Cv, s:2, 1935
Connors, Thomas. Merasheen, s:1, 1949

Corbin, William. Placentia, s:1, 1869
Cousins, James. Lamaline, s:1, 1876
Cronn, John. Famish Cv, PB, s:1, 1919
Crow, Thomas. Little Hbr, PB, s:1, 1889
Culleton, Thomas. Bar Haven, s:2, 1902-12
Cumbie, James. Bar Haven, r:1, 1929
Cumbie, John. Bar Haven, s:1, 1912
Curtis, Bernard. Salmonier, PB, s:1, 1872
Curtis, William. Salmonier, PB, s:1, 1887
Daley, Laurence. Salmonier, PB, s:1, 1881
Daley, Moris. Salmonier, PB, s:1, 1872
Darby, Samuel. Burin, s:1, 1866
Darby, Stephen A. Burin, s:1, 1901
Davis, James. Placentia, Fox Hbr, s:1, 1886
Davis, Philip. Fox Hbr, s:1, 1884
Davis, Richard. Fox Hbr, s:1, 1890
Denief, Thomas Jr. Little Hbr, Burin, s:1, 1883
Denty, William Henry. Boat Hbr, s:1, 1946
Denty, Wilson. Boat Hbr, Burnt Isl, Flat Isls, b:1, r:2, 1906-10
Dicks, Michael Joseph. Oderin, s:1, 1937
Dicks, Robert. Flat Isls, PB, s:1, 1907
Dicks, William. Haystack, s:1, 1910
Dinn, Laurence. Salmonier, PB, s:1, 1889
Dober, Dennis. Little Bay, PB, s:1, 1917
Dober, John & David. PB, s:1, 1865
Dober, Thomas. Beau Bois, PB, s:1, 1898
Doody, Edwin. Mosquito, Salmonier, s:1, 1926
Doody, John. Little Bay, Mortier Bay, s:1, 1934
Dowden, Eli. Rock Hbr, s:1, 1916
Dreddy, William. Fox Hbr, s:1, 1874
Duggan, Martin. Salmonier, PB, s:1, 1901
Duke, Isaac. PB, s:1, 1840
Dunphy, Joseph. Paradise, PB, s:1, 1903
Dunphy, Patrick. Placentia, Little Placentia, s:2, 1896-1900
Dutton, James. Petit Forte, s:1, 1891
Emberly, Patrick. North Hbr, s:1, 1876
Ennis, Lewis. Merasheen, s:1, 1889
Ennis, Thomas. Merasheen, s:1, 1833
Evans, Patrick V. Argentia, s:1, 1910
Evans, Robert. Hbr Buffett, s:1, 1841
Farrell, Bernard. Bar Haven, b:1, r:1, 1919-28
Farrell, John J. Little Bay, Mortier Bay, r:1, 1929

Farrell, Joseph. Mortier Bay, s:1, 1904
Farrell, Joseph. PB, Mortier Bay, s:1, 1834
Farrell, Martin. Marystown, s:1, 1906
Farrell, Michael P. Marystown, r:1, 1931
Farrell, Thomas Francis. Bar Haven, s:1, 1946
Farrell, William J. Marystown, r:1, 1925
Fewer, John P. Parker's Cv, s:1, 1967
Fewer, Patrick. Parker's Cv, r:1, 1930
Fillatre (?), William. Marystown, s:1, 1913
Fitzpatrick, John. Ship Hbr, s:1, 1885
Fitzpatrick, Pierce. Placentia, s:1, 1886
Fitzpatrick, William. Marystown, s:1, 1908
Fitzpatrick, William. St. Lawrence, Lawn, s:1, 1857
Fleming, James. Lamaline, s:1, 1877
Fleming, John. Lamaline, s:2, 1865-73
Flinn, John & Thomas. Barren Isl, Piper's Hole, s:1, 1877
Flinn, William. Petit Forte, s:1, 1887
Flynn, James Anthony. Petit Forte, St. Anne's, s:2, 1939-43
Flynn, James. St. Anne's, PB, s:1, 1943
Flynn, John (1st). Petit Forte, s:1, 1892
Flynn, John (2nd). Petit Forte, s:1, 1943
Flynn, Joseph Bernard. Bar Haven, s:2, 1939-47
Flynn, M. T. Mortier Bay, s:1, 1907
Flynn, Patrick. PB, s:1, 1912
Flynn, Thomas. Great Bonia, Great Paradise, Bickford's Cv, s:2, 1942-47
Foley, James. Mortier Bay, s:1, 1835
Follett, James. Clattice Hbr, s:1, 1948
Follett, Peter. Clattice Hbr, s:1, 1929
Foote, Charles. Oderin, r:1, 1925
Frampton, Thomas S. Flat Isls, PB, r:1, 1927
Gambin, Michael. Petit Forte, r:1, 1949
Garrett Hickey, St. Kyran's, s:1, 1914
Goddard, Thomas Jr. Burin, s:2, 1877-88
Grandy, Wilson Joseph. Bar Haven, s:1, 1947
Grant, Andrew. Placentia, s:1, 1897
Gregory, Peter. Admiral's Beach, Salmonier, Haricott SMB, s:2, 1925-35
Griffin, James. Placentia, s:1, 1889
Griffin, Thomas. Placentia, s:1, 1893
Griffiths, Patrick. Ship Hbr, r:1, 1926
Guy, Benjamin. Arnold's Cv, s:1 ship, 1914
Guy, George Albert. Arnold's Cv, s:1, 1967
Haley, Albert. Lamaline, s:1, 1881

Haley, William. Lamaline, s:1, 1888
Hann, James. Lamaline, s:1, 1879
Hann, John. Lamaline, s:1, 1879
Hann, Joseph. Rushoon, Boat Hbr, s:1, 1938
Hann, Thomas. Hbr Buffett, b:1, r:1, 1853-56
Harris, Edward. St. Joseph's, Mall Bay SMB, s:1, 1935
Harris, John. St. Jacques, s:1, 1902
Hawco, John. Salmonier, PB, s:1, 1897
Hawco, William. Hbr Buffett, r:1, 1869
Hawcoe, Thomas. Salmonier, PB, s:1, 1888
Hayden, Eric. Petit Forte, s:1, 1986
Hayden, Joseph. Rushoon, Petit Forte, s:1, 1979
Hayes, Edward. Dunville, Fox Hbr, r:1, 1917
Hayes, Patrick. Petit Forte, s:1, 1905
Hayes, Thomas. Sound Isl, PB, s:1, 1874
Hayes, William. St. Kyran's, s:1, 1876
Hayley, James. Lamaline, s:1, 1883
Healey, Patrick K. Fox Hbr, b:1, r:1, 1900-26
Healey, Patrick. Fox Hbr, s:1, 1900
Hearn, William. Hbr Buffett, s:1, 1898
Hennessy, Edward. Merasheen, s:1, 1850
Hepditch, Patrick. Clattice Hbr, s:1, 1946
Hepditch, Richard. Lamaline, s:1, 1853
Hickey, John. Little Paradise, s:1, 1905
Hickey, Patrick. Prowseton, s:1, 1942
Hillier, James. Lamaline, s:1, 1879
Hillier, William. Lamaline, Bay du Nord FB, s:2, 1862-81
Hiscock, Henry. Flat Isls, PB, s:1, 1906
Hoben, William. Burnt Isls, r:1, 1925
Hodder, George R. Marystown, b:1, r:1, 1924-32
Hodder, George R. Marystown, r:1, 1932
Hodder, John Cyrus. Creston, s:2, 1931-35
Hodder, Levi. Creston, s:1, 1958
Hodder, Richard. Rock Hbr, s:1, 1895
Hodder, Richard. Rock Hbr, s:1, 1898
Hodder, William (2nd). Rock Hbr, s:1, 1944
Hodder, William Robert. Rock Hbr, s:2, 1927-44
Hodder, William T. Marystown, b:1, r:1, 1912-28
Hollett, Gabrial. Baine Hbr, Come By Chance, s:3, 1888-1912
Hollett, John. North Hbr, s:1, 1934
Hollett, Thomas. Baine Hbr, Sound Isl, Little Hbr, s:2, 1875-78
Hollett, Wilson. Hbr Buffett, s:1, 1886

Hondrick, Michael. Placentia, s:1, 1878
Hooper, Charles. Creston, r:1, 1927
Houlihan, Edward P. Argentia, s:1, 1921
Houlihan, James. Little Placentia, s:1, 1903
Houlihan, Patrick. Argentia, s:1, 1911
Hynes, Maxwell. Southern Hbr, s:1, 1971
Ingram, Fred. Kingwell, s:1, 1950
Inkpen, James Jr. Great Burin, s:1, 1874
Inkpen, James. Burin, s:1, 1864
Inkpen, Robert. Burin, Grand Bank, s:1, 1875
Jarvis, William (2nd). Oderin, b:2, r:1, 1901-27
Joyce, Kenneth Gerald. Burin Bay Arm, s:1, 1991
Keating, David. Lamaline, s:1, 1884
Keating, James. Long Hbr, PB, r:1, 1926
Keating, Michael. Long Hbr, Placentia, s:1, 1892
Keating, Patrick. Long Hbr, PB, s:1, 1905
Keeping, Emanuel. Boat Hbr, s:2, 1940-50
Keeping, Enos. Boat Hbr, s:1, 1947
Keeping, James. Boat Hbr, s:1, 1913
Keeping, Nelson. Boat Hbr, s:1, 1940
Kelly, Daniel J. Little Bay, Marystown, b:1, r:2, 1947-59
Kelly, Gerard Majella. Beau Bois, s:2, 1954-64
Kelly, Joseph. Beau Bois, s:1, 1928
Kelly, Thomas. Burin, s:1, 1841
Kenway, Charles. Flat Isls, PB, s:1, 1922
Kerivan, Jeffrey. Dunville, r:1, 1931
Kielly, Michael. Oderin, s:1, 1936
Kiely, John & Patrick Dunphy, Presque, PB, s:1, 1834
King, Denis. Fox Hbr, r:1, 1924
King, Thomas. Oderin, r:1, 1878
Lake, Daniel. Darby's Hbr, s:1, 1945
Lake, Harry. St. Joseph's, s:1, 1910
Lake, Henry. Bay de Loo, s:1, 1908
Lake, Henry. St. Joseph's, s:1, 1902
Lake, John. Darby's Hbr, s:1, 1905
Lamb, George. Oderin, Fox Hbr, s:2, 1898-1901
Lamb, Patrick. Red Isl, s:1, 1861
Lawrence Brothers, Long Hbr, PB, s:1, 1965
Leonard, Edward Jr. Presque, s:1, 1933
Leonard, Edward Sr. Isle Valen, r:1, 1860
Leonard, William. PB, s:1, 1901
Lewis, John. Salmonier, PB, s:1, 1889

Lewis, Michael. Salmonier, PB, s:1, 1899
Lockyer, Charles. Boat Hbr, s:2, 1943-51
Lockyer, Earl. Boat Hbr, s:1, 1962
Lockyer, Heber. Woody Isl, r:1, 1931
Lockyer, Samuel. Isle Valen, s:1, 1944
Logner, William. Lamaline, s:1, 1881
Loughlan, William. Flat Isls, PB, s:1, 1898
Loughlin, Edward Sr. Flat Isls, PB, s:1, 1910
Loughlin, James Henry. Flat Isls, PB, r:1, 1930
Lynch, Daniel. Fox Hbr, s:2, 1900-11
MacKay, Patrick. PB, s:1, 1834
Maher, Daniel. PB, s:1, 1846
Manning, Fergus Patrick. Little Hbr, PB, s:1, 1949
Manning, John. Little Hbr, s:1, 1919
Manning, Peter J. Oderin, s:1, 1927
Manning, Ronald. Oderin, s:2, 1936-48
Manning, Thomas. Little Bay, s:1, 1899
Mansfield, James. Placentia, s:1, 1836
March, William. Hbr Buffett, Haystack, Tack's Beach, b:1, r:3, 1926-36
Martin, John. Burin, s:1, 1893
Masters, William Joseph. Port Elizabeth, s:1, 1966
Mayo, Gabriel. Creston, r:1, 1929
Mayo, William. Marystown, s:1, 1906
McCarthy, Daniel. PB, Beau Bois, s:1, 1833
McCrowe, Dennis (1st). Fox Hbr, s:1, 1900
McCrowe, Dennis. Oderin, r:1, 1932
McCue, Daniel Joseph. Fox Hbr, s:1, 1935
McCue, James Joseph. Bar Haven, s:1, 1949
McCue, John. Fox Hbr, s:1, 1930
McDonald, Michael F. Salmonier, PB, s:1, 1927
McGrath, Thomas. Burin, s:1, 1833
Meade, Patrick. Ship Hbr, PB, s:1, 1952
Melay, William. Boat Hbr, s:1, 1911
Messervey, William. Oderin, s:1, 1885
Miller, James. Kingwell, PB, s:1, 1888
Miller, John. Kingwell, PB, s:1, 1887
Mitchell, Joseph. Port au Bras, s:1, 1912
Mitchell, Nathan. Burin, s:1, 1883
Mitchell, William. Marystown, s:2, 1916-22
Molloy, Andrew. Mortier Bay, s:1, 1891
Molloy, Joachim. Mooring Cv, Mortier Bay, s:1, 1935
Molloy, Maurice. Little Hbr, PB, s:1, 1930

Monks, Charles. Monkstown, r:1, 1962
Monks, Harry. Tack's Beach, s:1, 1907
Monks, Henry. Prowseton, Brewley, s:2, 1928-42
Monks, James. Monkstown, s:1, 1906
Monks, John. Burin, Monkstown, s:2, 1926-48
Monks, John. Monkstown, s:1, 1952
Mooney, John. Placentia, s:1, 1903
Moore, John. Merasheen, Plant, s:1, 1835
Morash, Obadiah. Hbr Buffett, r:1, 1929
Morell, John. Merasheen, s:1, 1833
Moulton, Abel H. Burin Bay Arm, s:1, 1934
Mullett, Archibald. Oderin, s:1, 1947
Munden, Levi. Baine Hbr, s:1, 1906
Murley, George. Marystown, s:1, 1899
Murley, John. Creston, r:1, 1925
Murphy, Albert. Parker's Cv, r:1, 1931
Murphy, Alphonsus. Long Hbr, PB, s:1, 1904
Murphy, Denis. Long Hbr, PB, s:1, 1895
Murphy, Francis J. Placentia, s:1, 1900
Murphy, Frank. Placentia, s:2, 1899-1902
Murphy, James. Placentia, Argentia, s:1, 1843
Murphy, James. Placentia, s:1, 1892
Murphy, John. Placentia, s:1, 1912
Murphy, Leo. Mount Arlington Heights, s:1, 1983
Murphy, Peter (1st). Oderin, s:1, 1890
Murphy, Peter (2nd). Long Hbr, PB, r:1, 1935
Murphy, Thomas L. Long Hbr, PB, r:1, 1925
Murphy, Tobias. Ram's Isl, PB, s:1, 1888
Murphy, William. Long Hbr, PB, s:1, 1955
Nolan, Richard. Salmonier, PB, r:1, 1901
Norman, Thomas. Red Isl, r:1, 1928
Norris, Richard. Salmonier, PB, s:1, 1900
Novell, Louis. Merasheen, s:1, 1834
Novelle, James. Merasheen, s:1, 1877
O'Reilly, Edward. Corbin, PB, s:1, 1907
Pafford, Josiah. North Hbr, s:1, 1918
Pafford, Lewis. North Hbr, s:1, 1909
Pafford, William. Hbr Buffett, r:1, 1960
Pardy, Henry P. Port Anne, Tack's Beach, r:1, 1958
Parrott, Nicholas. Salmonier, PB, s:1, 1898
Parsons, James. Clattice Hbr, s:1, 1910
Parsons, John. Clattice Hbr, s:1, 1917

Pearson, Daniel. Great Paradise, Paradise, s:1, 1947
Peavie, Edmund Arthur. Come By Chance, s:1, 1977
Peavie, James. Arnold's Cv, s:1, 1981
Peavie, James. Burnt Isl, s:1, 1942
Peavie, Joseph. Port Anne, Arnold's Cv, s:2, 1960-77
Peavie, Joseph. St. Joseph's, s:1, 1935
Peavy, William. Gallows Hbr, Little Hbr, PB, s:2, 1897-1909
Peavy, William. Little Hbr, PB, s:1, 1909
Peddle, William. Flat Isls, PB, s:1, 1925
Penny, Peter. Clattice Hbr, s:1, 1902
Phipard, Richard. Placentia, s:1, 1848
Picco, John Joseph. St. Joseph's, s:1, 1937
Picco, Philip. Burnt Isl, Long Isl, s:1, 1873
Piercey, John. Long Hbr, s:1, 1912
Pitcher, Joseph. Merasheen, s:1, 1935
Pitcher, Winston. Burin Bay Arm, s:1, 1982
Pitman, James & William Edwards, Lamaline, s:1, 1835
Pitman, John. Chandler's Hbr, s:1, 1902
Pittman, John. Marystown, r:1, 1928
Pittman, Joseph. Red Isl, s:2, 1884-86
Pittman, Patrick. Merasheen, r:1, 1931
Pittman, Richard. Mortier Bay, s:1, 1876
Pittman, Robert. Marystown, s:1, 1899
Pittman, Thomas. Marystown, s:1, 1916
Pomeroy, Austin. Merasheen, s:2, 1939-43
Pope, Robert. Fox Hbr, s:1, 1928
Power, Bernard Patrick. Argentia, s:1, 1937
Power, Edward (of William), Ship Hbr, PB, s:1, 1938
Power, John Joseph. S. W. Clattice Hbr, s:1, 1947
Power, Patrick T. Placentia, s:1, 1899
Power, Peter. Placentia, s:1, 1887
Power, Philip. Little Placentia, s:1, 1898
Power, Philip. Merasheen, Lundy Hbr, s:1, 1835
Power, Pius. Clattice Hbr, S. E. Bight, b:1, r:1, 1949-74
Power, Robert. Mortier Bay, s:1, 1878
Power, Robert. Spanish Room, s:1, 1949
Power, Sebastian. Ship Hbr, PB, s:1, 1935
Power, William Joseph. Clattice Hbr, s:1, 1929
Power, William. Ship Hbr, s:1, 1928
Purchase, John. Lamaline, s:1, 1864
Quinton, William. Merasheen, PB, r:1, 1904
Read, Benjamin. PB, s:1, 1855

Read, Joshua. PB, s:1, 1891
Reid, Earl Hubert. Baine Hbr, s:1, 1956
Reid, Edwin. Arnold's Cv, s:1, 1918
Reid, John. North Hbr, b:1, r:1, 1927-28
Rielley, William. PB, s:1, 1845
Rielly, Edward. Great Placentia, Placentia, b:1, r:1, 1876-80
Riely, Michael & Garret. Placentia, PB, s:1, 1840
Rodway, John. Baine Hbr, s:1, 1890
Rogers, Henry. Creston, Marystown, s:3, 1914-35
Rogers, Thomas. Creston, Epworth, s:3, 1925-36
Rose, Jeremiah. Red Isl, s:1, 1892
Rourke, Michael. Salmonier, PB, s:1, 1914
Rowe, John F. Spanish Room, s:1, 1915
Ryan, Denis. Paradise, PB, s:1, 1901
Ryan, Garrett. Merasheen, s:1, 1833
Ryan, John. Presque, PB, s:2, 1885-86
Ryan, William & James Collins, PB, s:2, 1870-73
Sheasty (?), Richard. Mortier Bay, s:1, 1834
Slade, David. North Hbr, s:1, 1986
Slade, George. PB, s:1, 1905
Slade, Jocelyn. Indian Hbr, PB, s:1, 1928
Slade, Reuben. Port Royal Arm, PB, s:1, 1915
Smith, Benjamin John. Boat Hbr, s:1, 1928
Smith, Bert. Baine Hbr, s:1, 1942
Smith, Frank. Bar Haven, s:1, 1941
Smith, James W. Baine Hbr, s:1, 1910
Smith, Philip. Baine Hbr, s:1, 1902
Smith, Thomas (1st). Placentia, s:1, 1880
Smith, Thomas (2nd). Baine Hbr, b:1, r:1, 1912-28
Smith, William. Oderin, s:1, 1885
Spurvey, Dennis. Fox Hbr, s:1, 1979
Stapleton, Alexander. Marystown, s:1, 1912
Stevenson, John. Fox Hbr, s:1, 1917
Street, Earle W. Epworth, s:1, 1935
Street, Eric Maxwell. Epworth, s:1, 1935
Street, George V. R. Epworth, s:1, 1927
Street, Isaac & Abraham. Burin Bay Arm, s:1, 1875
Sullivan, Humphrey. Placentia, s:1, 1874
Sullivan, Patrick. Presque, PB, s:2, 1875-76
Taylor, Benjamin. Burin Bay Arm, r:1, 1927
Tobin, Patrick Michael. Dunville, r:1, 1935
Tobin, Richard John. Placentia, s:1, 1943
Travers, Edward Joseph. Brewley, s:1, 1942

Travers, James J. Brule, PB, s:1, 1928
Travers, Leo Joseph. Brewley, s:1, 1947
Turpin, Patrick. St. Lawrence, s:1, 1977
Upshall, Samuel Edward. Kingwell, Little Hbr, s:2, 1962-78
Vaters, George. Baine Hbr, s:1, 1889
Vaters, Patrick. Baine Hbr, s:1, 1946
Vaters, Walter. Baine Hbr, s:1, 1928
Vaters, William. Rushoon, s:1, 1909
Wakeham, Thomas & Joseph. Presque, s:1, 1898
Wakeham, William J. Placentia, s:2, 1973
Walsh, Ambrose. Little Placentia, s:1, 1870
Walsh, John. Oderin, s:1, 1903
Walsh, Kyran. Lamaline, r:1, 1925
Walsh, Matthew. PB, s:1, 1841
Walsh, Michael Joseph J. Petit Forte, s:1, 1935
Walsh, Michael P. Great Bonia, r:1, 1926
Walsh, Thomas (1st). Marystown, s:1, 1906
Walsh, Thomas (2nd). Bickford's Cv, PB, s:1, 1934
Walsh, Thomas (3rd). Little Hbr W., PB, s:1, 1964
Walsh, William Henry. Little Hbr W., s:1, 1949
Walsh, William. Little Hbr, b:1, r:1, 1919-29
Walters, Herman. Boat Hbr, r:1, 1946
Walters, Thomas Edwin. Boat Hbr, s:1, 1949
Ward, Ambrose. Spanish Room, r:1, 1931
Wareham, Chesley. Sound Isl, s:1, 1926
Wareham, George. Haystack, s:1, 1904
Wareham, John (1st). Mussel Hbr Arm, s:1, 1900
Wareham, Samuel. Hbr Buffett, s:1, 1905
Wareham, Wilson. Arnold's Cv, s:2, 1926
Weare, John. Burin, s:1, 1878
Whalen, Thomas. Long Hbr, PB, s:2, 1935-36
Whiffen, Herbert. Rushoon, b:1, r:1, 1907-28
Whiffen, Maurice. Fox Hbr, r:1, 1928
Whiffen, Robert. Rushoon, s:1, 1930
Whiffen, William. Hbr Buffett, r:1, 1930
White, John. Salmonier, Placentia, s:1, 1883
White, Joseph. Petit Forte, s:1, 1943
Williams, Melvin George. Isle Valen, s:1, 1947
Wilson, William Joseph. Merasheen, s:1, 1939
Withers, James. Rock Hbr, s:1, 1896
Withers, Joseph. Marystown, s:1, 1916
Wyse, Richard. Placentia, s:2, 1900-06
Young, James. Creston, Little Bay, b:1, r:1, 1927-28

APPENDIX TO CHAPTER EIGHT: SOUTH AND SOUTHEAST AVALON PENINSULA

SHIPBUILDER, RESIDENCE, PLACE(S) BUILT, NO. OF SHIPS, YEAR(S)

Allison, Edward. Riverhead SMB, s:1, 1981
Armstrong, Andrew. Bay Bulls, s:1, 1903
Boland, John J. Calvert, r:1, 1925
Bonia, Jeremiah. North Hbr SMB, s:1, 1935
Bonia, Patrick. North Hbr SMB, s:1, 1887
Bulger, John. Trepassey, Salmonier SMB, s:1, 1887
Burke, Michael. Mall Bay SMB, s:1, 1885
Carew, Benjamin. Witless Bay, s:1, 1885
Carew, Henry. Cape Broyle, s:1, 1879
Cashin, Lawrence V. Cape Broyle, s:1 ship, 1914
Cashin, Richard. Cape Broyle, s:1, 1870
Christopher, William. Mall Bay SMB, s:1, 1888
Corcoran, John F. Coots Pond SMB, s:1, 1965
Daley, Daniel. St. Mary's, s:1, 1880
Daley, Harold J. Mall Bay SMB, s:1, 1973
Daley, James W. St. Joseph's SMB, r:1, 1928
Daley, Maurice Joseph. Mall Bay SMB, s:1, 1965
Daley, Richard J. St. Joseph's SMB, s:1, 1966
Dalton, James. SMB, s:1, 1901
Daly, Denis. St. Joseph's SMB, s:1, 1926
Daly, James Joseph. Mall Bay SMB, s:1, 1937
Daly, James. Mall Bay SMB, s:2, 1965-66
Davis, Robert. Mobile, s:1, 1886
Deady, Maurice. Salmonier SMB, s:1, 1876
Devereaux, Thomas. Trepassey, s:1, 1877
Devereaux, William. Trepassey, s:1, 1859
Dillon, Francis. Mobile, s:1, 1883
Dinn, Michael. St. Mary's, s:1, 1851
Dobbin, Ronald Patrick. Admiral's Beach SMB, s:2, 1966-67
Dobbin, Sebastian. Mosquito, Salmonier SMB, s:1, 1926
Doody, Albert. Admiral's Beach SMB, s:1, 1973
Doody, Casimer. Colinet Isl SMB, s:1, 1927
Doody, Cassimer Patrick. Mosquito, Colinet Isl SMB, s:1, 1943
Doody, Denis. Colinet Isl SMB, s:1, 1923
Drew, Edward. Bay Bulls, s:1, 1881
Driscoll, Joseph. Tors Cv, s:1, 1899
Driscoll, Lawrence. Tors Cv, s:1, 1906
English, John. Branch SMB, s:1, 1885

Fenely, Patrick. Fermeuse, s:1, 1888

Finney, James. Renews, s:1, 1876

Fitzgerald, Patrick. Mobile, s:1, 1886

Foley, James. Renews, s:1, 1906

Fortune, Pat. Tors Cv, s:1, 1878

Fortune, Sylvester. Tors Cv, s:1, 1896

Fox, James P. Salmonier SMB, s:1, 1883

Furey, William. St. Joseph's SMB, s:1, 1925

Gregory, Peter. Harricott SMB, s:1, 1935

Gushue, William. St. Joseph's SMB, s:1, 1935

Harris, John. North Hbr SMB, s:1, 1935

Hartery, Michael. Cape Broyle, s:1, 1927

Hayes, Daniel. Brigus South, Ferryland, s:1, 1931

Hearn, Ambrose. Bay Bulls, b:1, r:1, 1914-15

Hewitt, John. Trepassey, s:1, 1853

Hickey, James J. Mussel Pond SMB, r:1, 1929

Jackman, Michael. Fermeuse, s:1, 1883

James, George. Trepassey, b:1, r:1, 1899-1925

James, William. Trepassey, s:1, 1900

Keating, William. Renews, s:1, 1882

Kennedy, David. Mobile, s:2, 1908-13

Kennedy, Thomas. Trepassey, Tors Cv, s:2, 1879-85

Kenny, Gerald. Riverhead SMB, Fermeuse, s:1, 1982

Keough, Michael. Caplin Bay, s:1, 1885

King, Denis. North Hbr SMB, s:1, 1935

Linehan, Edmund M. Admiral's Beach SMB, s:1, 1966

Linehan, Francis J. Admiral's Beach SMB, s:2, 1966-72

Linehan, Jeremiah. Salmonier SMB, s:1, 1876

Manning, John. Salmonier SMB, s:1, 1880

McDonald, John. Salmonier SMB, s:1, 1896

McDonald, Michael F. Salmonier SMB, b:1, r:1, 1909-27

Merry, Frank. Caplin Bay, s:1, 1907

Morry, Edward. Salmonier SMB, s:1, 1910

Mulcahy, John. Bay Bulls, r:1, 1887

Mullowney, Stephen. Witless Bay, s:2, 1877-86

Murray, John. Salmonier SMB, s:1, 1887

O'Brien, Vincent. Cape Broyle, s:1, 1928

O'Driscoll, Joseph. Tors Cv, s:1, 1905

Peevie, Joseph. St. Joseph's SMB, Riverhead, s:1, 1935

Power, Joseph. Regina, St. Joseph's SMB, s:1, 1935

Power, Leo. Regina, Salmonier SMB, s:1, 1926

Power, Michael. Caplin Bay, s:1, 1884

Power, Nicholas. Brigus South, s:1, 1891

Power, Patrick. Ferryland, s:1, 1879
Power, Stephen. SMB, s:1, 1925
Puddister, John Francis. Bay Bulls, s:1, 1963
Roach, Henry. Branch SMB, s:2, 1885-1903
Roach, Patrick. Branch, SMB, s:1, 1871
Ronayne, Edward. Tors Cv, s:2, 1896-1906
Rowe, Eli. Chance Cv, s:1, 1906
Ryan, Ambrose Joseph. North Hbr SMB, s:1, 1947
Ryan, Philip. Mall Bay SMB, s:1, 1926
Ryan, Thomas. Cape Pine, Biscay Bay, Trepassey Bay, s:2, 1882-89
Snow, Solomon. St. Mary's, s:1, 1887
Sutton, George G. Trepassey, r:1, 1897
Sutton, Michael. Trepassey, s:1, 1852
Sutton, Richard. Trepassey, s:1, 1873
Sutton, Thomas G. Trepassey, s:1, 1928
Tobin, William. Renews, s:2, 1881-88
Tremlett, Peter J. Salmonier SMB, s:1, 1924
Tremlett, Peter. SMB, s:1, 1887
Walsh, Martin. Fermeuse, s:1, 1886
Walsh, Nicholas. Fermeuse, s:1, 1926
Warren, Llewelyn. Chance Cv, s:1, 1916
Weeks, Hamilton. Bay Bulls, s:1, 1902
Whalen, Thomas. St. Mary's, s:1, 1880
Williams, Henry. Bay Bulls, s:1, 1901
Williams, Philip. Bay Bulls, s:1, 1877
Williams, Thomas G. Bay Bulls, s:1, 1914
Williams, William G. Bay Bulls, s:1, 1871
Windsor, John. Ferryland, s:1, 1896
Winsor, Montgomery. Aquaforte, PB, s:1, 1923
Yetman, Jeremiah. St. Mary's, s:1, 1966
Yetman, Matthew. St. Mary's, s:1, 1935

GLOSSARY
OF TERMS USED IN VOLUMES ONE & TWO

BARQUE (BARK): A three-masted ship square-rigged on the foremast and mainmast and fore-and-aft rigged on the mizzen mast.

BARQUENTINE: A three-masted ship square-rigged only on the foremast and fore-and-aft rigged on the other masts.

BOLLARDS: Strong posts or supporting beams on a ship for holding a hawser fast.

BOWSPRIT: A spar attached to the bow of a vessel that stretches forward.

BREAST HOOKS: Thick V-shaped timbers placed so as to connect and strengthen the sides of the hull of a ship.

BRIG: A square-rigged vessel with two masts.

BRIGANTINE: A two-masted vessel square-rigged on the foremast and fore-and-aft rigged on the mainmast.

BULKHEAD: Sections or partitions in a vessel's hull.

C-CLAMP: A fastening or holding device in the shape of a C.

CARVEL-BUILT: The planks of a vessel are laid flush and the seams are sealed with oakum.

CLINKER-BUILT: The planks of a vessel overlap; used especially in life-boats.

COPPER-FASTENED: Copper sheets covering a ship's planking.

CROSS-HANDED: A person working alone.

CUT-WATER HEAD: The head or prow of a ship which "cuts" the water.

CUTTER: A small boat which may be powered by motor or sails.

DEADWOOD: Blocks of wood laid upon and fastened to the keel of a ship.

FIGURE HEAD: A figure, statue, or bust placed at the bow of a ship underneath the jib-boom.

FORE-AND-AFT: The rig of a vessel along its length as opposed to across its width; not square-rigged.

FORELOCKED: Fastened with bolts.

FULL-TIMBERED: Positioning the timbers of a ship especially close together.

GALLEON: Sometimes a war ship but usually a trading vessel; square-rigged on its foremast and mainmast and lateen-rigged (triangular sail) on the mizzen.

GALLERIES: Balconies at the quarters or around the stern of an early sailing ship.

GUNWALE: The uppermost edge (or wale) of a ship's side.

HAWSER: A large rope or small cable by which a ship is anchored or towed.

JIB: A triangular sail attached to the bowsprit and the foremast.

JIB-BOOM: A boom stretching out beyond the bow of the ship.

KEEL: The main timber in a ship extending from stem to stern at the bottom (the ship's backbone) and a support for the entire frame.

KEELSON: A long beam fastened over and along the keel to add strength to the keel.

KETCH-RIGGED: A two-masted vessel fore-and-aft rigged on the mainmast and the mizzen with the mizzen being about one-half the size of the mainsail.

LUGGER: A small vessel fitted with a four-cornered lugsail not attached to a boom or lower yard.

MIZZEN: The aftermost mast of a three-masted vessel or the small aft mast of a ketch.

PINNACE: A sixteenth-century vessel square-rigged on two masts but of a size suitable for being rowed.

PLANK-SHEER: A timber around a ship's hull at the line of junction with the deck.

RIDER KEELSON: Ribs in a ship's hold which are opposite and bolted to some of the ship's timbers and which reach from the keelson to the beams of the lower deck.

SCARFED: The joining of timbers by notching, grooving, and overlapping and then bolting these together; used especially in extending the length of a ship's keel.

SCHOONER: A two-masted vessel rigged fore-and-aft; the foremast is shorter than the mainmast.

SHALLOP: A small light boat carrying oars or sails or both.

SHEERSTRAKE: The uppermost continuous line of planking in a ship under the gunwale.

SHIP: The strict traditional definition of a ship is a vessel with at least three masts, all of them square-rigged; here it usually means a decked vessel of any size.

SKYSAIL: A light sail attached above the third section of a mast.

SLOOP: A small one-masted vessel rigged fore-and-aft with jib, mainsail, and topsails or mainsails.

SLOOP-OF-WAR: Rigged in any of several ways and mounting from 10 to 32 guns.

SMACK: A small sailboat usually rigged as a sloop; used mostly for fishing or coasting.

SNOW: A ship with two masts plus a "snow" mast immediately behind the mainmast, carrying a small trysail or gaff and boom sail; generally bigger than a brig or a brigantine.

STANCHIONS: Pieces of wood or iron of different shapes placed so as to support the deck, the quarter rails, the nettings, awnings, etc.

STRINGERS: Horizontal timbers connecting upright posts in a frame.

STUDDING SAILS: Light auxiliary sails on a square-rigged vessel; used in fair weather and attached by an extended boom outside a working sail.

TERN SCHOONER: A three-masted vessel with all masts of the same height and extended by three topmasts of the same height; the rig is fore-and-aft.

TIMBERS: The curved frames which form the ribs of a ship.

TOPSAIL SCHOONER: A fore-and-aft rigged schooner which carries a square topsail and a topgallant sail on the foretopmast.

TRANSOM: Transverse beams attached to the sternposts of a wooden ship to produce a flat stern.

TREENAIL/TRENAIL/TRENNEL: Wooden pegs used to join planks to timbers in a ship; they swell with moisture; may be up to three and four feet long.

TRYSAIL: A small fore-and-aft sail hoisted when other canvas has been lowered so that the vessel's head is kept to the wind during a storm.

TUMBLE HOME: That part of a ship which curves inward above the extreme breadth.

WALES: Related to gunwale. Any of several strakes or heavy planks which are attached to the outside of a ship to strengthen the hull.

WATERWAYS: Thick planking on the outside of a ship's deck fitting over the ends of the beams and against the inside of the top timbers to which they are bolted; the inner edge is hollowed out so as to form a channel in which water will run off the deck.

BIBLIOGRAPHY

BOOKS, PAMPHLETS, AND PAPERS

Baker, Melvin, Robert H. Cuff and Robert D. W. Pitt, eds. *Dictionary of Newfoundland and Labrador Biography*. St. John's: Harry Cuff Publications, 1990.

Barkham, Selma. "Documentary Evidence for 16th Century Basque Whaling Ships in the Strait of Belle Isle," in G.M. Story, ed, *Early European Settlement and Exploitation in Atlantic Canada*. St. John's: Memorial University, 1982: 53-95.

Belanger, Real and Michael Cook, eds. *Dictionary of Canadian Biography*. 14 vols. Toronto: University of Toronto Press, 2000.

Bonnycastle, Sir Richard Henry. *The Canadas in 1841*. 2 vols. London: Henry Colburn, 1841.

-------. *Newfoundland in 1842: A Sequel to The Canadas in 1841*. 2 vols. London: Henry Colburn, 1842.

Butt, Barry. *Community History of Exploits*. St. John's: Maritime History Group, Memorial University of Newfoundland, 1973.

Cell, Gillian T. *English Enterprise in Newfoundland 1577-1660*. Toronto: University of Toronto Press, 1969.

Crewe, Nimshi C. *The Newhook Master Shipbuilders*. (The above monograph appeared in the *Evening Telegram*, St. John's, June 17 and 18, 1965, and a list of corrections in the June 25 issue. Copyright 1999 by Charles G. Strong. Last updated on February 14, 1999).

Crosbie, G. *The Manuels of Exploits, Burnt Island*. St. John's: Maritime History Group, Memorial University of Newfoundland, n.d.

Cunningham, R. J. and K. R. Mabee. *Tall Ships and Master Mariners*. St. John's: Breakwater Books, 1985.

Evans, Calvin D. *For Love of a Woman: The Evans Family and a Perspective on Shipbuilding in Newfoundland*. St. John's: Harry Cuff Publications, 1992.

-------. *Silk Sails: Women of Newfoundland and Their Ships*. St. John's: Breakwater Books, 2008.

-------. *Master Shipbuilders of Newfoundland and Labrador, Volume One: Cape Spear to Boyd's Cove*. St. John's: Breakwater Books, 2013.

Feild, Edward. *Journal of the Bishop of Newfoundland's Voyage of Visitation and Discovery...in the Ship 'Hawk' 1848*. London: S.P.C.N., 1849.

Fizzard, Garfield. *Unto the Sea: A History of Grand Bank*. Grand Bank Historical Society, 1987. Printed by Dicks & Company, St. John's.

Galgay, Frank and Michael McCarthy. *Shipwrecks of Newfoundland and Labrador*. Volume III. St. John's: Creative Publishers, 1995.

Gosling, William G. *Labrador: Its Discovery, Exploration and Development*. Toronto: Musson, 1911.

Handcock, W. Gordon. *So longe as there comes no women: Origins of English Settlement in Newfoundland*. St. John's: Breakwater Books, 1989.

Harvey, Rev. M. *Newfoundland in 1900*. New York: South Publishing. St. John's: S. E. Garland, 1900.

-------. *A Short History of Newfoundland: England's Oldest Colony*. London: William Collins, Son & Co., 1890.

Hatton, Joseph and Rev. M. Harvey. *Newfoundland: Its History, its Present Condition, and its Prospects in the Future*. Boston: Doyle & Whittle, 1883.

Head, C. Grant. *Eighteenth Century Newfoundland*. Toronto: McClelland & Stewart, 1976.

Hillier, James and Peter Neary, eds. *Newfoundland in the Nineteenth and Twentieth Centuries: Essays in Interpretation*. Toronto: University of Toronto Press, 1980.

Historical Atlas of Canada, Volume I: From the Beginning to 1800. Toronto: University of Toronto Press, 1987.

The History of Burin by its Senior Citizens. 4th ed. 1977.

Horwood, Andrew. *Newfoundland Ships and Men*. St. John's: Marine Researchers, 1971.

Howley, James P. *The Beothucks or Red Indians: The Aboriginal Inhabitants of Newfoundland*. Cambridge: Cambridge University Press. Reprint by Coles Publishing Co., 1974.

Jukes, J. B. *Excursions in and about Newfoundland during the years 1839 and 1840*. 2 vols. London: John Murray, 1842. Reprinted by Canadiana House, Toronto, 1969.

Kendall, Victor and Victor G. Kendall. *Out of the Sea: A History of Ramea*. St. John's: Harry Cuff Publications, 1991.

Lounsbury, Ralph G. *The British Fishery at Newfoundland 1634-1763*. New York: Archon Books, 1969.

Lumsden, Rev. James. *The Skipper Parson on the Bays and Barrens of Newfoundland*. Edited by Naboth Winsor, 1977. n.p.

McGrath, P. T. *Newfoundland in 1911*. London: Whitehead, Morris & Co., 1911.

Major, Kevin. *As Near to Heaven by Sea: A History of Newfoundland and Labrador*. Toronto: Penguin, 2001.

Mannion, John J., ed. *The Peopling of Newfoundland: Essays in Historical Geography*. St. John's: Institute of Social and Economic Research, Memorial University of Newfoundland, 1977.

Matthews, Keith. *Lectures on the History of Newfoundland, 1500-1830*. St. John's: Breakwater Books, 1988.

O'Flaherty, Patrick. *Lost Country: The Rise and Fall of Newfoundland, 1843-1933*. St. John's: Long Beach Press, 2005.

-------. *Old Newfoundland: A History to 1843*. St. John's: Long Beach Press, 1999.

Page, Graham, W. C. Wilton and Tony Thomas. *Forestry in Newfoundland*. St. John's: Newfoundland Forest Research Centre, 1974.

Parker, John P. *Cape Breton Ships and Men*. Ayles bury, Buckingham shire: Hazel, Watson & Viney, 1967.

-------. *Sails of the Maritimes: The Story of the Three- and Four-Masted Cargo Schooners of Atlantic Canada, 1859-1929*. Toronto: McGraw-Hill Ryerson, 1960.

Parsons, Robert C. *Lost at Sea. Volumes One and Two*. St. John's: Creative Publishers, 1991 and 1992.

-------. *Toll of the Sea: Stories from the Forgotten Coast*. St. John's: Creative Publishers, 1995.

-------. *Vignettes of a Small Town (Grand Bank)*. St. John's: Creative Publishers, 1997.

-------. *Wake of the Schooners: From Placentia to Port aux Basques*. St. John's: Creative Publishers, 1993.

-------. *Wind and Wave: Sea Tales from Around our Coasts*. St. John's: Creative Publishers, 2003.

Patey, Francis. *The Grenfell Dock: The log of the IGA Marine Railway which operated at St. Anthony from 1928-75*. St. Anthony: Bebb Publishing, 1993.

Pedley, Rev. Charles. *The History of Newfoundland from the Earliest Times to the Year 1860*. London: Longman, Green, Longman, Roberts & Green, 1863.

Peyton, Amy Louise. *River Lords, Father and Son (The Peytons)*. St. John's: Jesperson Press, 1987.

Pitt, Robert D. W. and Joseph R. Smallwood, eds. *Encyclopedia of Newfoundland and Labrador*. 5 vols. St. John's: Newfoundland Book Publishers (1967) Ltd., 1981-1994.

Prowse, Daniel W. *A History of Newfoundland from the English, Colonial and Foreign Records*. 2nd ed. London: Eyre and Spottiswoode, 1896.

Roberts, Dr. Harry D. *The Newfoundland Fish Boxes: A Chronicle of the Fishery*. Fredericton, N.B.: Brunswick Press, 1982.

Rothney, G. O. *Newfoundland: A History*. 2d ed. Ottawa: Canadian Historical Association, 1964, c1959. (Historical Booklet, no. 10).

Sager, Eric W. and Lewis R. Fischer. *Shipping and Shipbuilding in Atlantic Canada, 1820-1914*. Ottawa: Canadian Historical Association, 1986.

Seary, E. R. *Family Names of the Island of Newfoundland*. St. John's: Memorial University of Newfoundland, 1977.

Smallwood, Joseph R., ed. *The Book of Newfoundland*. 6 vols. St. John's: Newfoundland Book Publishers (1967) Ltd., 1937-75.

Story, G. M., W. J. Kirwin and J. D. A. Widdowsen, eds. *Dictionary of Newfoundland English*. Toronto: University of Toronto Press, 1982.

Story, G. M., ed. *Early European Settlement and Exploitation in Atlantic Canada*. Selected Papers. St. John's: Memorial University of Newfoundland, 1982.

Tocque, Rev. Philip. *Newfoundland: As it was, and as it is in 1877*. Toronto: John B. Magurn, 1878.

Townsend, Charles Wendell, ed. *Captain Cartwright and His Labrador Journal*. 3d ed. Boston: Dana Estes, 1911. Published by DRC Publishing, St. John's, 2003.

Watson, William. *Newfoundland and its Missionaries*. Cambridge, Mass.: Printed by Dakin & Metcalfe, Halifax, N.S., 1866.

Whitcomb, Edward A. *A Short History of Newfoundland and Labrador*. Ottawa: From Sea to Sea Enterprises, 2010.

Whiteley, William H. *James Cook in Newfoundland: His Life, Times and Legacy*. St. John's: Newfoundland Historical Society, 1975.

Winsor, Naboth. *Building on a Firm Foundation: A History of Methodism in Newfoundland 1825-1853*. Vol. 2, n.d, n.p.

-------. *Stalwart Men and Sturdy Ships: A History of the Prosecution of the Seal Fishery by the Sealers of Bonavista Bay North, Newfoundland*. Gander: Printed by Economy Printing Ltd., 1985.

Wix, Edward. *Six Months of a Newfoundland Missionary's Journal, from February to August 1835*. London: Smith, Elder, 1836.

PERIODICAL ARTICLES

Christensen, Ruth M. "The Establishment of S.P.G. Missions in Newfoundland, 1703-1783." *The Historical Magazine of the Protestant Episcopal Church* 20 (1951): 207-229.

Handcock, W. Gordon. "Spatial Patterns in a Trans-Atlantic Migration Field: The British Isles and Newfoundland During the Eighteenth and Nineteenth Centuries." *Proceedings of the 1975 British-Canadian Symposium on Historical Geography. The Settlement of Canada: Origins and Transfer*: 13-45.

Power, Bridget and Kathleen Lopez. "The Newhooks of England and Newfoundland." *Newfoundland Ancestor* 13, no. 2 (Summer 1997): 65-69.

Whiteley, William H. "James Cook and British Policy in the Newfoundland Fisheries." *The Canadian Historical Review* 54, no. 3 (1973): 245-272.

NEWSPAPERS AND MAGAZINES

Daily News, St. John's. 1895-96, 1914-15.

Decks Awash, St. John's.

Evening Telegram, St. John's. 1882-83, 1914-25.

Free Press, St. John's. 1903-05, 1907-14, 1916-17, 1921-22. Some years incomplete.

Newfoundland Ancestor, St. John's: Quarterly Journal of the Newfoundland and Labrador Genealogical Society.

Newfoundland Journal of Commerce, St. John's.

Newfoundland Quarterly, St. John's.

Newfoundlander, St. John's. 1837-42, 1882.

Public Ledger, St. John's. 1837-84.

Standard and Conception Bay Advertiser, Harbour Grace. 1863-73.

Times and General Commercial Gazette, St. John's. 1838-41, 1885-95.

Twillingate Sun, Twillingate. 1880-92, 1895.

DIRECTORIES

Hutchinson's Directory, Newfoundland. 1864-65.

Lovell's Directory, Newfoundland. 1870-71, 1894-97.

McAlpine's Directory, Newfoundland. 1870-71.

McAlpine's Maritime Business Directory, Newfoundland. 1880-81, 1894-97, 1904.

OTHER SOURCES

Newfoundland Ship Registers 1813-1939. Maritime History Archives, M.U.N. and National Archives, Ottawa.

Newfoundland Ship Registers 1935-1992. Registry of Shipping, St. John's.

Lloyd's Ship Registers 1764-1784 (listing ships built from 1752 onward).

INDEX

C

G

H

I

J

K

N

O

P

Q

R

S

Y

PHILIP EVANS (LEFT) WITH CALVIN D. EVANS (RIGHT)

CALVIN D. EVANS retired from dual careers as a university librarian and a United Church minister. He is the author of three books: *For Love of a Woman: The Evans Family and a Perspective on Shipbuilding in Newfoundland* (Harry Cuff, 1992), *Soren Kierkegaard Bibliographies* (McGill, 1993), and *Silk Sails: Women of Newfoundland and Their Ships* (Breakwater, 2008). He has also written several articles on library science and has been a contributing writer for the *Dictionary of Canadian Biography* and for the *Encyclopedia of Newfoundland and Labrador*. In 2005 he wrote the biographies of fifteen Newfoundland women for the Grand Falls-Windsor Chapter of the Council on the Status of Women. Calvin now lives with his wife, Goldie, in Wasaga Beach, Ontario. They have three children (plus one deceased), six grandchildren, and eight great-grandchildren. They spend their summers at a cottage in Pleasantview, Newfoundland.

As the Culture of Outports Program Director, PHILIP EVANS oversees the planning and execution of the annual study and community build along with its various supporters. Philip graduated from the University of Toronto with a Bachelor of Architecture in 2003. He is a Principal at E.R.A Architects Inc. and specializes in a wide range of projects from contemporary design, cultural and urban planning, adaptive reuse, and heritage building conservation. Philip lives in Toronto with his wife, Julie Di Cresce, and their two sons, Fletcher and Buckley.